Active Server Pages 3.0

BY EXAMPLE

201 West 103rd Street
Indianapolis, Indiana 46290

Bob Reselman

Active Server Pages 3.0 by Example

International Standard Book Number: 0-7897-2240-2

Library of Congress Catalog Card Number: 99-66448

Printed in the United States of America

First Printing: June 2000

01   00   99   4   3   2   1

Trademarks

Warning and Disclaimer

Associate Publisher
Tracy Dunkelberger

Acquisitions Editor
Todd Green

Development Editor
Laura Bulcher

Managing Editor
Thomas F. Hayes

Project Editor
Karen S. Shields

Copy Editor
Victoria Elzey

Indexer
Deborah Hittel

Proofreader
Harvey Stanbrough

Technical Editor
Bryan Scattergood

Team Coordinator
Cindy Teeters

Media Developer
Jay Payne

Interior Designer
Karen Ruggles

Cover Designer
Rader Design

Copywriter
Eric Borgert

Layout Technician
Cyndi Davis-Hubler

Contents at a Glance

Table of Contents

Dedication

I dedicate this book to my father, Joe. He took me to work with him on Saturdays, bought me milkshakes, and taught me things I never would have known otherwise.

About the Author

Bob Reselman is a nationally known software developer, writer, teacher, and a founding principal with Cognitive Arts and Technologies. In addition to his writing and development activities, Bob spends his time studying the integration of creative, artistic endeavor with the process of software development. In the recent past, Bob held positions as a principal consultant for the international consulting firm, Cap Gemini, and as platform architect for desktop systems for the computer manufacturer Gateway.

Now he resides in Des Moines, Iowa with his wife Dorothy Lifka and his daughters, Geneviève and Alexandra.

Bob enjoys working with others in the pursuit of making great software. He can be reached at bob@CogArtTech.com.

Acknowledgements

The more that I make software, the more I understand that the making of software really is an art. And through such understanding I have come to believe that the semantics of computer programming are as important, if not more so, than the syntax of the discipline. Code that has little meaning has little value—no matter how well it compiles.

Now that I have a written a few programming books, it's time to stop for a moment to reflect and acknowledge those people who have made a lifelong impact upon my thinking as a software developer.

When I need guidance about how to make creative, sound software that has balance, integrity, and thoughtfulness, I think back to the lessons of my teachers from an earlier era: Peter Skiff, Ben Boretz, Elie Yarden, and Joan Tower.

When I need a reminder about the nobility and greatness of software development, I cannot help but think of the lessons that Jim and Michele McCarthy taught me.

When I need a powerful example of how to write code that behaves in such a way that it changes the world for the better, I look to the woman whom I love and who has loved me for more than 20 years, my wife Dorothy Lifka.

An important thanks is due to Wayne Pruchniak for once again coming to help when the labor of the book was too much. He is a trusted colleague and a talented technical writer.

Finally, I want to express my deepest gratitude to the production team for this book, Bryan Scattergood, Laura Bulcher, Victoria Elzey, Karen Shields, and particularly Todd Green, the acquisitions editor. I committed myself to making a quality book that would be of real benefit to others. Todd shared, supported, and reinforced this commitment throughout the production of this book. I sincerely hope that our product bears evidence of our commitment. Every author should have the opportunity and the pleasure to work with people such as these. They made this book better than I could have ever imagined.

Tell Us What You Think!

As the reader of this book, *you* are our most important critic and commentator. We value your opinion and want to know what we're doing right, what we could do better, what areas you'd like to see us publish in, and any other words of wisdom you're willing to pass our way.

As an associate publisher for Que, I welcome your comments. You can fax, email, or write to let us know what you did or didn't like about this book—as well as what we can do to make our books stronger.

Please note that we cannot help you with technical problems related to the topic of this book, and that due to the high volume of mail we receive, we might not be able to reply to every message.

When you write, please be sure to include this book's title and author as well as your name and phone or fax number. We will carefully review your comments and share them with the author and editors who worked on the book.

Fax: 317-581-4666

Email: quetechnical@macmillanusa.com

Mail: Associate Publisher, Programming
           Que
           201 West 103rd Street
           Indianapolis, IN 46290 USA

Introduction

Greetings! In order to know where we are going, it's useful to know where we have been, even in the world of programming.

Fifteen years ago the desktop PC was king. The world was full of standalone applications, such as WordPerfect, Lotus 1-2-3, Dbase, and PacMan. Novell was the emerging giant of network operating systems. Macs were for artists and PC's were for accountants. Every desktop computer was master of its own domain.

That was then. This is now. The pendulum is swinging. The growth of the Internet is bringing us back to servercentric computing. Before the PC, the mainframe reigned supreme. It was the Big Server. One computer could service hundreds, maybe thousands, of users. However, each user had to be part of the given mainframe's "Club." And not just anybody would program a mainframe. Mainframe programmers were thought to be very, very special.

That was then. This is now. Now all you need to participate in the new world of servercentric computing is a networked PC running Windows NT over TCP/IP, a copy of Notepad (which comes free with every copy of Windows), an understanding of HTML, and a knowledge of Active Server Pages. That's it!

The *by Example* Series

How does the *by Example* series make you a better programmer? The *by Example* series teaches programming using the best method possible—examples. The text acts as a mentor, looking over your shoulder, providing example programs, and showing you new ways to use the concepts covered in each chapter. While the material is still fresh, you will see example after example, demonstrating ways to use what you have just learned.

The philosophy of the *by Example* series is simple: The best way to teach computer programming is with multiple examples. Command descriptions, format syntax, and language references are not enough to teach a newcomer a programming language. Only by taking the components, immediately putting them into use, and running example programs can programming students get more than just a feel for the language. Newcomers who learn only a few basics using examples at every step of the way will automatically know how to write programs using those skills.

How This Book Is Designed

This book is designed to give you the ASP knowledge you need to participate in the new world of distributed computing. Active Server Page technology allows you to write robust, distributed applications that can actually change the way the world plays, learns, and does business. ASP is that powerful. All you need is some patience and perseverance.

This book is example-based. After a few introductory chapters that lay a conceptual foundation for the work we are going to do, you'll find that every chapter is loaded with examples. I believe in the example-based approach to learning upon which this series is based. Whenever I get into a jam and need to learn a new programming technique, when I consult documentation, the first thing I do is check out the code examples. It's one of the fastest ways to learn. One snippet of tight, well-documented code is worth 10 paragraphs of "how to" writing.

Using Other Resources

ASP programming is a broad discipline. VBScript, the language you'll use to create Active Server Pages, is becoming very big and extraordinarily powerful. This book is not designed to be the sole provider for your learning needs. There are many free resources out there to help you become a great ASP programmer and you should use them all. The best complement to this book is probably the Microsoft ASP and VBScript Web sites. You should plan to visit them often.

You can find Microsoft's ASP documentation online at

```
http://msdn.microsoft.com/isapi/msdnlib.idc?theURL=/library/psdk/iisref/
comp59f8.htm
```

You can find the complete VBScript documentation at

```
http://msdn.microsoft.com/scripting/default.htm?/scripting/vbscript/doc/
vbstoc.htm
```

Who Should Use This Book

This book is for that reader who has a background in computer programming and has done some Web development. The programming background we expect is a basic familiarity with Visual Basic. The reader should know what a variable is, the different primitive data types, how to make conditional statements, how to use some of the common functions intrinsic to the Visual Basic runtime, and how to make a standard executable. References to Visual Basic programming resources outside of the book are provided within the book. This way, if you do not have VB programming experience, but some other type of programming background, COBOL for example, you can fill in the areas in which you are lacking in direct VB programming experience.

You should have some knowledge of the Internet. You should know what a URL is and how it relates to identifying content on the Web. We do expect that you know how to make a simple Web page using standard HTML either with or without an HTML Editor. You should know how to control font rendering using the <FONT> tag and page layout using the <P>, <BR>, and <CENTER> tags. In addition, if you can make Web pages that have graphics, tables, and links to other pages, you are well prepared to create the HTML features of an Active Server Page.

What the Reader Should Expect

When you are through with this book, you should expect to be able to

- Create dynamic client pages using ASP server-side technology

- Write simple ASP applications that can perform server-side data access using ActiveX Data Objects

- Program server-side data access using transactions

- Program using the ActiveX controls and components that ship with ASP 3.0, Internet Explorer 5, and Internet Information Server 5

What the Reader Should Not Expect

Every book on computer programming has limitations. It's almost impossible to teach every facet of a given technology with one volume. If you spread content too thin, you do no justice to the specific topic. Please be advised that there are topics that are not within the scope of this book. The following topics are outside the scope of this book:

- Windows NT/2000 security architecture and security mechanisms

- Creating ActiveX controls

- Creating ActiveX components

- Configuring objects under Microsoft Transaction Server

Conventions Used in This Book

This book uses several common conventions to help teach Active Server Pages. Here is a summary of those typographical conventions:

EXAMPLE

Examples are indicated by the icon shown at the left of this sentence.

OUTPUT

You'll find the icon shown to the left of this sentence to indicate output associated with the code listings.

Some of the typographical conventions used include the following:

- Commands and computer output appear in a special monospaced computer font.

- Words you type appear in a **boldfaced computer font**.

- Any lines of code that are too long to fit on a single line will be broken into two lines, and a code continuation character, ➥, will appear on the second line.

In addition to typographical conventions, the following special elements are included to set off different types of information to make them easily recognizable:

NOTE
Special notes augment the material you read in each chapter. These notes clarify concepts and procedures.

TIP
You'll find numerous tips offering shortcuts and solutions to common problems.

CAUTION
The cautions warn you about roadblocks that sometimes appear when working with Active Server Pages. Reading the caution sections should save you time and trouble, not to mention a few headaches.

Where to Find the Code

Please visit the following *by Example* Web site for example code and additional material associated with this book:

```
http://www.quecorp.com/series/by_example/
```

What's Next

Now that you have an idea of what your in for, let's move on to the first chapter, in which you'll learn about the nature of modern, distributed computing and the role ASP plays in this paradigm. And then, we'll do what we've come to do...program!

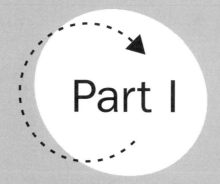

Part I

Part I: Introducing ASP

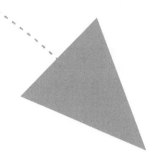

The Fundamentals of Distributed Computing Using ASP

You've probably heard some talk about Active Server Pages (ASP) being a technology enabling you to make Web pages that are truly dynamic, giving you the data you want, when you want it. Although this is undoubtedly a powerful characteristic of the technology, it's only the tip of a very big iceberg. The real big deal about ASP is that it's a significant part of the next generation of modern computing—the generation of inexpensive distributed computing. Using Active Server Pages is about computing over the wired planet. In an ASP environment it's possible to write code that executes on one or many systems and displays the results of that execution to another system anywhere in the world. ASP is part of a revolution that's changing the way the world works, a world in which any user can use any computer on the planet to plug into any system anywhere and access the information he or she needs instantaneously. And, this information can be anything from a play by Shakespeare, a real time stock quote, or a film on demand.

In this chapter you will

- Get an introduction to distributed computing
- Understand the role of the client and server
- Get an introduction to n-tier architecture
- Get an overview of the role of Active Server Pages

Working in the Distributed Computing Environment

Distributed computing using low cost PCs has been around for some time, since the mid 1980s. However, it's the emergence of the Internet that has really brought it into limelight.

What is distributed computing? Distributed computing is the opposite of standalone computing. You can think of a standalone environment as *monolithic*. In a monolithic environment you have one computer that accepts input, processes the input, and then returns the results of that processing to a monitor attached to it. For a long time most PC's were standalone. You had one computer that contained an application on its hard disk, Lotus 1-2-3 for example, and some data on that same hard disk. The application, data, user input, display, and output all lived on that one machine. If you had to move the output to another system you could put it "on the network." If your computer was not connected to a network, you could copy the data to a floppy disk and run it down the hall using SneakerNet.

As time passed, networks such as Novell and Banyan emerged that enabled data to be shared among different machines. This was the start of client-server computing. In the early days of client-server, the server might be a computer that served up files as you needed them or offered printing services. The client was the computer on your desktop that used the file and printing services. Early client-server computing made computing more efficient, particularly when it came to sharing a printer among many computers. But the ability for machines to really talk to one another was quite limited. And, even though data might be on another machine, input, computation, and display functionality still was contained within the monolithic PC.

Today, things are different. Most client-server network interaction is standardized on TCP/IP, the protocol that is the *lingua franca* of the Internet. TCP/IP is an addressing standard that allows all data to move consistently and reliably from one computer to another. TCP/IP uses a 12-digit addressing structure called an IP address. Every bit of data that travels through the Internet has an IP address attached to it, as you see in Figure 1.1. An IP address is similar to mailing a letter using a zip code—an addressing standard that everybody in the country agrees upon. When sending a letter, you don't have to spend a lot of time worrying about the details of routing and delivery; the zip code takes care of it. The same is true of IP addresses. If a computer adheres to the TCP/IP standard, any other computer on the planet that supports TCP/IP can find it. This means that because of TCP/IP, it now is possible for Novell servers to talk to NT servers and so forth.

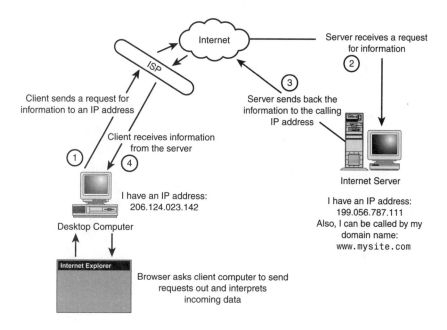

Figure 1.1: *The Internet is the framework for modern client-server networks.*

The removal of proprietary protocols in favor of a universal standard means that any client can work with any server. Hooking up to another computer is as easy as typing in a 12-digit IP address or a URL. Interaction is open and the cost to hook up is cheap. More importantly, the granularity of interaction is finer. Today you can have an environment in which Computer A uses data access services on Computer B in conjunction with processing functions that live on Computers C and D. Computer B might talk to five database computers. And for all we know, Computer A is a television set running WebTV (see Figure 1.2).

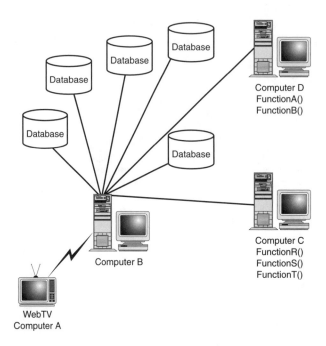

Figure 1.2: *Today the modern application lives throughout the enterprise.*

In earlier times the application was a program that lived and worked on one computer on your desktop, today the growing trend is for the application to live and work all over on the Internet or Intranet. Viewing the output of the application can take place on your desktop computer or your cell phone. However, as diverse as the distributed environment might be, in the end it boils down to one computer, no matter its size, being able to serve another.

Understanding the Client

A client is any computer or computing device that uses the services of another computer. As you read previously, in previous times a client computer was generally a standalone PC that might be on a Novell network using the file management and print services of another computer. For the most part, the client did not really depend on the server to get any of its application functionality. The average client had to have a whole lot of smarts built into it to get anything done. Most application processing took place on the client. A lot of data resided there, too. In addition, the client knew a whole lot about the server it was using in terms of operating system, functionality, and security. This sort of client is around still today. It is referred to as a *fat client*.

Modern Internet technology has changed the way the client works. In modern client-server computing the browser is becoming the main vehicle by which a client performs activity. And the activity the client performs is becoming more about displaying data than it is about processing data or computing logic. This delegation of processing and logic away from the client makes for what is know as a *thin client*.

Understanding the Server

A server is any computer that provides service to another. You can have servers that provide file management and print services. You can have servers that manage a network by coordinating user rights and access. You can have a server that provides database services, servers that feed you stock market quotes—the possibility of services is endless.

An important distinction you need to make when working with servers is to understand the difference between server hardware and server software. Most people think of the server as the box that sits out there on the network. Although it is true that there is a distinct box out there filled with hard drives and network cards, the real action is in the server software.

Server software is a service. It's possible for a server box to support many types of server software. You can have a service that provides file system security. You can have a service that provides printer access. You can have a service that accepts requests for data from the Internet and responds accordingly. You can have servers cooperating with each other. For example, you can use the base security services of the NT operating system to provide authentication to database servers. Things can get quite convoluted. The thing to remember is that the hardware server is quite different from server software. When someone says that he has a mail server, he is really saying he has a computer upon which mail server software is running. When someone says she has an Internet server, she is saying she has a computer upon which Internet server software is running. In these two cases, both servers might be running on the same computer.

INTERNET INFORMATION SERVER AND ACTIVE SERVER PAGES

Within the scope of this book, you are going to be dealing with Internet Information Server (IIS). IIS is software designed to handle all Internet services within a given box and to handle requests for Web pages. It can do file transfer under the FTP protocol, and also provides the engine for the Active Server Page technology. ASP is built right into IIS.

Servers have become the focal point of modern computing. As you read previously, where before the desktop computer unified a given application, now the trend is to have the application live in many computers, distributed throughout the network using Internet protocols to communicate with one another. It's no longer true that you have the logic and data of an application on the same machine that presents the application's output to the user. Any segment of an application can be anywhere. Designing applications that take advantage of the unlimited possibilities of modern distributed computing is what *n-tier architecture* is about.

Working Within an N-Tier Architecture

N-tier architecture is the segmentation of an application into parts and distributing these parts throughout a network. The virtue of using an n-tier architecture is that the ability to execute, maintain, and enhance large-scale applications is increased greatly. Let's look at a real world example to see the benefit of using an n-tier architecture rather than the traditional desktop-based, single tier solution.

EXAMPLE

Imagine that you were writing a program for the Happy Valley School District. The purpose of the program is to maintain student roster and attendance information within the School District and to keep track of each student's grades with regard to a given teacher's syllabus and grading system. Table 1.1 shows a list of the features of the Happy Valley School District application.

Table 1.1: Feature List for the Happy Valley School District Application

Feature	Description
Log in	Allows user to Log in to application.
Authenticate	Verifies that the username and password and grants use rights.
Choose service	Allows the user to select attendance or grading service.
Choose class	Allows user to select the class upon which to take attendance or administer grades.
Get class roster	Gets a roster for a specific class.
Display class roster	Displays a roster list.
Input attendance	Allows the user to enter attendance data for given day.
Record attendance	Stores the results of a given attendance taking.
Create grading scheme	Creates the structure by which an individual teacher will grade his students.
Store grading scheme	Stores the grading scheme.
Get grading scheme	Retrieves a grading scheme for a particular teacher or class.

Feature	Description
Display grading scheme	Displays the grading scheme for a given teacher or class.
Input grade	Allows user to enter grades.
Store grade	Stores grades entered by teacher.
Analyze grades	Performs processing that allows a teacher to determine a midterm and final grades.
Deliver grades	Either prints a grade sheet for student or emails the grade to a student and parent.

The previous table is by no means exhaustive, but it does give you a good sense of the high-level functionality that needs to be built into the application to make it useful.

We are going to draw up two architectural plans for the Happy Valley application. One plan designs the program as a standalone, desktop application. The other plan takes a distributed approach to design, spreading the functionality of the application throughout the school system. Before we begin, we need to talk about a design principle that pertains to all computer applications, whether standalone or distributed. This is the principle of application partitioning.

Partitioning the Application

Any application can be separated into three fundamental parts:

Presentation   The means by which an application displays output and accepts input.

Logic   The algorithmic computation that you program into the application.

Data   The quantities and values that your application processes and stores.

A feature can use one or all of these partitions when it comes time to implement it. We can map the features of the Happy Valley School District Application against these three partitions, as shown in Table 1.2.

EXAMPLE

Table 1.2: Partitioning the Happy Valley School District Application

	Presentation	Logic	Data
Login	X		
Authenticate		X	
Choose service	X		
Choose class	X		
Get class roster		X	

continues

Table 1.2: continued

	Presentation	**Logic**	**Data**
Display class roster	X		
Input attendance	X		
Record attendance			X
Create grading scheme		X	
Store grading scheme			X
Get grading scheme		X	
Display grading scheme	X		
Input grade	X		
Store grade			X
Analyze grades		X	
Deliver grades	X		

Partitioning an application gives us greater control over development and eventual distribution. Now let's take a look at various architectures that we can use to implement the application. We'll start with the standalone approach.

Single-Tier Approach

An application that runs on a single standalone computer is called a single-tier application. It is single-tier because all three of the application's partitions, Presentation, Logic, and Data reside on the same computer. In a single-tier application, the application uses the mouse and keyboard to accept user input and the monitor and printer to display output. The application uses the standalone computer's processor to do calculation. Data is stored on the computer's hard drive. Figure 1.3 shows the features of the Happy Valley School District Application implemented within a single-tier application.

The advantage of a standalone application is that everything is self-contained in one machine. The application does not require any connection to a network to work. The concept of online and offline is irrelevant. Using this architecture, users could easily put this application on a laptop computer and carry it with them to whatever class they were teaching.

There are some significant disadvantages to this architecture. The first and foremost disadvantage is the inability to assure that the data that is being used within the computer synchronizes with the data that is outside the computer. For example, consider class rosters. Within the Happy Valley School District students are assigned to a class by the building principal. That class list file is loaded onto the standalone machine at the beginning of the semester. However, if the principal adds a new student to the class, a new class list must be loaded onto the standalone system. This is a significant chore if the principal must update hundreds of classes. In addition, there is an interval of time in which the class list on the principal's computer will be different from the class list on the teacher's computer. That the data lists do not correspond, even for a short period, is a compromise of the enterprise's data integrity..

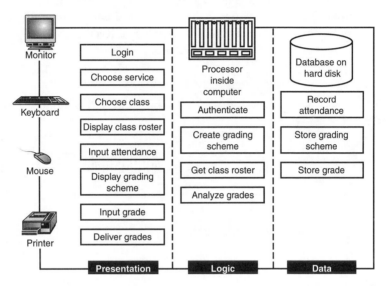

Figure 1.3: *Here is an example of a single-tier application architecture*

Another disadvantage is the chore of leveraging the application's logic. For example, imagine that a teacher comes up with a grading scheme that another teacher wants to use. The other teachers have no easy way of knowing the details of each other's grading scheme. Also, even if the teachers were aware of various grading schemes, there isn't any easy way by which to share the schemes with one another.

The last disadvantage is that the standalone application is platform dependent. For example, if the application is written to work on a Macintosh, quite common in an educational institution, a teacher who is using Windows would have to use a Windows version of the application, should one exist. If one doesn't exist, the teacher would have no recourse but to buy a Macintosh computer. Although it is true that most commercial grade applications have different versions for each operating system, in the world of custom application development, creating and maintaining a different version of software for each operating system is an extremely costly undertaking.

Let's see whether we can address these issues by altering the application's architecture.

Two-Tier Approach

A two-tier architecture is a simple client-server framework in which the Presentation and Algorithmic Logic partitions of an application live on a separate machine from an application's Data and Data Logic. Figure 1.4 shows the Happy Valley School District Application transformed from single-tier architecture to a two-tier architecture.

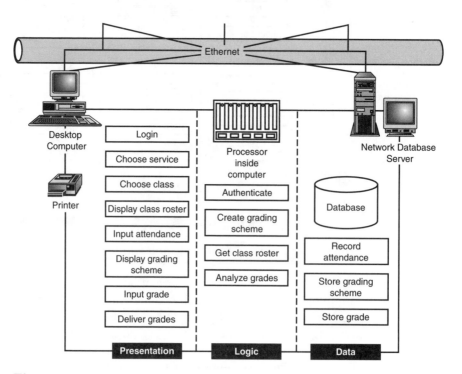

Figure 1.4: *In two-tier architecture, Data is separated from Presentation and Logic.*

In the two-tier architecture shown here, the data for the Happy Valley School District lives in a central database server. Client systems log in to the database over a network.

The most obvious advantage of a two-tier architecture is that all the data is centralized. If a building principal adds a student to a class, that information is posted almost immediately to the master database and available for use by any teacher whose system has rights to the database server.

The disadvantage is that system performance is subject to the conditions of the network and the utilization rate of the database server. In a single-tier architecture data access is very fast because everything is on the same machine. One user is accessing one database without having to negotiate a wired connection. However, after the data is relegated to another computer, data movement is subject to conditions of the line that connects the machines and the demands made upon the database server by all the systems using that server. If the database server is taking many requests for data, overall performance is going to be slow. In addition, if the database server goes down, the application becomes inoperative.

Three-Tier Approach

Three-tier Architecture separates the Presentation services of an application from Algorithm services completely. In a three-tier application architecture, the Presentation, Algorithm, and Data services of an application live on separate computers (see Figure 1.5).

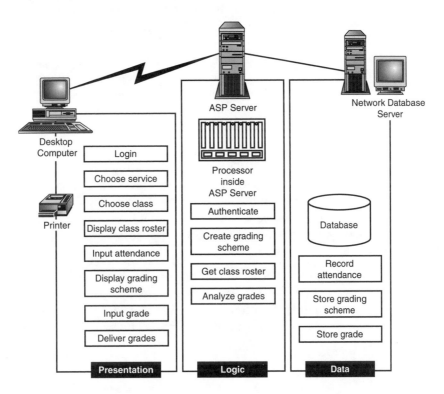

Figure 1.5: *A three-tier application architecture distributes Presentation, Logic, and Data services to separate computers.*

Be advised there are different types of a Presentation layer, with varying degrees of dependency. For example, at one end of the spectrum you can create an application that will run only on the Windows operating system. The presentation client is hard coded to look for a specific computer from which to get its application logic. The logic might be contained in remote ActiveX components that are accessed only through the enterprise's internal network. In a scenario such as this one, the end user could have to keep the Presentation component of the application on a laptop and move anywhere within the enterprise in which the internal network was available. He or she simply plugs in and logs in to the company network and access to the logic is readily available.

You might be wondering what the advantage of this architecture is given that the end user is bound to a private network. The biggest advantage is the ability to change a given piece of logic quickly without having to go through a massive redeployment. For example, imagine that the Analyze Grade feature of the Happy Valley School District application needed to change. For example, a directive was issued mandating that attendance was to be considered in the grading process, where previously it wasn't. If this were the case in a two-tier architecture, every client application would need to be changed to accommodate the new rule. In a three-tier scenario, a developer writes the new code that changes the grading rule, installs it on the computer that contains the application logic and that's it! The clients still go on utilizing the application and the rule is seamlessly implemented throughout the enterprise (see Figure 1.6).

Granted there are still problems with the type of three-tier implementation previously described. The client's operating system must match up with the Logic computer's operating system. There is still significant dependency on a dedicated network. Also, the actual rendering engine is still specific to the client. For instance, if the Presentation component supports 16-color graphics only, there is no way that the application will ever be able to display photos.

Let's look at the other end of the spectrum of three-tier architecture. Instead of having a Presentation component that is custom made and dedicated to one application, we use an Internet browser as the Presentation component. Why? Because the browser has one job, and one job only: to process ASCII text-based HTML and transform it into Web pages that contain text, graphics, and HTML elements to handle simple data input. The Internet browser is platform independent. It presents data from any operating system, using any processor, on any network. It doesn't matter whether the client is running on a Macintosh and the application logic resides on an NT server. As long as the logic source can generate HTML, the browser can render it into a graphical presentation. The ramifications of architecture are far reaching. To be operational, only two conditions need to exist. First, a browser must be on the desktop and second, the desktop needs to have access to the network that supports TCP/IP. If the Happy Valley School District uses a browser-based, three-tier architecture in its application, the teacher really could be sitting at home doing grading while not caring one iota whether the configuration of his or her computer supports the application or not. All that's needed on the client end is the browser and access to the IP address of the Logic server. Welcome to the Thin Client.

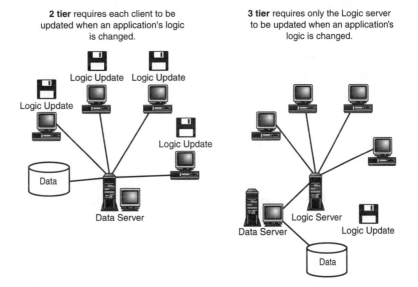

Figure 1.6: *Application update is a lot easier in a three-tier environment.*

Notice that the logic server in the three-tier diagram in Figure 1.5 is an ASP server. ASP is ideal for thin client computing.

Three-tier is a favorable architecture, but it's not a panacea that will make computing easier for everyone. By nature, this architecture is highly centralized. Although you have an unlimited number of clients that can access the application, you have one data source and one logic source. If the logic or database server goes down, you have big problems. And, you do not have a lot of flexibility in terms of development authority.

Suppose a group of elementary school principals in the Happy Valley School District wanted to develop their own grading policy, or even have their own way of displaying report cards. In the current three-tier architecture, the principals would have to get together and work with the District to see their ideas turned into code. They could not do it themselves. Remember, both the Logic and Data servers are the property of the District. Give and take bureaucratic negotiation with regard to the determination of network services might work in the short term for a small enterprise. However, what do you do if the District gets hundreds of change requests from hundreds of schools? Change would take forever. The solution is to decentralize into an n-tier architecture.

N-Tier Approach

An n-tier architecture is one in which there are an infinite number of logic servers and data servers from which a given client can access functionality and data. In a way, the Internet is one big n-tier environment. You can get your news services from CNN.com and your radio programs from Broadcast.com. The browser does no more than render these distinct services onto your desktop computer.

N-tier architecture brings an enhanced level of efficiency and autonomy to the enterprise. You can see in Figure 1.7 that the middle and elementary schools have been given their own servers from which to provide logic services. In this architecture, each server can set the policy for its domain. For example, the elementary schools can implement a different grading policy from the middle schools, yet both the middle and elementary school can enjoy the services of the district and each other. Should a new entity emerge, for example an alternative middle school, the new school can benefit from existing services as well a provide its own. All it needs to do is publish an IP address so that others in the enterprise might find it. Growth is easy and fast. All new members need to do to participate in the enterprise is to have access to the network using TCP/IP and speak HTML.

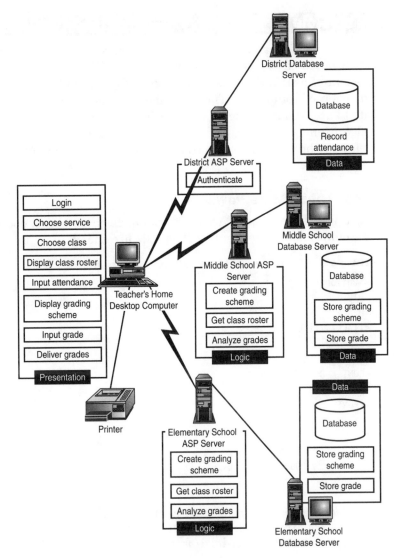

Figure 1.7: *An N-Tier architecture allows for easy, efficient growth of services within an enterprise.*

The Role of ASP

We've sort of glossed over things with regard to the role of ASP within the distributed enterprise. So now let's pick up the ball. The first and foremost benefit of ASP is that the technology truly takes advantage of thin client distributed computing. The core functionality of ASP is that it has the ability to access data using standard Microsoft data access methods, perform algorithmic computing and return its output in standard, vanilla HTML that any browser can support. ASP really is the dream of the thin client come true.

Less Labor, More Power

Listing 1.1 is a piece of ASP code that opens a database, does a query and outputs HTML. The results of the code are shown in Figure 1.8.

Listing 1.1: A Simple Piece of ASP Code Doing Data Access (`01asp01.asp`)

```
<%Option Explicit%>
<HTML>
<HEAD>
<TITLE></TITLE>
</HEAD>
<BODY>
<FONT FACE=ARIAL COLOR=Blue Size=4>
Returning a set of records using ASP
</FONT>
<P>
<%
    Dim cn 'Connection var
    Dim rs 'Recordset var
    Dim SQL 'SQL String

    'Write a SQL statement that says to get all the
    'records from the database table, tblStudents
    SQL = "SELECT * FROM tblStudents"

    'Create the data objects
    Set cn = CreateObject("ADODB.Connection")
    Set rs = CreateObject("ADODB.Recordset")

    'Open a Data connnection using ADO
    cn.Open "DSN=AriMiddleData"
    rs.ActiveConnection = cn
    'Open a set of records
    rs.Open SQL

    'Go through all the records that are
```

```
    'returned from the database
    While NOT rs.EOF
%>
<FONT FACE=ARIAL COLOR=Blue Size=3>
First Name: <%=rs("FirstName")%><BR>
Last Name: <%=rs("LastName")%>
</FONT>
<HR>
<%
rs.MoveNext
Wend
'Close the recordset and connection
rs.Clone
cn.Close
%>

</BODY>
</HTML>
```

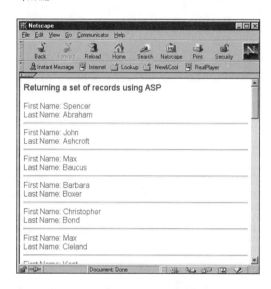

Figure 1.8: *ASP allows you to display data access output as HTML.*

Even though the details of the previous ASP code might be a little mystical, one thing should be readily apparent, there's Visual Basic code in there! Visual Basic is the scripting language of ASP. ASP provides you the leverage of Visual Basic to create very complex applications using VBScript, which is subset of VB. And, you can use third party and custom made, server-side COM components to increase your code reuse and lessen the burden of day-to-day hacking (see Figure 1.9).

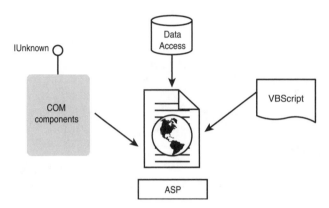

Figure 1.9: *ASP gives you the best of all worlds.*

ASP allows you to do all the things that you can do in the more difficult scripting environments, such as CGI programming using C++ or Perl, but with half the headache. You can do a lot with ASP in a very short time.

Dynamic Content

ASP is designed to maintain and generate dynamic content. Dynamic content is the up-to-the-moment data you want, when you want it. Let's look again at our Happy Valley School District example. Every school in Happy Valley records the attendance of the students present on a given day. Some schools at the middle and secondary level take attendance on a class-by-class basis. Everyday, an overwhelming amount of data is generated just to keep track of who is present or who is not. In the old days the school district would hire a complete staff just to maintain attendance records. Sadly the human solution was frightfully slow. The lag time between data in and data out could be hours, if not days. If a parent wanted to know whether her son or daughter really did make it to chemistry, that data was not readily available.

Even when the School District automated to a mainframe or minicomputer environment to handle data gathering and reporting, the cost incurred to give each teacher a terminal to enter data directly into the system was prohibitive. Although the environment was digital, the lag time between data in and data out was significant. Collating attendance input and reporting it was still pretty much paper based.

The advent of client-server architecture and cheap desktop computers meant that a teacher could indeed log in and view attendance data. But surprisingly there was still a lot of manual manipulation involved in getting the data in and data out. Even in an HTML-based Web environment, if there wasn't a way to report the attendance of the chemistry class that started five minutes prior to the request. If a teacher was indeed able to get the data sent to a central data source, getting the data out in a timely manner was still a chore. Without a way to generate data in real time, even in a Web environment, the lag time between data in and data out made efficient distributed computing a dream.

Luckily ASP makes the dream of real time client-server computing in a Web-based environment a reality. When you call an ASP page from your browser, the internal code internal of the page writes or reads the data you want from a data source in real time. There's no hard coding and no waiting. All computing is done in real time.

ASP bring enormous power to the computing enterprise. When you are using ASP, it doesn't take much code to change the dynamics of a whole enterprise. In the Happy Valley scenario above, data management that would have taken hours, if not days previously, now takes seconds. Now using ASP, any school within the Happy Valley System District can participate in the computing enterprise. All that's required are some desktop computers, Ethernet wire, a few hubs, and an NT server running Internet Information Server and SQL Server. The promise of inexpensive, comprehensive client-server computing is now becoming a reality.

Windows DNA and ASP

Windows DNA stands for Windows Distributed interNet Architecture. Windows DNA is the Microsoft initiative for distributed computing over the Internet, and it includes both an architectural model and a set of products to support the model. The Windows DNA architectural model is very similar to standard three-tier architecture. Microsoft is trying to flavor three-tier to be more accommodating to the Windows platform. Thus, Microsoft products come into play very quickly. ASP is positioned within Windows DNA as the fundamental technology to use to provide presentation services to non-Windows clients. However, if a client does support one of the Win32 operating systems (Window 95, Windows 98, Windows NT, or Windows 2000), Microsoft is suggesting that ActiveX controls be used on the client side to provide more robust interaction. The Windows DNA guidelines require that all distributed applications support both Windows and non-Windows clients as well as datasources that run in Windows and non-Windows environments.

Clearly, Microsoft is trying to play as large a part as it can in any enterprise configuration. It seems as if the company is moving beyond the mantra of "Windows Everywhere" to "Windows DNA Everywhere." The initiative is significant. Whether the enterprise is using solely Windows clients to access mainframe data or using Windows 2000 Advanced Server to control a cluster of servers in a client-server configuration, Microsoft wants to play a major role in any facet of an enterprise's configuration. Microsoft is devoting tremendous resource to promoting Windows DNA. The company understands the importance of distributed computing using the Internet and plans to have Windows play an important part in its growth.

The ASP Promise of Distributed Computing

Modern distributed computing is about being able to plug in anywhere to get the information that you need, when you need it. ASP is a central player in the modern distributed environment. It has the ability to access data, perform logical analysis upon the data, and then format output into HTML, which can be displayed on any computer that has a browser—any data, on any computer, at any time. That's the promise of distributed computing. The point of this book is to give you the basic facility you need with ASP so that you, too, can help make the promise of modern distributed computing a reality.

What's Next

Now that you have an overview of the nature of modern client-server computing and the role as ASP within n-tier environment, we need to get down to the nuts and bolts of working with ASP. The next chapter shows you how to create the servers upon which you'll run ASP. In addition, you'll learn the fundamentals of client-side and server-side scripting.

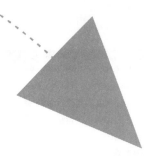

Migrating from Static Web Pages to Active Server Pages

The essential fact about migrating from static Web pages to Active Server Pages means you understand that you are going to write programs. Static Web pages are like the documents that you create in your word processor. You write the content, save the content to a file, and then put it on the Web server. If you need to make a change, you manually edit the document. Although it's true that creating static Web pages requires facility with HTML, the markup language affects the way content is displayed, not the content itself. Active Server Pages are different. ASP enables you to use the Internet server to program the creation of content without having to rely upon ongoing human interaction. Making the move from working with static Web pages to working with Active Server Pages is not terribly hard, but it does require a different way of thinking. Creating Active Server Pages requires that in addition to thinking like a writer, you think like a programmer.

In this chapter you will

- Receive an overview of Personal Web Server (PWS) and Internet Information Server (IIS)

- Learn how to create a simple, client-side script

- Learn how to create a simple, server-side script

- Learn about the ASP Application framework

Working with IIS, PWS, and ASP

An Active Server Page is a Web page that is processed by a Web Server. The role of the Web server when it comes to static pages is to open an HTML file, read it, and pass the contents of the file back to the calling browser. Active Server Pages are dynamic. The Web server opens the file, reads the contents, passes on the HTML to the client, but also executes parts of the content that are scripting instructions that have been written into special sections of the page.

ASP enables you to intersperse script within HTML. For example, the following Web page in Listing 2.1 reports the time. Figure 2.1 shows the page run in a browser. Please notice that the <% %> tags indicate server-side script.

EXAMPLE

Listing 2.1: A simple Active Server Page (02asp01.asp)

```
<HTML>
<HEAD>
<TITLE></TITLE>
</HEAD>
<BODY>
The time is: <%=Time()%>
</BODY>
</HTML>
```

OUTPUT

Figure 2.1: *Active Server Pages enables you to generate information at the moment you need it.*

You'll notice that the code in Listing 2.1 is almost all standard HTML, except for this:

```
<%=Time()%>
```

This code is an instruction that tells the Web server, "Hey, go get the time and put it in here." This instruction is called server-side script because the script is run by the server, not the browser on the client side.

As an ASP developer, you are going to interact with the Web server much more than you did when you writing static HTML. The Web server plays a much larger role. It's the server, with the help of the scripting engine, that executes scripting instructions. It's the server that generates the error messages you use when debugging your code. In addition, as you become more adept at programming ASP, you'll find that you can program the server such that you can share code between a variety of Active Server Pages.

✔ For information on using the server to work with multiple Active Server Pages, see the "Working with Applications" section in Chapter 7, "Intermediate ASP: Processing Data," p. 166.

Understanding the Web Server and ASP

A Web server manages the taking of requests for data from a browser on the Internet and responses to those requests.

As you previously read, requests for static HTML files on the server's side are a simple matter of opening the file, reading it, and sending its contents to the browser. However, Microsoft has enhanced two of its server products to do more than feed straight HTML files to requesting browsers. Internet Information Server (IIS) and its smaller-scale desktop cousin Personal Web Server (PWS) have the ability to process server-side scripts in Web pages. When either IIS or PWS see a file with the extension .asp on the filename, the server knows to be on the lookout for server-side scripts within the page, as you see in Figure 2.2.

CAUTION

You must use the extension .asp on your files that contain Active Server Page script. If you use the extension .htm or .html, the server assumes that all text within the file is to be sent to the calling browser. This means that your ASP code will be displayed in the browser.

Choosing a Development Environment

If you plan to program using ASP in a network environment, you must have access to a Windows NT 4.0 server running Internet Information Server 4.0. IIS 4.0 is a free product that ships under Windows NT Option Pack 4.0. You can download it from the following site:

http://www.microsoft.com/ntserver/all/downloads.asp?RLD=71

If your network is using Windows 2000 Server, you'll use Internet Information Server 5.0, which ships with the product.

If you are running Windows 95 or 98 on your desktop machine, you can use Personal Web Server (PWS). Personal Web Server installs on your local hard disk and enables you to work as if your desktop computer were an actual Web server. PWS is a good tool to use if you want to test your pages and scripts before you deploy them for broader use.

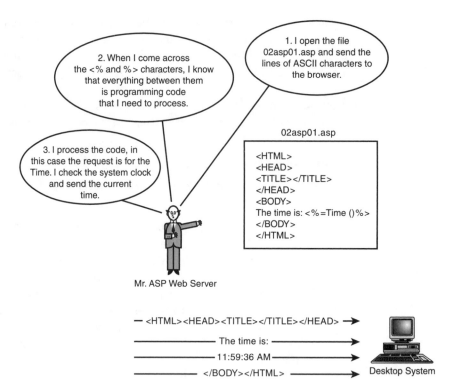

Figure 2.2: *Web servers supporting ASP know how to process scripts embedded in HTML.*

Personal Web Server is available free on the Windows NT Option Pack 4. Also, you can download it at the Microsoft Developer Web site at:

`http://www.microsoft.com/windows/ie/pws/default.htm?RLD=23`

If you are doing ASP development in a company or large organization, it is very unusual to be allowed direct control to an enterprise's IIS server. Most of the configuration tasks are handled by your company's Webmaster or system administrator. On the other hand, if you are working on your desktop machine using PWS, you have complete control over your environment and can configure PWS to your own liking.

Personal Web Server Overview

Figure 2.3 shows you the main dialog box of Personal Web Server.

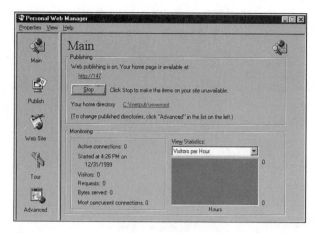

Figure 2.3: *You use the Personal Web Manager dialog box to start and stop the server.*

The Personal Web Manager dialog box has a number of features available to you. Table 2.1 shows an overview of these features.

Table 2.1: Personal Web Server Features

Feature	Description
Main	Allows you to start and stop the server as well as view usage statistics. Also tells you how to reference your computer as a URL and the location of your home page on your local system.
Publish	Provides a wizard enabling you to create a Web site automatically.
Web Site	Allows you to edit the home page and view data from the site that you made using the Publishing Wizard. You can view data such as the GuestBook and Dropbox.
Tour	Provides you with a guided tour about how to use PWS.
Advanced	Allows you to create virtual directories that represent your ASP Applications.

Starting Personal Web Manager

A basic activity you do with the Personal Web Server Manager window is to start and stop the server, which is the same as turning the server on and off. If the server is not running, the scripts in your Active Serer Page will not be processed. Therefore, if you find that your scripts are not executing, the first thing to do is check to make sure that the server is running. To start Personal Web Server, click the Start/Stop button in the Main dialog box.

Microsoft Management Console for Internet Information Server 4.0

In addition to processing ASP pages, IIS supports FTP, Web, and other Internet services and protocols. Windows NT organizes the control of the various services under a common toolbox known as the Microsoft Management Console (MMC). The MMC allows you to start, stop, and configure services. In addition, the MMC allows you to configure the rights and setting for directories and files in the master Web directory. Figure 2.4 shows you the Microsoft Management Console for Internet Information Server 4.0. If you are administering your own IIS server, you might want to spend some time studying the extensive help files that ship with the MMC.

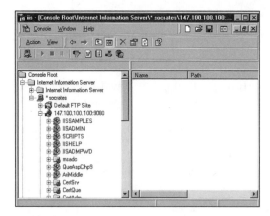

Figure 2.4: *You can administer the various IIS services using the Microsoft Management Console.*

Figure 2.5 shows you the Internet Information Services console for Internet Information Server 5.0 that ships with Windows 2000. This console is the upgrade from IIS 4.0. This new upgrade provides an enhanced Graphical User Interface that allows you take advantage of some of the new Internet networking features of Windows 2000.

Deploying Your Work on the Server

PWS and IIS designate a master directory on the hard drive that contains all data and script files for use by the Internet server. The default master directory is \InetPub, as seen in Figure 2.6.

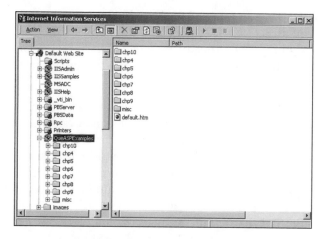

Figure 2.5: *The Internet Information Services console for IIS 5.0.*

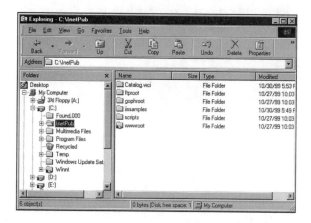

Figure 2.6: *You place Web pages in the* wwwroot *directory on* InetPub.

The wwwroot directory of InetPub contains all the Web pages that are used by IIS or PWS. IIS and PWS have built-in intelligence that knows to route a request for a Web page using the *Hypertext Transfer Protocol (HTTP)* to this directory. When making your Web site, you or your webmaster create a subdirectory in wwwroot that is dedicated specifically to your site. Then, as you create pages, you'll place them in your site's directory or in subdirectories of your site's directory.

If you are working on a network, most likely your network administrator will give you direct access to your site directory across the network. The site directory might not appear in your Network Neighborhood Explorer window as a subdirectory of wwwroot. It might appear as a root-level directory on the server.

Figure 2.7 demonstrates this type of directory representation. Figure 2.7 shows you an illustration of two Explorer windows. The Explorer window on the left shows the tree of an NT Server from its wwwroot directory. The window on the right is the Network Neighborhood tree on the client system that accesses the server. Notice that the directory QueAsp is in the wwwroot directory of the server system on the left and as a root level directory of the server representation in Network Neighborhood. (The server is named Socrates.) Both of these windows point to the same location on the server, C:\InetPub\wwwroot\QueAsp. When it comes time to deploy a Web page, all you would need to do is copy your work into the QueASP directory in the client Network Neighborhood Explorer window. Your work is copied to the server without any problem.

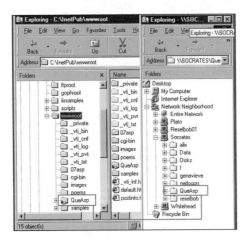

Figure 2.7: *A server can share a directory on a network (as seen in the right pane) without revealing the location of the directory within the server itself (as seen in the left pane).*

The ASP Application and Virtual Directories

As you become a more experienced programmer you'll find that many of the pages you make are related in some way or another. For example, you might have a login page that provides access to a main page. This main page, in turn, allows you access to a guestbook page, a news page, and a family tree page. You can consider all of the pages that make up your site to be a distinct application. IIS and PWS allow you to identify a group of Web pages as members of a common ASP Application (see Figure 2.8).

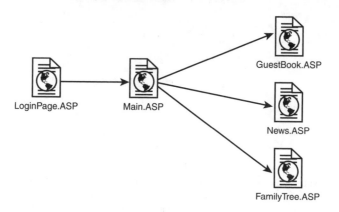

Figure 2.8: *A group of related pages can be organized into an ASP Application.*

✔ For information about the ASP Applications and the Global.ASA file, see Chapter 7, "Intermediate ASP: Processing Data," p. 153.

You create an ASP application by defining a *virtual directory* within IIS or PWS. When you create a virtual directory, the intelligence within IIS and PWS associates any reference to the files in the directory represented by the virtual directory and its subdirectories to be components of an ASP application. After you have an ASP application identified, you can add a Global.asa file to the virtual directory. The Global.ASA file provides data and functions that you can use throughout the many pages that make up your ASP application.

Figure 2.9 shows the Personal Web Manager. You click the Advanced icon in the left side of the manager window to display the dialog box that you use to create a virtual directory.

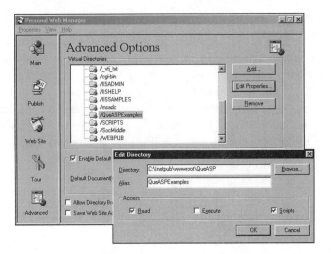

Figure 2.9: *You can create virtual directories within PWS by selecting the Advanced icon.*

CAUTION

When you create a virtual directory, you grant permission for the types of operations that files within the directory can perform. PWS supports the permissions Read, Scripts, and Execute. By default, permissions granted to a virtual directory's files are Read and Scripts. Read means that when a browser asks a Web server for a file, the server can open the file, read the contents, and pass the results back to the calling client. Scripts means that the server can run Active Server Page scripts within the file, passing the results of the script back to the calling browser. Execute means that your browser can invoke executable files (.EXE) and CGI scripts that the server runs in its memory.

If you experience trouble getting your ASP scripts to run, check the permissions of the virtual directory in which the file is stored to make sure that the appropriate permissions are selected.

Figure 2.10 show the first page in the IIS 4.0 Virtual Directory Wizard. You use the IIS Virtual Directory Wizard to create a virtual directory under IIS 4.0. This is the same under IIS version 5.0 also.

Please be advised that the property settings for a virtual directory available to you under IIS 4.0 and IIS 5.0 are much more complex than are those under Personal Web Server. Remember that Internet Information Server is designed to manage sites that support large applications with perhaps thousands of users who make tens of thousands of request an hour. The internal tools that are needed to manage such an enterprise are significant. Again, most enterprises delegate the administration of a site of this magnitude to an experienced Webmaster, well-versed in the intricacies of configuring Internet Information Server.

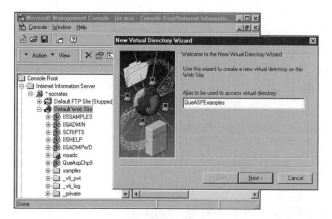

Figure 2.10: *IIS provides a wizard to create Virtual Directories.*

Figure 2.11 shows a virtual directory's properties page as it appears under IIS 5.0. You can see that configuration options are much greater than that of Personal Web Server.

Figure 2.11: *Virtual directory settings for IIS 5.0 (as shown in figure) and IIS 4.0 (not shown) are much more complex than are those for Personal Web Server.*

Referencing a Virtual Directory

After you create a virtual directory, you reference it in a URL as if it were a subdirectory of the Web server's virtual root. The virtual root directory is the directory that the Web server uses as an entry point when you call its domain name. The default virtual root directory that IIS and PWS use is \InetPub\wwwroot. Thus, were a Web server to have a domain name of MySite.Com, when you enter the URL, www.MySite.com into your browser, you are taken to the \InetPut\wwwroot directory of the computer that hosts the domain name, MySite. Should you want to call the virtual directory, QueASPExamples, you reference it by calling the following URL:

http://www.MySite.Com/QueASPExamples

Figure 2.12 illustrates this concept.

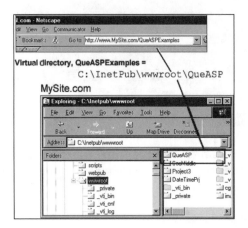

Figure 2.12: *Virtual directories allow you to map a directory anywhere on the server as a subdirectory to the server's domain name.*

It might sound a bit ironic, but many errors that occur in Web site development are not due to mistakes in the internal construction of the site's Web pages. Rather, the errors are due to mistakes in file placement. Many times a Web page will have a hypertext reference that jumps to another page. When the user clicks to make the jump he or she gets the infamous Page not found error. Upon investigation, sometimes the ASP developer finds that the error is caused by improper reference to a virtual directory in the jump's URL. Understanding virtual directories and being able to use them properly will save you headaches.

Your First Client-Side Script

As you might remember from the beginning of this chapter, a script is a series of commands that are executed from within a page of HTML code. Scripts come in two types, client-side and server-side. Client-side scripts are executed by the desktop browser. Server-side scripts are executed by the Internet server before the page content is passed on to the calling browser.

IS WRITING A SCRIPT LIKE WRITING A PROGRAM?

You can do a lot of programming using client-side scripts. It's possible to make Web pages that contain clocks, calendars, and calculators using nothing but script. In addition, you can write client-side script that does animation and performs complex mathematical computation. Don't be fooled by the term, `script`. Both JavaScript and VBScript, the languages you use to script pages, are full-fledged programming languages. Both support fundamental object-oriented programming principals. JavaScript is very similar syntactically to the C programming language and Java. VBScript is a subset of Visual Basic. If you are serious about learning how to write useful, effective scripts, you should plan on investing as much time to learning the scripting language of your choice as you would to learning any other programming language.

NOTE

To learn how to make a client-side calendar using JavaScript go to
`http://javascript.internet.com/calendars/dynamic.html`.

You declare a client-side script by using the <SCRIPT></SCRIPT> tags. Any text that is written between these tags is interpreted by the browser to be script, subject to the scripting language in which it is written. At the present time, the two most prominent browsers, Netscape Navigator and Internet Explorer, support the JavaScript scripting language. Internet Explorer supports VBScript also—Netscape Navigator does not! Keep in mind that if you are writing client-side scripts that you want to run on both Netscape Navigator and Internet Explorer browsers, you would do well to use JavaScript.

Listing 2.2 shows a simple piece of client-side script written in JavaScript. The script allows the user to click a button to show a message in a message dialog box. Figure 2.13 shows the results of the client-side script in a browser.

EXAMPLE

Listing 2.2: Simple Client-Side JavaScript (02asp02.htm)

```
<HTML>
<HEAD>
<TITLE>Simple Message</TITLE>
</HEAD>
<BODY>

<SCRIPT LANGUAGE=javascript>
    function GetMsg(){
    //Use the alert() method to display a message
    //dialog
        alert("Hello Reader");
    }
</SCRIPT>
```

continues

Listing 2.2: continued

```
<Form Name=MyForm>
<P><INPUT name=btnMsg
          type=button
          value="Get Message"
          onclick=GetMsg()></P>
</FORM>
</BODY>
</HTML>
```

OUTPUT

Figure 2.13: *Client-side script is executed within the browser.*

Let's review how the code operates. The page creates a button with the following code:

```
<Form Name=MyForm>
<P><INPUT name=btnMsg
          type=button
          value="Get Message"
          onclick=GetMsg()></P>
</FORM>
```

The code defines an HTML <FORM> with the name, MyForm. A <FORM> is an HTML element that you use to organize data that might later be submitted to a server for processing. We use the <FORM> element here because we want the page to be supported by both the Netscape Navigator and Internet Explorer browsers. Netscape Navigator requires that <INPUT> elements be declared within a <FORM> element. If we did not use the <FORM> element, the <INPUT Type=Button> button would not appear in Netscape Navigator. The need to use <INPUT> elements embedded within a <FORM> element is a peculiarity of the Netscape browser.

CAUTION

Please be advised that Microsoft supports JavaScript in its version of the language called JScript. For the most part, JScript behavior is the same as JavaScript. However, there are instances when JScript behaves differently than JavaScript, particularly when running under Netscape Navigator. You would do best to test your client-side scripts in both browsers before deploying your work.

NOTE

For an excellent online reference guide to JavaScript, go to
`http://developer.netscape.com/docs/manuals/js/client/jsref/index.htm`.

The following code is an extract from Listing 2.2. When the user clicks the button, `btnMsg`, the `onclick=GetMsg()` directive in the `<INPUT>` HTML element fires the `GetMsg()` function within the script tags:

```
<SCRIPT LANGUAGE=javascript>
    //Use the alert() method to display a message
    //dialog
    function GetMsg(){
        alert("Hello Reader");
    }
</SCRIPT>
```

`GetMsg()` displays an alert message bow with the characters `Hello Reader`.

Granted if you are new to scripting, this small demonstration might be mystifying. This little piece of code alone requires you to know a few things about writing script that are not readily apparent. Don't worry, you are going to get a good overview to scripting, particularly VBScript, later in this book. What's important right now is to understand that creating dynamic pages involves programming various parts of your Web page. In this case, we've programmed a button to display an alert message box.

✔ For information about client-side scripting using VBScript see Chapter 3, "The Fundamentals of VBScript," p. 51.

Your First Server-Side Scripts

You create Active Server Pages using server-side script. As you read previously, server-side script is script that is executed by the Internet server, the results of which are then passed on to the calling client.

There are two techniques that you use to define a block of server-side script. One way is to use the `<SCRIPT></SCRIPT>` tags, with the `RUNAT=Server` attribute. The other technique is to embed the line of script between the `<% %>` tags. When you use the `<% %>` tags, you can insert script within standard HTML (refer to Listing 2.1). When the server processes the Active Server Page, it processes the script as it encounters it within the HTML. When you use the `<SCRIPT></SCRIPT>` tags, the server processes the script within these tags after the body of HTML. It is a minor point now, but later as your scripting becomes more complex, this difference will have broader implications.

You can write server-side script in a variety of scripting languages. IIS supports server-side scripting in JavaScript, VBScript, and most recently in PerlScript. If you use the <SCRIPT> tag, you define the script's language by using the Language= attribute, as shown next.

```
<SCRIPT Language=VBScript RUNAT=Server>
```

The <% %> tags support VBScript by default.

Listing 2.3 shows you a simple Active Server Page that uses the <SCRIPT></SCRIPT> tags. The script uses the Response object to send a string of data that reports the current date. Notice the script uses the VBScript Date() function to create the date output dynamically. The Response object represents the data that the server is sending back to the calling client. (You'll cover the Response object in a later chapter.) Figure 2.14 shows the output of the script in a browser.

EXAMPLE

Listing 2.3: Enhancing Scripts with Language Functions (02asp03.asp)

```
<SCRIPT Language=VBScript RUNAT=Server>
    Response.Write "The date is : "
    Response.Write Date()
</SCRIPT>
```

OUTPUT

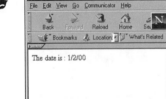

Figure 2.14: *Server-side script allows you to process data before it is sent to a client browser.*

✔ For information about the Response object, see Chapter 6, "Beginning ASP: Client Server Communication," p. 140.

Listing 2.4 shows you a simple Active Server Page that uses the <% %> tags. Please remember that you use the <% %> when you want to intersperse script output with HTML output. The script uses the Response object to send the string of characters, "I am script" to the browser. Figure 2.15 shows the output of the script in a browser.

EXAMPLE

Listing 2.4: Script interspersed within HTML (02asp04.asp)

```
<HEAD>
<TITLE>Simple Message</TITLE>
</HEAD>
```

```
<BODY bgcolor=black>
<FONT Face=ARIAL color=white size = 5>
<%
     Response.Write UCase("I am script")
%>
</FONT>
</BODY>
</HTML>
```

OUTPUT

Figure 2.15: *Combining HTML with script allows you write concise dynamic Web pages.*

Please notice that the HTML that appears in the browser displays all the characters in the string, "I am script" as uppercase. The reason all the characters are uppercase is because of the programming logic in the server-side script. UCase is a VBScript function that transforms all the characters in a string to its uppercase equivalents. The server-side script ran the function on the string, then returned the results. When you look at the client side code in Listing 2.5, you'll see no evidence of the server side script. All you see a string in uppercase characters.

Also notice that the HTML <FONT> tag is in force with regard to the script output. There is nothing in the script that causes the font color of the output to display white. The HTML causes the font to display white and the background color of the page to display black. Interspersing script with HTML leverages the power of both.

EXAMPLE

Listing 2.5: Client-side ASP Output (02asp05.txt)

```
<HTML>
<HEAD>
<TITLE>Simple Message</TITLE>
</HEAD>
<BODY bgcolor=black>
<FONT Face=ARIAL color=white size = 5>
I AM SCRIPT
</FONT>
</BODY>
</HTML>
```

A significant benefit of server-side script is that it allows you to protect your work from being adopted by others. Client-side script is easy for everyone to see. Most browsers allow you to view a page's source code quite easily. Thus, if you use client-side code to create a difficult, laborious algorithm, your hard work is readily available to anyone who wants it. However, implementing the algorithm on the server-side keeps your code private.

Another benefit of server-side script is that it allows you to centralize the logic of your applications to one location, making deployment and maintenance a simple affair. This becomes particularly useful when you use server-side script to get data from a database. After the script retrieves the data from the database, it can use HTML to graphically format the retrieved data—show different types of data in different color fonts and so forth. Should you need to update the data or the format of the data, you don't need to go to every client that uses the page. You simply go to the page on the server that contains the server-side script and alter the script at this central location. The change is transparent to the browser. In a distributed environment the server-based ASP application is the center of attention. The browser is nothing more than an ubiquitous viewing device.

What's Next

In this chapter you learned some fundamental concepts that you need to understand to migrate from writing static Web pages to dynamic Web pages using script. You learned about the different types of server products that Microsoft offers. You learned how to create, configure, and use virtual directories. Finally, you got an introduction to client-side and server-side scripting.

The next chapter gives you a detailed look at VBScript, the default scripting language that you use to write server-side script for ASP. You'll review some of the topics about scripting that we learned in this chapter. Then you'll get knee deep in the details of VBScript. You'll learn how to create variables, make statements, work with loop and conditional statements as well as write user-defined procedures. Last, you'll cover events and event procedures.

Part II

Part II: ASP Programming

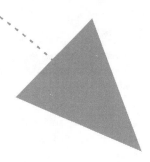

The Fundamentals of VBScript

VBScript and ASP go hand in hand. VBScript is one of the two most promi-nent languages you can use to program server-side, dynamic behavior into the ASP pages you create. You can use JavaScript to work on the server-side, however, many Windows programmers who have prior knowledge of Visual Basic find it easier to use VBScript to do server-side ASP program-ming. VBScript is not case sensitive and the syntax is easy to master. JavaScript, on the other hand, is case sensitive and although it is a more compact language, similar to C, sometimes beginning programmers have trouble getting the nuances of the syntax.

When it comes to writing script that executes on an unknown, client-side browser, JavaScript is the way to go. Remember, at the present time, Netscape Navigator does not support VBScript. Using JavaScript on the client side ensures that your code will execute regardless of whether the browser is Internet Explorer or Netscape Navigator. However, using VBScript on the sever side makes your programming effort a lot easier.

In this chapter you will

- Create variables using VBScript
- Work with Arrays and Collections
- Make statements in VBScript
- Create Subs and Functions
- Work with Event Procedures

VB, VBScript, JavaScript, and Data Types

Before we go on, let's make one thing perfectly clear: Programming is programming, regardless of whether you are writing code in Visual Basic, VBScript, JavaScript, C++, Pascal, or Java. Sometimes, developers who use a scripting language as their main means of expression feel as if they are not really programmers, that they are not as smart or as adept as developers who use other languages such as Java or C++. Don't be fooled. It takes just as much discipline, talent, thoughtfulness, and creativity to make a well-designed program in VBScript as it does in C++. Yes, mastery of language is important, but what you do with the language is more important.

Now that this little misconception is out of the way, let's take an overview of VBScript and a brief peek at JavaScript.

Using `<SCRIPT></SCRIPT>` tags

You use the `<SCRIPT></SCRIPT>` tags when you want to insert script in a Web Page. The `Language=` attribute defines the language in which the script within the tags is written. You have a choice of VBScript or the Microsoft type of JavaScript, JScript. You can use the `<SCRIPT></SCRIPT>` tags to denote both client-side or server-side script. If you want your script to be executed on the client side, use the `RUNAT=Server` attribute within the `<SCRIPT></SCRIPT>` tags.

Listing 3.1 shows you a set of `<SCRIPT></SCRIPT>` tags for some client-side VBScript. This script is executed when the user clicks a specific button, button1, on a Web page running in a client-side browser. Don't worry about the meaning of the code. The important thing to observe here is the use of the `Language` attribute.

EXAMPLE

Listing 3.1: `<SCRIPT></SCRIPT>` Tags Using VBScript (`03asp01.htm`)

```
<SCRIPT LANGUAGE=VBScript>
    Sub button1_OnClick()
        Alert text1.value
    End Sub
</SCRIPT>
```

Figure 3.1 shows the results of the code when the user clicks the button on the Web Page.

OUTPUT

Figure 3.1: *You can use VBScript to display a browser's Alert dialog box.*

<SCRIPT Language = VBScript RUNAT=Server>

You use the RUNAT attribute of the <SCRIPT> tag if you want to write VBScript code that runs on a server only. The <SCRIPT> tag HTML in Listing 3.2 uses the RUNAT attribute to indicate that the script is to be executed on the IIS server and then sent to the calling browser. Again, do not get too caught up in figuring out the script syntax. The important thing here is to understand that the RUNAT attribute makes the script run on the server side.

EXAMPLE

Listing 3.2: Using the RUNAT Attribute to Run Server-Side Script (`03asp02.asp`)

```
<HTML>
<HEAD>
<TITLE></TITLE>
</HEAD>

<BODY>
<SCRIPT LANGUAGE=VBScript RUNAT=Server>
    Response.Write("<FONT SIZE=6 FACE=ARIAL>")
    Response.Write("I am writing this from the server side")
    Response.Write("</FONT>")
</SCRIPT>
<P> </P>
</BODY>
</HTML>
```

The output of this script is shown in Figure 3.2.

Figure 3.2: *Server-side VBScript outputs HTML to the calling browser.*

<Script Language = JavaScript>

You read earlier that you can use JavaScript as your scripting language on both the server and client sides. If you want to use JavaScript as your programming language, set the Language attribute to JavaScript as shown in the first line of Listing 3.3.

Listing 3.3: Setting the Language Attribute to JavaScript (03asp03.htm)

```
<SCRIPT LANGUAGE=javascript>
function button1_onclick() {
    var r = text1.value;
    window.alert(r);
}
</SCRIPT>
```

Figure 3.3 shows the output of the code in Listing 3.3.

Figure 3.3: *The scripting language you use is transparent to the user.*

If you are familiar with the C or Java programming languages, you'll notice that the syntax of JavaScript is very similar to both. JavaScript uses the semicolon to indicate the end of a programming statement, curly brackets (also known as braces) to denote code blocks, and most importantly, JavaScript is case sensitive. When you use JavaScript you cannot use uppercase characters as you would use their lowercase equivalents.

The code in Listing 3.4, which is a variation of Listing 3.3, will not work. Notice in Listing 3.4, the line:

```
window.alert(R);
```

The code in this particular line uses an uppercase R. Whereas in Listing 3.3, the working code uses a lowercase r. Remember that if you are going to use JavaScript always be aware that the language is case sensitive.

EXAMPLE

Listing 3.4: JavaScript is Case Sensitive (`03asp04.htm`)

```
<SCRIPT LANGUAGE=javascript>
function button1_onclick() {
    var r = text1.value;
    window.alert(R);
}
</SCRIPT>
```

VBScript Versus VB

The scripting language that we are going to use in this book when it comes to server-side scripting is VBScript. As you might have heard, VBScript is a sub-set of Visual Basic. This means that VBScript shares many of the features of the parent language. The way you evaluate data, make statements, and control program logic in VBScript is almost identical to the way you do these things in Visual Basic. In addition, most of the functions internal to VB can be used in VBScript. However there are some important differences.

- VBScript explicitly supports one data type only, the Variant.
- VBScript is an interpreted language.
- VBScript cannot directly use the Windows API.
- There are a few syntactical differences in the use of some internal functions.

- You cannot use VBScript to create ActiveX Custom Controls.

- You do not use the Visual Basic programming workbench—the Integrated Development Environment (IDE)—to do VBScript programming.

You might come upon some other idiosyncrasies as you continue to work with VBScript. However, for now, these limitations are the ones with which you really need to be familiar. Outside of these limitations, programming in VBScript is not that different from programming in Visual Basic. And, if you decide to use Microsoft's Visual InterDev as your ASP development tool, you'll find that you can have the ease of a visual programming environment, too.

Now that you know how VBScript is positioned as a scripting language for both server and client scripting, let's get down to the nuts and bolts of VBScript programming.

VBScript, Variables, and Data Types

You read earlier that VBScript supports only one data type, the Variant. (Actually, there are situations where you can use specific data types in VBScript. However, you do not do this directly. It's sort of a behind the scenes type of thing. You'll learn more about this is in a bit.)

The Variant is a special data type. It represents all and any data type known to man. Thus you can use a Variant to represent a String, an Integer, and Object, and so on. This versatility does come at a price: the luxury of type safety does not exist in VBScript. Any variable can be of any type at any time.

Let's look at how to create variables in VBScript.

Creating Variables in VBScript

There are two ways to create a variable in VBScript. One way is to just use the variable. This is called *implicit declaration*. The following example shows you how to create a variable implicitly.

```
<SCRIPT LANGUAGE=VBScript>
    i = 1
</SCRIPT>
```

EXAMPLE
The other way to create a variable in VBScript is to do so explicitly, using the Dim <keyword>. For example, to create a variable, FirstName, you write the following code within a set of <SCRIPT> tags:

```
<SCRIPT LANGUAGE=VBScript>
    Dim FirstName
</SCRIPT>
```

EXAMPLE

Also, later on, after you learn to make classes using VBScript, you can create variables using the Public or Private <keyword>, such as:

```
<SCRIPT LANGUAGE=VBScript>
    Private InsideData
    Public OutsideData
</SCRIPT>
```

OBJECT-ORIENTED VARIABLE DECLARATION

Please be advised that the Private and Public <keyword> come into play when you start doing advanced scripting using the <CLASS> tag. The <CLASS> tag denotes a class. A class is an object-oriented data type that you use to make objects.

Variables that are declared as Public can be used by functions outside of the class in which they are declared. Variables that are declared Private have visibility only within the class.

You assign a value to a variable by using the equal sign as shown in the following lines:

```
Dim s
s = 2
```

Because all variables in VBScript are Variants, you can assign any type of data to a given variable. The variant data type is smart enough to figure out how to accommodate the assignment. For example, although you can create a variable and assign a number to it, you can just as easily assign a string value to it, as follows.

```
Dim s
s = 2
s = "I was a number. Now I am a string"
```

Listing 3.5 declares a variable, FirstName, that receives the value that a user enters into a Web Page's textbox, Text1. When the user clicks the button, an Alert dialog box displays the name entered in the textbox twice.

Listing 3.5: Declaring a Variable with Dim <keyword> (03asp05.htm)

```
<SCRIPT LANGUAGE=VBScript>
    Sub button1_OnClick()
        Dim FirstName
        FirstName =  text1.value
        Alert FirstName & " " & FirstName
    End Sub
</SCRIPT>
```

EXAMPLE

Figure 3.4 shows the output of the code in Listing 3.5.

OUTPUT

Figure 3.4: *Variables add versatility to your Web Page.*

Concatenating Strings

You can combine strings together and assign them to a variable by using the string concatenation operator, the ampersand, &, as follows:

```
s = "This is " & "really cool"
```

Also, in VBScript you can use the plus sign (+) to concatenate strings. The following code is quite valid:

```
s = "This is " + "really cool"
```

However, be advised that if you do use the plus sign, you do run the risk of error. The following code will cause an error in the script:

```
s = "This is " + 5
```

In the previous example, the raw data is made up of two primitive types, a string (`"This is "`) and an integer (5). The plus sign does not know how to reconcile the two different types to get them to work together. However, the ampersand has enough built-in smarts to reconcile the two different data types. Thus, this code works perfectly well:

```
s = "This is " & 5
```

Arrays and Loops

An array is a group of variables that share the same name. Each member of the group is called an *element*. You declare an array as you would a variable except that you add an index number within a set of parentheses in order to indicate how many elements are within the array. For example, to declare an array named Stooges that contains three elements, you write

```
Dim Stooges(2)
```

Usually, the first element of an array has the index number zero. Thus, the second element has the index number one and so on. This is why the array declared previously has an index of two, yet contains three elements. The code in Listing 3.6 shows you how to create the array, Stooges, assign a string as each element, and then display the output in an HTML Input element of type=text. You'll notice that a For...Next loop is used to create the text output. We'll cover For...Next loops in a moment.

LBOUND **AND** UBOUND **FUNCTIONS**

You use the LBound function to determine the lowest bound element of an array. You use the UBound function to determine the upper bound element of an array. The syntax is

```
LBound(ArrayVarName)
UBound(ArrayVarName)
```

For example, in an array MyArray(4)

```
LBound(MyArray) returns 0
UBound(MyArray) returns 4
```

EXAMPLE

Listing 3.6: Using an Array in Script (03asp06.htm)

```
<SCRIPT LANGUAGE=VBScript>
    Sub button1_OnClick()
        Dim Stooges(2)
        Dim i
        Dim OutStr

        Stooges(0) = "Moe"
        Stooges(1) = "Larry"
        Stooges(2) = "Curly"
        For i = 0 to UBound(Stooges)
            OutStr = OutStr + ": " + Stooges(i)
            text1.value = OutStr
        Next
    End Sub
</SCRIPT>
```

Figure 3.5 displays the output of the script shown in Listing 3.6.

OUTPUT

Figure 3.5: *When you use client-side script, you can output data to the HTML text Input element.*

Notice that in Listing 3.5 a For...Next loop is used to traverse an array. VBScript supports the looping statements that you find in standard Visual Basic. Table 3.1 shows you the standard looping statements available to you in VBScript.

Table 3.1: VBScript Looping Statements

Statement	Example
For...Next	For i = 0 to 5 r = 10 + i Next
While...Wend	While i <= 5 i = i + 1 Wend
Do...Loop	Do i = i + 1 Loop Until i > 5

For...Next LOOPS IN VBSCRIPT

When using a For...Next loop in VBScript please be aware that you do not need to include the counter variable in the Next statement as you do in standard Visual Basic.

VISUAL BASIC FOR...NEXT LOOP

```
For i = 0 to 10
    r = 10 + i
Next i
```

VBSCRIPT FOR...NEXT LOOP

```
For i = 0 to 10
    r = 10 + i
Next
```

Resizing Arrays

If you want to resize an array, you use the ReDim <keyword>. Please be advised that you can resize an array only if it has been created without declaring any elements in the array.

If you find that you need to continually re-dimension a given array, you use the Preserve <keyword> to keep the data in the array intact. If you do not use the Preserve <keyword>, all the data in the array will be removed.

Listing 3.7 shows you how to create an array, Stooges, resize it to accommodate three elements, then resize it again to accommodate an added element, while maintaining the data associated with the three previous elements.

EXAMPLE

Listing 3.7: Using the ReDim Statement (03asp07.htm)

```
<SCRIPT LANGUAGE=VBScript>
    Sub button1_OnClick()
        Dim Stooges()
        Dim i
        Dim OutStr

        Redim Preserve Stooges(2)

        Stooges(0) = "Moe"
        Stooges(1) = "Larry"
        Stooges(2) = "Curly"

        Redim Preserve Stooges(3)
        Stooges(3) = "Shemp"

        For i = 0 to UBound(Stooges)
            OutStr = OutStr + ": " + Stooges(i)
            text1.value = OutStr
        Next
    End Sub
</SCRIPT>
```

Figure 3.6 shows the output from Listing 3.7.

Figure 3.6: *The output from a re-dimensioned array.*

Now that you have an understanding as to how to declare variables and arrays, let's learn how to use them to make statements.

Statements and Expressions

A statement, also known as an *expression*, is an instruction that you create using VBScript, or any other language for that matter. You can create statements that assign a value to a variable. You can create statements that perform mathematical operations using variables. You can create statements that execute other statements, and so forth.

VBScript requires that a complete statement be written on a single line. If you do need to extend a statement over multiple lines, you can use the underscore character_, which VBScript interprets as the line continuation character. For example, both of the statements in Listing 3.8 are valid.

Listing 3.8: The Line Continuation Character _ (03asp08.htm)

```
<SCRIPT LANGUAGE=VBScript>
    Dim y
    Dim s
    s = (y + y) + (y + 1 + y + 1) + (y + 2 + y + 2)

    s = (y + y) + (y + 1 + y + 1) + _
                    (y + 2 + y + 2)
    Alert s
</SCRIPT>
```

CAUTION

You cannot use the line continuation character to break up a string within the quotation marks.

This will error:

```
<SCRIPT LANGUAGE=VBScript>
    Dim s
    s = "I am an erroneously _
        extended string"
</SCRIPT>
```

If you want to extend a string over two lines, you must truncate the string first, as follows:

```
<SCRIPT LANGUAGE=VBScript>
    Dim s
    s = "I am a properly" & _
        "extended string"
</SCRIPT>
```

Using Math Operators

VBScript supports the usual math operators. Table 3.2 shows you the math operators, with an example for each.

Table 3.2: VBScript Simple Math Operators

Operator	Description	Example
+	Addition	t = r + s
-	Subtraction	t = r -s
*	Multiplication	t = r * s
/	Floating point division	t = r / s
^	Exponent	t = 2 ^ 3
		(t evaluates to 8)
mod	Remainder	t = 3 mod 1
		(t evaluates to 1, the remainder of 3 divided by 2)

Inequality Operators

Inequality statements are what you normally think of as greater than and less than statements. VBScript supports the following symbols shown in Table 3.3.

Table 3.3: VBScript Inequality Operators

Operator	Description	Example	Evaluates
<>	Not equal	2 <> 3	True
<	Less than	2 < 3	True
<=	Less than or equal to	2 <= 2	True
>	Greater than	2 > 3	False
>=	Greater than or equal to	3 >= 3	True

Conditional Statements

A conditional statement is one that passes control to another statement when it evaluates to true. VBScript supports these statements: If...Then, If...Then...Else, If...Then...ElseIf...Else, and Select Case statements.

The following example demonstrates the syntax for a simple If...Then statement that executes one line of code and another that executes multiple lines of code.

EXAMPLE

```
<SCRIPT LANGUAGE=VBScript>
    If x = 5 Then y = 9

    If x = 5 Then
        'Send out an alert message
        Alert "x = 5, it really does!"
        y = 9
    End If
</SCRIPT>
```

Notice that the If...Then statement that executes multiple lines of code terminates with an End...If line.

The next example shows you how to write an If...Then...Else statement. You use an If...Then...Else statement when you need to have alternate code execute if the If condition is not met.

EXAMPLE

```
<SCRIPT LANGUAGE=VBScript>
    If x = 5 Then
        y =0
        i = 14
    Else
        y = 9
        i = 200
    End If
</SCRIPT>
```

You use the `If...Then...ElseIf` statement to test for multiple conditions. The following example shows you how to us the `If...Then...ElseIf` statement:

EXAMPLE

```
<SCRIPT LANGUAGE=VBScript>
    If y > 10 Then
        x = x + y
    ElseIf y > 100 Then
        x = x + x + y
    Else
        x = x
    End If
</SCRIPT>
```

COMMENTING IN VBSCRIPT

You comment a line in VBScript by using the single quote character, ', at the beginning of the line. Also, remember you can comment only lines that appear within a set of `<SCRIPT>` tags.

The following shows a commented line:

```
<SCRIPT LANGUAGE=VBScript>
    'Declare a variable
    Dim y
</SCRIPT>
```

Similarly, you write comments within in line script tags as follows

```
<%
    'Declare a variable
    Dim y
%>
```

Select Case Statements

The `Select Case` statement allows you to itemize blocks of code to execute according to a test variable, basically helping you to test against many conditions very efficiently. The following code in Listing 3.9 shows you how to use a `Select Case` statement, and Figure 3.7 shows the output of the code.

Listing 3.9: Using `Select Case` Statements (`03asp09.htm`)

EXAMPLE

```
<SCRIPT LANGUAGE=VBScript>

    Sub button1_OnClick()
        Dim TestVar
        Dim varTrait
        'Get the stooge that the user entered
        TestVar = text1.value
        'You start a Select Case statement with
        'the keyword Select Case and the given test
```

continues

Listing 3.9: continued

```
'variable. Please be advised that TestVar is
    'an arbitrary variable name.
    Select Case TestVar
        'Then use the keyword Case followed by
        'the value of the test variable to which
        'you want to respond. In this case, if
        'the test variable = "Moe", then assign the
        'value "Bossy" to another variable.
        Case "Moe":
            varTrait = "Bossy"
        'If the test variable = "Larry" assign the
        'string, "Whiney" to the variable, varTrait.
        Case "Larry":
            varTrait = "Whiney"
        'If the test variable = "Curly" assign the
        'string, "Funny" to the variable, varTrait.
        Case "Curly":
            varTrait = "Funny"
        'You use Case Else when there are no other
        'match can be found.
        'IMPORTANT: Don't forget to put the colon at
        'the end of each Case condition.
        Case Else:
            varTrait = "Unknown"
        'You end a Select Case construct with the End
        'Select keywords.
    End Select

    text2.value = varTrait
End Sub

</SCRIPT>
```

OUTPUT

Figure 3.7: *The output from the* Select Case *statement.*

Procedures

A procedure is a set of statements to which you assign a name. Then, when you want to execute the statements within the procedure you use the name that you assigned to the procedure. VBScript supports two kinds of procedures. The first kind is a `Sub`. The second kind is a `Function`.

Sub

A `Sub` is a procedure that executes the statements within its code block, but does not return a value when execution is complete. You create a `Sub` using the following syntax:

```
<SCRIPT LANGUAGE=VBScript>
    Sub SubName()
    ...statements
    End Sub
</SCRIPT>
```

Where `Sub` and `End Sub` are VBScript keywords. `SubName` is a user-defined name of the procedure. Parentheses are required following the `SubName`.

You've seen `Sub` throughout this chapter, in the guise of the `OnClick()` event procedure. (Event procedures are special `Subs` that you'll learn about later in this chapter.)

Listing 3.10 shows an example of a `Sub`, `GetBiggerNumber()`, which is called from another `Sub`, `button1_OnClick()`. Please notice that the `Call <keyword>` is used within the event procedure `button1_OnClick()` to execute the `Sub`, `GetBiggerNumber()`. The `Call <keyword>`, although optional to use to execute a `Sub`, is a good tool to use. It allows anyone viewing your code to see that a `Sub` rather than a variable is being accessed. For the most part, the order in which `Subs` are written is irrelevant in terms of precedent of execution (see Listing 3.10) .

EXAMPLE

Listing 3.10: A Simple `Sub` (03asp10.htm)

```
<HTML>
<HEAD>
<TITLE></TITLE>
</HEAD>
<SCRIPT LANGUAGE=VBScript>


    Sub GetBiggerNumber()
        Dim x
        Dim y
        'Get the First Number
        x = Cint(text1.value)
```

continues

Listing 3.10: continued

```
'Get the Second Number
    y = Cint(text2.value)

    If x > y Then
        text3.value = x
    Else
        text3.value = y
    End If

End Sub

Sub button1_OnClick()
    Call GetBiggerNumber
End Sub
</SCRIPT>

<BODY>

<P>First Number: <INPUT name=text1 size=15></P>

<P>Second Number:
<INPUT name=text2 size=15></P>

<INPUT type="button" value="Get Bigger Number" name=button1>

<P>Bigger Number: <INPUT name=text3 size=15></P>

</BODY>
</HTML>
```

Figure 3.8 displays the output of the code in Listing 3.10.

OUTPUT

Figure 3.8: *Using a Sub promotes code reusability.*

Function

A Function is a procedure that returns a value upon execution. You construct it very much in the same way that you do a Sub. However, instead of using the Sub <keyword> you use the Function <keyword>. Moreover and most importantly, you pass a value out of a Function by assigning the value to the function's name. Writing well-designed functions is the first step toward creating well-encapsulated code. Listing 3.11 shows you code in which the Sub GetBiggerNumber has been transformed to a Function called GetBiggerNumber(). The function returns a value, which depends on the larger value entered into text elements on a Web page.

EXAMPLE

Listing 3.11: Returning a Value from a Function (03asp11.htm)

```
<HTML>
<HEAD>
<TITLE></TITLE>
</HEAD>
<SCRIPT LANGUAGE=VBScript>


    Function GetBiggerNumber()
        Dim x
        Dim y
        'Get the First Number
        x = CInt(text1.value)
        'Get the Second Number
        y = CInt(text2.value)

        'Pass the larger number out of the
        'function by assigning the value to
        'the function's name.
        If x > y Then
            GetBiggerNumber = x
        Else
            GetBiggerNumber = y
        End If

    End Function

    Sub button1_OnClick()
        'Use the return of the function, GetBiggerNumber
        'as the value to assign to the text element,
        'text3.
        text3.value = GetBiggerNumber()
    End Sub
</SCRIPT>
```

continues

Listing 3.11: continued

```
<BODY>

<P>First Number: <INPUT name=text1 size=15></P>

<P>Second Number:
<INPUT name=text2 size=15></P>

<INPUT type="button" value="Get Bigger Number" name=button1>

<P>Bigger Number: <INPUT name=text3 size=15></P>

</BODY>
</HTML>
```

Listing 3.11 changes the internals of the page. However, the output of that listing is much the same as what is shown in Figure 3.8.

Working with Arguments

When you consider the code in Listing 3.11, you'll see there is a problem. For the function GetBiggerNumber to work in any other Web page, HTML text elements named text1 and text2 must be on the new page. Otherwise, the code will not work. This is very poor function design.

A function that is designed well maintains internal integrity even if the code is cut and pasted from one Web page to the next. We can remove the text elements' dependency on GetBiggerNumber by using arguments in the function.

An argument is a placeholder for data that you pass into a function. Using arguments makes your functions more independent and reusable. We are going to enhance the GetBiggerNumber function to take two arguments, ArgOne and ArgTwo. Then, when the function is used, we pass the numbers we want to be compared as values for ArgOne and ArgTwo.

Listing 3.12 shows the code for the enhanced version of GetBiggerNumber.

EXAMPLE

Listing 3.12: Enhancing Functions with Arguments (03asp12.htm)

```
<HTML>
<HEAD>
<TITLE></TITLE>
</HEAD>
<SCRIPT LANGUAGE=VBScript>


    Function GetBiggerNumber(ArgOne, ArgTwo)
        Dim x
```

```
        Dim y
        'Get the value from the first argument
        x = CInt(ArgOne)
        'Get the value from the second argument
        y = CInt(ArgTwo)

        'Pass the larger number out of the
        'function by assigning the value to
        'the function's name.
        If x > y Then
            GetBiggerNumber = x
        Else
            GetBiggerNumber = y
        End If

    End Function

    Sub button1_OnClick()
        'Call GetBiggerNumber and pass the
        'values in text elements, text1 and text2
        'as arguments to the function.
        text3.value = GetBiggerNumber(text1.value, text2.value)
    End Sub
</SCRIPT>

<BODY>

<P>First Number: <INPUT name=text1 size=15></P>

<P>Second Number:
<INPUT name=text2 size=15></P>

<INPUT type="button" value="Get Bigger Number" name=button1>

<P>Bigger Number: <INPUT name=text3 size=15></P>

</BODY>
</HTML>
```

Again, the output of this code will not look any different from what you see in Figure 3.8. The important thing here is to recognize that all the enhancements have taken place with regard to how the internals of the function work, not to the output behavior).

Beware of Types

Consider the following sample of code from Listing 3.10.

```
'Get the value from the first argument
x = CInt(ArgOne)
'Get the value from the second argument
y = CInt(ArgTwo)

If x > y Then
    GetBiggerNumber = x
Else
    GetBiggerNumber = y
End If
```

You might be wondering why the VBScript conversion function CInt() is used. CInt() converts string values that look like numerals into actual integers. Although it is true that all variables declared in VBScript are Variants, and Variants can represent any data type known to man, things are not always as easy or as universal as they seem.

Things get a little murky when data is assigned to the arguments. If the Variant ArgOne contains the value 12 and ArgOne decides to be a string, and the Variant ArgTwo contains the value 5 and decides to be a string also, the function returns the value 5. Mathematically the numeric value 5 is definitely not greater than 12. However in terms of string comparisons, 5 is greater than 12. It's the way strings work.

Therefore, to avoid this sort of inaccuracy, we need to be able to tell the Variants to interpret its value as an Integer. This is where the VBScript CInt() function comes in handy. When we apply the function to the Variant ArgOne, we are telling the variant to consider ArgOne to be an Integer. The process is called *typecasting*. We are transforming a variable from type Variant to type Integer.

VBScript provides a variety of type conversion functions. Table 3.4 shows you the ones most commonly used.

Table 3.4: Often-Used VBScript Conversion Functions

Function	Description
CInt(var)	Converts the variable to an Integer
CStr(var)	Converts the variable to a String
CDbl(var)	Converts the variable to a Double
CLng(var)	Converts the variable to a Long
CCur(var)	Converts the variable to Currency
CBool(var)	Converts the variable to a Boolean (True/False)
CDate(var)	Converts the variable to a Date

There will be many times when you will need to ensure that your variables are of a specific type, particularly after you assign ambiguous values to a variable. You'll find conversion functions to be a handy tool to help you ensure your data's integrity.

Event Procedures

There are a special group of procedures that you create that are executed automatically by the browser or Internet Information Server when an event is fired. These procedures are called event procedures.

An *event procedure* is code that you program, and that is run in response to a given event that is fired within a program, object or Web page. The event procedure you are probably most familiar with is the OnClick event, which is associated with the Click event of a button. Whenever a user clicks on a button on a Web page in a browser, a Click event is fired by the browser. After the event is fired, the browser will go off to look for an OnClick event procedure within the Web page's <SCRIPT> tags. If the event procedure exists, it is executed. If none is found, the browser goes on about its business. The same dynamic is in force for Internet Information Server when server side events are fired.

Most of the common events have an event procedure associated with each particular event. For instance, Click events are associated with OnClick event procedures. MouseMove events are associated with OnMouseMove event procedures, MouseDown events are associated with OnMouseDown event procedures, and so forth.

In VBScript you must create the event procedure for the event that you want to capture. This is very unlike standard Visual Basic where the Visual Basic IDE creates the skeleton of a given event's event procedure code for you. It's a little tricky to get used to doing all this from scratch. However, it is a skill easily mastered with a little practice.

CAUTION

If you do not name an event procedure just right, you might be in for a surprise. The code will not produce an error. It simply will be ignored by the browser or IIS as just another procedure sitting in a set of <SCRIPT> tags.

Event Procedure Naming Syntax

The syntax for naming an event procedure is

```
Sub ElementName_OnEventName()
    'statements and stuff
End Sub
```

Where

- The Sub and End Sub keywords denote a procedure.

- ElementName is the name of the HTML element or object that causes the event to be fired.

- The underscore character (_) relates the element to the event.

- On are the prefix characters that relate the event procedure to a given event.

- EventName is the event the event procedure is capturing.

The following code is an example of the code skeleton that you would write to capture the Click event of a button named MyButton.

```
Sub MyButton_OnClick()
    'Your code would be here
End Sub
```

This is the code skeleton that you would write to capture a MouseOver event for an Image element named MyImage:

```
Sub MyImage_OnMouseOver()
    'Your code would be here
End Sub
```

The important thing to remember is that you must use the prefix, On to identify the event of the event procedure for which you are creating the code skeleton. The following example is the code skeleton that you would not create to capture the Click event of a button named BigButton.

```
Sub BigButton_Click()
    'Your code would be here. But it
    'wouldn't execute anyway. You forgot
    'the On prefix for the Click.
End Sub
```

A browser can fire many different events. The code in Listing 3.13 shows you a Web page in which there are two event procedures, one to capture a Click event for a button element and another to capture a MouseOver event for an image element. The output of the code is shown in Figure 3.9.

EXAMPLE

Listing 3.13: Using Click and MouseOver Events (03asp13.htm)

```
<HTML>
<HEAD>
<TITLE></TITLE>

</HEAD>
<SCRIPT LANGUAGE=VBScript>
```

```
Sub image1_OnMouseOver()
    Dim s

    s = "You are moving over " & image1.name
    text1.value = s
End Sub

Sub button1_OnClick()
Dim s

s = "You have clicked a button"
text1.value = s
End Sub
</SCRIPT>

<BODY>

<P><INPUT name=text1 size=30></P>
<P>
<INPUT type="button" value="Click Me" name=button1>
</P>
<P>Mouse your mouse over the blue box: </P>
<P><INPUT type=Image src="box.gif" name=image1></P>

<P> </P>

</BODY>
</HTML>
```

OUTPUT

Figure 3.9: *Event procedures provide real-time functionality to your Web applications.*

Server-Side Events

This book is about ASP, therefore; most of the event procedures that you'll create in your scripts will be those that you program in response to server-side events. Luckily there are not as many events on the server side as there are on the client side. Actually, there are only two events that will take the bulk of your attention. One event is the `Start` event; the other is the `End` event.

The `Start` event is fired when an ASP Application or an ASP Session begins. The event procedures that you program are `Session_OnStart` and `Application_OnStart`.

The `End` event is fired when an ASP Application or ASP Session ends. You program the `Session_OnEnd` and `Application_OnEnd` event procedures. You'll learn more about the Application and Session objects later in this book. For now, the important thing to know is that IIS does fire events and that you can program server-side script to capture these events.

THE APPLICATION AND SESSION OBJECTS

The Application object is an ASP construct that encompasses all the Web pages that make up your ASP application. The Application object allows you to treat each Web page as a part of a larger program.

The Session object allows you to keep track of a given user's activities between pages.

✔ For more information on the Application and Session objects, see Chapter 7, "Intermediate ASP: Processing Data," p. 153.

Scope

VBScript supports variable scope. This means that the lifetime and visibility of a variable depends on the place in code in which you create it. Support for scope allows you to give different variables the same name and not have to worry about name collision if the variables are of different scope. Being able to give common names to variables with different scope promotes code reusability. You don't have to spend a lot of time worrying about a preexisting name for a variable you are about to create. It doesn't matter as long as the variable in not in the same scope.

Local Variables

Local variables are declared within a procedure. The variable lives only as long as the procedure is in force. After the procedure terminates, the variable is removed from memory and the value assigned to it vaporizes.

Please look at the code in Listing 3.11. Notice that the event procedures `image1_OnMouseMove()` and `button1_OnClick()` have a variable, s. These are two distinct variables. Each s variable is local to the specific event procedure. Each variable is created when the event procedure is run. When the event procedure ends, the s variable is removed from memory.

Script-Level Variables

If a variable is created outside of a procedure, it lives as long as the page is being processed and can be seen by any other variable within the page.

Listing 3.14 shows code that uses script-level code. Notice the variable y is created within the <SCRIPT> tags, yet outside of any one procedure. This means that the variable is in force for as long as the Web page is active and that it can be seen from anywhere in the page, from within any procedure. You use variables with script level scope when you need to share data between procedures.

Figure 3.10 displays the output of from Listing 3.14.

EXAMPLE

Listing 3.14: Using Script-Level Scope (03asp14.htm)

```
<HTML>
<HEAD>
<TITLE></TITLE>
</HEAD>
<SCRIPT LANGUAGE=VBScript>
    'Declare a variable with script level scope
    Dim y

    Sub button1_OnClick()
        Dim x
        x = 100
        y = text1.value
        text2.value = x + y
    End Sub

    Sub button2_OnClick()
        Dim x
        x = 50
        y = text1.value
        text3.value = x + y
    End Sub

</SCRIPT>

<BODY>

<P>The value of Y =    <INPUT name=text1 size=6></P>
```

continues

Listing 3.14: continued

```
<P><INPUT  name=button1 type=button value="Button 1 (x = 100)"></P>
<P><INPUT name=button2 type=button value="Button 2 (x = 50)"></P>
<HR>

<P>The value you get when you click Button1 is:
<INPUT name=text2 size=6></P>
<P>The value you get when you click Button 2 is:
<INPUT name=text3 size=6></P>
```

OUTPUT

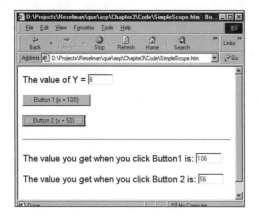

Figure 3.10: A script-level variable can be seen from anywhere within the page.

What's Next

This chapter provided a fast overview of VBScript. It is by no means exhaustive, as there is a lot to the language. As you move on with this book, we'll keep adding to your VBScript knowledge. However, be advised that Microsoft has put the complete documentation for VBScript online. It's comprehensive and it's free! You can locate it on the Microsoft Web site at

`http://msdn.microsoft.com/scripting/default.htm?/scripting/ vbscript/doc/vbstoc.htm`

The next chapter introduces you to the fundamentals of writing ASP script. You'll put the VBScript that you have learned here to use, but you will do so within a server side ASP framework. Therefore, you'll need to have access to a server running IIS minimally on Windows NT 4.0, if not Windows 2000. On the other hand, if you are developing ASP Pages on your desktop computer, you'll need a copy of PWS running.

NOTE

PWS is available for download at

`http://www.microsoft.com/windows/ie/pws/default.htm?RLD=23`

4

Writing Script for the Server Side

Writing server-side ASP script is different from writing script that is meant to run exclusively on client-side browsers. Server-side script is more abstract in the sense that you never really get to see your final work until all the logic in the page is run and HTML output is sent on to the calling client. Server-side scripting has a greater level of abstraction than that which you do on a sole client machine. ASP script makes a Web page's layout a framework into which you pour your data. The ASP code you write on the server-side rarely appears as identical HTML when it reaches the client.

In this chapter you will

- Learn how the server interprets script

- Write inline, server-side script

- Create procedures in your server-side script

- Execute script using the <SCRIPT> tag

- Make client-side calls back to functions on the ASP server

How a Server-Side Page Works

You can conceptualize an ASP page to be HTML interspersed with script that is executed as the page is called into memory by IIS (Internet Information Server). When the server comes across some script in an ASP page, it says to itself, "Hey I have some script coming up here. I am not going to pass this text on to the calling client. Instead I am going to interpret it as script and execute the statements accordingly" (see Figure 4.1).

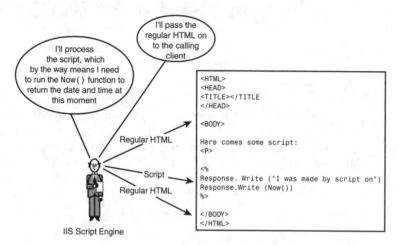

Figure 4.1: *Server-side script allows you to process VBScript functions and then transform the output into HTML output.*

NOTE

IIS identifies an Active Server Page as a file that has the filename extension, `.asp`.

There are two ways you can implement server-side script. One way is to write the script inline. The other way is to embed script between `<SCRIPT></SCRIPT>` tags.

Writing Inline Script

Writing server-side script inline means that the script is executed by the server-side scripting engine in the order that it appears in the ASP page. You indicate inline server-side script in your page by placing the programming statements between the following symbols `<% %>`.

Listing 4.1 shows a simple Active Server Page that has inline script.

Listing 4.1: An Active Server Page with a Simple Inline Script (04asp01.asp)

```
<HTML>
<HEAD>
<TITLE></TITLE>
</HEAD>

<BODY>

Here comes some script:
<P>
<%
Response.Write("I was made by script on ")
Response.Write(Now())
%>
<P> </P>

</BODY>
</HTML>
```

Notice that two lines of script are executed between the <% %> symbols. The script uses the Response object to send the line, "I was made by script on" to the calling client browser. (For now please consider the Response object to be a way to send data back to the calling browser. We'll cover the Response object in more detail in other chapters.) Then, the script executes the VBScript Now() function to retrieve the exact date and time at the moment the page was loaded into the server's memory for processing. The script transforms the output of the Now() function into a string, which it passes on to the calling browser. Figure 4.2 shows the script output that has been sent to the calling browser. Listing 4.2 shows the source code behind the client-side display.

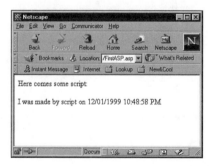

Figure 4.2: *ASP output can be browser-independent HTML.*

Listing 4.2: ASP Output on the Client (04asp02.htm)

```
<HTML>
<HEAD>
<TITLE></TITLE>
```

Listing 4.2: continued

```
</HEAD>

<BODY>

Here comes some script:
<P>
I was made by script on 12/01/1999 10:48:58 PM
<P> </P>

</BODY>
</HTML>
```

Interspersing Inline Script

You can intersperse inline script within an Active Server Page. The script is executed in the order in which it is encountered. The ASP code in Listing 4.3 shows you how to intersperse inline throughout a single Active Server Page.

EXAMPLE

Listing 4.3: Interspersed Active Server Page Script (04asp03.asp)

```
<HTML>
<HEAD>
<TITLE></TITLE>
</HEAD>

<BODY>

Here comes some script:
<P>
<%
Response.Write("I was made by script on ")
Response.Write(Now())
%>
<P><FONT Color=Red Size= 4>
Here comes some more script:
<P>
<%
Response.Write("Today's date in serial time is: ")
Response.Write(CLng(Date()))
%>
</FONT>
</BODY>
</HTML>
```

Figure 4.3 shows you the page's output. Please notice that the script output is subject to the color and size attributes of the <FONT> tag. The ASP engine respects tag directives outside the script symbols when creating script output.

Figure 4.3: *Serial time treats each day as 1 and starts counting days at December 31, 1899.*

Using Variables Inline

You declare variables within inline script symbols just as you would declare them with <SCRIPT></SCRIPT> tags. When you declare a variable inline, it has page level scope. It can been seen from anywhere in the page, unless you declare the variable within a procedure. (You'll learn how to use procedures within inline script in the section "Using Procedures" later in this chapter.)

You can use page-level variables to pass data between inline script blocks. Listing 4.4 shows you an Active Sever Page with two instances of inline script. The variable MyDate has been declared within one inline script block and used within another. Figure 4.4 shows the output of the Active Server Page content.

EXAMPLE

Listing 4.4: Using Variables in Server-Side Script (04asp04.asp)

```
<HTML>
<HEAD>
<TITLE></TITLE>
</HEAD>

<BODY>

Here comes some script:
<P>
<%
Dim MyDate
MyDate = CDate(Now() - 30)
Response.Write("Here is a secret date: ")
Response.Write(MyDate)
%>
<P><FONT Color=Red Size= 4>
Here comes some more script:
```

Listing 4.4: continued

```
<P>
<%
Response.Write("Here is a secret date, the day before: ")
Response.Write(CDate(MyDate -1))
%>
</FONT>
</BODY>
</HTML>
```

Here comes some script:

Here is a secret date: 11/02/1999 4:37:24 PM

Here comes some more script:

Here is a secret date, the day before:
11/01/1999 4:37:24 PM

Figure 4.4: Here is the output from Listing 4.4.

Using Procedures

You declare procedures within inline script just as you do within the
<SCRIPT></SCRIPT> tags.

Listing 4.5 shows you how to create a procedure within an inline script
block. The Sub GetSecretDate contains the code statements that were previously executed as strict inline script. A new piece of inline script has been
added that calls the procedure. Figure 4.5 shows the Active Server Page
output.

Listing 4.5: A Sub Procedure Within Inline Script (04asp05.asp)

```
<HTML>
<HEAD>
<TITLE></TITLE>
</HEAD>

<BODY>
<%
    Sub GetSecretDate()
        Dim MyDate
        MyDate = CDate(Now() - 30)
```

```
            Response.Write("Here is a secret date: ")
            Response.Write(MyDate)
      End Sub
%>
Here comes some script:
<P>
<%

      Call GetSecretDate
%>
<P><FONT Color=Red Size= 4>
Here comes some more script:
<P>
<%
Response.Write("Here is a secret date, the day before: ")
Response.Write(CDate(MyDate -1))
%>
</FONT>
</BODY>
</HTML>
```

EXAMPLE

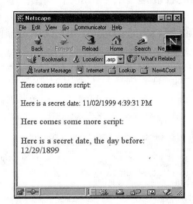

Figure 4.5: *Variables declared in a procedure are local to the procedure.*

Notice that the output from the last inline script block in Listing 4.5 is a little out of kilter with the logic of the previous two examples. The first block outputs 11/02/1999 as the secret date, yet the output is saying the day before is 12/29/1899, when logically the date should be 11/01/99. Why is this happening? No, it's not a Y2K problem. It's a scope problem.

You can think of *variable scope* as the level by which a variable is visible. Variables created within a procedure can be seen by statements within the procedure, only. Any statement outside of the procedure cannot see inside the procedure to work with the procedure's variables. In fact, statements outside of a procedure do not even know that variables inside a procedure exist. Hence, it's possible to use a single variable name on many variables without any sort of name collision, as long as the variables are not visible to one another.

ASP supports two levels of scope, page level and procedure level. Page level variables can be seen by any statement within the Active Server Page, regardless where in the page the statement is. Any variable created outside of a procedure, within the body of an Active Server Page script has page level scope. Procedure level variables, on the other hand, exist within the procedure in which they were created, only.

When you look at the procedure GetSecretDate() in Listing 4.5, you'll notice that a variable MyDate is created within the procedure. Later within the page you see MyDate used in the script block, in the line:

```
Response.Write(CDate(MyDate -1))
```

Although they share the same name, these are two different variables. The MyDate in the GetSecretDate() has scope local to that procedure. When the procedure ends, the variable vaporizes. The MyDate used in the script block has page level scope. When you create a variable, its initial value is zero. Thus, the value of the page level MyDate within the last script block is zero. The MyDate–1 expression evaluates to –1, which the CDate() function type-casts to 12/30/1899, the serial date equivalent.

CAUTION

VBScript does not require explicit variable declaration. Therefore "Dim"-ing a variable before you use it is optional. When you use a variable, you are declaring it.

Be careful, mistyped variables will just be considered new variables.

You can require explicit variable declaration within your Active Server Pages by using the Option Explicit keyword as the first statement within a set of script tags at the top of the Active Server Page. Like so:

```
<%Option Explicit%>
```

Writing Inline Functions

You write a function within an inline, server-side script block just as you would any other type of procedure. The only difference is that you use the Function keyword and that you return a value from the function by assigning the return value to the function's name. You can access a function declared inline from anywhere within the Active Server Page.

Listing 4.6 shows inline script in which the Sub GetSecretDate has been transformed to a function, GetSecretDate(). GetSecretDate() returns a Variant, which indicates the secret date. Figure 4.6 displays the output of Listing 4.6 in a browser.

EXAMPLE

Listing 4.6: A Function Within Inline Script (04asp06.asp)

```
<HTML>
<HEAD>
<TITLE></TITLE>
</HEAD>

<BODY>
<%
    Function GetSecretDate()
        Dim MyDate
        MyDate = CDate(Now() - 30)
        GetSecretDate = MyDate
    End Function
%>
Here comes some script using a function:
<P>
<%
Response.Write("The secret date is: ")
Response.Write(GetSecretDate())
%>
<P><FONT Color=Red Size= 4>
Here comes some more script:
<P>
<%
Response.Write("Here is a secret date, the day before: ")
Response.Write(CDate(GetSecretDate() -1))
%>
</FONT>
</BODY>
</HTML>
```

OUTPUT

Figure 4.6: *Using an inline function makes your code easier to maintain.*

Writing Inline Loops

You write server-side, inline loops by inserting the loop output between two related script blocks. One script block contains the loop generation statement). The other script block contains the loop iteration statement(s). Listing 4.7 shows an Active Server Page that contains inline, server script for a For...Next loop and a While...Wend loop. Figure 4.7 displays the output in a browser. Notice that the <% %> script symbols bound the For and Next lines of the For...Next loop, but that the inline script symbols do not appear around the line "I am in a For...Next loop." This standard HTML is repeatedly sent as output while the loop is in force. The same is true of the script construction for the While...Wend loop.

EXAMPLE

Listing 4.7: Server-Side Script with Loops(04asp07.asp)

```
<HTML>
<HEAD>
<TITLE></TITLE>
</HEAD>

<BODY>
<P><FONT Color=Red Size= 2>
Here comes some For...Next script:
<P>
<% For i = 1 to 10%>
    I am in a For...Next loop<BR>
<%Next%>
<P>
Here comes some While...Wend script:
<P>
<%While r <= 10%>
    I am in a While...Wend loop<BR>
<%
r = r + 1
Wend
%>
</FONT>
</BODY>
</HTML>
```

OUTPUT

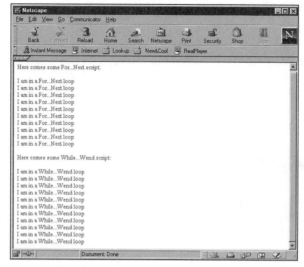

Figure 4.7: *Inline loops are a good way to generate large amounts of standard HTML quickly.*

Using RUNAT=Server

You learned in previous chapters that you can define server-side script in your Active Server Page by setting the RUNAT attribute of the <SCRIPT> tag as RUNAT=Server.

CAUTION

Please be advised that VBScript does not support an RUNAT=client attribute. There is only one use for the RUNAT attribute and that is RUNAT=server.

Listing 4.8 shows you a piece of script that was used previous in this chapter. However, this script is embedded into a set of <SCRIPT></SCRIPT> tags.

EXAMPLE

Listing 4.8: Load order of <SCRIPT></SCRIPT> (04asp08.asp)

```
<HTML>
<HEAD>
<TITLE></TITLE>
</HEAD>

<BODY>
<P><FONT Color=Red Size= 4>
Here comes some script:
<P>
<SCRIPT Language=VBScript RUNAT=Server>
    Response.Write("I was made by script on ")
    Response.Write(Now())
```

continues

Listing 4.8: continued

```
</SCRIPT>

<P>I am the last line in the Web Page.</P>
</FONT>
</BODY>
</HTML>
```

Figure 4.8 displays the output of Listing 4.7 in a browser.

OUTPUT

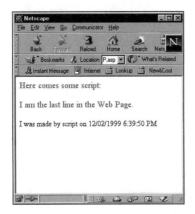

Figure 4.8: *Using the* <SCRIPT> *tag to implement inline behavior produces strange results.*

Understanding Execution Behavior

The ASP script engine processes script output between the inline <% %> symbols differently from script between <SCRIPT></SCRIPT> tags. Script output between the inline symbols is executed in the order the files are loaded into memory. However, script output within the <SCRIPT></SCRIPT> tags is processed after the complete page is loaded into memory.

Look at Listing 4.8 again. Notice that the script within the <SCRIPT></SCRIPT> tags comes *before* the line "I am the last line the Web Page". Now look at the output in Figure 4.8. Notice that the script output, "I was made by script...." comes *after* the line, "I am the last line in the Web Page". You can see that the script engine processed the HTML output first, then executed the script in the <SCRIPT></SCRIPT> tags.

Listing 4.9 shows an Active Server Page that has both inline script and script between <SCRIPT></SCRIPT> tags. Notice in the output in Figure 4.9, that the inline script is executed in the order in which it is positioned in the page. However the script in the <SCRIPT></SCRIPT> is processed after the script is loaded into memory and the output appears at the end of the page that is displayed.

Listing 4.9: Active Server Page with Inline Script and Tag-Based Script (`04asp09.asp`)

```
<HTML>
<HEAD>
<TITLE></TITLE>
</HEAD>

<BODY>
<P><FONT Color=Red Size= 4>
Here comes some script:
<P>
<%Response.Write("I am inline script.")%>
<P>
Here comes some SCRIPT tag script, not:
<SCRIPT Language=VBScript RUNAT=Server>
    Response.Write("I was made by SCRIPT tags on ")
    Response.Write(Now())
</SCRIPT>

<P>I am the last line in the Web Page.</P>
</FONT>
</BODY>
</HTML>
```

Figure 4.9: Here is a mixture of inline and tag-based script.

Calling Back to Script on the Server Side

It's possible to create client-side VBScript that calls back to code on the server side. You use the SRC attribute of the <SCRIPT> tag to accomplish this.

The SRC attribute allows you to define an external file that contains extra script that you can access from within your client code. For example, the following <SCRIPT> tag uses the SRC attribute to define a file Funcs.vbs.

```
<SCRIPT LANGUAGE=VBScript
  SRC="http://www.CogArtTech.com/Funcs/Funcs.vbs">
</SCRIPT>
```

EXAMPLE

When you define an external file in the `<SCRIPT>` tag, you have access to any function or sub in that file just as if it were written into your script (see Figure 4.10).

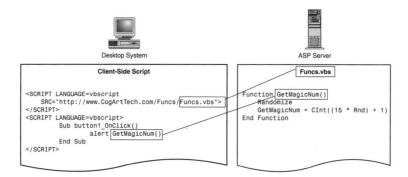

Figure 4.10: *You can use callbacks to functions on an ASP server to share the same code among different pages.*

You do not need to enclose VBScript subs and functions in eternal files within the `<SCRIPT></SCRIPT>` tags. Listing 4.10 shows the contents of the external script file, `Funcs.vbs`. This file contains the text of a VBScript function, `GetMagicNumber()`. The function returns a random number between 1 and 15.

Listing 4.10: An External VBScript Function (`Funcs.vbs`)

```
Function GetMagicNum()
    Randomize
    GetMagicNum = CInt((15 * Rnd) + 1)
End Function
```

EXAMPLE

You'll notice that defining the external file is the only purpose to this specific `<SCRIPT>` tag. This is perfectly acceptable scripting practice.

Listing 4.11 shows the Active Server Page that uses this external piece of script. Notice the function `GetMagicNum()` is not defined anywhere within the page. As you know now, it's defined within the external file, `Funcs.vbs`, which resides on the ASP server. Thus, all calls to `GetMagicNum()` (as is done in `button1_OnClick`) are made back to that ASP server.

EXAMPLE

Listing 4.11: Using Function Callbacks in ASP Script (04asp11.asp)

```
<HTML>
<HEAD>
<TITLE></TITLE>
</HEAD>
<BODY>
<SCRIPT LANGUAGE=vbscript
    SRC="http://www.CogArtTech.com/Funcs/Funcs.vbs">
</SCRIPT>

<SCRIPT LANGUAGE=vbscript>
    Sub button1_OnClick()
        'Call back to the GetMagicNum function which
        'is defined in the external file, Funcs.vbs
        alert GetMagicNum()
    End Sub
</SCRIPT>
<FONT FACE=ARIAL SIZE=5>
Calling back to functions<P>
<INPUT type="button" value="Magic Number" name=button1>
</FONT>
</BODY>
</HTML>
```

Figure 4.11 shows the output of Listing 4.11.

OUTPUT

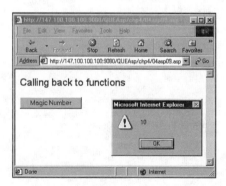

Figure 4.11: *Calling back to functions is transparent to the browser output.*

The benefit of keeping a library of subs and functions that you call back to, within one central file on your ASP server, is that many Active Server Pages can share common functionality. Upgrading the common behavior among many pages becomes an efficient task. You don't have to go from page to page to make changes. You simply go to the external callback file that contains the code you want to modify and implement the changes that you want to make.

NOTE

You can also call back to server-side functions from the client side using JavaScript as your scripting language. JavaScript convention asks that you name the external file with the extension, `.js`. Please remember to dedicate a callback file to a given language. You cannot mix and match functions from different scripting languages.

What's Next

This chapter showed you how the ASP engine interprets script. You learned how to write simple inline, server-side script. In addition, you learned to write Subs, Functions, and loops using inline script. You learned how to set the RUNAT attribute to make script in <SCRIPT></SCRIPT> tags execute on the server side. Lastly, you learned how to call back to a function on an ASP server.

Early in the chapter, you saw that we used the Response object. However, we haven't really talked about objects in any sort of detail. If you were a bit baffled, what follows should bring some clarity to the matter. In the next chapter we are going to talk about objects and object-oriented programming in general. In addition, we'll discuss some particular objects that ship with IIS and that you can use with ASP.

5

Fundamentals of Object-Oriented Programming

Object-oriented programming has become the standard methodology used in modern computer programming initiatives. Object-oriented programming, also known as OOP, requires you to think in a new way. It asks that you think not so much in terms of lines of code that are executed in sequence, but rather in terms of packets of code that can be used in one or many programs and can behave in one or many ways. ASP supports the object-oriented programming paradigm. You can use VBScript to create your own objects right in your Active Server Pages. In addition, ASP supports the use of objects that reside in custom and commercial ActiveX Components.

In this chapter you will learn how to

- Build class in VBScript using the Class and End Class keywords
- Use the Private and Public keywords
- Use the CreateObject() function
- Work the Properties, Methods, and Events of objects within Internet Explorer
- Work with the FileSystemObject

Understanding Objects and Classes

Object-oriented programming really isn't about programming as much as it is about thinking. Thinking in terms of objects means that you are able to look at a thing as a set of properties and methods. The properties of a thing are the data that are associated with it. For example, a bank account has Balance and Account Number data. The methods of a thing are its procedures. For example, a bank account has a Withdrawal procedure and a Deposit procedure. Thus, whenever you create a new bank account, by nature you create all the properties and methods that go along with it.

An object is related to an OOP construct called a class. In fact, an object is an instance of a class. You can think of a class as a template, a dress pattern for example. And you can think of an object as the specific thing made from the template—a dress made from a dress pattern. Thus, if you have a class, BankAccount, an object of this class would be a specific account, such as MyBankAccount or WifesBankAccount.

What is a class? A class is a group of variables and procedures, all of which are contained under the same name. In object-oriented programming we refer to the variables of a class as the properties and to the procedures as methods.

Let's make a class in VBScript and then talk about it.

Making a Class in Script

VBScript 5.*x* supports the construction of classes. The syntax you use to create a class is shown below:

```
Class ClassName
    'Class statements
End Class
```

Imagine that we want to make a class that describes a musician. A musician has first name and last name properties as well as a property, Instrument, that indicates the instrument the musician plays. Also, the musician has a method, Play(), which indicates an action he or she does with an instrument.

Listing 5.1 shows an example of a using VBScript to declare a class, Musician. Figure 5.1 shows the output of script that uses an object of that class. The sections that follow the example describe the particulars within Listing 5.1.

Listing 5.1: Defining Classes Using `Class` and `End Class` Keywords (`05ASP01.asp`)

```
<HTML>
<HEAD>
<TITLE></TITLE>
</HEAD>

<BODY>
<SCRIPT LANGUAGE=VBScript>
    '****************************************
    'A simple class that describes a musician.
    Class Musician
        Public FirstName 'The first name of the musician
        Public LastName 'The last name of the musician
        Public Instrument 'The instrument played

        'This is a method named, Play. The
        'method shows an alert box that that
        'reports the data of the Musician class.
        Function Play()
            Dim str ' As string buffer

            'NOTE: You use the Me keyword to indicate
            'the class that you use to indicate "this"
            'class. Me.Firstname means the FirstName
            'property of this class.
            str = "I am  " & Me.FirstName
            str = str & " " & Me.LastName & vbCrlf
            str = str & "I play the " & Me.Instrument
            Play = str
        End Function
    End Class
    '****************************************
    Sub button1_OnClick()
        Dim m
        'Create an object based on the class,
        'Musician
        Set m = New Musician
        'Populate the class's properties
        m.FirstName =text1.value
        m.LastName = text2.value
        m.Instrument =text3.value
        'Call the Play method of the class
        Alert m.Play()
    End Sub
</SCRIPT>
```

continues

Listing 5.1: continued

```
<CENTER>
<FONT Size=5 Color=blue Face=Arial>
Working with Simple Classes in VBScript
</FONT>
</CENTER>
<P>
<FONT Size=4 Color=blue Face=Arial>
<P>
Please enter data:
<P>
</FONT>
<FONT Size=4 Color=brown Face=Courier>
<P>First Name: <INPUT  name=text1></P>
<P>Last Name: <INPUT name=text2></P>
<P>Instrument: <INPUT name=text3></P>
<P><INPUT name=button1 type=button value="Play">
</P>
</FONT>
</BODY>
</HTML>
```

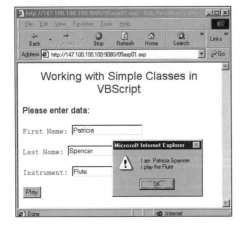

Figure 5.1: You can create classes on the client or server side.

Instantiating an Object

You create an object based on your class code by declaring a variable and then using the Set keyword in conjunction with the New keyword, like so:

```
Dim m
'Create an object based on the class,
'Musician
Set m = New Musician
```

Properties

A property is a member variable of class. A class can contain none, one, or many variables, each with a distinct name, that you can access when an instance of the class is made. As you learned earlier, when you create an instance of the class, the properties come along free, so to speak. Please look at the following snippet of code from Listing 5.1:

```
Class Musician
      Public FirstName 'The first name of the musician
      Public LastName 'The last name of the musician
      Public Instrument 'The instrument played
  .

  .

      End Class
```

Notice that the class contains variables named FirstName, LastName, and Instrument. These items are properties of the class. Now look at the following snippet of code from the button1_OnClick() event procedure.

```
'Populate the class's properties
m.FirstName =text1.value
m.LastName = text2.value
m.Instrument =text3.value
```

Notice that the code creates an object, m, which is an instance of the class Musician. Also, please notice that the code is assigning data to the FirstName, LastName, and Instrument properties of the object.

Methods

A method is a procedure, either a Sub or Function, that is a member of a class. In the example in Listing 5.1, the class, Musician has one method, Play(). The behavior programmed into the method is to return a string that reports the values of the properties of the class. Thus, when you instantiate an object based on the class, Musician, you access the Play method of the class just as you can any of the class's properties. The following snippet of code, which is from the button1_OnClick method from Listing 5.1, shows the call to Play() method using the object, m.

```
Alert m.Play()
```

Private and Public Scope

A fundamental principle of object-oriented programming is the principle of encapsulation. Encapsulated code uses properties and methods to reveal only the essential parts of a class to the "outside world." All other data and procedures are accessible inside the class only.

You use the keyword `Public` to indicate properties and methods that are visible outside the class. You use the keyword `Private` to indicate variables and procedures that can be seen from within the class.

Encapsulation is like a kitchen at McDonalds. When you order a burger and fries at any McDonalds, you don't care who made the bun for your hamburger. You don't care about what brand of oil was used to fry the fries. And you really don't care who the employees were who made the burgers. All you care about is the burger and fries—that they come out hot and taste good! This is a bit of an unusual analogy but it's highly descriptive.

You can think of the burger and fries as `Public` members of the class, `McDonaldsKitchen`. You can think of the bun manufacturers, oil type and kitchen employees as `Private` members of `McDonaldsKitchen`. You, the customer, are "outside" of the `McDonaldsKitchen`. Thus, all you see are the burger and fries, the `Public` members. You never get to "see" the `Private` members. If the bun manufacturer changes, it really doesn't affect your burger in a way that you can observe.

Listing 5.2 shows you a page that uses encapsulation to protect its data. Notice that the `Private` keyword is used to make certain pieces of data visible within the class only. Also, notice that a private `Class_Initialize()` event procedure initializes the private data variables. The `Private` keyword keeps data that is internal to the class from being altered by code outside of the class.

EXAMPLE

Listing 5.2: Using `Class_Initialize()`(`05ASP02.asp`)

```
<HTML>
<HEAD>
<TITLE></TITLE>
</HEAD>

<BODY>
<SCRIPT LANGUAGE=VBScript>
    '*****************************************
    'A simple class that describes a toy
    Class Toy
        Public Recipient 'The name of the recipient
        Public RetailPrice 'Non-discount price
        Public DiscountPrice 'Lowest price that you
                             'can sell this toy for
        Private mCost 'The cost of the toy
        Private mMinMarkup 'Minimum markup for selling
        Private mMaxMarkup 'The highest markup enforce on
                           'a toy

        'All classes have an event,Initialize which
        'is fired when an object of this class is
```

```
                'created. This event procedure, Class_Initialize
                'captures the Initialize event. All classes support
                'a Class_Initialize, event procedure.
                'You use the event procedure to "set up" the object,
                'before it is used by the outside code
                Private Sub Class_Initialize()
                    'Initialize the Private variables
                    mCost = 20
                    mMinMarkup = .10
                    mMaxMarkup = .50

                    'This discount price is calculated as
                    'the cost marked up by the minimum markup
                    DiscountPrice = mCost + CInt(mCost * mMinMarkup)

                    'This retail price is calculated as a
                    'the cost marked up by the maxiumum markup
                    RetailPrice = mCost + CInt(mCost * mMaxMarkup)
                End Sub
            End Class
            '****************************************
            Sub button1_OnClick()
                Dim t
                'Create an object based on the class,
                'Toy
                Set t = New Toy
                'Give the toy a recipient
                t.Recipient =text1.value
                'Get the prices from the object
                text3.value = CCur((t.RetailPrice) * CInt(text2.value))
                text4.value = CCur((t.DiscountPrice) * CInt(text2.value))
            End Sub
        </SCRIPT>

        <CENTER>
        <FONT Size=5 Color=blue Face=Arial>
        Working with Encapsulated Classes in VBScript
        </FONT>
        </CENTER>
        <P>
        <FONT Size=4 Color=blue Face=Arial>
        <P>
        Please enter data:
        <P>
        </FONT>
        <FONT Size=4 Color=brown Face=Courier>
        <P>Recipient: <INPUT   name=text1></P>
```

continues

Listing 5.2: continued

```
<P>Number ordered: <INPUT name=text2></P>
<P>Total Cost Retail: <INPUT name=text3></P>
<P>Total Cost Discount: <INPUT name=text4></P>
<P><INPUT name=button1 type=button value="Calculate Prices"></P>
</FONT>
</BODY>
</HTML>
```

OUTPUT

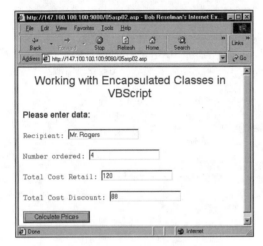

Figure 5.2: *You can use private data to do calculations internally in a class.*

USING `Class_Initialize()`

All classes have an event, `Initialize`, which is fired when an object of the given class is created. This event procedure, `Class_Initialize()`, captures the `Initialize` event. All classes have the `Class_Initialize()` event procedure implicitly. Whenever a class is created, the program goes out in search of a `Class_Intialize()` method. If none is found, the program goes on about its business.

You can use the `Class_Initialize()` event procedure to set start-up values and program start-up behavior for your class.

You'll notice that in Listing 5.2 the discount and cost data of the class is kept private, as shown below:

```
Private mCost 'The cost of the toy
Private mMinMarkup 'Minimum markup for selling
Private mMaxMarkup 'The highest markup enforce on a toy
```

This means that only procedures within the class, such as the `Class_Intialize()` event procedure, can use this data. (Read the sidebar on the `Class_Intialize()` to learn the details of the procedure's use.)

Also, notice that we use the private data to calculate the value of the properties `RetailPrice` and `DiscountPrice`. The calculation is performed within the `Class_Intialize()` event procedure, as shown below:

EXAMPLE

```
Private Sub Class_Initialize
    'Initialize the Private variables
    mCost = 20
    mMinMarkup = .10
    mMaxMarkup = .50

    'This discount price is calculated as
    'the cost marked up by the minimum markup
    DiscountPrice = mCost + CInt(mCost * mMinMarkup)

    'This retail price is calculated as
    'the cost marked up by the maxiumum markup
    RetailPrice = mCost + CInt(mCost * mMaxMarkup)
End Sub
```

Thus, we have used `Public` properties to return the result of calculations of private data. However, there is a problem in this example. Although we can report back private data through `Public` properties, we can still overwrite the data of the `Public` properties by simply assigning a value to it. For example, if you want to overwrite the value of the Toy class's `RetailPrice` property, you write the code:

```
t.RetailPrice = 23
```

This might not be the behavior that you want to have in your class. You might want the `RetailPrice` to be read-only, so that after it is calculated, it cannot be changed. How do you accomplish this? You enhance your code to use `Let` and `Get` property methods.

Enhancing Properties with `Let` and `Get` Property Methods

The principle of encapsulation dictates that members outside of a class never work directly with private members of the class. You saw this principle violated in the Toy class above. We created the `RetailPrice` property by declaring it as a `Public` variable. In the world of object-oriented programming this is bad business.

Fortunately we can use `Let` and `Get` property methods to shield private data from the outside, yet present a singular interface to that data. In VBScript every public property can be presented by two property methods that are associated with one private variable (also known as a data member). The `Let` property method is used to assign a property's value "in" to the associated private data member. The `Get` property is used to retrieve the value of the associated private data member and pass it "out" to the property name. Figure 5.3 illustrates this concept.

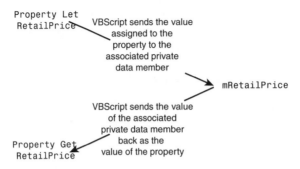

Figure 5.3: *Use* Let *and* Get *property methods to provide robust encapsulation for your classes.*

The syntax for the Let property method is

```
Property Let PropertyName (ValuePassedToAssign)
    mPrivateDataMember = ValueToAssign
End Property
```

Where

Property Let and End Property are the keywords indicating property method declaration.

PropertyName is the name of the property to which the property method is associated.

ValuePassedToAssign is the value that is assigned to the class's property.

mPrivateDataMember is the private data member associated with the property of the property method.

The syntax for the Get property method is

```
Property Get PropertyName ()
    PropertyName = mPrivateDataMember
End Property
```

Property Get and End Property are the keywords indicating property method declaration.

PropertyName is the name of the property to which the property method is associated.

mPrivateDataMember is the private data member associated with the property of the property method.

Please notice that you return data using the Get property method just as you would for a function, by assigning the return value to the name of the Get property method.

Listing 5.3 shows the code for the Toy class. The Toy class code has been enhanced to use Let and Get property methods instead of public variables to define Recipient, RetailPrice, and DiscountPrice properties. Please notice that the Class_Intialize() event procedure hasn't any calculation behavior. It sets the initial values of some of the private data members. Calculation activity has been moved to the Get property methods of the RetailPrice and DiscountPrice properties. The output behavior has not been affected. Thus, the output for Listing 5.3 is the same as shown in Figure 5.2.

EXAMPLE

Listing 5.3: Using Let and Get Property Methods (05ASP03.asp)

```
<HTML>
<HEAD>
<TITLE></TITLE>
</HEAD>

<BODY>
<SCRIPT LANGUAGE=VBScript>
    '*****************************************
    'A simple class that describes a toy
    Class Toy
        'Private data members
        Private mRecipient 'The name of the two
        Private mRetailPrice 'Non-discount price
        Private mDiscountPrice 'Lowest price that you
                               'can sell this toy for
        Private mCost 'The cost of the toy
        Private mMinMarkup 'Minimum markup for selling
        Private mMaxMarkup 'The highest markup enforce on
                           'a toy

        'Recipient Property Methods
        Property Let Recipient (NewValue)
            mRecipient = NewValue
        End Property

        Property Get Recipient()
            Recipient = mRecipient
        End Property

        'RetailPrice Property Method
        '(Read Only Property, notice there isn't any Let Property method
        'for Retail Price.)
        Property Get RetailPrice()
            mRetailPrice = mCost + CInt(mCost * mMaxMarkup)
            RetailPrice = mRetailPrice
```

continues

Listing 5.3: continued

```
        End Property

            'DiscountPrice Property Methods
            '(Read Only Property, again—no Let Property method))
            Property Get DiscountPrice()
                mDiscountPrice = mCost + CInt(mCost * mMinMarkup)
                DiscountPrice = mDiscountPrice
            End Property

            'Initialize the class
            Private Sub Class_Initialize
                'Initialize the Private variables
                mCost = 20
                mMinMarkup = .10
                mMaxMarkup = .50
            End Sub
        End Class
    '*****************************************
    Sub button1_OnClick()
        Dim t
        'Create an object based on the class,
        'Toy
        Set t = New Toy
        'Give the toy a recipient
        t.Recipient =text1.value
        'Get the prices from the object
        text3.value = CCur((t.RetailPrice) * CInt(text2.value))
        text4.value = CCur((t.DiscountPrice) * CInt(text2.value))
    End Sub
</SCRIPT>

<CENTER>
<FONT Size=5 Color=blue Face=Arial>
Working with Encapsulated Classes in VBScript
</FONT>
</CENTER>
<P>
<FONT Size=4 Color=blue Face=Arial>
<P>
Please enter data:
<P>
</FONT>
<FONT Size=4 Color=brown Face=Courier>
<P>Recipient: <INPUT   name=text1></P>
<P>Number ordered: <INPUT name=text2></P>
<P>Total Cost Retail: <INPUT name=text3></P>
```

```
<P>Total Cost Discount: <INPUT name=text4></P>
<P><INPUT name=button1 type=button value="Calculate Prices"></P>
</FONT>
</BODY>
</HTML>
```

Making Properties Read-Only

Notice that the properties RetailPrice and DiscountPrice in Listing 5.3 haven't any Let property method. The reason the Let property method was omitted was to make the properties read-only. Without a Let property method, you have no way to access private data members in order to write data.

Using Classes on the Server Side

You can create classes on the server side just as you would for the client side. In order to create a server-side class, the class declaration must be done within the inline, server-side tags <% %> or within the <SCRIPT></SCRIPT> tags using the RUNAT=Server attribute. In addition, if you are using Windows NT 4.0, you must have the Internet Explorer 5.0 script engine installed on the server.

Moving Beyond VBScript Classes

VBScript classes are useful, but they are limited. You don't have the benefit of creating custom events and raising them within your class. This is a feature of standard VB and other low-level languages that is used extensively. It's a powerful tool. In addition, VBScript's use of Variants does not make for the fastest, most efficient code in the world.

To get around these shortcomings, many programmers make custom classes in VB or C++ and then wrap them up in ActiveX DLL or ActiveX EXE Object Libraries they can use within VBScript. The next section shows you how to use VBScript to work with classes in this manner.

Working with ActiveX Components

You can use objects that exist in ActiveX DLLs and ActiveX EXE Object Libraries (also known as ActiveX Components) in the VBScript of your Active Server Pages. Object Libraries that exist in compiled code run faster. In addition, they provide the types of services you cannot get from stand-alone VBScript. For example, you can have an ActiveX DLL that contains code that works with the Windows API functions internally and passes out the results of these functions in a way that can be used by your Active Server Pages. Using ActiveX Object Libraries with VBScript is a technology that greatly enhances the scope of your ASP programming.

Internet Information Server ships with ActiveX Components that you can use in your VBScript. Table 5.1 shows you a list of ActiveX Components that ship with IIS 5.0.

Table 5.1: IIS 5.0 ActiveX Components

Component	Description
Ad Rotator	Rotates advertisement banners
Browser Capabilities	Reports information on the calling browser
Content Linking	Links Web pages together
Content Rotator	Rotates strings in a ticker tape manner
Counters	Counter utility
ADO Object Library	Allows you to work with databases
File System Object	Allows you to work with the server's file system
Logging Utility	Creates an HTTP activity log
MyInfo	Allows you to keep track and modify sys admin information
Page Counter	Creates a counter that measures page openings
Permission Checker	Provided password services
Tools	Generates random numbers, checks for files, processes HTML forms

TIP

For more information on these ActiveX Components, go to Microsoft's MSDN site at `http://msdn.microsoft.com/isapi/msdnlib.idc?theURL=/library/psdk/iisref/` `Âcomp59f8.htm`

If you want to work with any of these components, they must be installed on the server's hard drive and registered in the server's Windows NT Registry. After the component is registered, use the `CreateObject()` function to create objects from a given component in your Active Server Page.

The following section shows you how to use the `CreateObject()`function to work with a small custom object created using standard Visual Basic. Later in this chapter, you'll take a detailed look at how to work with the `FilesSystemObject` in the Scripting Object Library that ships with IIS.

Using `CreateObject()`

You use the `CreateObject()` function to create an object from an ActiveX component. The syntax for the `CreateObject()` function is

`Set obj = CreateObject("LibraryName.ObjectName")`

Where

`Set` and `CreateObject` are VBScript keywords

`obj` is an object variable to which the created object will be assigned.

LibraryName is the name of the ActiveX DLL or ActiveX EXE that is the object library.

ObjectName is the name of the object within the object library.

Please notice two things. First, you must use the Set keyword when assigning the object you are creating to the object variable. Second, the *LibraryName.ObjectName* parameter is a string and must be enclosed in quotation marks.

Working with CreateObject() in an Active Server Page

Listing 5.4 shows you how to use the CreateObject() function to work with an object in an ActiveX DLL. The ActiveX DLL you are going to access is a whimsical one, custom made for this book. The object's name is NameGen and it lives in the custom ActiveX DLL, UselessTools.DLL.

The object NameGen has one property, RandName. Every time you call RandName, a new name is generated as the property's value.

NOTE

You can download the setup files for the ActiveX DLL, Useless Tools from the MCP Web site dedicated to this book: http://www.quecorp.com/series/by_example/. After you download the files, run Setup.EXE using your NT server as the destination computer for the installation. If you are using Personal Web Server to run your Active Server Pages, use your desktop system as the destination for the ActiveX DLL files. Running Setup.EXE registers the component in your system Registry automatically.

EXAMPLE

Listing 5.4: Using CreateObject() (05ASP04.asp)

```
<HTML>
<HEAD>
<TITLE></TITLE>
</HEAD>
<BODY>
<CENTER>
<FONT Size=5 Color=blue Face=Arial>
Using ActiveX Components
</FONT>
</CENTER>
<P>
<FONT Size=3 Color=blue Face=Arial>
<P>
This name in the brown font is the output of an ActiveX
Component that generates names randomly. The object lives
on the server side.
<P>
The CreateObject() method is used to create an object
```

continues

Listing 5.4: continued

```
from the library.
<P>
And the name is.....
</FONT>
<FONT Size=5 Color=brown Face=Courier><B>
<%
     'Declare a variable for the object
     Dim n

     'Create the object and assign it to the object
     'variable
     Set n = CreateObject("UselessTools.NameGen")

     'Get a return from the RandName property and send
     'it back to the calling client.
     Response.Write(n.RandName)
%>
</B></FONT>
</BODY>
</HTML>
```

OUTPUT

Figure 5.4: *You can encapsulate functionality in ActiveX components and then use* CreateObject() *to access them.*

The code in Listing 5.4 is straightforward. There's not a lot of magic or a tremendous amount of difficulty in this example. The important things to remember when using CreateObject() is to use the Set keyword when assigning the returned object to the object variable and to enclose the ObjectLibrary.ObjectName parameter in quotation marks.

Scripting Objects on the Client Side: Working with the Window Object

Internet Explorer ships with a bunch of objects that you can use to do client-side programming. These objects are part of the *Document Object Model* (DOM). The DOM is a representation of all the objects that exist within a browser. These objects range from the history list of the browser to a specific element in a page of HTML. The DOM is voluminous and interwoven with *Dynamic HTML* (DHTML). The Document Object Model is worthy of a book all to itself, of which there are many. Thus, within the scope of this section, we are not going to drill down too deeply into the intricacies of the DOM. However, we are going to look at a few of the more prominent objects in order to show you how to program client-side objects to create dynamic pages.

The objects we are going to look at in this section are

- Window objects
- Document objects
- HTML Element objects

TIP

For more information on the Document Object Model and Dynamic HTML, go to Microsoft's MSDN site at `http://msdn.microsoft.com/workshop/author/dhtml/reference/objects.asp`

CAUTION

Please be advised that the Document Object Model is a standard supported by the *World Wide Web Consortium* (W3C). Thus, because it is an international standard, both Internet Explorer and Netscape Navigator support the object model. However, as is usual in the modern world of commercial Web development, the ways in which these competing browsers support the standard are alike in many ways and different in some ways. Therefore, you might encounter problems using the same code on different browsers. Also, please remember to use JavaScript to write script that is to execute on both Netscape and Internet Explorer.

Working with a Built-In Object's Properties

The DOM accommodates HTML elements as objects in their own right. In terms of the VBScript, you work with an attribute of a given HTML element as a property.

EXAMPLE

For example, the value of attribute of the following HTML button element

```
<INPUT type="button" value="Get the stuff" name=button1>
```

is referenced within the DOM as

```
button1.value = ="Get the stuff"
```

The VBScript code in the Active Server Page in Listing 5.5 shows you how to work with an HTML text element and button element as a set of DOM objects. This code applies to the text that you enter in the HTML text element and displays it on the face of the HTML button element. Figure 5.5 shows you the output of the script.

EXAMPLE

Listing 5.5: Working with Client-Side Objects (05ASP05.asp)

```
<HTML>
<HEAD>
<TITLE></TITLE>
<SCRIPT LANGUAGE=VBScript>

</SCRIPT>
</HEAD>
<SCRIPT LANGUAGE=VBScript>
    Sub button1_OnClick
        'Return the text in the text
        'element as the caption on the
        'button's face
        button1.value = text1.value
    End Sub
</SCRIPT>
<BODY>
<CENTER>
<FONT Size=5 Color=blue Face=Arial>
Working with Client Side Objects
</FONT>
</CENTER>
<P>
<FONT Size=3 Color=blue Face=Arial>
Enter some stuff:
</FONT>
<INPUT type="text" name=text1 size=20>
<P>
<INPUT type="button" value="Get the stuff" name=button1>
</BODY>
</HTML>
```

OUTPUT

Figure 5.5: *The Internet Explorer window on the lower right is the result of the button click.*

Working with a Built-in Object's Methods

Most client-side objects have methods you can use to build dynamic behavior into your Web pages. The Window object, the object that represents the browser in its entirety as opposed to the Document object, which represents the Web page within a browser, has a method that allows you to open new instances of the browser. This method is the Open() method.

The Open() method has the syntax

window.**open(**URL, Name, Features, Replace**)**

Where

> URL is an optional string parameter that indicates the URL of the new windows content.

> Name is an optional parameter that is the name of the window.

> Features is an optional string parameter that indicates how the window should be opened. For example, you can use the "fullscreen=yes" setting to open the new window so that it occupies the entire display area of you computer monitor.

> Replace is an optional parameter that indicates whether the new page should replace the "firing" page as the entry in the history list.

TIP

For more information about the Window object, go to Microsoft's MSDN site at

http://msdn.microsoft.com/workshop/c-frame.htm?944505439765#/workshop/
➥author/dhtml/reference/objects/obj_window.asp

The code in Listing 5.6 shows you how to use the Open() method of the Window object to make a new browser window by clicking a button. Figure 5.6 shows you the result of the code when executed.

EXAMPLE

Listing 5.6: Using the window.open() Method (05ASP06.asp)

```vbscript
<HTML>
<HEAD>
<TITLE></TITLE>
<SCRIPT LANGUAGE=VBScript>

</SCRIPT>
</HEAD>
<SCRIPT LANGUAGE=VBScript>
    Sub button1_OnClick
        Dim NewURL
        Dim WinFeatr
        'Get the value from the text element
        'as assign it as the new URL
        NewURL = text1.value
        'Make sure that the user entered something
        'in the text element
        If NewURL = "" then
            'If not, report the fact
            Alert "You must enter a valid URL"
            'Send the screen's mouse cursor back
            'to the text element
            text1.focus()
            'Leave townh
            Exit Sub
        'Make sure that the user has the
        'transfer protocol on the URL
        ElseIf UCASE(Left(text1.value, 7)) _
                            <> "HTTP://" Then
            'If the HTTP string is not there, add it
            NewURL = "http://" & NewURL
        End if
        'Create a string that contains the data for the
        'features parameter
        WinFeatr = "menubar=no,status=no,toolbar=no"
        WinFeatr = WinFeatr & ",resizable=yes,scrollbars=yes"
        'Open the window
        window.open NewURL,"MyWindow", Cstr(WinFeatr)
    End Sub
</SCRIPT>
<BODY>
<CENTER>
<FONT Size=5 Color=blue Face=Arial>
```

```
More Working with Client Side Objects
</FONT>
</CENTER>
<P>
<FONT Size=3 Color=blue Face=Arial>
Enter a URL:
</FONT>
<INPUT type="text" name=text1 size=20>
<P>
<INPUT type="button" value="Get to the URL" name=button1>
</BODY>
</HTML>
```

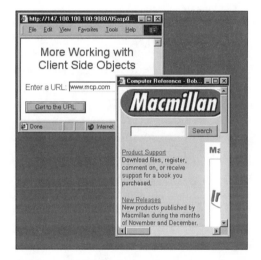

Figure 5.6: *Use the* Features *parameter of the* Window *object's* Open() *method to remove menu bars and tool bars from the browser window.*

Please notice that in the button1_OnClick() event procedure in Listing 5.6 the code uses the focus() method of the text object in the line

```
text1.focus()
```

When you call the focus() method of an HTML text element object, you are telling the browser to put the mouse cursor into the text area of the element. In this case, the method is called because the user did not enter valid data in the text element. The code analyzes the value of the variable that contains the new URL value (NewURL). If the value is a null string (""), an error message is displayed and the cursor is returned to the text element.

Also please notice that within the code, the Open() method of the Window object uses the Features parameter in such a way as to accommodate multiple feature settings:

```
WinFeatr = "menubar=no,status=no,toolbar=no"
WinFeatr = WinFeatr & ",resizable=yes,scrollbars=yes"
'Open the window
window.open NewURL,"MyWindow", Cstr(WinFeatr)
```

The key to understanding the Features parameter is to remember that the parameter is a single string that contains all of the *name=value* pairs that determine the given configuration of the new browser window. In the example above, the new window is created without any menubar or toolbar ("menubar=no,status=no,toolbar=no"). However, the window can be resized and you can move about the Web page within the window by using the windows scrollbars (",resizable=yes,scrollbars=yes").

Working with a Built-In Object's Events

The objects built into Internet Explorer fire events that you can capture with event procedures that you write within the <% %> or <SCRIPT></SCRIPT> tags. For example, if you want to capture the focus event of an object, you write an OnFocus() event procedure. If you want to capture the loss of focus, you create an OnBlur() event procedure. You write an OnClick() to capture a click event. The number of events an object can fire is quite large. Some events are common to all objects. Some are unique to each object.

Table 5.2 shows a list of event procedures for the more common events you'll capture. Again, the number of events that a given object can support can be quite large. You might want to go to the area of the Microsoft Developer's Network site given in an earlier tip to get details about a specific object's events.

Table 5.2: Common Client-Side Event Procedures

Component	Description
OnFocus	Captures when an object has the focus
OnBlur	Captures when an object loses focus
OnClick	Captures when an object is clicked
OnMouseUp	Captures when a mouse button is released
OnMouseDown	Captures when a mouse button is pressed down
OnMouseOver	Captures when the mouse cursor moves over an object
OnMouseOut	Captures when a mouse cursor moves out of the boundary of an object
OnLoad	Captures when a Window object loads a Web page
OnUnload	Captures when a Web page is unloaded from a Window object
OnError	Captures when an object error

Listing 5.7 shows you how to code behavior into a Window object's OnLoad and OnUnload event procedures. Figure 5.7 shows the browser window with the enhancements programmed in the OnLoad() event procedure. In addition,

the illustration shows the Alert dialog box that's displayed by the
OnUnload() event procedure as well as the new Web page that gets loaded
into the browser by the OnClick() event procedure of the button element.
You can program a Window object's OnLoad() event procedure to initialize the
browser.

EXAMPLE

Listing 5.7: Programming the Window_OnLoad and Window_OnUnLoad Event Procedures (05ASP07.asp)

```
<HTML>
<HEAD>
<TITLE></TITLE>
</HEAD>
<SCRIPT LANGUAGE=VBScript>
    Sub Window_OnLoad()
        'Put the presert time as the caption
        'in the browser window't title bar
        document.title = "Load Time = " & Cstr(Time())

        'If the this page is loaded after noon time
        If CDbl(Time()) > .5 Then
            'make the background color of the page
            document.bgColor = &Hffff00& 'Yellow
        Else
            'otherwise make the background color
            document.bgColor = &H00ff00& 'Green
        End if
    End Sub

    Sub Window_OnUnLoad()
        Dim s
        'Send out an alert telling the user
        'the time of day that he or she is leaving
        'this page.
        s = "You are leaving this page at: "
        s= s & Cstr(Time())
        Alert s
    End Sub

    Sub button1_OnClick()
        'Reassign the secret Web page to the document's
        'URL property. When you do this, you call the new
        'Web page to be the contents of this window.
        document.url = "http://www.pionet.net/~reselbob"
    End Sub
</SCRIPT>
<BODY>
<CENTER>
```

continues

Listing 5.7: continued

```
<FONT Size=5 Color=blue Face=Arial>
Working with Events
</FONT>
</CENTER>
<P>
<FONT Size=3 Color=blue Face=Arial>
</FONT>
<P>
<INPUT type="text" id=text1 name=text1>
<INPUT type="button" value="Get secret URL" name=button1>
</BODY>
</HTML>
```

NOTE

When you want to access the Window or Document objects in a Web Page or Active Server Page, you refer to them by their object names directly. You do not need to assign the object to an object variable.

Thus, if you want to set the title property of the document object to hello, you write document.title = "Hello"

If you want to call the Close() method of the Window object, you write window.close()

OUTPUT

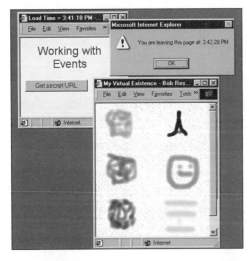

Figure 5.7: *The* Document *object's URL property allows you to redefine the Web page that's displayed within the browser.*

There are a number of interesting things about the code in Listing 5.7. First notice that the Window_OnLoad() method configures the browser's title bar by using the document object's `title` property to show the time of day upon which the page was loaded.

```
document.title = "Load Time = " & Cstr(Time())
```

The `Document` object's `bgColor` represents the color of the browser's *client area*. The code in the event procedure runs an `If…Then` statement to test for the time of day when the page was loaded into the browser. If the time is after noon (.5 of a day), the `bgColor` property is assigned the hexadecimal value that turns the background color to yellow. If the time is before noon, the background color of the document is turned to green.

```
If CDbl(Time()) > .5 Then
    'make the background color of the page
    document.bgColor = &Hffff00& 'Yellow
Else
    'otherwise make the background color
    document.bgColor = &H00ff00& 'Green
End if
```

The `Window_OnUnload()` event procedure captures when the document presently in the browser is being removed. Before the removal happens, an `Alert` message reporting the time of removal is shown to the end user.

```
s = "You are leaving this page at: "
s= s & Cstr(Time())
Alert s
```

Finally the document object's `URL` property is put to use in the button element's `OnClick()` event procedure.

```
Sub button1_OnClick()
.

.

.

    document.url = "http://www.pionet.net/~reselbob"
End Sub
```

The `URL` property reports the URL of the current page in the browser. If you want to change the page and not open a new browser window to do so, you assign the `URL` of the new page to the URL property. The browser senses this change in the property, gets the new page out on the Internet and loads it into the browser.

You can embed client-side script in an Active Server Page and have it work perfectly well in a browser. You've seen this. All of the client-side examples in this chapter are in ASP files. However, this is an ASP book, and as an ASP programmer you are going to be concerned with working on the server side. So let's look at how to use objects on the server side.

Scripting Objects on the Server Side: Working with the `FileSystemObject`

As you saw in Table 5.1, Internet Information Server ships with many ActiveX Components that you can use in your Active Server Pages. This section focuses on how to use the `FileSystemObject`. The `FileSystemObject` allows you to work with the drive and file system of a given computer. You can use the `FileSystemObject` to determine how many drives a computer has, as well as the size and type of those drives. The Active Server Page shown in Listing 5.8 shows you how to use the `FileSystemObject` to determine the number of drives on a computer as well as the size and usage of each drive. Figure 5.8 shows you the HTML display of the ASP in a browser.

EXAMPLE

Listing 5.8: Using the `FileSystemObject` to Report Hard Disk Statistics (`05ASP08.asp`)

```
<HTML>
<HEAD>
<TITLE></TITLE>
</HEAD>
<BODY>
<CENTER>
<FONT Size=5 Color=Blue Face=Arial>
Server System Information
</FONT>
</CENTER>
<FONT Size=4 Color=Brown Face=Arial>
  <%Dim fso 'files system object var
    Dim drvs 'drives collection var
    Dim drv 'variable for the letter of a given drive
    Dim i, j 'counter vars
    Dim pct 'String for percentage
    Dim str 'String buffer var

    'Create a file system objec
    Set fso = CreateObject("Scripting.FileSystemObject")

    'Query the Count property of the Drives collection
    'of the FileSystemObject in order to determine
    'how many drives you have. Then make some output
    'display which reports the
    Response.Write("<B>This server has " &  fso.Drives.Count)
    Response.Write(" drives</B>.<HR>")
```

```
'Isolate the drives collection into its own variable
'just to make the code easier to read
Set drvs = fso.Drives

'Traverse the drives collection in order to extract
'information about each drive.
For Each d in drvs
        'Get the drive letter
        drv = d.DriveLetter
        'Make sure the drive is ready.
        If d.IsReady Then
            'Create a string that....
            str = "Drive " & UCase(drv) & ": has a capacity "
            '...reports the capacity of the drive...
            str = str & "of " & d.TotalSize
            '...how much space is available.
            str = str & " bytes of which " & d.AvailableSpace
            str = str & " bytes are free."
            str = str & "<P>Drive " & UCase(drv)
            str = str & ": has used "
            'Figure out how many space has been used
            j = CDbl(d.TotalSize) - CDbl(d.AvailableSpace)
            'Convert it to a percentage of the drive
            pct = (CDbl(j)/CDbl(d.TotalSize)) * 100
            'Report back the percentage.
            str = str & CInt(pct) & "% of its capacity."
        Else
            'If the drive is not ready, kick off an error
            'message
            str = "Drive " & UCase(drv) & ": is not ready."
        End if
        'Pass the string that contains information on this
        'particular drive back to the calling browser
        Response.Write(str & "<HR>")
        'Do some clean up work
        str = ""
        set d = nothing
    Next
%>
</FONT>
<P> </P>

</BODY>
</HTML>
```

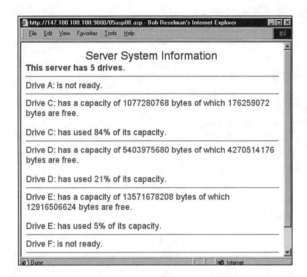

Figure 5.8: *The* FileSystemObject *allows you to make a System Information Page.*

TIP

For detailed information about the FileSystemObject, go to Microsoft's MSDN site at
http://msdn.microsoft.com/scripting/vbscript/doc/vsobjFileSystem.htm

---

The following sections discuss the features of the FileSystemObject as used in the code shown in Listing 5.8.

Working with the Drives Collection

The FileSystemObject has one property, the Drives property. The Drives property is a collection that contains one or many Drive objects. (A Drive object represents a drive in a computer.) We really haven't talked about how ASP uses collections yet, so let's take a moment to go over it.

If you are familiar with programming standard Visual Basic, you no doubt have encountered Collections. A Collection object is like a "smart" array. It can hold groups of variables or even groups of other objects. To increase the size of the collection, you don't have to go through all the trouble of redimensioning it as you do with an array. Whenever you want to add a value or an object to a collection, you call the Add method of the Collection object.

Collection objects have a Count property that reports the number of items in the Collection. If you want to work with a specific object within the Collection, you use the Collection's Item(Index) method. Thus, if you want to get the first object in a `Drives` collection of a `FileSystemObject` named fso, you use the code

```
Set d = fso.Drives.Item(1)
```

Please be advised that although you can process `Collection` objects in VBScript, you cannot create them as a data type. You can use them only when they are return values from other objects. The code in Listing 5.8 does this in the line

```
Set drvs = fso.Drives
```

The above line assigns a Collection of `Drive` objects from the `FileSystemObject` to the variable drvs. Nowhere in the code is drvs created as a collection. It can only take references to existing collections of other objects.

Using For...Each

The For...Each statement is a looping mechanism, similar to the For...Next statement. The For...Each statement enables you to traverse a `Collection` object in order to work with each object in the collection. The syntax for the For...Each loop is

```
For Each obj In objCollection
... 'Do something with obj
Next
```

Where

> For Each and In are keywords indicating the For...Each loop
>
> obj is an object within the collection to process
>
> objCollection is the collection of objects
>
> Next is a keyword continuing the loop

Listing 5.8 uses the following For...Each statement to access each `Drive` object in the `Drives` collection:

```
For Each d In drvs
    'Get the drive letter
    drv = d.DriveLetter
.
.
Next
```

The For...Each loop "extracts" a `Drive` object, d, from the Collection, drvs. Then, within the loop, the variable drv is assigned the drive letter for a given drive. The `Drive` object has a property, `DriveLetter`, which returns the logical drive letter for the drive.

Getting System Information Using the `FileSystemObject`

Let's take a step by step walk through the code in Listing 5.8 in order to get a thorough understanding of the functionality of the script.

The first thing the script does is declare some variables that will be used throughout the code. This is standard stuff. Next, the code uses the `CreateObject()` function to open the ActiveX Object Library, Scripting to get the `FileSystemObject`. An instance of the `FileSystemObject` is assigned to the variable, `fso`. This is done in the line of code

```
Set fso = CreateObject("Scripting.FileSystemObject")
```

After the `FileSystemObject` is in play, things get interesting. The page needs to report how many drives are on the server. As you already know, the `FileSystemObject` has a property, `Drives`. `Drives` is a `Collection` object that represents the drives on a computer. (The `FileSystemObject` is smart enough to work with Windows to figure out how many drives are on the computer.) We query the `Drives` collection to find out how many drive objects it contains by using the collection's `Count` property:

```
Response.Write("<B>This server has " &  fso.Drives.Count)
```

In addition, we use the `Response` object to send a string back to the calling browser reporting the number of drives.

Next, the page needs to get statistics about each drive on the computer. The script uses a `For…Each` loop to traverse the `Drives` collection, isolating a drive on each trip through the collection:

```
For Each d in drvs
```

The script gets the drive letter of a `Drive` object using the object's `DriveLetter` property. The `DriveLetter` value is assigned to a variable, `drv`.

```
drv = d.DriveLetter
```

Then the script calls the `IsReady` method to determine the readiness of the drive. If the drive is a floppy drive, Zip drive, or CD-ROM and there isn't any disk media in the drive, `IsReady` returns `False`. If the drive is a failing hard drive, `IsReady` returns `False` also. Otherwise `IsReady` returns `True` if the drive is functioning properly, with appropriate disk media inserted.

```
If d.IsReady Then
```

NOTE

If a function or method returns a True/False value, you can simply use the function or method name as a condition in an If…Then statement. The return value is implied. For example

```
If d.IsReady Then DoSomething
```

is the same as

```
If d.IsReady = True Then DoSomething
```

If the disk is ready, the script that gathers the statistical information is run. If not, a string indicating that the drive is not ready is created:

```
str = "Drive " & UCase(drv) & ": is not ready."
```

The script gathers drive space and drive usage statistics using the TotalSize and AvailableSpace properties of the Drive object. TotalSize returns the total size of a given drive in bytes:

```
str = "Drive " & UCase(drv) & ": has a capacity "
'...reports the capacity of the drive...
str = str & "of " & d.TotalSize
```

AvailableSpace returns how much space is still open on the drive:

```
str = str & " bytes of which " & d.AvailableSpace
str = str & " bytes are free."
```

The amount of space that has been used is calculated. The typecasting function, CDbl() is used in order to make the script accommodate the very large numeric values of the gigabyte size drives:

```
j = CDbl(d.TotalSize) - Cdbl(d.AvailableSpace)
```

Then the percentage of the drive that has been used is determined. The value is multiplied by 100 in order to make the numbers appear greater than zero and less than 100, for percentage display purposes:

```
pct = (CDbl(j)/CDbl(d.TotalSize)) * 100
```

Finally, the percentage is reported as a string that is concatenated onto the master string:

```
str = str & CInt(pct) & "% of its capacity."
```

The string is sent on to the calling browser with an HTML hard return line tag attached:

```
Response.Write(str & "<HR>")
```

The script does some clean up work. The string buffer variable, str is set to empty. And the object variable that represents the Drive object is set to Nothing. The keyword Nothing removes any reference to any drive object. It's a habitual safety measure on the part of the programmer. Setting object variables to Nothing when you are through with the object being referenced is a good programming practice.

```
str = ""
set d = nothing
```

If there are still Drive objects within the Drives collection, the whole process is reiterated. Otherwise, the For…Each loop is terminated.

Working with Files on Disk

The `FileSystemObject` is a very versatile tool. In addition to determining statistics about the drives on your computer, you can use the `FileSystemObject` to open text files to read and write data. The Active Server Page in Listing 5.9 shows script that opens a text file on a computer's hard disk. The text file contains a poem. A different poem is opened, given the time of day that the page is called. Figure 5.9 shows the output of the Active Server Page.

Listing 5.9: Using the `FileSystemObject` to Read Files (`05ASP09.asp`)

```
<HTML>
<HEAD>
<TITLE></TITLE>
</HEAD>


<BODY>
<%
    Function GetPoem(PoemType)
        Dim fso 'files system object var
        Dim filename 'filename var
        Dim str 'String buffer variable
        Dim fPath 'Complete file path variable
        Const ForReading = 1 'indicates how to access open files

        'The Select Case statement decided the
        'poem file to use, given the value of
        'the argument Poem type
        Select Case PoemType
            Case "MORNING":
                filename = "poems/morning.txt"
            Case "MIDMORNING":
                filename = "poems/midmorning.txt"
            Case "AFTER NOON":
                filename = "poems/after noon.txt"
            Case "EVENING":
                filename = "poems/evening.txt"
        End Select

        'Create a FileSystemObject
        Set fso = CreateObject("Scripting.FileSystemObject")
        'Set the path of the poem file by getting
        'the path of this file using the Server object's
        'MapPath method and passing the poem's filename
        'as an argument to the MapPath method.
        fPath = Server.MapPath("/" & filename)
```

```
                        'Check to make sure that the file really
                        'is where it is supposed to be. Use the
                        'FileExists method of the FileSystemObject
                        If fso.FileExists(fPath) Then
                                'Use the OpenTextFile method to open
                                'the text file that contains the poem.
                                'When you use OpenTextFile, the method
                                'returns a TextSteam object automatically
                                Set f =fso.OpenTextFile(fPath, ForReading)

                                'Traverse the TextStream. When you get to the
                                'end of the file, the EndOfSteam property will
                                'return False.
                                While Not f.AtEndOfStream
                                        'Read the TextSteam a line at a
                                        'time using the File object's ReadLine method
                                        str = str & f.ReadLine
                                        'Add an HTML line break tag
                                        'to the end of each line
                                        str = str & "<br>"
                                Wend
                        Else
                                'If the file does not exist, return
                                ' a generic error message
                                GetNewsFile = "File access error"
                                'Leave this function. There is no more
                                'to be done.
                                Exit Function
                        End if
                        'Return the result of processing the
                        'TextStream out of the function.
                        GetPoem = str
                End Function
%>


<CENTER>
<FONT Size=5 Color=Blue Face=Arial>
The Daily Poem
</FONT>
</CENTER>
<P>
<FONT Size=4 Color=Blue Face=Arial>
<P>
This page displays a special poem depending on the
time of day the page is called.
```

continues

Listing 5.9: continued

```
<P>
</FONT>
<FONT Size=4 Color=Brown Face=Courier>
  <%
    Dim fil 'String buffer var
    Dim tm 'time var

    'Take a time stamp of when this
    'file was used by the server
    tm = CDbl(Time())
    'Use an If...ElseIf...Else statement
    'to determine the time of day that
    'this file was opened. Remember that
    'the Time() function returns a value between
    '0 and 1 that reports the  portion of a 24
    'hour day in which the function was called.
    'The value .5 represents noon, .25 = 6 AM,
    '.75 = 6 PM, etc....
    If tm > 0 AND tm <= .25 Then
        fil = UCase("Morning")
    ElseIf tm > .25 AND tm <= .5 Then
        fil = UCase("Midmorning")
    ElseIf tm > .5 AND tm <= .75 Then
        fil = UCase("Afernoon")
    ElseIf tm > .75 AND tm <= 1 Then
        fil = UCase("Evening")
    End if
    'Call the GetPoem function that is defined
    'above to get the poem and return it as a
    'string that you pass back to the calling client
    'using the Response object.
    Response.Write(GetPoem(fil))
  %>
</FONT>
<P> </P>

</BODY>
</HTML>
```

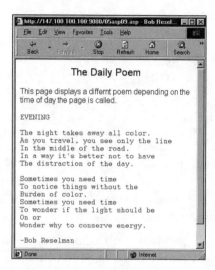

Figure 5.9: *The* `FileSystemObject` *streamlines the whole business of working with text files.*

The way the page works is that an inline server-side script takes a time stamp. The time is compared in an `If…ElseIf` statement. The result of the `If…ElseIf` is a string that is passed as an argument to the function, `GetPoem()`:

```
If tm > 0 AND tm <= .25 Then
    fil = UCase("Morning")
ElseIf tm > .25 AND tm <= .5 Then
    fil = UCase("Midmorning")
ElseIf tm > .5 AND tm <= .75 Then
    fil = UCase("Afernoon")
ElseIf tm > .75 AND tm <= 1 Then
    fil = UCase("Evening")
End if
.
.
.

Response.Write(GetPoem(fil))
```

The function `GetPoem()` creates a `FileSystemObject` and assigns it to an object variable, `fso`.

```
'Create a FileSystemObject
Set fso = CreateObject("Scripting.FileSystemObject")
```

```
'Set the path of the poem file by getting
'the path of this file using the Server object's
'MapPath method and passing the poem's filename
'as an argument to the MapPath method.
fPath = Server.MapPath("/" & filename)
```

Also, the `Server` object's `MapPath` property is to determine the location of this Active Server Page on the server's hard disk. Granted, we haven't covered the `Server` object yet. However, we will do so in later chapters. Right now, just consider the `Server` object to be the way we find out the filepath of this Active Server Page is on disk.

✔ For information about the `Server` object see the section "Using the Server Object" in Chapter 10, "More on Objects and ASP" on page 247.

We use the `FileSystemObject`'s `FileExist` method to determine whether the file we want to open is really on the disk. The file to open is determined as result of the `Select Case` statement within the `GetPoem()` function. The method takes the location of the file as an argument:

```
If fso.FileExists(fPath) Then
```

If the file exists, we use the `FileSystemObject`'s `OpenTextFile` method. `OpenTextFile` returns a `TextStream` object. You can think of `TextStream` as a connection that you attach to the file, through which you access the text of that file.

```
Set f =fso.OpenTextFile(fPath, ForReading)
```

We run a `While…Wend` loop against the `TextStream` object's `EndOfStream` property. The `EndOfStream` goes to `False` when the end of the file is reached.

```
While Not f.AtEndOfStream
```

The `ReadLine` method reads characters from a `TextStream` object a line at a time. A master string is constructed by concatenating the output of the `ReadLine` method:

```
str = str & f.ReadLine
```

Finally, the script concatenates an HTML line break tag (<br>) at the end of each line of the text file in order to have a new line presented when the text is displayed in the calling browser.

```
str = str & "<br>"
```

The `While…Wend` statement terminates when the end of the `TextStream` is reached. The master string is returned out of the `GetPoem()` function.

What's Next

This chapter has been your foray into the world of object-oriented programming using VBScript and Active Server Pages. You've learned how to create our own classes using the `Class` and `End Class` keywords. You've learned how to program with a few of the object built into Internet Explorer. In addition, you've learned how to use the `FileSystemObject` on the server side.

As of this point, we've been using the `Response` object without really paying too much attention to its purpose and operation. Now it's time to look at the details. The next chapter takes an in-depth look at the `Response` object as well as the `Request` object. The relationship between the `Response` and `Request` objects is the keystone in Active Server Page programming and distributed computing.

Part III

Part III: Working with ASP on the Server

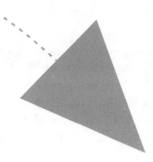

Beginning ASP: Client-Server Communication

In the world of Active Server Page programming client-server communication is encapsulated within two different yet equally important objects—the Request object that represents the Internet browser on the client computer and the server-side Response object, which returns processed data to the calling client. The purpose of this chapter is to give you an overview of the Request and Response objects with an introduction about how to use each.

In this chapter you will

- Learn about the properties and methods of the Request object
- Learn about the properties and methods of the Response object
- Learn how to use the Request object to get client-side system information
- Send data to a client using the Response object

Introduction to the `Request` Object

The `Request` object *encapsulates* the information that the calling client sends to an Internet server within the scope of every Internet conversation. This information is diverse. It ranges from information about the browser that the client is using to the data that the browser wants to have processed by the Internet Server (see Figure 6.1).

Although the `Request` object is unique to IIS and ASP, the information that is sent from the browser to the Internet server is not. The format for this information has been around for a while and is specified by the *World Wide Web Consortium (W3C)* under the *Common Gateway Interface* specification (CGI). The `Request` object is a wrapper that allows you do work with the CGI quickly and easily. Also, the `Request` object is a wrapper for other information, such as that transmitted under the secure version of the *Hypertext Transport Protocol*, HTTPS. (HTTPS is an acronym for *Secure Hypertext Transport Protocol*.)

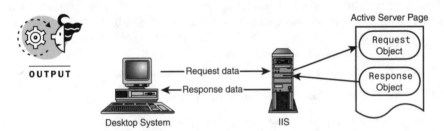

OUTPUT

Figure 6.1: The `Request` and `Response` objects encapsulate incoming and outgoing data, respectively.

THE INTERNET CONVERSATION

The interaction between a browser and an Internet server can be understood in terms of an Internet conversation.

The browser contacts the Internet server using the URL of the server. During the initial contact, the browser passes the IP address of the calling client. (Other data is passed also. However, the IP address is most important. Without the IP address of the client, the server has no way to return a response.)

The Internet server responds to the initial contact by sending data back to the IP address the calling client provided. Usually, the response is data that makes up a particular Web page. After the data is sent, the conversation is terminated.

The `Request` Object and CGI

What is the Common Gateway Interface? CGI is the standard format to which a browser adheres when it sends data to an Internet server. When the

Internet server receives transmission data from a browser, it parses the data out and assigns the information to predefined *environmental variables*. This data can be accessed by scripts and executable programs on the server. An example of an environmental variable is HTTP_USER_AGENT. This variable contains information that indicates the type of browser that the client used to submit a request to the Internet server.

Every time a user sends a request to an Internet server, the browser he uses packages up a lot of data about the browser and the computer upon which the browser resides. This is done behind the scenes. Then, the information that the browser packages is shipped off to the URL on the Internet server, along with other information specific to the request. Again, this data is sent every time a browser contacts an Internet server, and the data that is sent is structured according to the CGI standard.

You don't need to concern yourself too much with the intricacies of CGI and CGI programming to work with the Request object. The important thing to remember is that information is sent between a client browser and an Internet server in a predictable way, according to a predefined format and that the Request object is a wrapper for this interaction.

TIP

For more information on the Common Gateway Interface specification, go to World Wide Web Consortium site at http://www.w3.org/CGI/

Referencing the Request Object

The Request object is a global object within ASP. You use the object by referring to it directly by name. There is no need to access the Request object indirectly by assigning an instance of it to an object variable. For example, to call the TotalBytes property of the Request object within the script, you write Request.TotalBytes.

Using the Request Object

Table 6.1 shows a summary of the properties, methods, and collections that make up the Request object. Please take a moment to review it.

Table 6.1: IIS 5.0 Properties, Methods, and Collections of the **Request** *Object*

Name	Item	Description
TotalBytes	Property	Reports the number of bytes sent by the client in the body
BinaryRead	Method	Reads the body of an HTTP transmission on a byte-by-byte basis

continues

Table 6.1: continued

ClientCertificate	Collection	Contains security information
Cookies	Collection	Contains persistent cookie information
Form	Collection	Contains data sent in an HTTP form
QueryString	Collection	Contains name=value pairs in an HTTP QueryString
ServerVariables	Collection	Contains the set of server-side environmental variables

For the purposes of ASP programming, most of your activity is going to be to use the Request object to retrieve specific query data from a calling client using the Form, Cookies, and QueryString collections. For example, if you were to create an Active Server Page that retrieves telephone number and address information, you would use the Request object to determine the person or business for which the calling clients want you to get a specific telephone number and address. Most likely, you would use the Forms or QueryString collection. (You'll learn how to do this in later chapters.) In cases like this example, you are not going to need great facility working with the "under the hood" environmental data. But there are times when being able to determine client-side system information, such as the computer that is making a request, is useful. For example, you might need to know what type of browser a calling client is using to deliver specific data back to the browser of a given type.

Working with ServerVariables

The Request object organizes CGI environmental variables under a Collection object named ServerVariables. The way the ServerVariables collection works is that you supply the given CGI variable name as an index value. For example, if you want to find the client's IP address value, you use the server variable index named REMOTE_ADDR like so:

```
ServerVariables("REMOTE_ADDR")
```

For the most part the Index values that you pass to the ServerVariables collection are equivalent to the name of the corresponding CGI Environmental Variable.

EXAMPLE

TIP

For more information about the server variables that you can access from the ServerVariables collection, go to the Microsoft Developers Network site that lists these at http://msdn.microsoft.com/library/psdk/iisref/vbob5vsj.htm.

Listing 6.1 shows you an Active Server Page that reports the IP address of the calling client's computer using the Request object's ServerVariables collection. Also, the page uses the ServerVariables collection item, HTTP_USER_AGENT, to determine the browser type that the client is using.

Listing 6.1: Using the ServerVariables Collection to Get Information About a Calling Client (06ASP01.asp)

```
<HTML>
<HEAD>
<TITLE></TITLE>
</HEAD>
<FONT SIZE=5 FACE=ARIAL COLOR=Brown>
Things the Request object can find out about you:
</FONT>
<P>
<FONT SIZE=4 FACE=ARIAL COLOR=Green>
The IP Address of your browser is:
</FONT>

<FONT SIZE=4 FACE=ARIAL COLOR=Blue>
<%
Response.Write(Request.ServerVariables("REMOTE_ADDR"))
%><P>

</FONT>
<FONT SIZE=4 FACE=ARIAL COLOR=Green>
The type of browser that you use is:
</FONT>
<FONT SIZE=4 FACE=ARIAL COLOR=Blue>
<%
Response.Write(Request.ServerVariables("HTTP_USER_AGENT"))
%><P>
</BODY>
</HTML>
```

This output for Listing 6.2 is shown in Figure 6.2

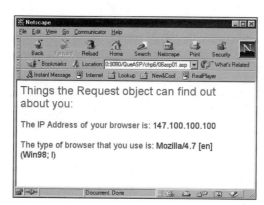

Figure 6.2: *Mozilla/4.7 indicates the browser Netscape Navigator version 4.7.*

Introduction to the Response Object

The Response object encapsulates data that a script sends to the calling browser. Table 6.2 displays a summary of the properties, methods and collections of the Response object.

Table 6.2: IIS 5.0 Properties, Methods, and Collections of the **Response** *Object*

Name	Item	Description
Buffer	Property	Set to TRUE if you want the server to process all the script before sending data on to the client
CacheControl	Property	Used for working with proxy servers
Charset	Property	Lets the client know what type of alphabet the server uses
ContentType	Property	Lets the client know the HTTP type/subtype information that the server is sending
Expires	Property	Length of time, in minutes, that a page should be cached on the client side
ExpiresAbsolute	Property	Expiration date and time for page caching
IsClientConnected	Property	TRUE, if the client is still connected to the server (Read Only)
PICS	Property	A string that indicates the PICS label, (Platform for Internet Content Selection), a rating system for Web content
Status	Property	Returns HTTP status code number
AddHeader	Method	Adds a variable to the HTTP header
AppendToLog	Method	Sends data to the Web server's log
BinaryWrite	Method	Sends pure bytes to the client instead of characters
Clear	Method	Clears the buffer. (To use this, make sure that Response.Buffer is set to TRUE.)
End	Method	Terminates script processing
Flush	Method	Sends script output immediately, without buffering
Redirect	Method	Sends output from another Web site
Write	Method	Outputs a string to the browser
Cookies	Collection	Reads or writes data for client-side cookies

As you can see, the Response object has a broad set of properties, methods, and a collection. We are not going to go into a detailed description of the use of every property, method, and collection at this time. This book is designed so that we continually revisit the Response object as well as the Request object in various chapters. Each time we revisit an object, we'll give attention to a previously unexamined feature.

Using the Write Method

The most often used method of the Response object is the Write method. The Write method sends a string back to the calling client, to be written to the browser that the calling client used to open the Internet conversation.

The syntax of the `Write` method is

```
Response.Write("String to send back to the calling client.")
```

This syntax might be familiar to you. We've been using the `Write` method of the `Response` object liberally up to this point.

You can use the `Write` method to return a constant string value back to a browser. In addition, you can use the `Write` method to return a string value from a function. The content of the string is irrelevant when using the `Write` method. The string can represent a set of HTML tags as well as text to be displayed in the browser. For example, this string returned by the `Response` object will appear bold.

```
Response.Write("<B> Bold string to send back to the calling client.</B>")
```

Sending a String

Listing 6.2 shows you how to use the `Write` method of the `Response` object to return a string within some HTML code. Figure 6.3 shows you the output of this listing.

EXAMPLE

Listing 6.2: Outputting HTML with the `Write` Method (`06ASP02.asp`)

```
<SCRIPT LANGUAGE=vbscript RUNAT=Server>
    Response.Write("<FONT SIZE=6 FACE=ARIAL COLOR=Blue>")
    Response.Write("String to send back to the calling client.")
    Response.Write("</FONT>")
</SCRIPT>
```

OUTPUT

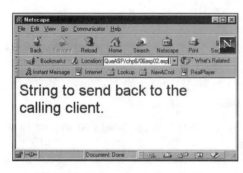

Figure 6.3: *You can use the* `Write` *method to return HTML tags as well as static text.*

Returning Values from Visual Basic Functions

As mentioned previously, you can use values returned from a function as the output parameter for the `Response` object's `Write` method. For example, if you want to return the present time, you use the VBScript `Time()` function with the `Write` method, like so:

```
Response.Write(Time())
```

Listing 6.3 is an enhanced version of Listing 6.2. Listing 6.3 uses the `Time()`, `Date()`, `Weekday()`, and `WeekdayName()` VBScript functions to produce output that is sent to the calling client using the `Response` object's `Write` method. The results of Listing 6.3 are displayed in Figure 6.4.

EXAMPLE

Listing 6.3: Using VBScript Functions Within the `Response.Write` Method (`06ASP03.asp`)

```
<SCRIPT LANGUAGE=vbscript RUNAT=Server>
    Response.Write("<FONT SIZE=4 FACE=ARIAL COLOR=Blue>")
    Response.Write("This page was processed at: ")
    Response.Write(Time())
    Response.Write("</FONT><P>")

    Response.Write("<FONT SIZE=4 FACE=ARIAL COLOR=Green>")
    Response.Write("This page was processed on: ")
    Response.Write(Date())
    Response.Write("</FONT><P>")

    Response.Write("<FONT SIZE=4 FACE=ARIAL COLOR=Brown>")
    Response.Write("This page was processed on this day: ")
    Response.Write(WeekdayName(Weekday(Date())))
    Response.Write("</FONT><P>")
</SCRIPT>
```

OUTPUT

```
Netscape
File  Edit  View  Go  Communicator  Help

Back  Forward  Reload  Home  Search  Netscape  Print

Bookmarks  Location: ASP/chp6/06asp03.asp   What's Related
Instant Message  Internet  Lookup  New&Cool  RealPlayer

This page was processed at: 7:18:53 AM

This page was processed on: 12/13/99

This page was processed on this day: Monday

Document: Done
```

Figure 6.4: *You can use the* `Date()` *and* `Time()` *functions to timestamp a page.*

Notice that the code in both Listing 6.2 and Listing 6.3 is pure script, that the code is not contained within the boundaries of `<HTML></HTML>` tags. ASP allows you to make pages that contain nothing but script output. You simply embed the script you want to execute within `<SCRIPT></SCRIPT>` tags and save the page with the `.asp` extension. Then call the page from a browser as you would any other Active Server Page.

Working with the Request and Response Objects

As you saw in Listing 6.1, you can work with the ServerVariables collection of the Request object to determine the type of browser that sent IIS a request for data. Let's put this feature to work for us to do some simple decision making.

Listing 6.4 shows a standard Web page that contains an HTML button only. When the user clicks the button, the client-side JavaScript behind the button click event procedure opens a new browser window into which the data from the Active Server Page shown in Listing 6.5 is returned. The Active Server Page returns a different Web page depending on the type of browser that made the request for data. Figure 6.5 displays both the calling client and the response under Netscape Navigator. Figure 6.6 displays the client and response under Internet Explorer. (Please be advised that the domain name, www.SomeWebSite.com, used in this example is fictitious.)

EXAMPLE

Listing 6.4: Using the Open Method to Open New Windows (06ASP04.htm)

```
<HTML>
<HEAD>
<TITLE></TITLE>

<SCRIPT LANGUAGE=javascript>
<!--
    function button1_onclick(){
        window.open("http://www.SomeWebSite.com/chp6/06asp05.asp");
    }
//-->
</SCRIPT>

</HEAD>
<FORM Name=MyForm>

<INPUT type="button"
    value="Click me to get this browser's developer's help"
    name=button1
    onclick="button1_onclick()">
</FORM>
<BODY>

<P> </P>

</BODY>
</HTML>
```

OUTPUT

Figure 6.5: When you know the calling browser, you can return information specific to that browser.

EXAMPLE

Listing 6.5: Using the `Redirect` Method of the `Response` Object (`06ASP05.asp`)

```
<%
    Dim MyBrowser
    Dim pos

    'Get the browser information
    MyBrowser = Request.ServerVariables("HTTP_USER_AGENT")

    'See if the Internet Explorer substring in there.
    'If the substring is in there, Instr returns a value
    'which indicates the position of the substring within the
    'string, If the value is zero, no substring is found.
    pos = Instr(UCase(Cstr(MyBrowser)), "MSIE")

    If pos = 0 then
        Response.Redirect("http://www.netscape.com")
    Else
        Response.Redirect("http://msdn.microsoft.com/default.asp")
    End if
%>
```

The interesting thing about the code in the Active Server Page is that it uses the `Request` object to determine which browser requested the page.

The way a browser type is identified from the contents of the string returned when the `ServerVariables("HTTP_USER_AGENT")` collection item is called. The return from Internet Explorer is

```
Mozilla/4.0 (compatible; MSIE 5.0; Windows 98; DigExt):
```

The return from Netscape Navigator is

```
Mozilla/4.7   (Win98; I)
```

Thus, the code tests to see if the characters "MSIE" appear in the output of the `ServerVariables("HTTP_USER_AGENT")` collection item. If they do, we know we are working with an Internet Explorer client.

OUTPUT

Figure 6.6: *The ASP code is able to determine the calling browser and respond accordingly.*

Working with the `Response.Redirect` Method

As you can see, the code in Listing 6.5 tests to discover the type of browser the client is using. If the client browser is Netscape Navigator, the request is redirected to the developer's page at the Netscape site. If the client browser is Internet Explorer, the call is redirected to Microsoft Developer Network Web site. Let's look at how the `Redirect` method works.

The `Response` object's `Redirect` returns an alternate Web site to the calling client. The syntax for the `Redirect` method is

```
Response.Redirect(NewURL)
```

where *NewURL* is a string that contains the full URL of the site to which the response should be redirected.

CAUTION

Please be advised that it's best to use the complete URL when defining a new Web site using the `Redirect` method. This means that you should include the `http://` part of the URL string. For example, if you want to redirect a request to www.mcp.com, define the URL as `http://www.mcp.com`. If you don't, the call has a good chance of producing an error.

The code in Listing 6.5 redirects users with Netscape browsers to the developer's site by using the `Redirect` method as follows:

```
Response.Redirect("http://www.netscape.com")
```

What's Next

This chapter introduced you to the `Request` and `Response` objects, which are the fundamental building blocks for facilitating client-server interaction in a distributed environment, using ASP. We'll be revisiting these objects many times throughout the book. You used the `Request` object to work the `ServerVariables` collection. Also, you learned how to use the `Response` object return data to a calling client, based on information in the `Request` object.

The next chapter shows you how to process data using ASP. You'll take a look at how ASP works with HTML forms and relates them to the `Forms` collection of the `Request` object. Also, you'll look at how to work with a group of ASP pages under the ASP Application structure.

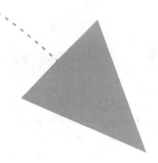

Intermediate ASP: Processing Data

One of the powerful features of ASP is the ability to process data quickly and efficiently. Before ASP came along, handling data submission from a calling client was a chore, a significant chore. You needed to work with CGI directly using a language such a PERL or C/C++. Using ASP allows you to spend more time thinking about the services you want to offer to make your site a great site than having to worry about the syntactical hoops you will need to jump through to implement them.

In this chapter you will

- Learn how to work with data in HTML forms
- Learn to make applications that maintain state
- Learn how to use client-side cookies
- Learn how to make applications that consist of many Active Server Pages
- Learn how to use the Session object

Working with Data in a Form

You use an HTML `<FORM>` element to submit data to an Internet server. The `<FORM>` element is an HTML element that collects and organizes data. Listing 7.1 shows an example of the HTML `<FORM>` element. Figure 7.1 shows the output of the HTML.

EXAMPLE

Listing 7.1: A Simple Use of the `<FORM>` Element (07asp01.htm)

```
<HTML>
<HEAD>
<TITLE>Simple Form</TITLE>
</HEAD>
<BODY>
<FORM
    Name=frmMain
    Method="POST"
    Action = "http://www.anysite.com/scripts/myscript.asp">

    Your Name: <INPUT Type=Text Name=txtName>
    <P>
    <INPUT Type="Submit" Value="Submit" Name="Submit">

</FORM>
</BODY>
</HTML>
```

OUTPUT

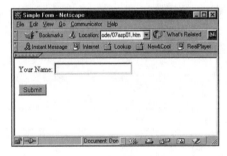

Figure 7.1: *A simple login page that uses the* `<FORM>` *element.*

The fundamental syntax for the `<FORM>` element is

```
<FORM Name=MyName Action=URL Method=POST|GET></FORM>
```

Where:

> `Name=` takes a text value that is the name of the form element (optional).
>
> `Action=` takes a text value, a URL that is the location of an executable file or script that will process the data submitted by the form (optional).

Method= takes the text POST or GET, indicating the HTTP submission method. This pertains to the way data is submitted to the Internet server. The default is GET (optional).

THE DIFFERENCE BETWEEN THE GET AND POST METHODS

The difference between the GET and POST methods is that the GET method tells the Internet server to send the incoming data to the standard CGI variables. The POST method tells the Internet server to send the data directly onto its incoming data stream to be processed.

The previous is the fundamental syntax you need to make a useful <FORM> element. Other attributes are part of the <FORM> tag, events for example. They are useful, but not critical to know at this time.

Submit buttons are commonly used within a form. A submit button is created by using the HTML <INPUT Type=Submit> element. When a user clicks a submit button, the intelligence built into the browser collects data that is associated with the form's <INPUT> elements and sends the data onto an Internet server. Submit buttons are dedicated specifically to submission behavior.

The browser knows the server to which to send the data based on the URL assigned to the Action attribute of the <FORM> tag. Please look at Listing 7.1 again. Notice that the data entered in the <Input Type=Text Name=txtName> element will be sent to server-side script at the URL, http://www.anysite.com/scripts/myscript.asp.

Using the Form Input Elements

The purpose of an <INPUT> element is to provide a mechanism that allows the user to enter data into an HTML form, for eventual submission to an Internet Server. When the user enters data into an <INPUT> element, a name=value pair is created. The Name of the pair corresponds to the Name attribute of the <INPUT> element. The name=value pairs of the form are passed by the browser to the server when the user clicks the submit button.

WHAT IS AN ATTRIBUTE?

An attribute identifies a specific feature of the tag and describes how it is to be set. For example, in the tag <FONT SIZE=4>, SIZE is the attribute that describes the size of the font. Tags can have none, one or many attributes.

The fundamental syntax for an <INPUT> element is

<INPUT Type=InputType, Name=FriendlyName Value=SomeValue>

Where:

Type is the element type (see Table 7.1).

`Name` is the name of the `<INPUT>` element

`Value` is the data entered in element or the default value shown in the element.

Table 7.1 lists the different types of `<INPUT>` elements with a description and remark about each. Listing 7.2 is a Web page that shows the code to display these `<INPUT>` elements. The output from this code is shown in Figure 7.2.

Table 7.1: Various **`<INPUT>`** *Elements*

Type	Description	Remarks
Text	Standard text box	Use the `SIZE=` attribute to set the length of the text input
Password	Similar to Text but input characters are masked with a "*"	None
Checkbox	A box that you can check·on and off; more than one checkbox can be checked at one time	Use the `CHECKED` attribute to set a check in the checkbox
Radio	A circle that you can click on and off; only one radio can be selected at one time	Use the `CHECKED` attribute to show selection
Hidden	Invisible, holds a predefined value	This type is used to pass data from browser to server and back again; however, this data is accessible only to the server
File	Similar to a textbox but allows the user to browse for files on the hard drive	None
Submit	Button used for submitting data from all input fields	None
Reset	Button that clears the value of all input fields	None
Button	A standard button	Set the `VALUE=` attribute to enter a caption in the button face
Image	A graphic with the behavior of a SUBMIT input type	Use the `SRC` attribute to assign a graphic to the element
TextArea	An element that allows you to input multiple lines of text	`<TEXTAREA>` is a separate element that is used for creating scrollable text boxes that have variable size and height; this element is not an attribute of the `<INPUT>` element—the `<TEXTAREA>` element uses a `</TEXTAREA>` end tag.

WHAT IS A NAME=VALUE PAIR?

A Name=Value pair is the way that HTML structures data that is passed on to a server over the Internet. The name part of the pair is the identifier of the pair, whereas the value part of the pair is the quantity or text that the pair is sending. For example, say you wanted to pass the first name of a person on to an Internet server. You construct a Name=Value pair:

Firstname=Bob,

Firstname identifies the pair and Bob is the text assigned to be the value of the pair. If you want to pass a first name of Bill, you would enter the following:

FirstName=Bill

When it's time to send data back to a server over the Internet, the browser collects all the Name=Value pairs it has to send and groups them into one piece of very long text for submission. For example, the Name=Value pairs:

FirstName=Bob

LastName=Reselman

Would be sent over the Internet as:

FirstName=Bob&LastName=Reselman

Name=Value pairs are used in Internet programming because the only thing that is ever passed along the Internet when using HTTP is text. Name=value pairs are an easy, reliable way to pass data around.

EXAMPLE

Listing 7.2: A Web Page with Standard <INPUT> Elements (07asp02.htm)

```
<HTML>
<HEAD>
<TITLE>HTML Elements</TITLE>
</HEAD>
<BODY>
<FORM Name=frmMain>
<P>I am a Text: <INPUT name=text1 type=text></P>
<P>I am a TextArea: <TEXTAREA name=textarea1 rows=4 cols=20></TEXTAREA></P>
<P>I am a Password: <INPUT name=password1 type=password></P>
<P>I am a CheckBox: <INPUT name=checkbox1 type=checkbox>
I am a Radio Button: <INPUT name=radio1 type=radio></P>
<P>I am a Submit Button:
<INPUT name=submit1 type=submit value=Submit>
I am a Reset Button:
<INPUT name=reset1 type=reset value=Reset></P>
<P>I am a plain old button:
<INPUT name=button1 type=button value=Button></P>
<P>I am a File:<INPUT name=file1 type=file></P>
<P>I am an Image:
<INPUT name=img type=image src="button.gif">
<P>I am Hidden:
```

Listing 7.2: continued

```
<INPUT  name=hidVar type=hidden value="MyHiddenVar">
</FORM>
</BODY>
</HTML>
```

OUTPUT

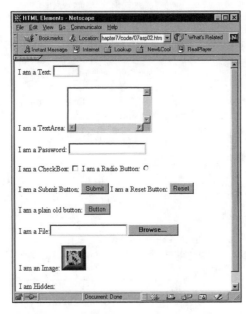

Figure 7.2: *The HTML* <INPUT> *elements allow you to pass data from a Web page to an Internet server.*

Mapping <FORM> Input to ASP

ASP uses the Form collection of the Request object to work with data submitted in a <FORM> element from the calling client. The Form collection represents all the <INPUT> elements within a given HTML <FORM>.

The syntax for using the Form collection is

```
str = Request.Form(elementName)
```

Where:

> str is an arbitrary variable containing a value passed from an element within the form.

> *elementName* is a string that represents the name of the element within the Form collection.

Thus, to access the data in the <INPUT TYPE=Text> element in the following HTML:

```
<FORM Name=MyForm>
Enter Data: <INPUT Name=myText TYPE=text>
</FORM>
```

You would write the following code:

```
s = Request.Form("myText")
```

The important concept to understand when using the Form collection is that only one form is submitted to an Internet server at any one time. Some beginning ASP programmers assume that the Form collection represents all the forms on a given Web page. This is not the case.

FORM.COUNT

The Form collection supports the Count property, which returns the number of entries in the collection.

Working with Request.Form()

Now that you have an understanding of the syntactical structure of Form collection, let's put this knowledge to work in code. We are going to submit some data to an Active Server Page on an Internet server using an HTML <FORM>. Then, within the Active Server Page, we are going to use the Form collection of the ASP Request object to determine general and specific information about the submission.

Listing 7.3 shows a page of HTML that contains an HTML <FORM> that passes data to an Active Server Page. The <FORM> is made up of some text elements and a submit button. Figure 7.3 displays the HTML in a browser. Please notice that the page already has data to submit>.

EXAMPLE

Listing 7.3: A Web Page with a Form Element (07asp03.htm)

```
<HTML>
<HEAD>
<TITLE>Simple Form</TITLE>
</HEAD>
<BODY>
<FONT COLOR=Brown SIZE=5 FACE=ARIAL>
Tell us about yourself:
</FONT>
<P>

<FONT COLOR=BLUE SIZE=4 FACE=ARIAL>
<FORM
    Name=frmMain
    Method="POST"
    Action =
    "http://www.SomeWebSite.com/QueAsp/chp7/07asp04.asp">
```

continues

Listing 7.3: continued

```
    Your Name: <INPUT Type=Text Name=txtName>
    <BR>
    Favorite Color: <INPUT Type=Text Name=txtColor>
  <BR>
    Favorite Movie: <INPUT Type=Text Name=txtMovie>
    <BR>
    <INPUT Type="Submit" Value="Submit" Name="Submit">
</FORM>
</FONT>
</BODY>
</HTML>
```

OUTPUT

Figure 7.3: *You can use an HTML form on your page to gather information about your visitor.*

Listing 7.4 shows the Active Server Page that processes the data submitted by the code in Listing 7.3. The output from the ASP code is shown in Figure 7.4

EXAMPLE

Listing 7.4: Using the Forms Collection in ASP (`07asp04.asp`)

```
<HTML>
<HEAD>
<TITLE></TITLE>
</HEAD>
<BODY>
<CENTER>
<FONT SIZE=5 FACE=ARIAL COLOR=Red>
Working with a Form
</FONT>
<P>
</CENTER>
<FONT SIZE=4 FACE=ARIAL COLOR=Green>
The number of elements
in the form of the calling client is: <BR>
</FONT>
```

```
<FONT SIZE=4 FACE=Courier COLOR=Green>
<%=Request.Form.Count%>
</FONT>
<P>
<FONT SIZE=4 FACE=ARIAL COLOR=Blue>
Here is all the data: <BR>
</FONT>
<FONT SIZE=4 FACE=Courier COLOR=Blue>
<%=Request.Form%>
</FONT>

<P>
<FONT SIZE=4 FACE=ARIAL COLOR=Red>
Here is each piece of data: <br>
</FONT>
<FONT SIZE=4 FACE=Courier COLOR=Red>
<%
    Dim i
    Dim str
    'Use a For...Next loop to traverse
    'all the elements within the form.
    For i = 1 to Request.Form.Count
        str = Request.Form(i) & "<br>"
        Response.Write(str)
    Next
%>
</FONT>
```

OUTPUT

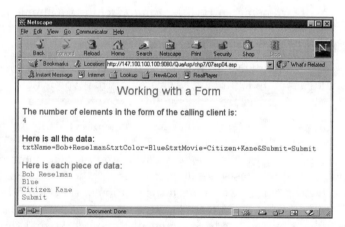

Figure 7.4: *The* Form *collection contains the elements in the form, even the* Submit *button.*

Let's take a moment to analyze some aspects of the ASP code in Listing 7.4.

Please notice that you can determine the number of elements within the Form collection by using the Count property, as shown in the following line of code:

```
<%=Request.Form.Count%>
```

After we can determine the number of entries in a collection, we can traverse the collection using a For...Next loop to find the value of each entry.

```
For i = 1 to Request.Form.Count
    str = Request.Form(i) & "<br>"
    Response.Write(str)
Next
```

You'll find this technique useful when you need to work with groups of data in a predefined structure, such as a registration form.

Last, notice the you can display all the data in the Form collection in its raw name=value pair format by calling output from the Form directly:

```
<%=Request.Form%>
```

RESPONSE.WRITE SHORTHAND

You can use the equal sign before an expression within in line script tags <% %> to output the value of that expression as a response to the calling client. For example,

```
<%=Request.Form%>
```

is the same as:

```
<%Response.Write(Request.Form)%>
```

Let's move on to using an HTML form to facilitate a simple login process.

Making a Simple Login Process

Many programmers use HTML forms to process some sort of login data. So let's make a simple login page. A project of this type is an easy, applicable way to get your arms around using forms to process data.

Our login process contains two pages: a page of HTML to submit data and an Active Server Page to process the data that is submitted. The login page contains a Text <INPUT> element, a Password input element, and a Submit button. We use the Password element to mask the characters that the user enters in the form. We've changed the caption of the submit button to display the string, "Login." Please be advised that although the Value attribute of the Submit button has been changed to display "Login," the behavior of the button is still to submit data gathered in the form. Listing 7.5 shows the HTML code for the login page, and Figure 7.5 displays the login page.

Listing 7.5: An HTML Form Using a Password Element (`07asp05.htm`)

```
<HTML>
<HEAD>
<TITLE>Simple Login Form</TITLE>
</HEAD>
<BODY>
<FONT COLOR=Brown SIZE=5 FACE=ARIAL>
Please Login
</FONT>
<P>
<CENTER>
<FONT COLOR=BLUE SIZE=4 FACE=ARIAL>
<FORM
    Name=frmMain
    Method="POST"
    Action =
    "http://www.SomeWebSite.com/chp7/07asp06.asp">

    UserID: <INPUT Type=Text Name=txtUserID>
    <P>
    Password: <INPUT Type=Password Name=txtPWD>
    <P>
    <INPUT Type="Submit" Value="Login" Name="Submit">
</FORM>
</FONT>
</CENTER>
</BODY>
</HTML>
```

Figure 7.5: *Password elements mask the data that a user enters.*

The ASP, to which data is submitted, checks to make sure that neither the UserID nor password is less than six characters (see Listing 7.6). This is admittedly a very limited validation criterion. However, it suffices to demonstrate the programming techniques at hand. If you were to use this code in a full blown production environment, of course you would build in processing behavior that is much more substantial. Figure 7.6 shows the ASP output for valid and invalid login data. Generally you use red fonts to indicate an error situation. In this case, the text in the valid login window is in blue and the invalid login text is red.

EXAMPLE

Listing 7.6: Valid Script Without <HTML></HTML> Tags (07asp06.htm)

```
<SCRIPT LANGUAGE=vbscript RUNAT=Server>
    Function DoLogin(UserID, PWD)
    'Processes login behavior
        Dim str
        str = "Processing " & UserID & ", "
        str = str & "and your password."
        DoLogin = str
    End Function

    Dim UserID
    Dim PWD
    Dim errDesc(1)
    'Get the values from the login
    UserID = Request.Form("txtUserID")
    PWD = Request.Form("txtPWD")

    'Check to make sure the UserID data in
    'the form is more than 6 characters
    If Len(UserID) < 6 then
        errDesc(0) = "UserID length not supported"
    End if

    'Check to make sure the UserID data in
    'the form is more than 6 characters
    If Len(PWD) < 6 then
        errDesc(1) = "Password length not supported"
    End if
    'Check to see if the error message array has any
    'values in it
    If errDesc(0) = "" AND errDesc(1) = "" then
        'If it does not, call the processing function
        Response.Write("<FONT COLOR=Blue SIZE=5>")
        Response.Write(DoLogin(UserID, PWD))
        Response.Write("</FONT>")
    Else
        'Othewise issues an error message
        Response.Write("<FONT COLOR=RED SIZE=5>")
        Response.Write("Invalid Page <P>")
        Response.Write("Reasons: <P>")
```

```
        'Get the messages out of each array element
        If errDesc(0) <> "" then
            Response.Write(errDesc(0) & "<HR>")
        End if

        If errDesc(1) <> "" then
            Response.Write(errDesc(1) & "<HR>")
        End if
        Response.Write("</FONT>")
    End if
</SCRIPT>
```

OUTPUT

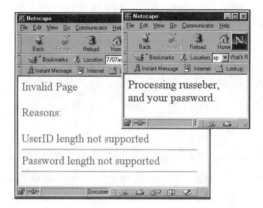

Figure 7.6: The window on the left indicates an invalid login attempt that produces an error message, whereas the window on the right is a successful login.

Please notice that the code in Listing 7.6 extracts the login data form using the Form collection referring to the name attribute of each HTML <INPUT> element:

```
'Get the values from the login
UserID = Request.Form("txtUserID")
PWD = Request.Form("txtPWD")
```

The rest of the code is straightforward VBScript. An array, errDesc(), is used to contain the error description strings, one for the UserID, the other for the password.

```
.
errDesc(0) = "UserID length not supported"
.

.
errDesc(1) = "Password length not supported"
```

If both elements of the array are NULL, then the data is valid. Subsequently control of the program is passed to the function, DoLogin().

```
If errDesc(0) = "" AND errDesc(1) = "" then
    Response.Write(DoLogin(UserID, PWD))
.
.
```

Otherwise, an error is in force and a report of the error is made to the calling client.

```
'Otherwise issues an error message
Response.Write("<FONT COLOR=RED SIZE=5>")
Response.Write("Invalid Page <P>")
Response.Write("Reasons: <P>")
'Get the messages out of each array element
If errDesc(0) <> "" then
    Response.Write(errDesc(0) & "<HR>")
End if

If errDesc(1) <> "" then
    Response.Write(errDesc(1) & "<HR>")
End if
Response.Write("</FONT>")
```

Again, the script is a little slight on login functionality. The point of the code is to show you how to work with the Form collection.

The Form collection is a powerful tool for processing data. You will be using it repeatedly, particularly if you are writing ASP applications that use multiple pages.

Working with Applications

ASP provided you with the ability to work with multiple pages as a group. When you use Active Server Pages that are interdependent, you have what is called an ASP Application. The last section gave modest evidence of this. For example, we needed to use a static HTML page (07asp05.htm) to call the associated ASP login page (07asp06.asp) to send it data. The ASP login page provided the logic by which the data from the form page was processed. Using multiple pages to make ASP Applications brings a whole new level to ASP programming. Under ASP, a page becomes a component of a larger whole. Of course, as we all know, any new solution produces at least one new question.

Understanding Session and Application Scope

The first question that arises when we work with multiple pages is how do you pass data between pages? By definition variables declared in a script or a procedure of script have scope only to the page in which the variable is made. We need to have a way to pass variable values from page to page. For example, imagine that you have a page the needs to know a UserID value that was defined in another page, a login page for instance. The variables defined under page level scope won't work. We need to be able to declare a variable that the whole application can see. These variables need to have a level scope greater than that of the page.

ASP supports levels of scope that supercede the page level. The first level above the page level is the Session level. You can conceptualize the Session level as being all the pages a given user uses when using your ASP application during a specific visit to the site. Variables that have Session scope are visible from page to page during a session that a user spends with your application.

NOTE

Every Session object is given a unique identification number by IIS. You access this number using the Session.SessionID property, such as

```
Response.Write Session.SessionID
```

The next level of scope above the Session level is the Application level. Variables with Application scope live throughout the application in its entirety. If you declare a variable with Application scope, it will exist for a session now, tomorrow, and for the life of the application. Figure 7.7 illustrates the concept.

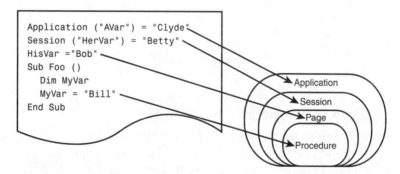

Figure 7.7: *Session variables live throughout the session. Application variables are always available anywhere in the application, at any time.*

Declaring a Session Variable

You declare a Session level variable using the Session object. The Session object describes the page to page interaction that a user does when working with you application. The syntax for declaring a Session level variable is

```
Session("VarName") = SomeValue
```

Where:

> VarName is a string the represents the name of the session level variable.
>
> *SomeValue* represents a value that you assign to the session variable.

Thus, if you want to create a Session variable, UserID, that takes the value "ebwhite", you write

```
Session("UserId") = "ebwhite"
```

If you want to write a Session variable, CreditLimit, that takes a value 6000, you write

```
Session("CreditLimit") = 6000
```

THE SESSION.ABANDON METHOD

If you want to destroy all Session level variables and objects, call the Session.Abandon method.

THE SESSION.CONTENTS COLLECTION

The Session.Contents collection contains all the session data for a given session. Session variables are part of this collection. If you want to find the values of each variable in the Session object, you traverse the Contents collection using a For...Each loop, like so:

```
For each str in Session.Contents

    'Report the session variable name
    Response.Write str & "="
    'Report the value of the session variable
    Response.Write Session(str)
Next
```

Declaring an Application Variable

You declare Application level variables using the Application object. The Application object represents your ASP application in its entirety. Application level variables persist from session to session.

You declare an Application variable very much in the same way you declare a Session variable. The following lines of code are two declarations of Application level variables. One takes a numeric value. The other stores a string value.

```
Application("NumberOfPlanets") = 9
Application("CurrentPrez")= "Clinton"
```

Working with Global.ASA

We need to look at one more topic before we can move on to the nuts and bolts of building ASP applications. ASP has a special file named Global.ASA.

Global.ASA is the file where you declare Session level and Application level variables independent of any page. Global.ASA is a central location in which you can create Session level and Application level variables that are in force for any given session or throughout the application. Using Global.ASA means that you do not need to use random Web pages to create and initialize variables. ASP is designed to "look" for Global.ASA to get global data.

Using Global.ASA does not mean that you cannot declare Session and Application levels at the page level. You can. However, using a high level structure for global data within your ASP application is good business in terms of software design. Making up Session and Application level data as you go along might put the integrity of your application's architecture at risk. Generally, when declaring variables, you should stay as low as you can go when defining scope. You want to declare a variable to have limited scope, preferably at the page and procedure level. An application that is designed well will have a limited number of Session and Application level variables that are essential for the application overall.

Any application on your Web site can have its own Global.ASA. You place a Global.ASA file in root directory of your ASP application.

ASP APPLICATION STRUCTURE

The structure of an ASP application is based on the directory-subdirectory tree structure. An ASP application is requited to a root directory that contains essential Active Server Pages and can have subdirectories containing additional pages that your application uses.

You register the root directory of your ASP application as a virtual directory under IIS or Personal Web Server. Registering your application activates the Global.ASA file dedicated to the application.

Listing 7.7 shows a bare bones Global.ASA file. Figure 7.8 shows the position of the file in the IIS Web site directory dedicated to this chapter.

EXAMPLE

Listing 7.7: Global.ASA Contains Session-level and Application-Level Variables (global.ASA)

```
<SCRIPT LANGUAGE=vbscript RUNAT=Server>
'********************
'Filename: Global.ASA
'
'Programmer: Bob Reselman
'
'Copyright 1999 Macmillan Computer Publishing
'********************
    Sub Application_OnStart()
        Application("CompanyName") = "A Good Company"
    End Sub
    Sub Session_OnStart()
        Session("SesMsg") = "Welcome to the Session"
```

continues

Listing 7.7: continued

```
    End Sub

    Sub Application_End()
        'Your code here

    End Sub

    Sub Session_End()
        'Your code here

    End Sub


</SCRIPT>
```

Figure 7.8: Global.ASA *must be in the root directory of your application.*

Notice that the Global.ASA shown in Listing 7.7 contains OnStart event procedure for the Application and Session objects. Let's look at what these are.

OnStart **Event Procedures**

As you learned earlier, the Application object represents your ASP application in its entirety, independent of the number of users interacting with your site. The Session object represents each particular set of page-to-page interactions that are a result of a given user's session. When your application starts, a Start event is fired for the application. When a user visits your site, a Start event is fired for that particular Session. Both of these events can be captured in Global.ASA. Application_OnStart() captures the Start event that is fired when the application starts. Session_OnStart() captures the Start event that is fired when a new user starts a session with your application.

The Global.ASA files in Listing 7.7 contains OnStart event procedures for the Application and Session objects. Please notice that the Application_OnStart() creates an application level variable, CompanyName and sets a value to it. Also, Session_OnStart() creates a session level variable, SesMsg and sets a value to that variable.

Listing 7.8 shows the code for an Active Server Page that calls the Application and Session variables defined and initialized in the Global.ASA file for this application. Figure 7.9 displays the output of the file.

EXAMPLE

Listing 7.8: Using Application and Session Variables (07asp08.asp)

```
<SCRIPT LANGUAGE=vbscript RUNAT=Server>
    'Call and output the Session variable
    Response.Write(Session("SesMsg") & "<BR>")
    'Call and output the Application variable
    Response.Write(Application("CompanyName"))
</SCRIPT>
```

OUTPUT

Figure 7.9: You can display the value of Application and Session variables defined in Global.ASA using Active Server Page script.

***

CAUTION

Don't forget to register your application's root directory as a virtual directory on IIS or Personal Web Server. If you do not, the Session and Application event procedures will not be in force.

***

OnEnd Event Procedures

Just as a Start event is fired when the Application and Session objects start, an End event is fired when the Application and Session objects terminate.

The Application object terminates when the Internet Information Server is shut down or when the Global.ASA file is replaced. Terminating the application is not an easy thing to do. When you do terminate it, you should use extreme caution. You program the Application_OnEnd() procedure when you need to do application level clean up before the application terminates.

You program the Session_OnEnd() event procedure when you want to do clean up as the user leaves the application or when the session times out. A session time out usually occurs when a script encounters a processing error that is not resolved in a set amount of time.

Listing 7.7 has skeleton code for the OnEnd event procedures for the Application and Session objects.

You'll see the OnEnd event procedures used later in the book when we build full-fledged ASP applications.

Keeping State in an ASP Application

A fundamental problem faced by all programmers who create programs that run over the Internet is the problem of state. *State* is the ability to persist data over time.

EXAMPLE

For example, imagine you have a desktop program that reports the total number of files on your hard drive. Every time you add a file to the drive, the program increases the number. Every time you delete a file, the program decreases the number. This desktop program is a stateful program. Whenever the state of the number of files on your hard drive changes, the program knows about the change and accommodates this change in state.

Now, imagine that your desktop program has been modified to be a client-server Internet application. Instead of keeping track of changes on the local hard disk, the program keeps track of the number of files on a server's hard disk. For every change in the state of the number of files on the server to be reported, the client portion of the application must be connected to the server. Otherwise, any state change will go unnoticed. Running this program as a Web application using standard HTTP/HTML is difficult because programs that run on the Internet using HTTP/HTML are stateless. The client connects to the server when it needs to and the connection lasts only for one Internet Conversation. The connection is not continuous. Thus in our scenario, every time the server wants to update file information, it needs to wait for a connection. The *asynchronous* nature of the interaction is a problem.

Understanding an Internet Conversation

The way an Internet Conversation works is that a client calls a server for a Web page. The server returns the page and the connection closes. The server forgets about the call. It forgets about the data passed to it or the data it returned. It's analogous to a series of short, absent minded, telephone conversations. Here is an analogy:

EXAMPLE

Bob: Hello, Ralph. I'd like to order a hamburger.

Ralph: OK, I'll have one sent right over.

Conversation ends.

New conversation:

Bob: Hello Ralph, This is Bob. Will you put some pickles on that hamburger?

Ralph: What hamburger? I don't know anything about a hamburger.

Conversation ends.

Ralph knows nothing about the hamburger that Bob ordered because the hamburger was ordered during a separate Internet conversation.

Solving the Problem of State

In our Web-based, client-server file reporting example, if the server wanted to report to the client the names of new files that it had on its disk, such reporting would be a problem. The server doesn't know what files the client considers new or old because it has no idea what the last file loaded to the local drive was. The server would need to keep a list of all the filenames that it sent to the client at any given time. This is a chore.

But, fortunately, it is not an impossible chore. There are a few ways to solve this problem. At the core of things the server needs to know the name, date, and file size of the last file it sent to the client. We could create a set of unique application-level variables for each client that would contain the file information data that the server needed. However, if we had to support millions of clients this would be a problem. What if some users did not want to use the program anymore? We might have thousands of orphan application variables lying around. This is not good business.

A more elegant solution would be to keep a record on the client machine the indicated the name, date, and size of the last file downloaded to it. Then, when the client calls the server, it could just pass this "last file downloaded" information to the server along with its other standard data. The server would look at this data and say, "Hey, this is the last file I gave this client. I'll report all the new files since this one."

Under the Hypertext Transfer Protocol (HTTP, the standard upon which Web interaction is based) a server can write a little record of data to a special area of the client's hard drive. The record of data is called a *cookie*.

Working with Cookies

A cookie is a packet of information that is shared between a Web server and a Web browser. Typically, if an Active Server Page wants the Web browser to remember a piece of information, it will send a cookie as part of the *HTTP header* in its response to a page request. When the browser receives the cookie, it stores it in memory. Cookies have an expiration date that determines how long the cookie can live on the client machine. If the cookie has an expiration date that will cause it to live beyond the current browser session, it is written to the user's hard disk.

The next time the browser requests a page from the same Web server, it sends any unexpired cookies that were originally sent from that server back as part of the request. The requested Active Server Page might then utilize the information it receives via the cookies, if appropriate.

CAUTION

It is possible to set both the Internet Explorer and Netscape Navigator browsers to not accept cookies. If the user's Web browser does not allow the use of cookies, the techniques described in this section cannot be used.

Writing Data with `Response.Cookies()`

A cookie is part of the `Response.Cookies` collection. The `Cookies` collection represents all of the cookies that a given Internet server writes on a given client. If you want to instruct a client browser to store a simple bit of information in a cookie, you use the following syntax:

```
Response.Cookies(cookie) = value
```

Where:

> `cookie` is the name of the cookie to be set.

> `value` is the information that you want to store in the cookie.

To set a cookie that indicates that the caller has a musical preference for Jazz, you can create the following cookie, `MusicPref`, like so:

```
Response.Cookies("MusicPref") = "Jazz"
```

You can use function returns for cookie values. For example, to store the date and time of the user's last visit to your Web site in a cookie named `LastVisit`, you can include the following line in an Active Server Page:

```
<% Response.Cookies("LastVisit") = Now() %>
```

When the client browser receives the HTTP response, it will create or update the appropriate cookie with the value that was sent.

Using `Response.Cookies().Expires`

Often, you will want to store information that can be retrieved by a later session; in fact, this is one of the most common uses of cookies. To do this, you must set the `Expires` attribute of the cookie that you are sending. You can set the `Expires` attribute with the following syntax:

```
Response.Cookies(cookie).Expires = value
```

where *value* in this case represents the date and time that you want the cookie to expire.

For example, to cause a cookie to remain available until 2:00 p.m. on December 31, 2000, you would use the following syntax:

```
Response.Cookies("LastVisit").Expires = "12/31/2000 14:00"
```

In this case, the `LastVisit` cookie will be available to subsequent visits to this site that take place on or before 2:00 p.m. on December 31, 2000.

As mentioned earlier, cookies where the `Expires` attribute is set to cause the cookie to live beyond the current session are saved to the user's hard drive. The exact storage location for cookies varies depending upon the browser type and version, as well as the client operating system. Internet Explorer typically stores each cookie in a separate text file. The cookie's filename consists of the username of the user currently logged in to windows, followed by an @ symbol and part of the name of the cookie's domain. Netscape Navigator stores all of a user's cookies in one text file named `cookies.txt`, located within the Netscape program directory structure. See Table 7.2 for some common cookie storage locations.

Table 7.2: Cookie Storage Locations

Browser	Operating System	Cookie Location
Internet Explorer	Windows 95/98	`C:\Windows\Cookies`
Internet Explorer	Windows NT	`C:\WINNT\Profiles\ username\Cookies`
Internet Explorer	Windows 2000	`C:\Documents and Settings\username\ Cookies`
Netscape	All	`C:\Program Files\Netscape\Users\ username\cookies.txt`

Working with Cookie Keys

Juggling several cookies in a single page might get unwieldy. You can organize your cookies somewhat by using *keys* to create *cookie dictionaries*. Simply put, a cookie dictionary is a group of cookies that all have the same name, and are identified by a *key*, a sort of sub-name. Think of it like a family; all of the family members share a common last name, but the individual members are identified by unique first names.

The syntax for using a keys with a cookies is

```
Response.Cookies (cookie)(keyname) = value
```

Where

> `cookie` is the cookie that contains keys
>
> `keyname` is the name of the key that is a distinct value within the cookie
>
> `value` is the assignment to the cookie

Listing 7.9 shows a cookie dictionary named `User`. The `User` cookie dictionary contains three keys, `Name`, `LastVisit`, and `ZIPCode`. Note that the `Expires` attribute is set for all of the cookies at once by setting it at the cookie dictionary level.

EXAMPLE

Listing 7.9: Organizing with Cookie Keys

```
<%
   Response.Cookies("User")("Name") = "June Thomas"
   Response.Cookies("User")("LastVisit") = Now()
   Response.Cookies("User")("ZIPCode") = "72301"
   Response.Cookies("User").Expires = "12/31/2000 14:00"
%>
```

Reading Data with `Request.Cookies()`

You use the `Request` object's `Cookies` collection to access the value of a cookie. For example, if you want to read the value of a cookie named, LastVisit, you would write

```
Response.Write Request.Cookies("LastVisit")
```

If you want to access values from cookies that use keys, such as the `User` cookie and the `Name` key, you would write

```
Response.Write Request.Cookies("User")("Name")
```

COOKIES.HASKEYS

The `Cookies` collection of the `Request` object has an attribute named `HasKeys`. This read-only attribute reports `True` if the cookie in question is a cookie dictionary (and therefore contains keys), or `False` if it is a standalone cookie.

Using Cookies

Now it's time to turn our conceptual framework of cookies into useful real world technology. First let's create a way to report all of the cookies that a server has generated.

Listing 7.10 shows an Active Server Page that reports all the cookies a client's cookies for a particular server. Figure 7.10 shows the output of the Active Server Page.

Listing 7.10: Using For…Each Loops to Access Cookies (07asp08.asp)

```
<HTML>
<HEAD>
<TITLE></TITLE>
</HEAD>
<BODY>
<CENTER>
<FONT face=ARIAL size=3 Color=Blue>
The following cookies are contained in the
Request object's Cookies collection:<BR>
<HR>
<%
'Display the entire cookie
Response.Write Request.Cookies()
%>
</CENTER>
<P></FONT>
<!--Create aTable-->
<TABLE align=center border=1>
  <TR>
    <TH>Cookie Name</TH>
    <TH>Contents</TH></TR>
<%
  'Traverse the cookies collection of the
  'Request object.
  For Each cookie In Request.Cookies
    'Start a new table row
    Response.Write "  <tr>" & VbCrLf
    'Check to see if the cookie has keys
    If Request.Cookies(Cookie).HasKeys Then
      'Create a new table cell for the data
      Response.Write "    <td align='center'>" & cookie & "<br>"
      Response.Write "(Cookie Dictionary)</td>" & VbCrLf
      'Start a new cell
      Response.Write "    <td>"
      'Put a label in this cell
      Response.Write "Keys:<br>" & VbCrLf
      'If the cookie does have keys, traverse
      'each key and write out the contents of the key
      For Each key In Request.Cookies(Cookie)
        Response.Write key & " = " & Request.Cookies(Cookie)(key) & "<br>"
      Next
      'Close off the cell
      Response.Write "    </td>" & VbCrLf
    Else
      'If you get to here, this is a standalone cookie
      Response.Write "    <td align='center'>" & cookie & "</td>" & VbCrLf
      Response.Write "    <td>"
```

Listing 7.10: continued

```
        Response.Write Request.Cookies(cookie)
        Response.Write "      </td>" & VbCrLf
      End If
      'Close off the row
      Response.Write "   </tr>" & VbCrLf
    Next
%></TABLE></P>

</BODY>
</HTML>
```

OUTPUT

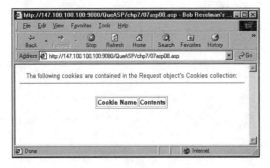

Figure 7.10: *This server hasn't created any cookies on this browser.*

You'll notice that when the Active Server Page was run, it reports that the browser hasn't any cookies written to it. That's because there aren't any cookies on this browser yet! So let's write some.

The following demonstration sets some user input to cookies. The demonstration requires that we use three Active Server Pages. One page to display cookie information (07asp08.asp), one page to take user input (07asp09.asp), and one to process user input and set it to cookies (07asp10.asp). Figure 7.11 shows you the three pages, their function, and relationship to each other.

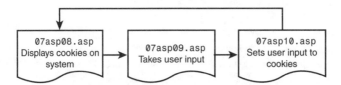

Figure 7.11: *These pages work together to display set and display cookies.*

Listing 7.11 shows the ASP code for the user input page. The page uses an HTML <FORM> to collect data input about the user. Figure 7.12 displays the page in a browser.

EXAMPLE

Listing 7.11: Collecting Data to be Processed into Cookies (`07asp09.asp`)

```
<HTML>
<HEAD>
<TITLE>Using Cookies</TITLE>
</HEAD>
<BODY>
<FONT SIZE=5 FACE=ARIAL COLOR=blue>
<CENTER>
Using Cookies<P>
</CENTER>
</FONT>

<FONT SIZE=5 FACE=ARIAL COLOR=blue>
<Form Name=MyForm
      Method=Post
      Action="http://www.SomeWebSite.com/QueAsp/chp7/07asp10.asp">
<P>
Name: <INPUT name=txtName><P>
Favorite Color: <INPUT name=txtColor><P>
Favorite Car: <INPUT name=txtCar><P>
Favorite Music:<INPUT name=txtMusic><P>
<INPUT type="submit" value="Submit" name=submit1>
<FORM>
</FONT>
</BODY>
</HTML>
```

Figure 7.12: *The data collection form with visitor information entered.*

The page shown in Listing 7.11 submits the data to the Active Server Page shown in Listing 7.12. Listing 7.12 processes the data from the form and assigns the form values to cookies. Figure 7.13 shows the page displayed in a browser).

EXAMPLE

Listing 7.12: Using Cookies with Keys to Organize Related Data

```
<%
Response.Cookies("LastVisit")=Now()
Response.Cookies("LastVisit").Expires = "12/31/2000 14:00"
Response.Cookies("LastIP") = _
    Request.ServerVariables("REMOTE_ADDR")
Response.Cookies("LastIP").Expires = "12/31/2000 14:00"
Response.Cookies("LastBrowser") = _
    Request.ServerVariables("HTTP_USER_AGENT")
Response.Cookies("LastBrowser").Expires = "12/31/2000 14:00"

Response.Cookies("Info")("Name") = Request.Form("txtName")
Response.Cookies("Info")("Music") = Request.Form("txtMusic")
Response.Cookies("Info")("Color") = Request.Form("txtColor")
Response.Cookies("Info")("Car") = Request.Form("txtCar")
Response.Cookies("Info").Expires = "12/31/2000 14:00"
%>
<HTML>
<HEAD>
<TITLE></TITLE>
</HEAD>
<BODY>
<CENTER>
<FONT SIZE=5 FACE=ARIAL COLOR=BLUE>
<A HREF="http://www.SomeWebSite/QueAsp/chp7/07asp08.asp">
Click here to set the secret cookies
</A>
</FONT>
</BODY>
</HTML>
```

Figure 7.13: *You can call Active Server Pages by using standard HTML* <A HREF> *tags.*

Notice that the script writes the cookies before processing any other HTML output. This is very important!

CAUTION

When creating Active Server Pages, cookies writing must come before the <HTML> tag, always. Writing cookies after the <HTML> tag will make code that creates an error!

Also notice that the code in Listing 7.12 uses the hypertext anchor elements <A HREF ....></A> to recall the Active Server Page that displays the cookie data on a client machine as shown in Listing 7.10. Figure 7.14 shows the page that you saw in Figure 7.10, only this time it's populated with data from the newly added cookies.

OUTPUT

Figure 7.14: *The top portion of the page shows the entire Cookies collection, which is a single string that is parsed by the ASP scripting engine into the Cookies collection.*

What's Next

This chapter showed you how to use process data supplied by a calling client. You learned to work the HTML <FORM> submissions. In addition, you were shown how to make variables with Session and Application level scope in order to work with data between pages. We discussed the nature of ASP Applications and the Session object. Lastly, you learned how to use cookies to persist data between the Web page and the Web server.

The next chapter takes you to the next level of ASP programming—working with data on databases. Next, you'll learn how to write ASP scripts that work with data access objects to manipulate data on a variety of data sources.

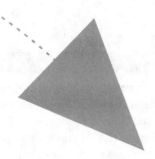

Moving Forward with ASP: Working with Data

One of the most powerful aspects of Active Server Pages programming is the capability of working with information stored in databases. A Web server running ASP connects to databases through ActiveX Data Objects (ADO) technology. ActiveX Data Objects makes data access a simple affair. In addition, ADO allows you to work with many different types of datasources, not just data in databases.

In this chapter you will

- Learn the ADO framework
- Learn how to create Active Server Pages that use OLE DB datasources
- How to work with ADO's Connection, Recordset, and Command objects
- Learn the fundamentals of SQL
- Learn how to use HTML to create and format reports from a database

The ADO Framework

ADO, or ActiveX Data Objects, is a collection of objects that allow applications to communicate with data sources in a consistent manner. Each object in the ActiveX Data Objects model represents a particular piece that is used when a program works with data. For example, the `Connection` object represents the hookup to the datasource from which you will get data. The `Recordset` object represents the particular data you retrieve from a data source. The `Command` object represents instructions you want to invoke upon a database—deleting data, for example. These objects haven't any graphical user interface. You use ActiveX Data Objects in pure code. The bulk of the work you do with ADO is going to be configuring the properties of each object. Then you call the methods of the objects in order to tell the data source to retrieve the data you want, add new data, and delete or change existing data.

You follow a four-step process when you use ActiveX Data Objects to work with databases:

1. Connect to the database.

2. Define the data you want.

3. Manipulate that data.

4. Display the data.

The code you write to use ADO will always implement some, but usually all, of these four steps.

Working with ADO, ODBC, and OLE DB

Before we go into the nuts and bolts of coding ActiveX Data Objects, you need to understand ADO relationship to OLE DB. Understanding OLE DB is important because when you configure the `Connection` object to hook up to a database, you are going to declare a provider from which you will get data. The formal name for the provider is the *OLE DB Provider*. If you don't understand what OLE DB is about and how the ADO technology relates to an OLE DB Provider, you run the risk of configuring your data connection improperly.

Understanding ODBC

OLE DB is a "next generation" technology that enhances ODBC. ODBC (Open Database Connectivity) allows databases from different manufacturers to work together. ODBC is an interpreter that makes all databases seem the same to one another and to programs that have to interact with them, regardless of the inner working of each database (see Figure 8.1).

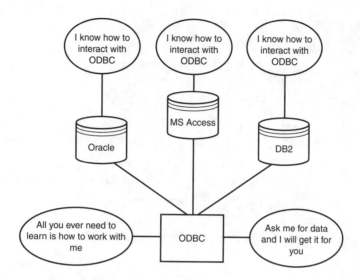

Figure 8.1: *Databases such as Oracle, MS Access, and DB2 provide software that allows them to interact with ODBC.*

The benefit of using ODBC is that you need to learn only one methodology to work with many different databases. Practically all the database manufacturers provide software that you install that allows their databases to work with ODBC. This software is called an *ODBC driver.*

Using the ODBC Datasource Administrator

You install ODBC drivers on the given computer that is going to access the ODBC-compliant database. With regard to Web servers, sometimes the database and the Web server reside on the same computer. Sometimes the database is on a different computer altogether. The ODBC Datasource Administrator applet is the tool you use to allow a given computer to have access to any number of ODBC databases, regardless of where the database resides. Of course, when you use databases that reside on the same computer as the Web server, overall performance between the database and Web server is a lot faster.

Usually the Web Master or Database Administrator is the person who configures ODBC datasources to a Web Server by using the ODBC Datasource Administrator application. The ODBC Datasource Administrator is located in the Control Panel of the computer upon which the Web Server runs (see Figure 8.2).

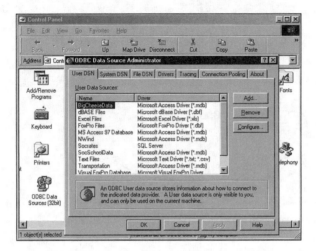

Figure 8.2: *The ODBC Datasource Administrator enables access to different ODBC-compliant databases.*

Understanding OLE DB

OLE DB picks up where ODBC leaves off. As powerful as ODBC is, it has a significant shortcoming. It only works with databases. There are other types of datasources out there. For example, there are email systems, index servers that search and index various types of documents on a hard disk, and the files system of your computer. OLE DB allows you to work with these datasources in very much the same way you work with standard databases (see Figure 8.3).

OLE DB is the first important step toward implementing Microsoft's vision of Universal Data. *Universal Data* is a model in which all data can be treated the same way regardless of the source. In the Universal Data model there is little difference between querying data in an SQL Server database or querying data in an email server. Data is data, regardless of source.

OLE DB is a set of standard objects and methods (also know as interfaces) that are exposed for any given data source. The nice thing about OLE DB is that you work with the same set of objects and methods regardless of the datasource behind the objects. What this means in real life is that you do not have to worry too much about the idiosyncrasies of datasources.

NOTE

For more information about ODBC, ADO, Universal Data Access, and Microsoft Data Access Components (MDAC), go to the Microsoft Developers Network Web Site at

```
http://msdn.microsoft.com/library/devprods/vs6/vstudio/mdac200/
mdac3sc7.htm
```

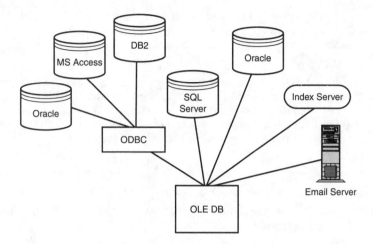

Figure 8.3: *Some databases can be accessed directly by OLE DB or indirectly by using the OLE DB Provider for ODBC; such is the case with the Oracle database in this figure.*

Working with OLE DB Providers

OLE DB interacts with data through a layer of software called the *OLE DB Provider*. The OLE DB Provider is similar to an ODBC driver in that it provides a mechanism for translating data structures to adhere to a widely supported, common standard. Datasource manufacturers publish OLE DB Providers, just as they do for ODBC drivers. Table 8.1 shows a list of the more common OLE DB Providers.

Table 8.1: Connecting the OLE DB Provider String

Datasource	Provider String
ODBC Data Sources	Provider=MSDASQL
Microsoft Index Server	Provider=MSIDXS
Microsoft Active Directory Service	Provider=ADSDSOObject
Microsoft Jet databases	Provider=Microsoft.Jet.OLEDB.3.51
Microsoft SQL Server	Provider=SQLOLEDB
Oracle databases	Provider=MSDAORA

> **NOTE**
>
> Some database manufacturers provide ODBC drivers and OLE DB Providers for its products. This means you can use OLE DB to access the database directly through the OLE DB Provider or you can access the database indirectly using the OLE DB Provider of ODBC.

You'll notice that table 8.1 shows each Provider String value for each OLE DB Provider. You'll use Provider String when you configure the

ConnectionString or Provider property of the Connection object to indicate the Connection object type of OLE DB Provider in force.

CAUTION

In order to be able to work with ADO, you must have the ADO Object Library installed on the Web Server upon which your Active Server Pages run. If the ADO Object Library is not installed, you can download it from the Microsoft Developers Network Web Site. The ADO Object Library components are part of Microsoft Data Access Components (MDAC) download. The Web page from which you can download them is

`http://www.microsoft.com/data/download.htm?RLD=68`

The following sections show you the details of the objects you need to use to do simple data access. In addition, you'll build a small Web Application that retrieves data from a data source.

Using CreateObject() to Make a Connection Object

As you read earlier, creating a connection to a datasource is the first thing you need to do when using ADO. You connect to a datasource using a Connection object. In order to create a Connection object you use the CreateObject() function. CreateObject() takes one parameter, a string indicating the object to create. The format for this string is the object library name and a period followed by the object within the object library that you want to create. The name for the ADO Object Library is ADODB. The following code creates a Connection object:

EXAMPLE

```
Dim cn 'Create a variable to hold a reference to the object
Set cn = CreateObject("ADODB.Connection")
```

WHERE DOES AN OBJECT LIBRARY LIVE?

An Object Library lives in an *ActiveX DLL* or an *ActiveX EXE*.

An ActiveX DLL is a *Dynamic Link Library*. An ActiveX DLL contains object code that other programs can use just as if it were their own. The same is true of an ActiveX EXE. ActiveX DLLs and ActiveX EXEs register information in the computer's System Registry about the object libraries they contain. This information is entered when the component is installed.

ActiveX DLLs and ActiveX EXE are referred to as *ActiveX Components*.

Using the Connection Object

In order to have a viable Connection object you need to have a "live" link to a datasource. You use the Open method of the Connection object to link to a datasource. There are a few ways to use the Open method. One way is to set a valid connection string value to the Connection object's ConnectionString property and call the object's Open method. The other way is to use the Open method only, passing a valid connection string as a parameter of the method. You use the `Close` method of the `Connection` object to sever the link between the object and the datasource.

✔ For more information about the properties, methods and collections of the Connection object, see Appendix B, "ADO Object Model" p. 505.

Understanding the Connection String

A connection string provides the information to a `Connection` object that it needs in order to link to a datasource. A connection string is composed of a series of `name=value` pairs. Each `name=value` pair is separated by a semicolon. These `name=value` pairs tell the `Connection` object the datasource to use, which type of OLE DB Provider to use as well the user ID and a password needed for access to the datasource, should the datasource require such information.

Creating the Connection String

The following code is an example of a connection string that allows a `Connection` object to link to datasource, `AriMiddle`, using an OLE DB Provider for ODBC. (`AriMiddle` is the ODBC datasource name for a fictitious school, the Aristotle Middle School. We'll use data about this school throughout the chapter.)

EXAMPLE

```
Dim cnn
Dim str str ="Provider= MSDASQL; Data Source=AriMiddle;
User ID=;Password="
cnn.ConnectionString = str
```

The string shown above uses the full provider string syntax. Please notice that in this case the datasource does not require a user ID and password for access.

The OLE DB Provider, user ID, and password `name=value` pairs are optional. For example, should the OLE DB Provider `name=value` pair be omitted, by default the `Connection` object uses the OLE-DB Provider for ODBC. If the user ID and password are omitted, the OLE DB Provider assumes that none are necessary. Thus, we can abbreviate the connection string down to one `name=value` pair and let the default values provided the addition information that is required, like so:

```
str = "Data Source=AriMiddle"
```

NOTE

Each OLE DB Provider has certain configuration requirements that are provided in the connection string. Therefore, the connection strings for different OLE DB Providers will vary somewhat. Within the scope of this book, we will be using the connection string for the OLE DB Provider for ODBC. ODBC is the default OLE DB Provider and is common for many applications. Using this OLE DB Provider allows us to make simple connection strings that are easy to configure and easy to use.

Listing 8.1 shows an Active Server Page that contains code that links to the datasource, AriMiddle, using the Open method of the Connection object with the two techniques discussed above. Figure 8.4 shows the output of the page.

EXAMPLE

Listing 8.1: ASP Script Accessing an OLE DB Datasource (08asp01.asp)

```vbscript
<SCRIPT LANGUAGE=vbscript RUNAT=Server>
'*****************************************
'An Active Server Page that shows
'two ways of opening a link to a datasource
'using the Open method of the Connection object
'*****************************************

Dim cnn 'A variable that references the connection
         'object
    Dim str 'A variable that references the connection
             'string

    'Create the Connection object
    Set cnn = CreateObject("ADODB.Connection")

    'Create the connection string
    str = "Provider=MSDASQL.1;Data Source=AriMiddle;"
    str = str & "User ID=;Password="

    'Assign the string to the connection string property
    'of the Connection object.
    cnn.ConnectionString = str
    'Open a connection
    cnn.Open
    'Close the connection
    cnn.Close

    'Send out a success notification
    Response.write "Opened and closed "
    Response.write "using full connection string.<BR> "

'Abbreviate the connection string using
    'the default OLE DB Provider
    str = "Data Source=AriMiddle"

    'Open a connection using the connection string
    'as a parameter to the Open method.
    cnn.Open str
```

```
'Send out another success notification
Response.write "Opened and closed "
Response.write "using DSN only. "

'Close the connection
cnn.Close
```

</SCRIPT>

OUTPUT

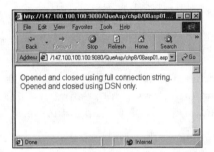

Figure 8.4: *This is the output of a page that reports a* Connection *object being opened and closed.*

The Recordset Object

After you've created a Connection object that has an open link to a datasource, you can retrieve data from it. The data you retrieve from a datasource is returned to you in a Recordset object. A Recordset object is a collection of records. You can think of a record as a row of data from an Excel spread sheet. The columns in the Recordset are called *fields*. The rows are *records* (see Figure 8.5).

The way you retrieve data is to execute a *SQL statement* against the datasource to which the Connection object is linked. The database processes the SQL statement and returns data that conforms to specification of the SQL statement. You pass the SQL statement as a parameter of the Recordset object's Open method. You'll learn how to do this in a moment, but first let's get a fast introduction to SQL so you can use it in your ADO programming.

Recordset

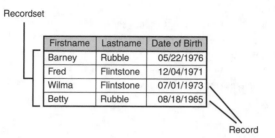

Firstname	Lastname	Date of Birth
Barney	Rubble	05/22/1976
Fred	Flintstone	12/04/1971
Wilma	Flintstone	07/01/1973
Betty	Rubble	08/18/1965

Record

Figure 8.5: *A recordset is a collection of records. Each column in the record-set is called a field.*

Understanding SQL

SQL is an acronym for Structured Query Language. SQL is a widely supported database language that allows you to define specific criteria that you use to retrieve, modify, add or delete data in a database.

SQL is a clause-based language. You construct statements that are a combination of specific clauses. The fundamental clauses are the SELECT FROM clause and the WHERE clause.

The syntax for the SELECT and WHERE clause is

```
SELECT TableName.FieldName, TableName.Fieldname_n FROM TableName WHERE TableName
= CriteriaValue AND TableName.Fieldname_n = CriteriaValue
```

Where:

SELECT, FROM, and WHERE are keywords indicating SQL clauses

TableName is the name of the table from which to select records

FieldName, FieldName_n are one or many fields from which to select values

CriteriaValue is the string that represents criteria that you define and to which the return values must comply. You can use the AND and OR keywords to make combinations of criteria.

For example, if you want to write a SQL statement that retrieves all the records in the table, Employees (see Figure 8.6), in which the field Branch contains the value "Riverside," you would write

```
SELECT Employees.EmployeeID, Employees.FirstName,
Employees.LastName, Employees.Position, Employees.Branch
FROM Employees
WHERE Employees.Branch)= 'Riverside'
```

EXAMPLE

CAUTION

When writing a SQL statement use the single quote character, ', to define strings.

EmployeeID	Firstname	Lastname	Position	Branch
1	Perry	White	Vice President	East Side
2	Sherman	Potter	Loan Officer	Central
3	Hawkeye	Pierce	Teller	Central
4	John	MacIntire	Teller	West Side
5	Clark	Kent	Loan Officer	Central
6	Lois	Lane	Vice President	Riverside
7	Jimmy	Olson	Teller	Riverside
8	Lana	Lang	Teller	Riverside
9	Margaret	Hoolihan	Loan Officer	Riverside
10	Frank	Burns	Teller	East Side
11	Bugs	Bunny	President	Headquarters

Figure 8.6: *Here is a fictitious table, Employees.*

✔ For more information about SQL, go to the Web Site for this book and download the tutorial called "The Fundamentals of SQL."

You can use SQL to join data among different tables and among different databases. SQL allows you to create and delete tables within databases. Its use is quite broad. As you can see, SQL is a large language.

The intent of this section is to show you enough SQL to give you a feel how it works within the code you are going to see used with the Recordset object. Clearly, a comprehensive review of the language is beyond the scope of this book. Later, as your ASP skills grow, you might benefit by studying SQL in a more detailed manner.

Retrieving Records Using the Recordset Object

You use the Recordset object to store data returned from the database defined in the Connection object. There are five steps that you take in order to extract data from a datasource and display it in an Active Server Page. These steps are

1. Create a Recordset object using CreateObject().

2. Create a SQL statement that defines the data you want to retrieve.

3. Define a Connection object for the Recordset object to use as the active connection.

4. Use the Recordset object's Open method, passing the SQL statement, to populate the Recordset with data from the data source.

5. Traverse the Recordset in order to create HTML that formats the display of the data.

Creating a `Recordset` Object

You create a `Recordset` object using the `CreateObject()` method. A `Recordset` is a distinct object within the ADO object library. The following code creates a `Recordset` object and assigns it to the variable, `rs`.

EXAMPLE

```
Dim rs      'Variable for a Recordset object

'Create a recordset object
Set rs = CreateObject("ADODB.Recordset")
```

NOTE

Don't forget to use the `Set` keyword when assigning an object as the value of a variable.

Using `Recordset.ActiveConnection`

A `Recordset` object needs to have an open `Connection` object in order to know the database that it's to work with. You use the `ActiveConnection` to associate a `Connection` object with a `Recordset` object. The following code creates a `Connection` object and a `Recordset` object. Then it assigns the `Connection` object to the `ActiveConnection` property of the `Recordset` object.

EXAMPLE

```
Dim cnn      'Variable for a Connection object
Dim rs       'Variable for a Recordset object

'Create the Connection object
Set cnn = CreateObject("ADODB.Connection")

'Create a recordset object
Set rs = CreateObject("ADODB.Recordset")

'Associate the Connection object to the
'Recordset object
rs.ActiveConnection = cnn
```

CAUTION

If you do not define an active `Connection` for the `Recordset` object, the object will generate an error when you try to access data.

Using `Recordset.Open`

After you have a `Connection` object set as the active connection for the `Recordset`, you can run a SQL statement against the database using the `Open` method of the `Recordset` object. The `Open` method takes as an argument the SQL statement that describes the data to retrieve, like so:

```
Dim SQL
SQL= "SELECT tblCourses.CourseName From tblCourses"
rs.Open SQL
```

If you want to condense your code, you can pass both the SQL statement
and the active Connection as arguments to the Open method like so:

```
Dim cnn      'Variable for a Connection object
Dim rs       'Variable for a Recordset object
Dim SQL

'Create the Connection object
Set cnn = CreateObject("ADODB.Connection")

'Create a recordset object
Set rs = CreateObject("ADODB.Recordset")

SQL= "SELECT tblCourses.CourseName From tblCourses"

rs.Open = SQL, cnn
```

Working with Data in a Table

The AriMiddle database contains the table, tblCourses, from which we are
going to retrieve data. We are going to want to return the name of each
course in the table. Figure 8.7 shows the structure and data of the table.

In order to return the title of each Course Name tblCourses we are going to
write a SQL statement that says, "return all the values in the field named
CourseName in the table named tblCourses. The SQL statement is as
follows:

```
SELECT tblCourses.CourseName FROM tblCourses.
```

After we have the SQL statement constructed, we pass it as a parameter
to a Recordset object.

Listing 8.2 shows an Active Server Page that is an enhancement of the one
shown in Listing 8.1. This Active Server Page shows you how to use the
Recordset object to retrieve and display data from a table in a database
using a SQL statement.

ClassID	CourseName	TeacherID
div101	Introduction to Divinity	reselbob
film101	Russian Cinema	eisenseg
film102	French Cinema	eisenseg
hist301	Western Civilization	russeber
hist302	Asian Civilization	russeber
hist312	The French Revolution	tallycha
homec101	Home Economics	brilljea
homec212	Pastries	brilljea
math301	Differential Equations	pascalbla
math312	Linear Algebra	pascalbla
math314	Logic	russeber
music203	Counterpoint	weberant
music203	Harmony	weberant
music401	Twenty First Century Music	weberant
phil101	Intro to Philosophy	aquintho
phil201	Ethics	wattsala
phil222	Empiricism	aquintho
polisci101	Introduction to Political Science	tallycha
polisci212	Diplomacy	tallycha
psych212	Abnormal Psychology	freudsig
psych101	Introduction to Psychology	freudsig

Figure 8.7: *Here is a fictitious table, `tblCourses`, from the sample database, AriMiddle. The values in the fields `ClassID` and `TeacherID` are codes that correspond to values in other tables.*

EXAMPLE

Listing 8.2: Populating the Recordset Object Using a SQL Statement (`08asp02.asp`)

```
<SCRIPT LANGUAGE=vbscript RUNAT=Server>
    Function GetCoursesData(cnn)
    '****************************************
    'Returns a string in which each value of in the
    'Field ClassName of the table, tblCourses is
    'displayed as a line of HTML.
    '****************************************

        Dim rs 'A variable for a Recordset object
        Dim SQL ' A variable for the SQL statement
        Dim str ' A variable for a string buffer

        'Create a SQL statement
        SQL= "SELECT tblCourses.CourseName From tblCourses "

        'Create a recordset object
        Set rs = CreateObject("ADODB.Recordset")

        'Bind the Connection to the Recordset object
        'by setting the value of Recordset's
```

```
                    'ActiveConnection property to the Connection
                    'object passed into the function
                    rs.ActiveConnection = cnn

                    'Open the recordset using the SQL
                    'statement
                    rs.Open SQL

                    'Traverse the recordset using a While
                    'loop that tests for the EOF property being
                    'TRUE. EOF becomes true when you pass the last
                    'record in the Recordset object.
                    While Not rs.EOF
                        'Extract the value of the course name
                        'in the current record. Then add the
                        'HTML line break tag
                        str = str & rs("CourseName") & "<BR>"
                        'Move to the next record
                        rs.MoveNext
                    Wend

                    'Return the string out of the function
                    GetCoursesData = str
                End Function

            Dim cnn 'A variable that references the connection
                    'object
            Dim str 'A variable that references the connection
                    'string

            'Create the Connection object
            Set cnn = CreateObject("ADODB.Connection")

        'Abbreviate the connection string using
            'the default OLE DB Provider
            str = "Data Source=AriMiddle"

            'Open a connection using the connection string
            'as a parameter to the Open method.
            cnn.Open str

            'Display a list header
            Response.write "<FONT COLOR=Blue "
            Response.write "SIZE=4 FACE=Arial> "
            Response.write "Courses offered "
            Response.write "at the Aristotle Middle School: <P>"
```

continues

Listing 8.2: continued

```
        Response.write "</FONT> "
        Response.write "<FONT COLOR=Green "
        Response.write "SIZE=3 FACE=Arial> "

        'Get class data using the function
        Response.Write GetCoursesData(cnn)
        Response.write "</FONT> "
        'Close the connection
        cnn.Close
</SCRIPT>
```

Let's analyze the Active Server Page script in Listing 8.2. The ASP script opens a Connection object, creates some HTML output, then acts as a caption to a list of courses that will be displayed by the function, GetCourseData(cnn), like so:

EXAMPLE

```
Dim cnn 'A variable that references the connection
            'object
    Dim str 'A variable that references the connection
            'string

    'Create the Connection object
    Set cnn = CreateObject("ADODB.Connection")

'Abbreviate the connection string using
    'the default OLE DB Provider
    str = "Data Source=AriMiddle"

    'Open a connection using the connection string
    'as a parameter to the Open method.
    cnn.Open str
    .
    .
    .
.  'Get class data using the function
    Response.Write GetCoursesData(cnn)
```

GetCourseData(cnn) takes a Connection object as an argument. The function creates a Recordset object and runs its Open method using the SQL statement that retrieves all the values from the table, tblCourseName.

EXAMPLE

```
Dim rs 'A variable for a Recordset object
        Dim SQL ' A variable for the SQL statement
        Dim str ' A variable for a string buffer

        'Create a SQL statement
        SQL= "SELECT tblCourses.CourseName From tblCourses"

        'Create a recordset object
```

```
Set rs = CreateObject("ADODB.Recordset")
.
.
.
rs.ActiveConnection = cnn

'Open the recordset using the SQL
'statement
rs.Open SQL
```

The `Recordset` object is populated with data retrieved from the datasource defined in the `Connection` object. A `While...Wend` loop is run using the value of `EOF` property or the `Recordset` as the terminating condition. The code looks at the value in the `ClassName` field of the current record and adds an HTML line break tag (`<BR>`) to the string buffer, `str`, which is used to store the output string. After the data is added to the string buffer, the `Recordset` object's `MoveNext` method is called. `MoveNext` moves the position of the current record to the next record in the `Recordset`. The process continues building the buffer string and adding an HTML line break for each new record until the end of the `Recordset` is reached. The value of the string buffer variable is passed as the return value of the function.

(`EOF` stands for End of File. When the position within the `Recordset` object is past the last record, the `EOF` property is set to TRUE.)

EXAMPLE

```
While Not rs.EOF
    'Extract the value of the classname
    'in the current record. Then add the
    'HTML line break tag
    str = str & rs("CourseName") & "<BR>"
    'Move to the next record
    rs.MoveNext
Wend

'Return the string out of the function
GetCoursesData = str
```

ACCESSING A FIELD'S DATA IN A RECORDSET

A data in a `Recordset` object is organized into fields. If you want to access a given field for a record within the `Recordset`, you use the following notation:

`rs("FieldName")`

Where `rs` is an arbitrary variable name representing a `Recordset` object and `FieldName` is the name of a given file.

If you wanted to read the data in a field, Teacher, in a Recordsset object, rs, you would write

`str = rs("Teacher")`

Figure 8.8 displays the result of running the Active Server Page shown in Listing 8.2

OUTPUT

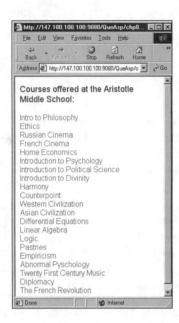

Figure 8.8: *Using HTML and a browser to display the output of a database simplifies the process of report writing.*

Working with Data in Multiple Tables

You can use ADO and ASP to work with data that exists in multiple tables. A database that allows you to access and unify data across multiple tables is called a *relational database*. If you refer back to Figure 8.7, you'll notice that the values in the TeacherID field seem to have no immediate meaning. There really isn't any way that you can tell which teacher is assigned to a given course. All you have is an identification code. For example, The French Revolution is taught by a teacher with the identification code, tallycha. So who is tallycha? Figure 8.9 shows you another table from the database, AriMiddle. The table is named tblTeachers. It contains a list of teachers at the Aristotle Middle School.

Notice that when you look up the value of the identification code, tallycha, in the TeacherID field of the table, you find that the teacher associated with the identification code has a first name Charles and a last name Tallyrand.

TeacherID	Firstname	Lastname	HireDate
aquintho	Thomas	Aquinas	9/12/1983
brilljea	Jean	Brillat-Savarin	9/23/1992
eisenseg	Segei	Eisenstein	8/20/92
freudsig	Sigmund	Freud	1/3/1990
mathecot	Cotton	Mather	12/21/1995
pascalbla	Blaise	Pascal	8/29/1996
reselbob	Bob	Reselman	8/21/199
russeber	Bertrand	Russel	9/03/1987
tallycha	Charles	Tallyrand	9/7/1994
wattsala	Alan	Watts	8/30/1991
weberant	Anton	Webern	7/11/1990

Figure 8.9: *Tables in a relational database are concise, containing only the most pertinent information to a given scope of information.*

It's possible to combine the information in the tables tblCourses and tblTeachers to create a new "virtual" table that reports the first and last name of the teacher as well as the course name for any given course. All we need to do is relate the tables using the value in the TeacherID field. The field TeacherID is common to both tables (see Figure 8.10).

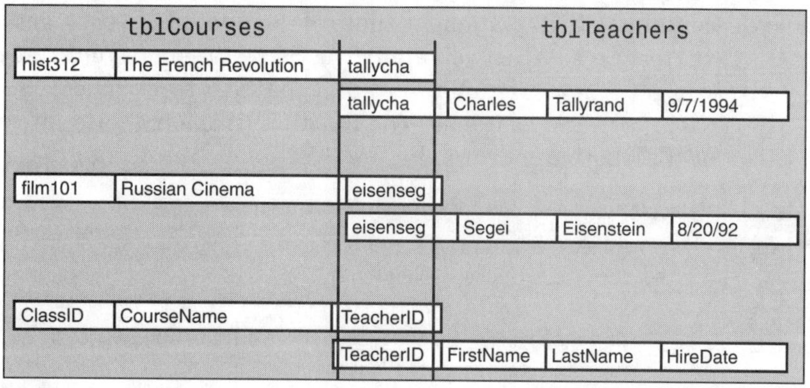

Figure 8.10: *The field that relates the data in two or more tables is called the key field.*

You use ADO to relate two tables by writing a SQL statement that says, "get me all the data in the field CourseName, in table, tblCourse, and the fields FirstName and LastName in the table, tblTeachers. Use the common field, TeacherID to relate the two tables". The statement you write in SQL that describes this *query* is

```
SELECT tblCourses.CourseName, tblTeachers.FirstName,
tblTeachers.LastName
```

```
FROM tblTeachers
INNER JOIN tblCourses
ON tblTeachers.TeacherID = tblCourses.TeacherID
```

NOTE

Please don't be anxious if the SQL statements constructed in this chapter seem mystical. SQL is a language that takes a while to master, like any other. The goal for using SQL in this chapter is to give you an introductory feel for it as well as providing you insight into the capabilities of the language. At some point, you might want to study the language in a more detailed manner.

After you have created a SQL statement that relates the tables for the data you need, you pass it to a `Recordset` object's `Open` method as for any other SQL statement.

Listing 8.3 shows you an Active Server Page that contains code that relates the tables `tblCourses` and `tblTeachers`. The resulting Web page displays the courses the Aristotle Middle School offers as well as the first and last names of the teacher assigned to teach each course.

The code is an enhancement of that which you saw in Listing 8.2. A new function `GetAllCourseData()` is a substitute for the function, `GetCoursesData()` in the previous listing. The function `GetAllCourseData()` contains a SQL statement that relates the tables `tblCourses` and `tblTeachers`. When you apply the SQL statement to the `Recordset` object, you get a new "virtual table" that contains three fields, `CourseName`, `FirstName` and `LastName`. The function wraps the data into a collection of HTML `<TABLE>` rows. Figure 8.11 shows the output of the code.

EXAMPLE

Listing 8.3: Relating Data in Separate Tables (08asp03.asp)

```
<SCRIPT LANGUAGE=vbscript RUNAT=Server>
    Function GetAllCourseData(cnn)
    '*****************************************
    'Returns a string in that is set of HTML <TABLE>
    'rows which contains the Course Name
    'as well as the First Name and Last Name
    'of the instructor
    '*****************************************

        Dim rs 'A variable for a Recordset object
        Dim SQL ' A variable for the SQL statement
        Dim str ' A variable for a string buffer

        'Create a SQL statement that relates the
        'tables tblCourses and tblTeachers
        SQL= "SELECT tblCourses.CourseName, "
        SQL= SQL & "tblTeachers.FirstName, "
```

```
        SQL= SQL & "tblTeachers.LastName "
        SQL= SQL & "FROM tblTeachers "
        SQL= SQL & "INNER JOIN tblCourses "
        SQL= SQL & "ON tblTeachers.TeacherID = "
        SQL= SQL & "tblCourses.TeacherID"

        'Create a recordset object
        Set rs = CreateObject("ADODB.Recordset")

        'Set the active connection
        rs.ActiveConnection = cnn

        'Open the recordset using the SQL
        'statement
        rs.Open SQL

        'Traverse the recordset
        While Not rs.EOF
            'Create a new <TABLE> row
            str = str & "<TR>"
            'Add the Course Name <TABLE> cell
            str = str & "<TD><FONT FACE=ARIAL SIZE=2>"
            str = str & rs("CourseName") & "</FONT></TD>"
            'Add the First Name <TABLE> cell
            str = str & "<TD><FONT FACE=ARIAL SIZE=2>"
            str = str & rs("LastName") & "</FONT></TD>"
            'Add the Last Name <TABLE> cell
            str = str & "<TD><FONT FACE=ARIAL SIZE=2>"
            str = str & rs("FirstName") & "</FONT></TD>"
            'Close off the <TABLE> row
            str = str & "</TR>"
            'Move to the next record
            rs.MoveNext
        Wend


        'Return the string out of the function
        GetAllCourseData = str
    End Function


Dim cnn 'A variable that references the connection
         'object
    Dim str 'A variable that references the connection
             'string

    'Create the Connection object
```

continues

Listing 8.3: continued

```
    Set cnn = CreateObject("ADODB.Connection")

'Abbreviate the connection string using
    'the default OLE DB Provider
    str = "Data Source=AriMiddle"

    'Open a connection using the connection string
    'as a parameter to the Open method.
    cnn.Open str

    'Display a list header
    Response.Write "<FONT COLOR=Blue "
    Response.Write "SIZE=4 FACE=Arial> "
    Response.Write "Courses offered "
    Response.Write "at the Aristotle Middle School "
    Response.Write "with instructors: <P>"
    Response.Write "</FONT> "
    Response.Write "<FONT COLOR=Green "
    Response.Write "SIZE=3 FACE=Arial> "
    'Create a HTML table
    Response.Write "<TABLE Border=0 Width=100%>"
    'Create the HTML table header
    Response.Write "<TH>"
    Response.Write "<FONT FACE=ARIAL SIZE=3 COLOR=Blue>"
    Response.Write "Course</TH>"
    Response.Write "<TH>"
    Response.Write "<FONT FACE=ARIAL SIZE=3 COLOR=Blue>"
    Response.Write "Instructor</TH>"
    Response.Write "<TH></TH>"
    'Get course data using the function
    Response.Write GetAllCourseData(cnn)
    'Close off the HTML table
    Response.Write "</TABLE>"
    Response.write "</FONT> "
    'Close the connection
    cnn.Close

</SCRIPT>
```

OUTPUT

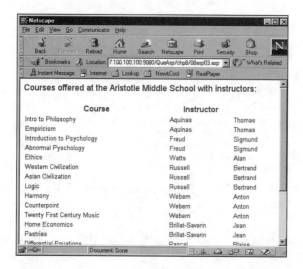

Courses offered at the Aristotle Middle School with instructors:

Course	Instructor	
Intro to Philosophy	Aquinas	Thomas
Empiricism	Aquinas	Thomas
Introduction to Psychology	Freud	Sigmund
Abnormal Pyschology	Freud	Sigmund
Ethics	Watts	Alan
Western Civilization	Russell	Bertrand
Asian Civilization	Russell	Bertrand
Logic	Russell	Bertrand
Harmony	Webern	Anton
Counterpoint	Webern	Anton
Twenty First Century Music	Webern	Anton
Home Economics	Brillat-Savarin	Jean
Pastries	Brillat-Savarin	Jean
Differential Equations	Pascal	Blaise

Figure 8.11: *Relating tables allows you to unify data easily.*

Using the Command Object to Write Data

You use the ADO Command object to add data to an ODBC datasource. The Command object represents a statement that you want to execute against a database. You use the Command object to add new data or modify and delete existing data.

You use the Command object in conjunction with SQL statements that you construct to describe the functionality you want to execute. After you have the SQL statement defined, you assign the text of the SQL statement to the CommandText property of the Command object. Then you call the Command object's Execute method.

Inserting Data into a Table Using SQL

You use the INSERT clause to add a record to an ODBC datasource using SQL. Figure 8.12 shows syntax for a SQL statement with an INSERT clause.

For example, if you want to add a new instructor, John Adams, to the table tblTeachers, you need to add data for the TeacherID, FirstName, LastName, and HireDate fields. The SQL statement that you write is

```
INSERT INTO tblTeachers(TeacherID, FirstName, LastName, HireDate)
VALUES ('adamsjoh', John, 'Adams', #12/12/1999#)
```

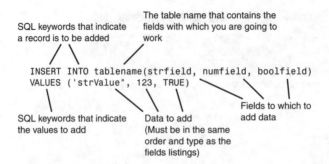

Figure 8.12: *You use the SQL INSERT clause to add a record to an ODBC datasource.*

Notice that in the field names section of the INSERT clause, each field name is not treated as a string. Rather, you use the field name without enclosing it in single quotes. However, the values that you are going to add to the datasource are to be indicated as strings and must be enclosed in single quotes. Numeric values are entered without quotes. Dates must be enclosed by pound characters (#).

Using Command.CommandText

Using the Command object with SQL statements is straightforward. You assign the SQL statement to the CommandText property, like so:

```
Dim SQL
Dim cmd
Set cmd = CreateObject("ADODB.Command")
SQL = INSERT INTO Books(BookTitle)
SQL = SLQ & VALUES('Tale of Two Cities')
cmd.CommandText = SQL
```

Using Command.ActiveConnection

Before you can call the Execute method of the Command object, you must assign a Connection object to be an active connection for the Command object. The Command object has an ActiveConnection property just as the Recordset object does.

```
Dim cnn
Set cnn = CreateObject("ADODB.Connection")
cnn.Open "Data Source = Media"
cmd.ActiveConnection = cnn
```

Using Command.Execute

After you have the Command object wired up by assigning values to the CommandText property and ActiveConnection property, you're ready to call the Execute method, like so:

```
cmd.Execute
```

Using ASP to Add a Record to an ODBC Datasource

Listings 8.4 and 8.5 show you HTML and ASP code that add a record to an ODBC datasource. Listing 8.4 is an HTML file that contains a <FORM> element into which a user inputs data (see Figure 8.12). The user submits the data to the Active Server Page shown in Listing 8.5.

EXAMPLE

Listing 8.4: HTML Element to Accept Data> Containing a <FORM> Element to Accept Data (08asp04.htm)

```
<HTML>
<HEAD>
<TITLE></TITLE>
</HEAD>
<BODY>
<CENTER>
<IMG src="ari.gif"><BR>
<FONT Color=Blue Size=5 Face=Arial>
<BR>Aristotle Middle School
</FONT>
<FONT Color=Blue Size=4 Face=Arial>
</CENTER>
<P>Add an instructor:</P>
</FONT>
<FORM    Name=frmMain
    Method="POST"
    Action = "http://localhost/QueAsp/chp8/08asp05.asp">
<FONT Color=Green Size=3 Face=Arial>
<P>TeacherID <BR>
<INPUT   name=txtTeacherID>
<P>First Name <BR>
<INPUT name=txtFirstName>
<P>Last Name <BR>
<INPUT name=txtLastName>
<P>
<INPUT type="submit" value="Add an instructor" name=submit1>
</FONT>
</FORM>

</BODY>
</HTML>
```

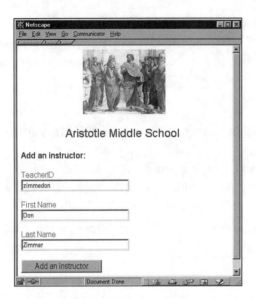

Figure 8.13: *A Web page that allows a user to enter data in a database.*

When you look at the code in the function, `AddInstructor()` of the Active
Server Page in Listing 8.5, you'll see that the procedure uses a `Command`
object to execute an SQL `INSERT` clause.

USING THE ASTERISK IN SQL

You can use an asterisk (*) as a way to way show "all fields and all records with the
table of a datasource". For example, the SQL statement

`SELECT * FROM Authors`

says, "show me all the records with all the fields in the table, Authors."

EXAMPLE

Listing 8.5: Adding Data Using a `Command` Object (`08asp05.asp`)

```vbscript
<SCRIPT LANGUAGE=vbscript RUNAT=Server>
    Function AddInstructor(cnn, _
                          TeacherID,_
                          FirstName, _
                          LastName)
    '*****************************************
    'Adds a record to the table, tlbTeachers
    '*****************************************

        Dim cmd 'A Command object
        Dim SQL ' A variable for the SQL statement


        SQL = "INSERT INTO tblTeachers "
```

```
    SQL = SQL & "(TeacherID, FirstName, LastName, HireDate)"
    SQL = SQL & " VALUES ('"
    SQL = SQL & TeacherID & "', '"
    SQL = SQL & FirstName & "', '"
    SQL = SQL & LastName & "', #"
    SQL = SQL & Cstr(Date())& "#)"

    'Create a recordset object
    Set cmd = CreateObject("ADODB.Command")

    cmd.CommandText = SQL
    cmd.ActiveConnection = cnn
    cmd.Execute

    'Report that the write was successful
    AddInstructor = True
    Exit Function
    On Error Resume Next
    AddInstructor = False
End Function


Function GetTeachers(cnn)
'*****************************************
'Returns an HTML string that shows all the teachers
'*****************************************
    Dim rs 'A variable for a Recordset object
    Dim SQL ' A variable for the SQL statement
    Dim str ' A variable for a string buffer

    SQL = "SELECT * FROM tblTeachers"

            'Create a recordset object
    Set rs = CreateObject("ADODB.Recordset")

    'Set the active connection
    rs.ActiveConnection = cnn

    'Open the recordset using the SQL
    'statement
    rs.Open SQL
    str = "<TABLE Width=100%>"
    'Traverse the recordset
    While Not rs.EOF
        'Create a new <TABLE> row
        str = str & "<TR>"
        'Add the Course Name <TABLE> cell
```

continues

Listing 8.5: continued

```
                str = str & "<TD><FONT FACE=COURIER SIZE=2>"
                str = str & rs("TeacherID") & "</FONT></TD>"
                'Add the First Name <TABLE> cell
                str = str & "<TD><FONT FACE=ARIAL SIZE=2>"
                str = str & rs("LastName") & "</FONT></TD>"
                'Add the Last Name <TABLE> cell
                str = str & "<TD><FONT FACE=ARIAL SIZE=2>"
                str = str & rs("FirstName") & "</FONT></TD>"
                'Close off the <TABLE> row
                str = str & "</TR>"
                'Move to the next record
                rs.MoveNext
        Wend
        str = str & "</TABLE>"
        GetTeachers = str
    End Function


'++++++++++++++++++++++++++++++++++
'SCRIPT ENTRY POINT
'++++++++++++++++++++++++++++++++++
    'Page level variables
    Dim cnn 'A variable that references the connection
            'object
    Dim str 'A variable that references the connection
            'string
    'Variables to store form data
    Dim TeacherID
    Dim FirstName
    Dim LastName

    'Get the data from the form an assign it
    'to the page level variables
    TeacherID = Request.Form("txtTeacherID")
    FirstName = Request.Form("txtFirstName")
    LastName = Request.Form("txtLastName")

    'Create the Connection object
    Set cnn = CreateObject("ADODB.Connection")

    'Abbreviate the connection string using
    'the default OLE DB Provider
    str = "Data Source=AriMiddle"

    'Open a connection using the connection string
    'as a parameter to the Open method.
    cnn.Open str
```

```
'Call the AddInstructor() function to add a
'new teacher to the database
If AddInstructor(cnn,TeacherID, FirstName, LastName) Then
    'Return the new list, with the new teacher
    'Display a list header
    Response.Write "<FONT COLOR=Green Size=5 FACE=ARIAL>"
    Response.Write "Addition Successful!!!" & "<P>"
    Response.Write "</FONT>"
    Response.Write "<FONT COLOR=Blue Size=5 FACE=ARIAL>"
    Response.Write "Aristotle Middle School<BR>Teacher Roster"
    Response.Write "<P></FONT>"
    Response.Write GetTeachers(cnn)

Else
    Response.Write "<FONT COLOR=Red Size=5 FACE=ARIAL>"
    Response.Write "Addition Failed!!!" & "<P>"
    Response.Write "</FONT>"
End if
  'Close the connection
  cnn.Close
</SCRIPT>
```

OUTPUT

Figure 8.14: *The ASP code behind this page requires the datasource for a list of teachers after a new teacher is added.*

Using the Command Object to Populate a Recordset Object

Please be advised that you can use the Command object's CommandType property in conjunction with the CommandText property to define different ways of working with ODBC data sources.

For example, if you set the value of the `Command` object's `CommandType` property to the constant value, `adCmdTable` (the numeric value of constant `adCmdTable` is 2), you can set the `CommandText` property. In addition, you can use the `Command` object's `Execute` method to return a `Recordset` object.

Listing 8.6 shows you how to configure the `Command` object to return the records with a specific table. The output of the Listing 8.6 displayed in Figure 8.15.

EXAMPLE

Listing 8.6: Returning Whole Tables Using the Command Object (08asp06.asp)

```
<SCRIPT LANGUAGE=vbscript RUNAT=Server>
Dim cnn
Dim cmd
Dim rs
Const adCmdTable = 2

Set cmd = CreateObject("ADODB.Command")
Set rs = CreateObject("ADODB.Recordset")
Set cnn = CreateObject("ADODB.Connection")

str = "Data Source=AriMiddle"

cnn.Open str

cmd.ActiveConnection = cnn
'Configure the command object to
'use interpret the CommandText
'value to be a table name
cmd.CommandType = adCmdTable '2
cmd.CommandText = "tblTeachers"

Set rs = cmd.Execute

Response.Write "<FONT FACE=ARIAL SIZE=4>"
Response.Write "Teachers" & "<P>"
Response.Write "</FONT>"
Response.Write "<FONT FACE=ARIAL SIZE=3>"
While not rs.EOF
    Response.Write rs("FirstName")
    Response.Write " "
    Response.Write rs("LastName") & "<BR>"
    rs.MoveNext
Wend
Response.Write "</FONT>"
</SCRIPT>
```

USING Recordset.Open TO OPEN A WHOLE TABLE

You can use the Open method of the Recordset object to open a complete table. In order to open a complete table using the Open method, you must use the expanded syntax of the method.

The complete syntax for Recodset.Open is

```
Recordset.Open Source, ActiveConnection, CursorType, LockType, Options
```

Where

Source is the datasource. When you are opening a whole table, this parameter is the name of the table to open.

ActiveConnection is the name of an active Connection object.

CursorType is a Visual Basic constant indicating the type of cursor you want to use. The supported constants are

```
adOpenForwardOnly (Default)
AdOpenKeyset
adOpenDynamic
adOpenStatic
```

LockType is a Visual Basic constant that indicates what type of row locking you will use when you open the Recordset object. The supported constants are

```
adLockReadOnly
adLockPessimistic
adLockOptimistic
adLockBatchOptimistic
```

Options is a Visual Basic constant that indicates how the Source parameter is to be considered. When you are opening a whole table, use the constant adCmdTable. The supported constants are

```
adCmdText, indicates a SQL statement
adCmdTable, indicates a table name
adCmdStoredProc, indicates the name of a stored procedure
adCmdUnknown, indicates a command specific to the OLE DB Provider
```

For example for the Recordset object named rs to open the table, tblStudents within the datasource, AriMiddle, you would code the Open method as follows:

```
rs.Open "tblStudents", cn, adOpenDynamic, adLockOptimistic, adCmdTable
```

CAUTION

If you have prior experience using ADO in Visual Basic, please beware that ASP and VBScript do not support the ADO constants for the Command object's CommandType property. You must declare them in your script. If you plan to use any CommandType value other than adCmdText, which is the default, and you do not declare these constants within your script or within Global.asa, your code will return an error!

The values of the ADO Command object constants are as follows:

Constant	Value
adCmdText	1
adCmdTable	2
adCmdStoredProc	4
adCmdFile	256
adCmdUnknown	8

OUTPUT

Figure 8.15: *Working with a table directly can sometimes save you effort.*

CLEANING UP IS GOOD BUSINESS

It's good practice to destroy the ADO objects that you create after you are finished using them. By default, when a data object goes out of scope, your ASP script will disconnect it from the datasource and remove the object from memory. However, as your code becomes more voluminous and complex, you might find that you have created data objects that are still connected. Therefore, you when you no longer need an object such as a Recordset connected to a datasource, use the Close method to disconnect it from the data source. If you want to remove an object variable reference from the object, use the Nothing keyword like so:

```
Dim rs

Set rs = CreateObject("ADODB.Recordset")

'Some code that does something here

.

.

.

'Close the Recordset, we no longer need it.

rs.Close


'Remove the object variable from the Recordset object

Set rs = Nothing
```

What's Next

This chapter showed you how to work with data in various datasources using ActiveX Data Objects (ADO). You learned about the Connection object, the Recordset object and the Command object. You used these objects in conjunction with SQL to create server-side scripts that generated reports that you could display in a client-side Web browser. In addition, you learned how to add data to a database using a client-side HTML <FORM> which submitted data to a server-side script. This script did the bulk of the work necessary to add data to an ADO datasource.

ActiveX Data Objects are considered Installable Components that ship with Internet Information Server. You install them on the server to make your ASP work easier. Internet Information Server ships with other Installable Components. The next chapter shows you how use some of them to control advertising banners, keep track of Web Page usage, and organize the way a user traverses the pages in your Web site.

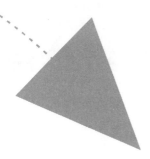

9

Working with the Installable Components for Internet Information Server

As you become more experienced at programming real-world Web sites that use Active Server Pages, you start to notice that various applications seem to require a common set of features. For example, mass market, commercial sites tend to derive revenue from advertising for other third parties. If you work on these types of sites, many times you'll find yourself building functionality that shows different ads at different times. Also, it's common that most sites want to keep track of the number of times that a page is used or to offer "what do you think" voting capabilities that allow users to report their preferences on certain topics and products. Granted you could build these features from scratch using VBScript and ASP. The technology is that powerful. However, implementing common features repeatedly gets old, fast.

Microsoft understands that most Web sites require certain features and functions repeatedly. The company has responded accordingly by creating a set of ActiveX components, which you can use to implement these often-needed functions. These components are called Installable Components for Internet Information Server. These ActiveX components ship free with Internet Information Server.

In this chapter you will learn how to

- Create pages that implement advertising rotating banners using the Ad Rotator Component

- Create Web pages with voting functionality using the Counters component

- Keep track of a Web page's usage with the Page Counter component

- Control the way visitors to your site traverse pages using the Content Linking component

Accessing ActiveX Components

Internet Information Server ships with a variety of ActiveX components that you can use to take the chore out of ASP programming.

The components we are going to look at in this chapter are

- Ad Rotator Component
- Content Linking Component
- Page Counter Component
- Counter Component

These components are built in distinct DLLs, which are registered in the System Directory when you install IIS. Also, please be advised that some of these components are upgrades that ship with IIS Version 5.0 and are not available in earlier versions. Table 9.1 shows a summary of the components we are going to examine in this chapter with pertinent information about each.

Table 9.1: Installable ActiveX Components to Use with ASP

Component	DLL	Version Support	CreateObject string
Ad Rotator Component	Adrot.dll	IIS 4.0, IIS 5.0	"MSWC.AdRotator"
Content Linking Component	NextLink.dll	IIS 4.0, IIS 5.0	"MSWC.NextLink"
Page Counter Component	Pagecnt.dll	IIS 5.0	"MSWC.PageCounter"
Counters Component	Counters.dll	IIS 5.0	"MSWC.Counters"

NOTE

IIS 5.0 ships with additional Installable Components. For a complete listing, go to the Microsoft Developer Network Web site at `http://msdn.microsoft.com/isapi/msdnlib.idc?theURL=/library/psdk/iisref/comp59f8.htm`

✔ For information about the Data Access Component—Data Access Objects—see Chapter 8, "Moving Forward with ASP: Working Data," p. 183.

Working with the Ad Rotator

The Ad Rotator component allows you to create an Active Server Page that displays an advertising banner randomly every time a calling client makes a request to a page. The graphic is picked from a list contained in an independent text file called a Schedule file (see Figure 9.1) .

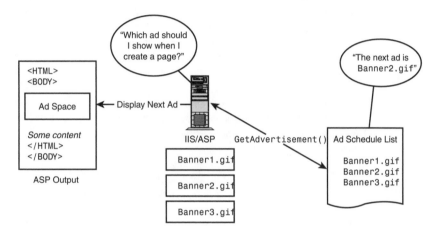

Figure 9.1*: The Ad Rotator component retrieves and keeps track of graphics to display as advertising banners in a Web Page.*

This is how the Ad Rotator works: After creating the object, you use the object's one and only method, GetAdvertisement(*ScheduleFilename*). GetAdvertisement() takes one argument, a string that indicates the name and location of a Schedule file. The Ad Rotator component consults the Schedule file to determine which graphic to display. In addition to a list of graphics to use, the Schedule file contains information about how to weigh the randomness of when the advertising banner will be displayed. Let's take a look at how the Schedule file works.

Creating the Rotation Schedule File

The Rotation Schedule file is a text file that contains a list of URLs and associated information. That list represents a list of graphics that are to be displayed as advertising banners in a Web page. Listing 9.1 shows an example of a typical Schedule file.

EXAMPLE

Listing 9.1: The Schedule File of the Ad Rotator Component (09asp01.txt/adrot.txt)

```
REDIRECT 09asp02.asp
WIDTH 402
HEIGHT 102
BORDER 0
*
```

continues

Listing 9.1: continued

```
http://localhost/QueAsp/chp9/ads/truth.gif
http://localhost/QueAsp/chp9/ariHome.htm
The Aristotle Middle School: Truth
1
http://localhost/QueAsp/chp9/ads/know.gif
http://localhost/QueAsp/chp9/ariHome.htm
The Aristotle Middle School: Knowledge
1
http://localhost/QueAsp/chp9/ads/courage.gif
http://localhost/QueAsp/chp9/ariHome.htm
The Aristotle Middle School: Courage
1
http://localhost/QueAsp/chp9/ads/wisdom.gif
http://localhost/QueAsp/chp9/ariHome.htm
The Aristotle Middle School: Wisdom
1
http://localhost/QueAsp/chp9/ads/beauty.gif
http://localhost/QueAsp/chp9/ariHome.htm
The Aristotle Middle School: Beauty
1
```

NOTE

You can use the keyword `localhost` as the IP address of a Web page when calling the page from a browser on the computer upon which IIS or PWS is running.

For example, the URL

`http://localhost/QueAsp/chp9/ariHome.htm`

says, "Hey, Internet server running on this computer, get me the Web page `QueASP/chp9/ariHome.htm`."

The Schedule file has a particular structure to which you must adhere. The file is divided into two parts. An asterisk separates each part. The top half contains information that applies to all graphics listed in the file. The bottom half contains information specific to each graphic in the rotation schedule.

Each piece of information in the top half of the file is associated with a specific keyword, as follows:

REDIRECT `09asp02.asp`

The `REDIRECT` keyword indicates the location of the Active Server Page that contains redirection instructions that the server follows, should the user click on the advertising banner. When you set this parameter, the component generates behind-the-scenes HTML that calls the indicated ASP file when the user clicks the graphic. Using global redirection is useful if you want all advertisements to revert to a common script that keeps record of which advertisement banners were clicked and redirects the user to a page of your choice. The redirection file is referenced relative to the filepath of the Active Server Page calling the `Ad Rotator` object. In the previous example, the `REDIRECT` file, `09asp02.asp` is in the same directory as the ASP file referencing the Schedule file.

WIDTH 402

The `WIDTH` keyword indicates the overall width by which the browser displays the graphics. The default is 440 pixels.

HEIGHT 102

The `HEIGHT` keyword indicates the overall height by which the browser displays the graphics. The default is 60 pixels.

BORDER 0

The `BORDER` keyword indicates thickness of the border that surrounds the graphics in the browser. The default is a 1-pixel border. Set the value to 0 if you do not want any border displayed.

The bottom half of the Schedule file contains information specific to each graphic. The format for each graphic's entry in the file is

- `adURL`—The location of the graphic file

- `adHomePageURL`— A specific home page, usually the home page of the advertiser. This URL information is passed to the redirection page defined in the top of the Schedule file. You can program the redirection page to extract the home page URL and redirect the user to that page.

- `Text`—Text that is displayed when a user moves his or her mouse over the graphic; also displayed if the browser does not support graphics.

- `Impressions`—The weighing of randomness. This entry is a numeric value between 1 and 10,000. You can assign impression values so that some ads are displayed more than others. For example, if you have three graphics entered and give each graphic an Impression value of 1, each graphic will be displayed an equal amount over time. However, if the graphics are assigned 1, 3, and 6, respectively, the first will be displayed 10% of the time, the second 30% of the time, and the last 60% of the time.

EXAMPLE

The following is an excerpt from the Schedule file shown in Listing 9.1:

```
http://localhost/QueAsp/chp9/ads/wisdom.gif
http://localhost/QueAsp/chp9/ariHome.htm
The Aristotle Middle School: Wisdom
1
```

In this example, the graphic that the page displays is found at

```
http://localhost/QueAsp/chp9/ads/wisdom.gif
```

The home page of the advertiser is

```
http://localhost/QueAsp/chp9/ariHome.htm
```

The text for the ad is

```
The Aristotle Middle School: Wisdom
```

Because all ads have an impression of 1, this ad is given equal display weight to all other ads.

Using the Ad Rotator

Listing 9.2 shows an Active Server Page that uses the Ad Rotator component. After the Ad Rotator object is created, the GetAdvertisement() method is called. The Schedule file that is called, adrot.txt, is the one shown in Listing 9.1. Figure 9.2 shows an illustration that is a composite of two calls to the same Web page. The Web page is constructed using the code in Listing 9.2. Notice that the pages display a different advertisement.

EXAMPLE

Listing 9.2: Using the CreateObject() Method to Make an Ad Rotator Object (09asp01.asp)

```
<HTML>
<HEAD>
<TITLE></TITLE>
</HEAD>
<BODY bgColor=#ffe4b5>
<FONT face="Arial" size=4 color=Blue>
Of Man's first disobedience, and the fruit<BR>
Of that forbidden tree whose mortal taste <BR>
Brought death into the world, and all our woe.<BR>
<P Align=Right>—John Milton, Paradise Lost. Book i. Line 1.
<P>

</FONT>
<HR>
<FONT face="Arial" size=3 color=Blue>
Please support our advertisers. Click the
advertisement to visit them...
</FONT>

<P>
<CENTER>
<%
Dim ad
```

```
Set ad = Server.CreateObject("MSWC.AdRotator")
Response.Write ad.GetAdvertisement("./adrot.txt")
%>
</CENTER>
</BODY>
</HTML>
```

OUTPUT

Figure 9.2: *The Ad Rotator displays a different ad each time a page is opened.*

When you look in Listing 9.2 you see that two lines of code are all that is needed to use the Ad Rotator component. One line uses `CreateObject()` to make the object and another line calls the `GetAdvertisement()` method of the `Ad Rotator` object.

NOTE

When you use the `Server` object's `CreateObject()` method, you are creating an object that lives throughout the lifetime of the page.

Listing 9.3 shows the client-side source code that `GetAdvertisement()` generates. Please notice that the code `GetAdvertisement()` generates contains standard `<HREF>` and `<IMG>` tags. The code within the `<HREF>` tag contains a call to the redirection page, `09asp02.asp`, which is defined in the Schedule file. In addition, the URL for the home page and banner graphic are passed back to the server within the URL's context string. The <IMG> tag contains the source URL for the graphic as well as the alternate text defined in the Schedule file. The alternate text is assigned to the ALT attribute of the <IMG> tag. Again, all this information is defined in the Schedule file. You can see how using the GetAdvertisement() method simplifies the whole process of rotating ads. One method call produces all the client-side HTML you need easily and consistently.

EXAMPLE

Listing 9.3: Using the GetAdvertisement Method

```
.
.
<FONT face="Arial" size=3 color=Blue>
Please support our advertisers. Click the advertisement to visit them...
</FONT>

<P>
<CENTER>
<A
HREF="09asp02.asp?url=http://localhost/QueAsp/chp9/ariHome.htm&image=http://local
host/QueAsp/chp9/ads/know.gif" ><IMG
SRC="http://localhost/QueAsp/chp9/ads/know.gif" ALT="The Aristotle Middle School:
Knowledge" WIDTH=402 HEIGHT=102 BORDER=0></A>
</CENTER>
.
.
```

NOTE

In HTML convention, within a URL, the question mark character (?) separates the Web address from the context string. A context string is the data passed to the server to process. The ampersand (&) separates name=value pairs. The plus sign (+) indicates a blank space. Thus, in the URL

   www.MySite.com?FirstName=Bob&LastName=Reselman&City=New+York

The Web site address is

   www.MySite.com

The context string is

   FirstName=Bob&LastName=Reselman&City=New+York

The name=value pairs are

   FirstName=Bob

   LastName=Reselman

   City=New+York

Now that we know how to display advertisements automatically using the Ad Rotator component, let's take a look at how we can use the redirection file to divert the user to the Web page associated with the advertisement. In addition, we'll keep track of the number of times an ad is selected within a Web page.

Processing Data from the Ad Rotator

Figure 9.3 is a flow chart that illustrates the logic of the code within the Redirection file. The contents of the Redirection file are shown in Listing 9.4.

USING SERVER.QUERYSTRING

The `QueryString` collection of the `Server` object contains all the name=value pairs that are passed to a server in a URL call from a client-side browser. Sometimes name=value pairs can be passed from a client-side HTML <FORM>. Other times they can be passed from a predefined <HREF> tag. All the name=value pairs are passed as one string. The `QueryString` collection parses out each name=value pair automatically.

The way you use the `QueryString` collection is to pass the name part of the name=value pair as an index to the collection to access the value part. Thus, to access the values in the following `QueryString`:

    FirstName=Bob&LastName=Reselman&City=New+York

You could write the following code:

```
Response.Write QueryString("FirstName") & ", "
Response.Write QueryString("LastName") & ", "
Response.Write QueryString("City")
```

The output is

```
Bob, Reselman, New York
```

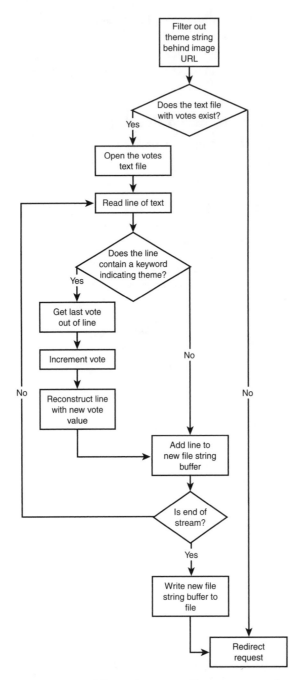

Figure 9.3: *The redirection file examines the query string using the* `Request.QueryString()` *collection to keep a record of referring advertisements.*

Listing 9.4: Keeping record of ad referrals (`09asp02.asp`)

```
<%
    Dim ImgURL 'The URL of the image clicked.
    Dim virtue 'banner selected
    Dim fso 'File System Object var
    Dim fPath 'Filepath var
    Dim ts 'var for TextStream object
    Dim str 'string buffer var
    Dim strFile 'string that contains the contents
               'of the voting file
    Dim voteNum 'the current number of votes in
               'on record
    Dim pos 'position var
    Const ForReading = 1 'TextStream constant
    Const ForWriting = 2 'TextStream constant

    'Assign the URL of the clicked banner's
    'image to a local variable
    ImgURL = Request.QueryString("image")

    'Use the Instr function to filter out the
    'ad theme from the URL server variable, image
    If Instr(ImgURL,"truth.gif") > 0 then
        virtue = "Truth"
    Elseif Instr(ImgURL,"know.gif") > 0 then
        virtue = "Knowledge"
    Elseif Instr(ImgURL,"courage.gif") > 0 then
        virtue = "Courage"
    Elseif Instr(ImgURL,"wisdom.gif") > 0 then
        virtue = "Wisdom"
    Elseif Instr(ImgURL,"beauty.gif") > 0 then
        virtue = "Beauty"
    End if

    'Make a record of the selected theme using a
    'text file and the File System Object

    'Create a FileSystemObject
    Set fso = CreateObject("Scripting.FileSystemObject")
    'Set the path of the text file that you are using
    'to keep record of banner choices using the Server
    'object's MapPath method and passing the filename
    'as an argument.
    fPath = Server.MapPath("/QueAspChp9/ads/" & "voterecs.txt")
```

continues

Listing 9.4: continued

```
'Check to make sure that the file really
     'is where it is supposed to be. Use the
     'FileExists method of the FileSystemObject
     If fso.FileExists(fPath) Then
          'Use the OpenTextFile method to open
          'the text file that contains the vote records.
          'When you use OpenTextFile, the method
          'returns a TextStream object automatically
          Set ts =fso.OpenTextFile(fPath, ForReading)
          'Traverse the TextStream looking for the
          'line that contains the chosen theme
          Do While ts.AtEndOfStream <> TRUE
               'Read the TextStream a line at a
               'time.
               str = ts.ReadLine
               'See if the line has the theme keyword
               If Instr(UCase(str), UCase(virtue)) > 0 Then
                    'If it does, create a new string with
                    'an incremented theme vote.

                    'Find the position of the comma
                    pos = Instr(str, ",")
                    'Get the current vote number value
                    'from the string
                    VoteNum = Right(str, len(str) - pos)
                    'Create a new line entry for the theme
                    'vote with an incremented vote number
                    str = UCase(virtue) & "," & Cstr(CInt(VoteNum) + 1)
               End if
                'Concatenate the string that contains
                'the new file information.
                strFile = strFile & str & vbCrlf
          Loop
          'Open the file again to do the write
          Set ts =fso.OpenTextFile(fPath, ForWriting)
          'do the write
          ts.Write strFile
          'Close up shop
          ts.Close
     End if
     'Redirect the user on to the home page defined
     'in the Schedule File. You get this information
     'from the QueryString index, "url" of the Request object.
     Response.Redirect Request.QueryString("url")
%>
```

The redirection file keeps a record of referring advertisements by using the `FileSystemObject` to write voting data to a text file. The structure of the voting data file is that each line contains a keyword indicating a voting category followed by a comma, followed by a number indicating the number of votes. Listing 9.5 shows the contents of the votes text file.

EXAMPLE

Listing 9.5: A text file record of ad referrals

```
BEAUTY,0
COURAGE,1
KNOWLEDGE,2
TRUTH,1
WISDOM,0
```

The bulk of the labor in the code shown in Listing 9.5 is to determine which advertising banner the user clicked. This is done using the `Instr()` function to identify substring values within the Image URL passed back to the server. (Remember, the Ad Rotator component inscribes the image's URL within the <HREF> tag that anchors to the image when displayed. Thus, the URL is passed back to the server.)

After all the data identification work is done, a `FileSystemObject` opens the voting text file as a `TextStream` object, finds the theme keyword and increments the value associated with the keyword. After the vote has been recorded, the `Response` object redirects output to another page indicated by the `"url"` value in the `Request` object's `QueryString` collection.

✔ For more detailed information about the `FileSystem` Object, see Chapter 5, "Fundamentals of Object-Oriented Programming," p. 99.

Protecting Your Code During File Writes

Although this code is useful, it does have some problems that need to be overcome to use this code in an industrial-strength environment. Most importantly, we need to build some safety mechanism into the code to make sure that it doesn't try to open a file for writing, if the file is open already. Trying to open an already open file can cause big, big headaches in terms of system crashes and data validity. We can prevent the concurrent opening of files by setting an Application-level variable in Global.asa that serves as a logical gate. When the gate is open, you can open the file. When it is closed you cannot. We set the logical gate in the `Application_OnStart` event procedure:

```
Sub Application_OnStart
    Application("IsVoting") = FALSE
End Sub
```

Before trying to open the file, check to make sure the gate is open. If it is, close the gate and open the file. When the gate is shut, no other code can access the file. The other code has to wait around until the gate opens (see Figure 9.4).

Close the gate by writing

```
Application("IsVoting") = True
```

After we are through writing to the file, we open the gate to let others in. Open the gate by writing

```
Application("IsVoting") = FALSE
```

Force code to wait around until the gate opens by setting an infinite, yet harmless loop as follows:

```
While Application("IsVoting") = True
    X = 1
Wend
```

After the variable `Application("IsVoting")` changes to `FALSE`, the code can move beyond the loop.

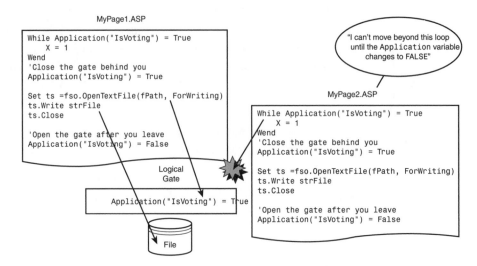

Figure 9.4: *Using an Application-level variable as a logical gate protects against disparate code sources opening a file for writing simultaneously.*

This might seem like a lot of energy to exert to implement a simple counting feature to record page usage. However, Internet Information Server 5.0 offers two components that simplify this whole business: the Counters and Page Counters components.

Working with Counters

Internet Information Server ships with two components that ease the burden of implementing counting functionality in your Active Server Pages. These are the Counters component (Counters.dll) and the Page Counter component (Pagecnt.dll).

The Counters component allows you to create Application-level Counters objects. A Counters object is a collection that contains one counter or many counters within it. Any number of pages can share a Counters object and a counter can persist forever or until you call the Remove method for a particular counter within the collection. Each counter is given a friendly index name which identifies it within the collection.

The Page Counter component allows you to create an object that keeps track of the number of times a page has been hit. All the mechanics of keeping track of each page's counter is encapsulated within the object. All you need to do to increment a page counter for a specific page is to create an object form the component and call the object's PageHit method. If you want to find out how many times a page has been hit, you query the Hits property.

Declaring the Counters Component

To create a Counters object that is shared among many pages in your application, create the object in your ASP application's Global.ASA file. Listing 9.5 shows a Global.ASA file that creates a Counters object.

EXAMPLE

Listing 9.5: Creating a Counters Object in Global.asa

```
<SCRIPT LANGUAGE=vbscript RUNAT=Server>
'********************
'Filename: Global.ASA /Chapter 9
'
'Programmer: Bob Reselman
'
'Copyright 1999 Macmillan Computer Publishing
'********************
    Sub Application_OnStart()
        'Add your most excellent code here

    End Sub
    Sub Session_OnStart()
        'Add your most excellent code here

    End Sub
```

continues

Listing 9.5: continued

```
Sub Application_OnEnd()
    'Add your most excellent code here

End Sub
Sub Session_OnEnd()
    'Add your most excellent code here

End Sub
</SCRIPT>
<OBJECT RUNAT=Server
        SCOPE=APPLICATION
        ID=MyCounter
        PROGID="MSWC.Counters">
</OBJECT>
```

Notice that the Counters object is implemented using the <OBJECT> tag and that the object is implemented outside of the <SCRIPT></SCRIPT> tags. When declaring an object in Global.asa, it is very important that you declare the object outside of the <SCRIPT></SCRIPT> tags.

USING THE <OBJECT> TAG

You can use the <OBJECT> tag to create a server-side object. The syntax for using the tag is

```
<OBJECT RUNAT=Server SCOPE=APPLICATION|SESSION ID=SomeInstanceName
➥PROGID="Library.Object">
```

After you create the object, reference it in the code as you would any other object variable. The following code shows you how to use the object declared previously:

```
SomeInstanceName.MyProperty = 4

SomeInstanceName.MyMethod()
```

Processing Data Using the Counters object

The Counters object supports four methods:

- **Get**—Retrieves the value of the counter.

- **Increment**—Increments the counter by 1.

- **Remove**—Deletes the counter from the application.

- **Set**—Applies a specific value to a counter.

After declaring an instance of the Counters object, MyCounter, for example, you invoke methods of a specific counter by passing its name as an argument to the method. For example, if you want to increment a counter named "visits" within the MyCounter instance declared in Listing 9.5, you write

```
MyCounter.Increment("visits")
```

If the counter "visits" does not exist, calling the Increment method will create it and set its initial value to zero.

If you want to get the current value of "visits", you write

```
x= MyCounter.Get("visits")
```

Again, all the details of keeping track of each specific counter is done internally within the Counters object.

Listing 9.6 shows code that uses the Counters object MyCounter, to keep track of the number of times a particular banner was selected within an advertisement. This code has the same functionality that was implemented in Listing 9.4. However, you notice that one line of code using the Counters object produces the same results that took numerous lines previously. (Please remember that MyCounter is declared globally in Global.ASA.)

EXAMPLE

Listing 9.6: Measuring Usage with the Counters Object (09asp03.asp)

```
<%
    Dim ImgURL 'a value indicating
               'the URL of the banner image
    Dim virtue 'var containing the counter name

    'Assign the URL of the clicked banner's
    'image to a local variable
    ImgURL = Request.QueryString("image")

    'Filter the image filename out of the
    'image URL server variable
    If Instr(ImgURL,"truth.gif") > 0 then
        virtue = "Truth"
    Elseif Instr(ImgURL,"know.gif") > 0 then
        virtue = "Knowledge"
    Elseif Instr(ImgURL,"courage.gif") > 0 then
        virtue = "Courage"
    Elseif Instr(ImgURL,"wisdom.gif") > 0 then
        virtue = "Wisdom"
    Elseif Instr(ImgURL,"beauty.gif") > 0 then
        virtue = "Beauty"
    End if

    'Increment a counter for the specific theme
    MyCounter.Increment(virtue)
```

continues

Listing 9.6: continued

```
        'Redirect the user on to the home page defined
        'in the Schedule File. You get this information
        'from the Server Variable, URL
        Response.Redirect Request.QueryString("url")
%>
```

Using the Page Counter Component

As you read previously, the Page Counter component allows you to create `Page Counter` objects that keep track of how many times a given page has been visited. You declare the `Page Counter` object within an Active Server Page using the `Server.CreateObject()` method. The following code is server-side script for incrementing and reporting a page count for the page in which it is run:

```
<%
Set MyPageCounter = Server.CreateObject("MSWC.PageCounter")
'Increment the counter on the page
MyPageCounter.PageHit
'Report the number of times a page has been hit
Response.Write "You are visitor number: " & MyPageCounter.Hits
%>
```

Working with Content Linking

The Content Linking component provides an object that allows you to traverse a set of HTML or ASP pages easily using the same code in all pages. The `Content Linking` object, which you create from the Content Linking component library works similarly to the Ad Rotator in that it uses an independent, external file that contains a list of URLs that represent the pages to link together in sequence. Figure 9.5 illustrates the concept.

Creating the Content Linking List

The format for the Content Linking list isn't nearly as complex as the Schedule list for the Ad Rotator component. Each Web page in the Content Linking list sequence is entered in order, with each Web page on a separate line. A page can be referenced by its full URL, `http://www.MySite.com/MyPage.htm`. Or, you can reference a page by its path relative to the directory in which the Content List file resides. You can enter a short description next to the Web page entry. The description must be separated from the Web page reference by a tab character. The following line of code shows a Content List entry for a Web page, `MyPage.HTM`, which is in a subdirectory, MyLinks, of the current directory:

```
MyLinks\MyPage.HTM    A short description about MyPage
```

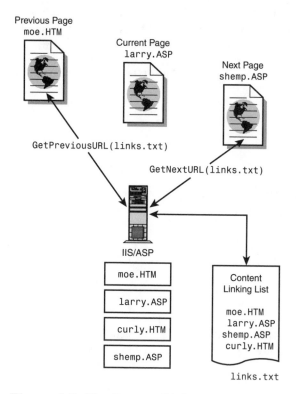

Figure 9.5*: The Content Linking component enables you to organize the sequence in which pages in your Web site flow.*

Listing 9.7 shows the Content Linking list named `arilinks.txt`. The list links the Web pages of the example Web site for this chapter, the Aristotle Middle School.

Listing 9.7: A Content Linking List (`arilinks.txt`)

```
ari_1.asp      The State and the Community
ari_2.asp      Action and Good
ari_3.asp      Friendship
default.asp  Aristotle Middle School Home Page
```

EXAMPLE

The Web pages as entered in the Content Linking list are in the same directory as the list itself.

Calling the Next and Previous Page

The code in Listing 9.8 shows you how to call pages using a Content Linking object. The page support a Previous button graphic (<) and a Next button graphic (>). Depending on the button that the user clicks, either the previous page in the Content Linking list, (the file, `arilinks.txt`, shown in Listing 9.7) or the next page in the list is called. Figure 9.6 shows how the pages are traversed starting from the lower-left and moving clockwise.

Listing 9.8: Using the Content Linking Component's `GetListIndex()`, `GetPreviousURL`, and `GetNextURL` Methods (`ari_1.asp`)

```
.
.
.
<TABLE Width="90%">
<TR>
<%
  Set NextLink = Server.CreateObject ("MSWC.NextLink")
    If (NextLink.GetListIndex ("./arilinks.txt") >= 1) Then
%>
<TD>
<A HREF="  <%= NextLink.GetPreviousURL ("./arilinks.txt") %>  ">

 <IMG src="prev.gif"></A></TD>
<%  End If  %>
<TD ALIGN=right>
<A HREF="  <%= NextLink.GetNextURL ("./arilinks.txt") %>
"><IMG src="NEXT.gif"></A>
</TD>
</TR>
</TABLE>
.
.
.
```

***Figure 9.6**: A Content Linking object allows many pages to share the same navigation code.*

Here's how the code works. The code in Listing 9.7 declares a Content Linking object, NextLink, using the CreateObject() method.

```
Set NextLink = Server.CreateObject ("MSWC.NextLink")
```

Then the code calls the GetListIndex() to determine the position of the current page within the Content Linking list. GetListIndex() takes the Content Linking list as an argument.

```
If (NextLink.GetListIndex ("./arilinks.txt") >= 1) Then
```

The code looks to make sure that the return value of GetListIndex() is greater than or equal to one. This is done to make sure that the current page is not at the top of the Content Linking list. If the page is not at the top of the Content Linking list, the If...Then logic within the ASP script displays a Previous button. Otherwise, we do not display a Previous button. Not displaying a Previous button on the first page is an arbitrary design decision. The page is designed so that you can move forward only from the first page.

The behind-the-scenes code for the Previous button is a server-side script call to GetPreviousURL() and a call to GetNextURL() for the Next button. The URLs that are returned as a result of these method calls are embedded in HTML <A HREF...> anchor tags. These tags give the graphics that represent buttons (prev.gif and next.gif) hypertext jump behavior. All the code is contained within an HTML <TABLE> for graphical layout purposes.

```
<A HREF="  <%= NextLink.GetPreviousURL ("./arilinks.txt") %>  ">

 <IMG src="prev.gif"></A></TD>
<%  End If  %>
<TD ALIGN=right>
<A HREF="  <%= NextLink.GetNextURL ("./arilinks.txt") %>
"><IMG src="next.gif"></A>
```

Listing 9.9 shows the client-side code that the Content Linking component generates.

EXAMPLE

Listing 9.9: The Result of Content Linking Code

```
.
.
.
<TABLE Width="90%">
<TR>

<TD>
<A HREF="  default.asp  ">

 <IMG src="prev.gif"></A></TD>
```

continues

Listing 9.9: continued

```
<TD ALIGN=right>
<A HREF="  ari_2.asp
"><IMG src="next.gif"></A>
</TD>
</TR>
</TABLE>
.
.
.
```

When it comes to adding a new Web page to the sequence, all you need to do is create the content for the Web page and add the navigation code in Listing 9.8 to the page. Finally, add the filename and location of the new page to the Content Linking list.

For example, if you want to add a new Web page, ari_4.asp, to your site and make it so that the page comes after ari_1.asp yet before ari_2.asp, you will modify the Content Linking list as follows:

EXAMPLE

```
ari_1.asp     The State and the Community
ari_4.asp     Some new data to review
ari_2.asp     Action and Good
ari_3.asp     Friendship
default.asp   Aristotle Middle School Home Page
```

Besides making the entry in the Schedule file and adding the navigation script common to all the pages, there is no need to add any extra code to the new Web page. The existing code accommodates the new page easily.

What's Next

This chapter showed you how to use four of the Installable Components that come with IIS 4.0 and 5.0. You learned how to use the Ad Rotator component to display banner ads. In addition, you saw some fairly complex code that showed you how to use the FileSystemObject to keep track of banner preference. You learned how to use the Counters component to simplify the work you did previously with the FileSystemObject. You learned how to use the Page Counter component to keep track of how many hits your page has had. Finally, you learned how to use the Content Linking component to organize the manner in which users traveled your site.

The next chapter shows you some more advanced programming practices and features of ASP. You'll learn how to use the Dictionary object to organize data easily and you'll extend your knowledge of the Server object. In addition, you learn how to make your code more robust by using error traps and error-handling procedures. Finally, you'll extend your knowledge of how to make more robust code by learning how to use transactions to make data writes to various datasources more reliable.

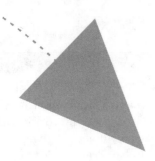

10

More on Objects and ASP

There's a lot to Active Server Technology in terms of the variety of objects you can use to create industrial strength production code. This chapter presents a potpourri of topics that bring together more of the tools you can use to enhance the reusability and robustness of your code. This chapter takes a deeper look at the Server object, shows you how to handle errors, and how work with the Dictionary object.

In this chapter you will learn how to

- Use the Dictionary object to organize data more easily

- Use the Server object to work with code in other Active Server Pages

- Use the Server object to enhance your control of Active Server Page output

- Use the Err object to write robust code that prevents your Active Server Pages from crashing

Working with the `Dictionary` Object

The `Dictionary` object allows you to simplify the way you work with arrays of data, particularly `name=value` pairs. The `Dictionary` is an object that is very much like a `Collection` object. The `Dictionary` allows you to add values to it. Each value that you assign to the `Dictionary` object is given a friendly key name of type String. For example, you can create a `Dictionary` object with an entry key named `"FirstName"`. Then, you can assign a value, `"Bob"` to that entry key name.

Creating a `Dictionary` Object

The `Dictionary` object is found in the Scripting Object Library. You use the `CreateObject()` method to make a `Dictionary` object available to your code. After you have the `Dictionary` object created, you use the `Add` method to make an entry in the `Dictionary`. The `Add` method takes two arguments, the key name of the entry and the value that you want to associate with the entry's key name.

The following code creates a `Dictionary` object, `dct`, and assigns a value to the key name, `"FirstName"`.

EXAMPLE

```
Dim dct 'Dictionary Var
'Create a dictionary object
Set dct = CreateObject("Scripting.Dictionary")
'Create a key FirstName and assign it the value, Bob
dct.Add "FirstName", "Bob"
```

Working with Keys

If you want to refer to a value associated with a specific key within the `Dictionary` object, use the key name as an argument to the object. The following code shows you how to extract the value associated with the `"LastName"` key name from the `Dictionary` object, `dct`:

```
Dim str
str = dct("LastName")
```

Traversing the `Dictionary` Object

As you read earlier, the `Dictionary` object is a collection of entries in which each entry is a named value. You can use a `For...Each` loop to traverse the `Dictionary` object to determine the name and value of each entry in it. The format for the `For...Each` loop is

```
For Each KeyVarName In DictionaryObj
    str = DictionaryObj(KeyVarName)
Next
```

Where

> KeyVarName is a variant that represents a key's name within the Dictionary object.
>
> DictionaryObj is a valid Dictionary object.

The following example shows you how to traverse a Dictionary object, dct:

EXAMPLE

```
For Each k in dct
    Response.Write dct(k)
Next
```

WHY TRAVERSE A COLLECTION?

Traversing a collection to work with data within the collection is something advanced programmers do as a matter of habit. It's not uncommon when working in a larger programming initiative to be given programmatically a collection of "stuff" you need to manipulate. The only thing you might really know about the thing you have been given is that you have a collection. That's it. You don't really know exactly what's in the collection. The collection might be useful or not. At some point, you have to go through each item in the collection to look at the keys and values to see whether anything in it is useful. The only way to meet this need is to traverse the collection.

For example, you might get a Dictionary object from which you are supposed to get a "FirstName" and a "LastName" value. However, you might not know if indeed there are such key names in there. In a case like this, it's absolutely essential that you be able to traverse the keys just to make sure "FirstName" and "LastName" key names exist in that collection. If such key names do not exist, you know the collection is invalid.

The Dictionary object contains a Keys collection. The Keys collection represents all the key names of the entries in the Dictionary. You can traverse the Keys collection of the Dictionary object in very much the same way you traverse the Dictionary object itself. The following example shows you how to traverse the Keys collection of the Dictionary object, dct:

EXAMPLE

```
For Each k in dct.Keys
    'Write the Key name and semi-colon separator
    Response.Write k & ":"
    'Write the value associated with the key
      'and skip a line
    Response.Write dct(k) & "<BR>"
Next
```

NOTE

When you use a For...Each loop to traverse a Dictionary object, the Dictionary object knows you are looking for each key in the Dictionary. This is true for any collection that is dedicated to a given object. For example, when you run a For...Each loop on the Request object's Cookies collection, the collection knows you are looking for each Cookie in the collection.

Listing 10.1 shows ASP code that creates a `Dictionary` object, adds two key names, FirstName and LastName, and assigns values to each key name. Then, the code uses a `For...Each` loop to traverse the `Dictionary`, extracting the key name and value of each entry. The output of the code is shown in Figure 10.1.

EXAMPLE

Listing 10.1: Organizing Data Using a `Dictionary` Object (`10asp01.asp`)

```
<HTML>
<HEAD>
<TITLE>Simple Dictionary</TITLE>
</HEAD>
<BODY>

<%
Dim dct 'Dictionary object variable
'Create a dictionary object
Set dct = CreateObject("Scripting.Dictionary")
'Create a key FirstName and assign it the value, Bob
dct.Add "FirstName", "Bob"
'Create a key Last and assign it the value, Reselman
dct.Add "LastName", "Reselman"

'Use a For Each loop to traverse each key (k)
'in the Keys collection of the Dictionary object
For Each k in dct.Keys
    'Get the Key
    Response.Write k & ": "
    'Get the  value associated with the key
    Response.Write  dct(k) & "<BR>"
Next
%>
</BODY></HTML>
```

Figure 10.1: Using the `Dictionary` object is transparent to the client browser.

You'll find the Dictionary object a useful tool, particularly when you need to process data submitted from an HTML form. The friendly name/key name feature of the Dictionary object makes it very adaptable to working with the name=value pairs of a form. Listings 10.2 and 10.3 show you how to use a Dictionary in an Active Server Page that receives data from an HTML form. Listing 10.2 shows you the form code. Listing 10.3 shows you the ASP that uses a Dictionary object to make processing the submission data easier. Figure 10.2 shows you a composite illustration of the input form and the ASP output.

EXAMPLE

Listing 10.2: A Simple Registration Form (10asp02.HTM)

```
<HTML>
<HEAD>
<TITLE>Win Something</TITLE>
</HEAD>
<BODY>
<FONT FACE=Arial Color=Blue Size=5>
<P>Register to Win!</P>
</FONT>
<FORM
    Name=MyForm
    Method="Post"
    Action="http://www.reselman.com/Chp10/10asp03.asp">
<FONT FACE=Arial Color=Blue Size=3>
<P>First Name: <INPUT name=FirstName></P>
<P>Last Name: <INPUT name=LastName></P>
<P>Address: <INPUT name=Address></P>
<P>City: <INPUT name=City></P>
<P>State: <INPUT name=State></P>
<P>Zip: <INPUT name=Zip></P>
<P>Email: <INPUT name=Email></P>
</FONT>
<P>
<INPUT type="submit" value="Submit" name=submit1>
</FORM>
</BODY>
</HTML>
```

Listing 10.3: Processing HTML Form Data Using a Dictionary Object (10asp03.ASP)

```
<HTML>
<HEAD>
<TITLE>You've Won!</TITLE>
</HEAD>
<BODY>

<%
Dim dct 'Dictionary Var
'Create a dictionary object
Set dct = CreateObject("Scripting.Dictionary")

'Get the data from the Form and put it
'into the Dictionary. (The variable, k, is the
'element name of each input element in the
'form
For Each k in Request.Form
    dct.Add   k, Request.Form(k).item
Next
%>

<FONT FACE=Arial Color=Blue Size=5>
Congratulations <%=dct("FirstName")%> !
</FONT>
<P>
<FONT FACE=Arial Color=Green Size=4>
You've won an all expense paid trip to
the tropical island of your choice!
<P>
The tickets to this 7 day, 6 night extravaganza
will be sent to:
</FONT>

<HR>

<FONT FACE=Arial Color=Purple Size=4>
<%=dct("FirstName")%>  <%=dct("LastName")%> <BR>
<%=dct("Address")%><BR>
<%=dct("City")%><BR>
<%=dct("State")%>,  
<%=dct("Zip")%><BR>
</FONT>
</BODY></HTML>
```

OUTPUT

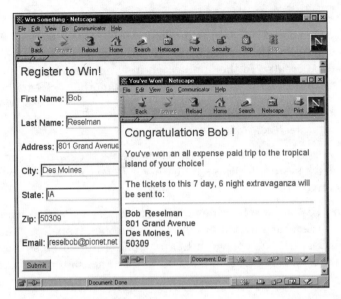

Figure 10.2: Dictionary objects make working with HTML form data much easier.

Using the Server Object

The Server object represents the Internet Information Server software on the server computer that executes your Active Server Pages. IIS acts as the traffic cop for all Internet requests upon your site. You use methods of the Server object to control how output is sent to the calling browser, to pass program control between various Active Server Pages, and to call code between Active Server pages. This section shows you how to use the following property and methods of the Server Object.

- Server.Transfer method

- Server.Execute method

- Server.HTMLEncode method

- Server.URLEncode method

- Server.MapPath method

- Server.ScriptTimeout property

Server.Transfer

The Server object's Transfer method, which is new to IIS 5.0, passes control from one Active Server Page to another. Any variables and objects that have been created in the application in which the original page resides will be maintained, even if the new page is in another ASP application.

The syntax for the Transfer method is

```
Server.Transfer(PagePath)
```

Where *PagePath* is a variant that represents the path on the server's hard drive system for the Active Server Page to which you want to transfer control.

Listing 10.4 shows the code for an Active Server Page in which the Server.Transfer method is called. The method transfers control to the Active Server Page shown in Listing 10.5. Figure 10.3 shows the result of using the Server.Transfer method to combine content in both listings.

EXAMPLE

Listing 10.4: Using the Server.Transfer (10asp04.ASP)

```
<HTML>
<HEAD>
<TITLE>Using Server.Transfer</TITLE>
</HEAD>
<BODY>


<FONT FACE=Arial Color=Blue Size=4>
This is the present file: <BR>


<%=server.mapPath(Request.ServerVariables("PATH_INFO"))%>
<P>
We will now transfer to this file, 10asp05.asp:
<HR>
</FONT>


<%Server.Transfer(".\10asp05.asp")%><BR>


</BODY></HTML>
```

EXAMPLE

Listing 10.5: Code Called by Server.Transfer (10asp05.ASP)

```
<HTML>
<HEAD>
<TITLE>Win Something</TITLE>
</HEAD>
<BODY>


<FONT FACE=Arial Color=Red Size=4>
Well, we've transferred to this file: 10asp05.asp
```

```
</FONT>
<P>
</BODY></HTML>
```

OUTPUT

Figure 10.3: *The* Server.Transfer *method makes content in multiple pages appears as one Web page.*

When you use the Server.Transfer method, be sure you identify the method's PagePath parameter correctly. If the page to which you want to transfer control is in the same directory as the page implementing the Server.Transfer method, all you need to do is enclose the external page in quotes, like so:

```
Server.Transfer(".\MyPage.asp")
```

If the page to which you want to pass control is in a directory below the one that contains the calling page, you would write

```
Server.Transfer(".\SomeDirectory\MyPage.asp")
```

If the page to which you want to pass control is in a directory above the one that contains the calling page, you would write

```
Server.Transfer("..\MyPage.asp")
```

Server.Execute

The Server object of Internet Information Server 5.0 provides an Execute method, which causes an ASP page to execute code contained in a second ASP page, and then returns control to the original page. This allows you to develop script routines that can be called by many pages. For example, you might develop a code that displays copyright information for your pages. You can store this routine in a page by itself and use Server.Execute to execute the routine from any other page in your ASP application.

The syntax for the Server.Execute method is

```
Server.Execute(PagePath)
```

Where `PagePath` is the name and location of the Active Server Page on the server hard disk containing the code you want to execute.

Listing 10.6 shows ASP code that creates a copyright notification string, then outputs that string using the `Response.Write` method.

EXAMPLE

Listing 10.6: Outputting Copyright Information Using Character Code &#169 (10asp06.ASP)

```
<SCRIPT LANGUAGE=vbscript RUNAT=Server>

    Dim str
    'Create a string that indicates a copyright
    'notification
    str = "<FONT Face=Courier Size=3 Color=Blue>"
    str = str &  "&#169 1999 Bob Reselman"
    str = str & "</FONT>"
    'Output the string
    Response.Write str
</SCRIPT>
```

Listing 10.7 shows another Active Server Page that calls the code in Listing 10.6 using the `Server.Execute` method. Figure 10.4 shows the result of the browser calling Listing 10.7.

EXAMPLE

Listing 10.7: Using the `Server.Execute` Method (10asp07.ASP)

```
<HTML>
<HEAD>
<TITLE>Another Poem</TITLE>
</HEAD>
<BODY>
<FONT FACE=ARIAL Color=Blue Size=5>
<P>My Kid Wants the Car</P>
</FONT>

<FONT FACE=Courier Color=Green Size=4>
My kid<BR>
wants the car<BR>
To feel grown up,<BR>
Showing to all her friends,<BR>
That she is invincible.<BR>
I fear she'll<BR>
wreck it.
</FONT>
<P>
<%Server.Execute("10asp06.asp")%>

<IMG Src=car.gif>

</BODY>
</HTML>
```

OUTPUT

Figure 10.4: *Using* `Server.Execute` *is transparent to the browser.*

Notice that the line of code `<IMG SRC="car.gif>` appears after the call of the `Server.Execute` method:

```
<P>
<%Server.Execute("10asp06.asp")%>

<IMG Src=car.gif>
```

This small bit of code demonstrates an important distinction between the `Server.Transfer` method and the `Server.Execute` method. The `Server.Execute` method allows program control to pass from a called page back to the calling page. The `Server.Transfer` method passes control to an external Active Server Page and does not return control back to the calling page. The code above passes control to the code in the external Active Server Page shown in Listing 10.6. Then, control is passed back to the calling page, at which time the HTML that shows the image graphic is run. Were the `Server.Transfer` method called instead of the `Server.Execute` method, the image would not be displayed because control would not return to the calling page.

The `HTMLEncode` Method

There is some text that is tricky to handle when it comes to writing it out in HTML. For example, suppose you want to display the following text in its entirety using

```
The <P> tag represents a paragraph break.
```

Initially you might write the following code:

```
<%
  str = "The <P> tag represents a paragraph break."
  Response.Write str
%>
```

However, when the browser runs the HTML, it interprets the <P> as an actual HTML paragraph tag, rather than the literal <P> character that you were expecting. The browser output in this case looks like this:

```
The

tag represents a paragraph break.
```

Use the Server object's HTMLEncode method to overcome this text display problem. The HTMLEncode method applies HTML encoding to a string, replacing special characters (such as the < and > characters in this example) with the HTML equivalents (< and > here). Consequently, the receiving browser will not attempt to interpret special characters as HTML tags, but will display the characters themselves.

The syntax of the HTMLEncode method is

```
Server.HTMLEncode(string)
```

where *string* represents the string to be encoded. HTMLEncode acts like a function. Its return value is the encoded string.

The ASP code in the example above should be rewritten as follows to achieve the desired results:

```
<%
str = "The <P> tag represents a paragraph break."
  Response.Write Server.HTMLEncode(str)
%>
```

Listing 10.8 shows you code that demonstrates how to use the Server.HTMLEncode method. The page presents one set of lines of code that does not use Server.HTMLEncode and one set of lines of code that does use the method. Figure 10.5 illustrates the before-and-after output of the code.

EXAMPLE

Listing 10.8: Using Server.HTMLEncode (10asp08.ASP)

```
<HTML>
<HEAD>
<TITLE>Using Server.HTMLEncode</TITLE>
</HEAD>
<BODY>
<FONT face=Arial size=4 Color=Blue>
Here is some text that does NOT use HTMLEncode:
</FONT>
<P>
```

```
<FONT face=Arial size=3 Color=Green>
<%
Dim str
str = "Here is a paragraph tag: <P>"
Response.write str & "<BR>"

str = "Here is a break tag: <BR>"
Response.write str & "<BR>"
%>
</FONT>

<HR>
<FONT face=Arial size=4 Color=Blue>
Here is some text that does use HTMLEncode:
</FONT>
<P>
<FONT face=Arial size=3 Color=Green>
<%
str = "Here is a paragraph tag: <P>"
Response.write Server.HTMLEncode(str) & "<BR>"

str = "Here is a break tag: <BR>"
Response.write Server.HTMLEncode(str) & "<BR>"
%>
</FONT>
</BODY>
</HTML>
```

OUTPUT

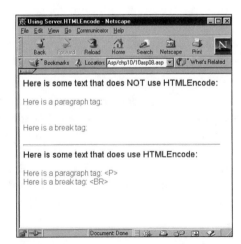

Figure 10.5: *The* `Server.HTMLEncode` *method is useful when you need to demonstrate HTML within a browser.*

The URLEncode Method

Any information contained in a URL must be presented in a specific format. For example, a URL cannot contain spaces or many other special characters. When working with "simple" URLs, such as Web addresses, this is not a problem. However, as you learned in previous chapters, it is common for a URL to include a query string, the purpose of which is to pass information from one page to another. In some cases, a programmer manually assembles a query string to pass predefined information to another page. The following example shows a line of code in which the programmer has used an <A HREF> anchor tag to pass a query string on to another page.

```
<A
HREF="http://www.reselman.com/Chp10/10asp10.asp?Sub=Bard&Pgr=Bob+Reselman">
Click me for an excerpt from Shakespeare</A>
```

> ✔ For information about the QueryString and the Request.QueryString collection, see the sidebar in Chapter 9, "Working with Installable Components for Internet Information Server," titled, "Using Server.QueryString," page 225.

Sometimes this information is mangled, usually because of typographical errors. For example, in the query string shown below, the anchor tag has a misspelling in which a space character is used instead of the plus sign between Bob and Reselman.

```
<A
HREF="http://www.reselman.com/Chp10/10asp10.asp?Sub=Bard&Pgr=Bob Reselman">
Click me for an excerpt from Shakespeare</A>
```

HTTP convention demands that you distinguish a space character between data by using a plus sign (+). Two values that are not concatenated with the plus sign are treated as separate values. When you pass this errant query string shown above to the server, only the Bob part of the value is processed.

However, we can use the Server.URLEncode method to avoid this sort of error. We process parts of the URL using the Server.URLEncode method. Server.URLEncode transforms the space character to a plus sign automatically. Listing 10.9 shows an Active Server Page in which the query strings are embedded in an <A HREF> anchor tag. The Server.URLEncode method is used in process strings in which spaces occur to transform them into plus signs, thus ensuring the overall integrity of the query string.

EXAMPLE

Listing 10.9: Using Server.URLEncode (10asp09.ASP)

```
<HTML>
<HEAD>
<TITLE>Old Poems</TITLE>
</HEAD>
<BODY>
<FONT FACE=ARIAL Color=Blue Size=5>
```

```
Some Poems
</FONT>
<HR>
<FONT FACE=Courier Color=Green Size=4>
<%
Dim str
'Create a string that is a URL that contains both
'Web page address and query string that the page is to process
str = "http://www.reselman.com/QueAsp/Chp10/"
str = str & "10asp10.asp?Poem=Bard&Pgr="
str = str & Server.URLEncode("Bob Reselman")
%>
<A HREF=<%=str%>>
Click me for an excerpt from Shakespeare</A>
<P>
<%
str = "http://www.reselman.com/QueAsp/Chp10/"
str = str & "10asp10.asp?Poem=Juntoku&Pgr="
str = str & Server.URLEncode("Bob Reselman")
%>
<A HREF=<%=(str)%>>
Click me for an old poem</A>
</FONT>
</BODY>
</HTML>
```

Listing 10.10 shows the source code that the browser receives from the Active Server Page in Listing 10.9. Notice that the space between Bob and Reselman now has a plus sign substitute. Figure 10.6 shows the output of the code.

EXAMPLE

Listing 10.10: Code Transformed Using Server.URLEncode

```
<HTML>
<HEAD>
<TITLE>Old Poems</TITLE>
</HEAD>
<BODY>
<FONT FACE=ARIAL Color=Blue Size=5>
Some Poems
</FONT>
<HR>
<FONT FACE=Courier Color=Green Size=4>

<A HREF=http://www.reselman.com/QueAsp/Chp10/10asp10.asp?
➥Poem=Bard&Pgr=Bob+Reselman>
Click me for an excerpt from Shakespeare</A>
<P>
```

continues

Listing 10.10: continued

```
<A HREF=http://www.reselman.com/QueAsp/Chp10/10asp10.asp?
➡Poem=Juntoku&User=Bob+Reselman>
Click me for an old poem</A>
</FONT>
</BODY>
</HTML>
```

OUTPUT

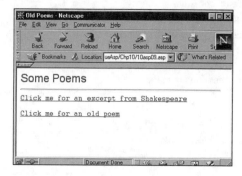

Figure 10.6: *It's not unusual to hard code a query string to a URL when using an* <A HREF> *tag.*

Listing 10.11 shows the Active Server Page code called by the <A HREF> tag in Listing 10.10. The script is straightforward. Items within Server.QueryString collection are used in conjunction with a Select Case statement to determine the Sub call that outputs HTML to the calling client. Figure 10.7 shows the output of Listing 10.11.

EXAMPLE

Listing 10.11: Using Server.QueryString with a Select Case Statement (10asp10.ASP)

```
<SCRIPT LANGUAGE=vbscript RUNAT=Server>
    Sub DoJuntoku()
        'An ancient poem
        Dim str
        str = "Royal dwellings  <BR>"
        str = str & "but<BR>"
        str = str & "today <BR> "
        str = str & "the eaves<BR>"
        str = str & "are overgrown —  <BR>"
        str = str & "yearning <BR>"
        str = str & "for the then,<BR>"
        str = str & "living<BR>"
        str = str & "in the snow.<BR>"
        str = str & "<P Align=Right>Retired Emperor Juntoku"
        str = str & "<P Align=Right>(1197 - 1242)"
        Response.Write str
    End Sub
```

```
Sub DoTheBard()
    'A verse from Shakespeare
    Dim str
    str = "Now would I give a thousand "
    str = str & "furlongs of sea for an <BR>"
    str = str & "acre of barren ground, long heath, "
    str = str & "brown furze, any <BR>"
    str = str & "thing. The wills above be done! "
    str = str & "but I would fain <BR>"
    str = str & "die a dry death."
    str = str & "<P Align=Right>The Tempest, Act 1, Scene 1"
    Response.Write str
End Sub
'Make a salutation
Response.Write "<FONT Color=Blue Face=Arial Size=5>"
Response.Write "Here is a poem for: "
Response.Write Request.QueryString("Pgr")
Response.Write "<P>"
Response.Write "</FONT>"

Response.Write "<FONT Color=Green Face=Courier Size=4>"
'Process the query string passed from the
'calling Active Server Page
Select Case Request.QueryString("Poem")
    Case "Juntoku":
        Call DoJuntoku()
    Case "Bard":
        Call DoTheBard()
End Select
Response.Write "</FONT>"
</SCRIPT>
```

The MapPath Method

You can use the Server object's MapPath method to convert a relative or virtual path (that is, the name of a file or folder) to the actual physical path
where the file or folder is (or would be) stored on the server's hard disk.
The syntax of the MapPath method is as follows:

```
Server.MapPath(path)
```

where *path* specifies the relative or virtual path whose location you wish to
determine. If *path* starts with a forward or backward slash, it is interpreted
as a virtual path and the mapping begins at the server's root. A *path* that
does not begin with a slash is interpreted as being relative to the folder
where the current Active Server Page is stored.

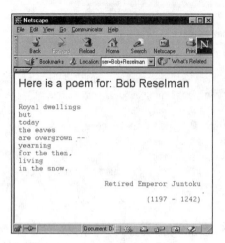

Figure 10.7: *This page was generated dynamically by analyzing data in the* `Request.QueryString` *collection.*

For example, if you want to know the physical directory in which a file named `default.asp` in your server's Web root would be stored, you can use the following line:

```
<% Response.Write Server.MapPath("/default.asp") %>
```

The output of this line would be something like the following, no matter where the current page is stored:

```
d:\inetpub\wwwroot\default.asp
```

However, if you eliminated the leading slash, the result would be a path that begins wherever the calling page is located, which might or might not start at the Web root. For example, if the current ASP page is located at `http://www.`*servername*`.com/QueASP/mappathtest.asp`, and it contains the line

```
<% Response.Write Server.MapPath("default.asp") %>
```

(notice the missing leading slash), the output would be something like this:

```
d:\inetpub\wwwroot\QueAsp\default.asp
```

The `MapPath` method can be very handy when an Active Server Page needs to know the physical location of a file on the server's hard drive, as you do not have to assume you know where the server keeps its Web files.

NOTE

MapPath does not check to see whether the file actually exists. For this reason, you can use MapPath to gather information to be passed to a component that will, in turn, create a file.

The ScriptTimeout Property

By default, Active Server Page scripts will be terminated by the server (and return an error) if they run longer than 90 seconds. If you have a script that legitimately might run longer than 90 seconds, a query on a very large database for example, you can use the Server object's ScriptTimeout property to increase the amount of time the server will allow ASP scripts to run. The value of the ScriptTimeout property is the number of seconds that will be allowed for a script; for example, the following line of code will change the ScriptTimeout property to 120 seconds:

```
<% Server.ScriptTimeout = 120 %>
```

NOTE

The default ScriptTimeout property is governed by the Web server's AspScriptTimeout property, which can be modified by the server administrator if necessary. An Active Server Page cannot set Server.ScriptTimeout to a value lower than the server's default.

Listings 10.12 and 10.13 demonstrate the use of the Server.ScriptTimeout property. Both pages contain VBScript code that uses a loop to cause a 120-second delay.

Listing 10.12 does not change the value of ScriptTimeout, so the default value of 90 seconds is in effect. Because the script runs longer than 90 seconds, the server will return an error before the script has time to finish.

However, Listing 10.13 changes ScriptTimeout to 180 seconds. Because the ScriptTimeout property is set at a value greater than the 120 seconds the script needs to complete the loop, the page is allowed to complete normally.

Figures 10.8 and 10.9 show the results of running these two sample pages.

EXAMPLE

Listing 10.12: Generating a Script Timeout Error (10asp11.ASP)

```
<HTML>
<HEAD>
<TITLE>More Timeout Stuff</TITLE>
</HEAD>
<BODY>
<FONT FACE=ARIAL Color=Blue Size=4>
This page uses Server object's ScriptTimeout
default value of 90 seconds.<br>
It contains a loop that runs for 120 seconds
before the page ends.<br>
<HR>
<%
```

continues

Listing 10.12: continued

```
  StartTime = Time()
  EndTime = DateAdd("s", 120, StartTime)
  Response.Write "I started at " & StartTime & "..."
  Response.Write "Here are the seconds:<br>"
  LastSec = Second(Now)
%>
</FONT>
<FONT FACE=Courier Color=Blue Size=3>
<%
  Do While Time() < EndTime
       'Make sure that you are not reporting the
       'same second
       If LastSec <> Second(Now()) Then
            'If it is a new second, reset the
            'second variable
            LastSec = Second(Now())
            'Increment the second counter
            i = i + 1
            'Print out the second
            Response.Write i & ", "
       End if
  Loop
%>
</FONT>
<FONT FACE=ARIAL Color=Blue Size=4>
<%
  Response.Write "<BR>" &  "I finished at " & Time()
%>
</FONT>
</BODY>
</HTML>)
```

Listing 10.13: Avoiding Script Timeout Errors by Increasing the `Server.ScriptTimeout` Value
(10asp12.ASP)

EXAMPLE

```
.
.
.
<%
  'Reset the timeout value in order to
  'let the loop run to its course.
  Server.ScriptTimeout = 180
  StartTime = Time()
  EndTime = DateAdd("s", 120, StartTime)
  Response.Write "I started at " & StartTime & "..."
  Response.Write "Here are the seconds:<br>"
  LastSec = Second(Now)
```

```
%>
```
.
.
.
.

OUTPUT

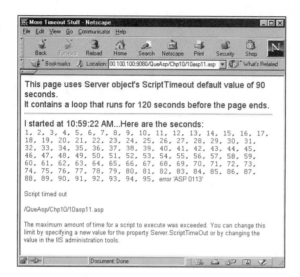

Figure 10.8: ASP sends the calling browser an error when a script times out.

OUTPUT

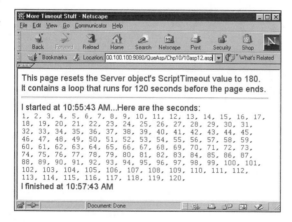

Figure 10.9: Resetting the value ScriptTimeout *property allows long loops to process.*

Handling Errors

Errors happen. They always have. They always will. However, this doesn't mean that your ASP code has to behave poorly when an error does occur.

Instead, you can use the error handling capabilities of Active Server Pages to make your code work reliably and predictably.

Using On Error Resume Next

Let's create an error.

```
Dim i
i = CInt("Hello World")
Response.Write "The value of i is: " & i
```

The code above generates an error because the CInt function cannot convert the non-numeric string constant, "Hello World" into a valid integer value (see Figure 10.10).

OUTPUT

Figure 10.10: Although the default data type is a variant, VBScript generates type mismatch errors when you use the type conversion functions improperly.

Clearly, the error generated above is serious and at some point should be addressed. However, the way the script is presently written, the script engine has no alternative but to terminate execution when it encounters the error. If we want to keep the script in force in spite of this error, we use the On Error Resume Next statement as shown below:

```
Dim i
On Error Resume Next
i = CInt("Hello World")
Response.Write "The value of i is: " & i
```

The On Error Resume Next statement tells the script engine to ignore any error it encounters and to execute the line of code directly following the given error.

The good news is that the script keeps running in spite of an error. The bad news is that the script keeps running in spite of an error. Granted, keeping the script up and running is important. Therefore, using On Error Resume

Next provides a significant error handling feature. However, in the example above, the result of the error handling is to display an empty value for i (see Figure 10.11). Should the script require a valid integer for the value i, the result of the error could have far reaching implications.

OUTPUT

Figure 10.11: *A variant that hasn't any value returns empty when called.*

Having the ability to identify an error and react to it increases the robustness and viability of your code. You can use the Err object to catch errors, identify them, and then write code that accommodates the error encountered.

Working with the Err Object

The Err object is a global object internal to VBScript that is populated with data every time an error is committed in code. Table 10.1 shows the properties and methods of the Err object.

Table 10.1: The Properties and Methods of the **Err** *Object*

Name	Item	Description
Description	Property	Returns or sets the friendly language description of the error.
HelpContext	Property	Returns or sets the context identification number, which is the location of a help topic in a help file associated with the error.
HelpFile	Property	Returns or sets the help file location, which is a WinHelp or HTML document that provides help information for the user.
Number	Property	Returns or sets a specific number that identifies the error. You can use defined error numbers, which you can associate with custom errors. The values 0 to 65,535 are valid error numbers. If you want to create a user-defined error number, add the specific user-defined number to the internal VBScript constant, vbObjectError.

continues

Table 10.1: continued

Name	Item	Description
Source	Property	Returns or sets the name of the object creating the error.
Raise	Method	Allows you to generate an error. The format is Err.Raise(Number, Source, Description, Helpfile, Helpcontext).
Clear	Method	Clears out the error object of all settings and data.

You use the `Err` object to catch errors by checking the object at critical times in your code.

Listing 10.14 shows you a sample of code that uses the `Err` object to trap an error. In this case, the error trap checks to see whether the `CInt` conversion function executed properly. If the code raises an error, an error message is created and returned to the calling client. Figure 10.12 shows the result of the script in which the error handling code has been added.

EXAMPLE

Listing 10.14: Using the `Err` Object to Trap Errors (10asp13.ASP)

```
<%
Dim i

On Error Resume Next 'Turn on error handling
i = CInt("Hello World")
'Check to see if the Err object
'has be generated
If Err Then 'Build in an error trap
    'If so, report an Error
    Response.Write "<FONT Color=Red Face=Arial Size=5>"
    Response.Write "You have an error.<BR>"
    Response.Write "The error is: "
    Response.Write Err.description & "<BR>"
    Response.Write "Please contact the web master."
    Response.Write "</FONT>"
Else
    Response.Write "The value of i is: " & i
End if

Response.Write "<FONT Color=Blue Face=Arial Size=4>"
Response.Write "<P>Thanks for using this site!"
Response.Write "</FONT>"
%>
```

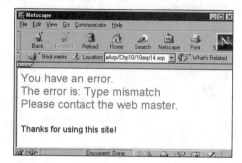

Figure 10.12: *You can use the* Err *object's description field to report the nature of an error.*

Creating Error Handling Procedures

You can dedicate a specific procedure in your script to handle errors (see Figure 10.13). Isolating error handling into a central area of your script is a wise thing to do, particularly if your script is large. Listing 10.15 shows an Active Server Page using a user-defined error handling Sub ErrorHandler() to process errors generated in the page. Figure 10.14 shows the result of Listing 10.15.

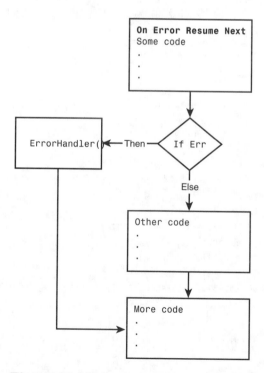

Figure 10.13: *A common error handling procedure makes your script easier to manage.*

Listing 10.15: Concentrating Error Handling for Your Active Server Page (10asp14.ASP)

```
<%
Sub ErrorHandler()
 Dim str 'Buffer
 Dim errMsg 'General Error Message
 Dim errCause 'Cause of error
 Dim errSol 'Probable solution

 Select Case err.Number
     Case 13: 'Type MisMatch
             'Solution
             errSol = "You cannot address this error. "
             errSol = errSol & "The cause is internal to the program. "
             errSol = errSol & "We sincerely apologize."
             'Greeting
             errMsg = "We apologize. An error has occurred. "
             errMsg = errMsg & "Please understand that "
             errMsg = errMsg & "it is not due to your use. "
         Case Else: 'Default handler
             'Solution
             errSol = "Please contact the webmaster at: "
             errSol = errSol & "webmaster@reselman.com "
             'Greeting
             errMsg = "Again, we apologize. An error has occurred. "
 End Select
 'Set the cause to the Err object Description
 errCause = Err.description

'Make an Error Report
 str = "<FONT Color=Red Face=Arial Size=5>"
 str = str & "<CENTER>"
 'Report that an error has occurred and it is
 'not due to user error
 str = str & errMsg
 str = str & "<P>"
 str = str & "</CENTER>"
 str = str & "</FONT>"
 str = str & "<FONT Color=Blue Face=Arial Size=4>"
 'State the cause of the error
 str = str & "The cause of the error is: "
 str = str & "</FONT>"
 str = str & "<FONT Color=Blue Face=Courier Size=4>"
```

```
    str = str & errCause & "<P>"
    str = str & "</FONT>"
    str = str & "<FONT Color=Blue Face=Arial Size=4>"
    'Offer a solution
    str = str & errSol & "<P>"
    str = str & "</FONT>"
    Response.Write str

    'Clear out the error object
    Err.Clear
End Sub

Dim i

On Error Resume Next 'Turn on error handling
i = CInt("Hello World")
'Check to see if the Err object
'has be generated
If Err Then 'Build in an error trap
        'If so, call the error handler
    Call ErrorHandler()
Else
    Response.Write "The value of i is: " & i
End if
Response.Write "<FONT Color=Blue Face=Arial Size=4>"
Response.Write "<P>Thanks for using this site!"
Response.Write "</FONT>"
%>
```

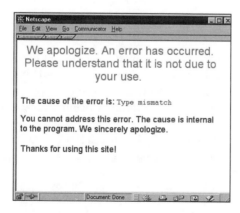

Figure 10.14: *Considerate, forgiving error messages make your code fun and desirable to use.*

THE THREE RULES OF ERROR MESSAGES

If you believe the most important person in the software development process is the end user—the person who will eventually use the program you are writing—then you can understand easily how important it is to provide error messages that consider the end user first.

It's not unusual when end users encounter an error in a program to think they have done something terribly wrong and maybe even destroyed the program. Most often, computer errors are the result of some programming oversight and not the result of user error at all. It's important that the user understands his or her innocence in the matter and that the program acknowledge this.

Therefore, one of the easiest, most important things you can do to make your program accommodating to the end user is to provide considerate error messages. Every error message you write should deliver three pieces of information:

1. That an error has occurred. If the error is not the fault of the user, the user needs to be informed of that.
2. The cause of the error.
3. The most likely solution that will address the error.

Programs that are considerate of the end user in their error messaging are fun to use and have wider acceptance than programs that are terse and cryptic when communicating with users. End users tend to be as forgiving of ill-behaved programs as those programs are forgiving of them.

Maintaining Error Scope

The On Error Resume Next statement is subject to the same rules of scope as variables. On Error Resume Next can apply to a whole page or it can apply to a specific procedure. The useful thing about subordinating On Error Resume Next to the procedure level is that it gives you a greater degree of control over the administration of your error handling.

Every time you use the On Error Resume Next statement, you reset the Err object. Thus, when you call On Error Resume Next within a procedure, operationally the Err object appears to be unique to that procedure. This means you are trapping only the errors particular to that procedure.

WELL-STRUCTURED CODE IS ROBUST CODE

Remember that VBScript is not like standard Visual Basic in that there isn't any On Error GoTo statement. When an error occurs, you cannot automatically transfer program control to a specific line of code. To make your code as robust as possible, you need to segment your code into as many procedures as possible and enforce reliable error trapping within those procedures.

However, if you use a central error-handling Sub, you have a problem. The problem arises when you enforce error checking on the error handler procedure itself.

If you use an `On Error Resume Next` statement in your error handling procedure, you are effectively wiping out any error information in the `Err` object. The error handling procedure cannot use the `Err` object to determine errors in outside procedures. Figure 10.15 illustrates this problem.

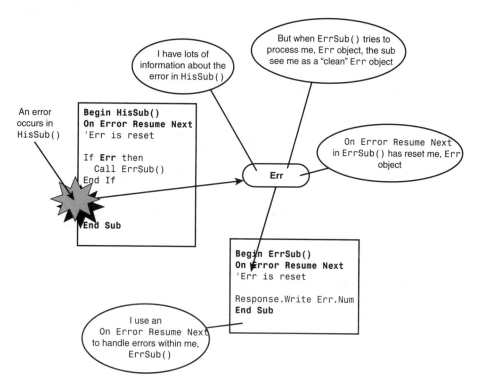

Figure 10.15: *The global* `Err` *object is used by all code within an Active Server Page.*

If we want to use a central error handler to administer error correction within an Active Server Page, we need a way to keep track of different states of the global `Err` object as it moves throughout a given script.

The easiest way to maintain error information about the particular state of the `Err` object is to pass the `Err` object as an argument to the error handling procedure. When you pass the `Err` object as an argument, you are really passing a copy of the `Err` object.

Operationally, you are taking a snapshot of the `Err` object. The snapshot contains the information in the `Err` object at the moment the error is raised. The error handling procedure processes the information in the snapshot. The `Err` object is left free to capture error information in other procedures. Should other procedures encounter errors, these procedures call the error handling procedure too, passing the Err object as an argument. Figure 10.16 illustrates this concept.

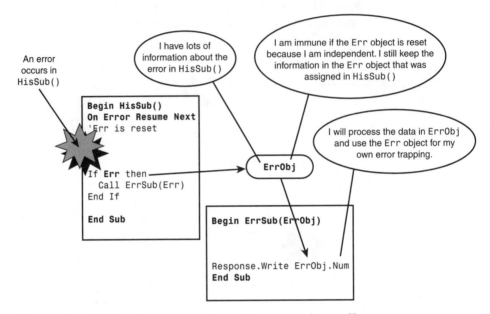

Figure 10.16: *Creating a snapshot of the error object allows you to pass error information among procedures.*

Listing 10.16 shows you an Active Server Page in which the code is partitioned in a procedure, Main(), and a central error handling procedure, ErrorHandler(). There is single entry point in this page, which does nothing more than call the procedure Main().

```
'====Entry Point==========
Call Main()
'=========================
```

The procedure Main() encapsulates the body script, shown in Listing 10.15, excluding the error handling procedure, Error Handler(). You'll notice that in the procedure, Main(), the code calls the error handling procedure, ErrorHandler(), passing the Err object as an argument. This creates the snapshot mentioned previously.

```
If Err Then 'Build in an error trap
     'If so, call the error handler
     Call ErrorHandler(Err)
  Else
     Response.Write "The value of i is: " & i
End if
```

After the `Err` object is passed to the error handling procedure, `ErrorHandler()`, its data is processed separately from the `Err` object.

The output from Listing 10.16 is identical to the output from Listing 10.15 as shown in Figure 10.14.

The benefit of using the code that is shown in Listing 10.16 is that the overall construction of the script is more structured. The code is partitioned into discrete procedures, making it easier to follow and easier to maintain. In addition, error detection is dedicated to each procedure. Doing error handling in this way allows you a finer degree of control and an easier way to maintain the code in the long run. Should you need to accommodate a new type of error in a later version of this, all you need to do is trap the error within the procedure as it occurs. Then write error-handling code in the central error handling procedure.

EXAMPLE

Listing 10.16: A Well-Encapsulated Error-Handling Procedure (10asp15.ASP)

```
<%
Sub ErrorHandler(ErrObj)
'=========================
'Error handling sub
'
'ErrObj is a snapshot
'of an error raised in another procedure,
'passed to this procedure for processing.
'=========================
  Dim str 'Buffer
  Dim errMsg 'General Error Message
  Dim errCause 'Cause of error
  Dim errSol 'Probable solution

'Process the phantom object
  Select Case ErrObj.Number
    Case 13: 'Type MisMatch
      'Solution
      errSol = "You cannot address this error. "
      errSol = errSol & "The cause is internal to the program. "
      errSol = errSol & "We sincerely apologize."
      'Greeting
      errMsg = "We apologize. An error has occurred. "
      errMsg = errMsg & "Please understand that "
      errMsg = errMsg & "it not due to your use. "
    Case Else: 'Default handler
      'Solution
      errSol = "Please contact the webmaster at: "
      errSol = errSol & "webmaster@reselman.com "
```

continues

Listing 10.16: continued

```
'Greeting
        errMsg = "Again, we apologize. An error has occurred. "
End Select
'Set the cause to the Err object Description
errCause = ErrObj.description

'Make an Error Report
str = "<FONT Color=Red Face=Arial Size=5>"
str = str & "<CENTER>"
'Report that an error has occurred and it is
'not due to user error
str = str & errMsg
str = str & "<P>"
str = str & "</CENTER>"
str = str & "</FONT>"
str = str & "<FONT Color=Blue Face=Arial Size=4>"
'State the cause of the error
str = str & "The cause of the error is: "
str = str & "</FONT>"
str = str & "<FONT Color=Blue Face=Courier Size=4>"
str = str & errCause & "<P>"
str = str & "</FONT>"
str = str & "<FONT Color=Blue Face=Arial Size=4>"
'Offer a solution
str = str & errSol & "<P>"
str = str & "</FONT>"
Response.Write str

'Clear out the error object
ErrObj.Clear
End Sub

Sub Main()
'=========================
'This Sub contains the initial code that
'the script runs.
'=========================
Dim i
On Error Resume Next 'Turn on error handling
i = CInt("Hello World")
'Check to see if the Err object
'has be generated
If Err Then 'Build in an error trap
  'If so, call the error handler
    Call ErrorHandler(Err)
Else
```

```
        Response.Write "The value of i is: " & i
    End if
    Response.Write "<FONT Color=Blue Face=Arial Size=4>"
    Response.Write "<P>Thanks for using this site!"
    Response.Write "</FONT>"
End Sub

'====Entry Point==========
Call Main()
'=========================
%>
```

What's Next

In this chapter you learned how to use the Dictionary object to organize data. You took a detailed look at the Transfer, Execute, HTMLEncode, URLEncode, and MapPath methods of the Server object, as well as the object's ScriptTimeout property. Finally, you learned how to use the On Error Resume Next statement and Err object to perform error handling.

This chapter brings us to the end of Part Three. The next chapter begins Part Four, "Client-Server Applications Using ASP." In Chapter 11, "Working with Security and Transactions," you'll learn how to make ASP applications that are secure. You'll learn how to authenticate users to make sure the right personnel have access to your ASP applications at the right time while making sure the data is kept safe within the application itself.

Part IV

Part IV: Client-Server Applications Using ASP

11

Working with Security and Transactions

Not all hackers are nice people who have a law-abiding passion for computer technology. Sadly, some people will go to a great deal of trouble to break into your site to steal your data and cause you harm. Crime in cyberspace is real. Nevertheless, you can take precautions. Internet Information Server architecture, in conjunction with ASP and Internet Explorer, offers many ways to make your site safe and secure. This chapter shows you some of these techniques.

In this chapter you will learn how to

- Configure your server to control user access

- Create a login program using Active Server Pages

- Work with the Windows Script Encoder

- Program Active Server Pages to work with Microsoft Transaction Server

Security Overview

There are many ways you can be the victim of foul play on the Internet. One way is to have the data that is sent between the server and the browser *sniffed*. Another way is to have unwanted intruders trespass into your server or a client machine.

Sniffing is the act of tapping into the flow of data across the Internet to detect certain types of data—credit card information being the most desirable. Most data sent over the Internet is ASCII text. This means that without proper precautions, the data sent between a browser and a client is exposed for the whole world to see. For example, if you submit some data that takes the format "cc=124534567891", it doesn't take too much of a rocket scientist to figure out that you might be sending out some credit card information. It's not that hard to make or buy sniffing software that watches all the traffic on the Internet in search of patterns such as credit card numbers, user IDs, and passwords. Sniffing is a significantly automated activity. All a digital eavesdropper needs to do is to put the sniffing agent in place and write credit card information it discovers to a log file. Later, perpetrators can read this information at their criminal leisure.

Invasion is unauthorized access to your server or your client system. Please remember that the structure of an Internet conversation opens up access to your computer to complete strangers. Granted, the various protocols that we use to communicate with one another over the Internet are supposed to prevent others from getting into our machines or sending us harmful computer viruses. However, as recent history bears evidence, sometimes the precautions just don't work.

So, what's to be done to make our computing environment safe?

Using a Secure Site

In terms of protecting sensitive data moving over the wire, the best thing you can do is configure IIS to use Secure Sockets Layer (SSL) on designated portions of your site to encrypt data. SSL is an encryption standard proposed to the World Wide Web Consortium (W3C). Therefore, both Netscape Navigator and Internet Explorer browsers support it on the client end. IIS supports SSL on the server side.

To use SSL you must get a digital certificate from a trusted authority. A trusted certificate authority is a third party that issues digital certificates to Web site owners. The best-known, trusted authority is Verisign.

A digital certificate testifies that you are indeed a legitimate business. After you have a certificate, you can use a public-private key scheme to implement a secure connection. Using keys allows you to encrypt and decipher data transmitted over the Internet.

NOTE

For information about using SSL under Windows NT and Internet Information Server, go to the Microsoft Developer Site at `http://support.microsoft.com/support/kb/articles/Q174/4/24.ASP`

You apply SSL by selecting the Properties item for the context menu of a standard or virtual directory from within the Internet Information Server Management Console under NT 4.0 or the Internet Services Management Console of Windows 2000.

Figure 11.1 shows the MMC context menu that you use to access the Directory Properties dialog of an Internet directory with the Directory Security tab selected. Please notice that the Secure Communication section in the middle of the dialog box contains a button with the caption, Key Manager. You click this button to access the Key Manager Wizard. The Key Manager Wizard helps you through the steps you need to take in order to use a digital certificate to provide validation for your site. Figure 11.2 shows the Properties dialog under Windows 2000.

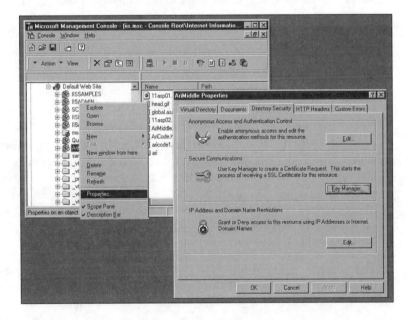

Figure 11.1: *Click the Key Manager button to access the Key Manager Wizard that assists you in getting a digital certificate for your site.*

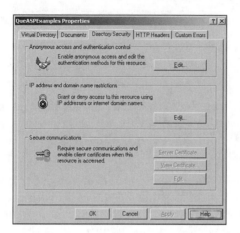

Figure 11.2: Under Windows 2000, if you do not have a digital certificate, the Secure communications buttons are disabled.

If you plan to conduct transactions on your site using sensitive data, a SSL and a digit certificate is the best way to ensure a secure, safe environment.

NOTE

For information about digital certificates and SSL, visit the Verisign Web site at `http://www.verisign.com/`

Configuring the Server to Protect Your Site

Revealing the structure of the data on a site to unauthorized persons is a common security breach. When someone calls a given directory on a Web server, you want the caller to be taken to a default Web page, not shown the contents of the directory. Figure 11.3 shows a Web browser calling a site at the IP address 147.100.100.100, in which the server is configured to allow anyone to view the contents of the current directory, the parent directory, and any subdirectory. Revealing the entire contents of a directory is not a good idea.

The way you prevent a visitor from your site to view the contents of a directory is to make sure that the Directory browsing allowed option in the middle of the IIS Directory properties dialog is not checked.

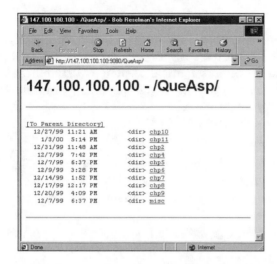

Figure 11.3: *Allowing a visitor to view a directory's contents is a security risk.*

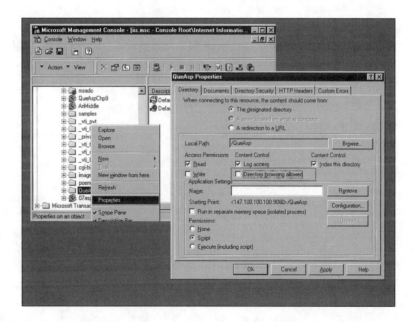

Figure 11.4: *The directory properties dialog allows you to set permissions for file and directory access.*

Using Default Pages

It's good business to configure the directories that are part of your wwwroot tree to display a default page in case of a directory call. A default page is a Web page that is shown automatically when a URL indicates a directory on your Web site without specifying a Web page. For example, the URL www.MySite.com/MyDirectory references a directory only, whereas the URL www.Mysite.com/MyDirectory/MyPage.htm references a file, in this case a fictitious Web page, MyPage.htm, within the directory, MyDirectory.

If directory browsing is disabled and a directory is enabled to support a default Web page, but a default Web page is not present in the directory, the server will deny you access to the directory (see Figure 11.5).

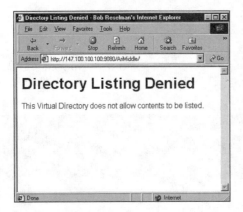

Figure 11.5: *IIS denies a user entry to a directory automatically when directory browsing is disabled.*

Internet Information Server allows you to define a list of specific Web pages as default pages for a directory. You define these pages within the Documents tab of the Directory's properties page. Figure 11.6 shows you the Documents tab for a Windows 2000 directory properties dialog box. This dialog box configures the directory to support default Web pages. In this case, the IIS searches the directory for the presence of Web pages named Default.htm, Default.asp, or iisstart.asp. If more than one of these pages is present, the page that is displayed is determined by the order of list. Pages at the top of the list have a higher priority.

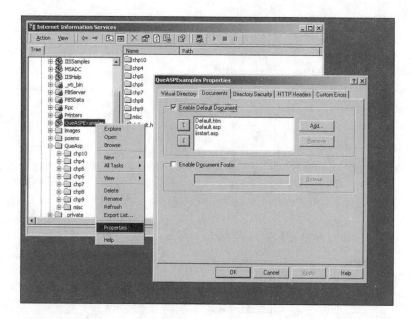

Figure 11.6: *You add a default page name to the supported page list by clicking the Add button.*

Creating a Simple Login Page

Protecting data flowing between a server and a client as well as barring unstructured access to directories on a Web page are good steps to take to make your Web site secure. The next level of security is *authentication,* the process of allowing access only to those whom you can identify as having the right to enter your Web site. To accomplish authentication we need to create a login process for your site.

Designing a Login Infrastructure

For small-scale sites, the design of our login infrastructure is straightforward. A login page is created as the entry point to the Web site. After the visitor is authenticated by providing a valid UserID and a valid password, he is granted access to a default Web page for the site. The content of the page is structured so that the visitor moves from the default page to other pages within the site in a linear fashion. The pages contain no hypertext jumps that allow the visitor to leave the predefined sequence of pages. Figure 11.7 illustrates the architecture of this sort of site.

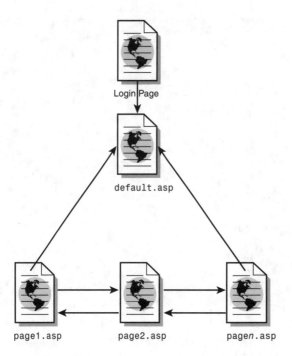

Login Page

default.asp

page1.asp   page2.asp   page*n*.asp

Figure 11.7: *This simple login infrastructure allows for controlled access to your Web site.*

Authenticating Users

In an authentication scenario, a person wanting entry to a Web site is granted access if he provides a valid UserID and password. One way to keep track of UserID and password information is to store it in a database that is registered as an ODBC datasource on the Web site's computer. With regard to the login program we are creating, when the user enters the site, he is presented with a Login page. The user enters a UserID and password. The data is submitted to an Active Server Page to be authenticated against data in the database. If the authentication proves valid, the user is redirected to the default page for the Web site. The site uses a Global.ASA file to provide the name of the datasource and the present URL of the Web Site. Figure 11.8 illustrates this idea.

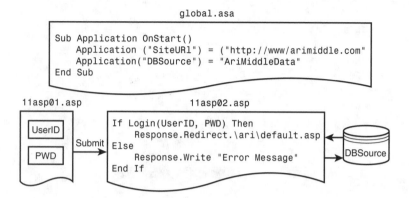

```
                              global.asa
  Sub Application OnStart()
      Application ("SiteURl") = ("http://www/arimiddle.com"
      Application("DBSource") = "AriMiddleData"
  End Sub
```

```
  11asp01.asp                    11asp02.asp
  ┌────────┐           If Login(UserID, PWD) Then
  │ UserID │               Response.Redirect.\ari\default.asp
  └────────┘  ┌──────┐  Else                                      ┌──────────┐
              │Submit│       Response.Write "Error Message"        │ DBSource │
  ┌────────┐  └──────┘  End If                                     └──────────┘
  │  PWD   │
  └────────┘
```

Figure 11.8: Some authentication architectures use a database to hold
UserID and password information.

Implementing the Login Page

Our login page for the Web site uses standard HTML <INPUT> elements
within a <FORM>, one for the UserID and one for the password. A Submit button is used to send the data on to the Active Server Page that processes the
authentication data. Listing 11.1 shows the HTML for the site's login page.
Figure 11.9 shows the page in a browser.

EXAMPLE

Listing 11.1: A Simple Login Page (11asp01.asp)

```
<HTML>
<HEAD>
<TITLE></TITLE>

</HEAD>
<BODY bgcolor=#000060>
<CENTER>
<img src="head.gif">
<font face="Arial" size=5 color=white>
<B>The Aristotle Middle School:Login</B><BR>
</font>
<FORM name=MyForm
      method=post
      action="<% =Application("SiteURL") & "/11asp02.asp"%>">

<font face="Arial" size=3 color=white>
LoginID<BR>
<INPUT type="text" name=LoginID>
<P>
Password<BR>
```

continues

Listing 11.1: continued

```
<INPUT type="password" name=PWD>
<P>
<INPUT type="submit" value="Login" name=submit1>
</FORM>
</font>
</CENTER>
</BODY>
</HTML>
```

OUTPUT

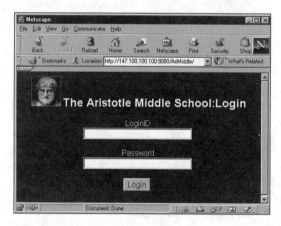

Figure 11.9: *A login page should be the default page for a Web site.*

Processing the Login Data

In our Web site, an Active Server Page has been dedicated to validate login data (see Listing 11.2). This validation page is called by the browser when the user submits login data by clicking the Submit button on the login page. The work of validating the UserID and password takes place in the programmer defined Login() function of that page, and Figure 11.10 shows a flow chart illustrating the programming logic for the Login() function.

(Listing 11.2 shows the source code for the Active Server Page that performs validation.)

Listing 11.2: Validating a Password Stored in an ADO Datasource (11asp02.asp)

```
<%
Function Login(LoginID, Password)
'**************************
'Parameters: LoginID  A String that indicates the
'                       LoginID of the User
'
'
'            Password A String that indicates the
```

```
'                     the password to be validated against
'                     the LoginID
'
'Return:  True,  if the LoginID and Password coincide
'
'Remarks: This method uses data kept in an external
'         database to do LoginID/Password validation.
'         The function retrieves a record from the
'         Access file under ODBC, indicated by the variable,
'         Application("DBSource"). The record is retrieved
'         according to the LoginID. If a record is
'         retrieved and if the LoginID and Password match
'         up, the method returns True.
'
'Programmer: Bob Reselman
'Copyright: 1999
'
'History: Created 11/28/1999
'
'**************************


    Dim cn 'Connection var
    Dim rs 'Recordset var
    Dim strSQL 'SQL Statement var
    Dim strCn 'Connection String var

    'Create a Connection Object
    Set cn = CreateObject("ADODB.Connection")
    Set rs = CreateObject("ADODB.Recordset")
    'Make the SQL statement that returns
    'the user with password, should one exist
    strSQL = "SELECT * FROM tblLogin WHERE LoginName = '"
    strSQL = strSQL & LoginID & "'"

    'Set error trapping
    On Error Resume Next
    'Open the Connection
    cn.ConnectionString = "DSN=" & Application("DBSource")

    cn.Open
    If Err Then Exit Function

    'Get the user from the DB
    rs.Open strSQL, cn
    If Err Then Exit Function
    'If the passwords match up, return TRUE
    If rs("PWD") = Password Then
```

continues

Listing 11.2: continued

```
        Login = True
    Else
        Login = False
    End If
    'Leave town
    rs.Close
    cn.Close
    Exit Function
End Function

If Login(Request.Form("LoginID"), Request.Form("PWD")) Then
    'If the login data is good, redirect the visitor
    'to the site's content directory
    Response.Redirect "ari/default.asp"
Else
    Response.Redirect "ari/err.asp"
End If
%>
```

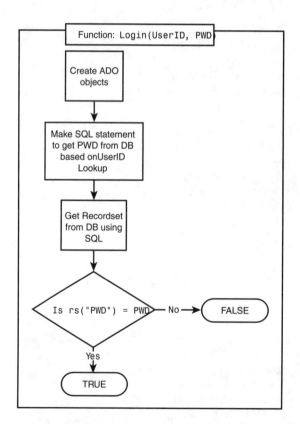

Figure 11.10: *The* Login() *function validates a provided password against one registered in the site's database.*

The code in Listing 11.2 uses ADO to access the datasource as defined in the Application-level variable Application("DBSource"). Keeping data access information in a central location allows many pages to share the datasource location information. Should you need to change the datasource for the site, you can do so easily while not having to rewrite code in every page. In addition, keeping the datasource information stored in a variable prevents others from viewing sensitive information about your data infrastructure. Granted, should someone crack your Global.ASA file, this information would be immediately viewable. However, if you use script encoding, this sort of security exposure can be avoided. (You'll look at script encoding later in this chapter.)

Notice that the Err object is used to provide error trapping for those points in the code where the Connection object and the Recordset object are opened. ADO Open methods tend to be places where data access code is vulnerable to errors.

✔ For details about the Err object, see "Handling Errors" in Chapter 10, "More on Objects and ASP," on page 261.

If a user enters valid login data, he is redirected to the default page for the site (default.asp). Figure 11.11 shows the pages that result from a successful login.

OUTPUT

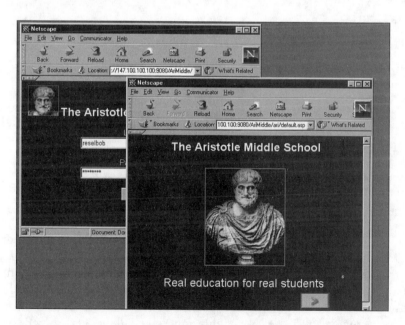

Figure 11.11: *An authenticated user is redirected to the site's content directory.*

Creating an Enhanced Login Page

Although the login page scheme provides a straightforward way to authenticate users wanting access to your site, a noteworthy problem exists that needs to be solved. Here is the problem: After a visitor is allowed into your site, the URL for each page he visits is visible in the location textbox of the visitor's browser. Thus, should the visitor's password be made invalid later, he can still get access to the site. All he needs to do to gain access is enter the URL of the Web page into the browser's location textbox. It's that easy. Figure 11.12 illustrates the problem.

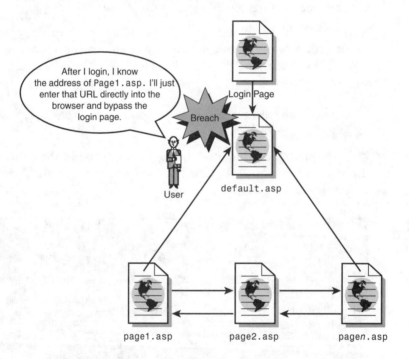

Figure 11.12: *Without proper precautions, a user can break into your site simply by entering the URL of an exposed Web page.*

One way to prevent unauthenticated visitors from viewing private pages on your Web site is to set a Session-level variable that indicates whether the visitor has indeed been authenticated to use a page on your Web site. You might remember that a Session-level variable is valid during the period when a visitor uses your ASP Application. When the user closes the browser, the session is over and all Session variables are removed from memory. We'll set a variable that says, "This user is good," which is visible for the duration of the session. Each page looks to this variable to see that the user is good before displaying the page contents. If the variable does not exist or is a null value, the user is denied access. After the session is over, the "This user is good" variable vaporizes. A new instance of "This user is good" must be created when a new session starts.

MAKING LOGIN UNIVERSAL

There is another method for having your user brought to a login page regardless of what page he calls within your site. You program the Session_OnStart event procedure in the site's Global.ASA file to redirect the user to the login page. The code below shows you how accomplish this:

```
Sub Session_OnStart
    Response.Redirect "MyLoginPage.asp"
End Sub
```

First, we'll modify the Global.ASA file to create and initialize a Session variable IsUserGood in the OnStart event procedure of the Session object. We'll add the following code:

```
Sub Session_OnStart()
    Session("IsGoodUser") = False
End Sub
```

Adding this code creates a Session-level variable, IsUserGood, for this particular user and session. The variable is initialized False. We'll set this variable to True after the visitor successfully logs in.

The following sample of code shows the modification made to the login page code shown in Listing 11.2 that sets the Session variable to True upon successful login.

```
<%
.
.
.
If Login(Request.Form("LoginID"), Request.Form("PWD")) Then
    'If the login data is good, redirect the visitor
    'to the site's content directory
    Response.Redirect "ari/default.asp"
    Session("IsGoodUser") = TRUE
Else
    Response.Redirect "ari/err.asp"
End If
%>
```

The last task we need to perform is to add the code shown in Listing 11.3 to each page in the application. This code checks the Session variable to make sure the visitor is authenticated to view the page. If the user is not authenticated, the code refuses access to the page by redirecting him to a Web page that notifies the visitor that he has been denied access to the site. This code must be added to the top of each Web page before the <HTML> tag because it contains a call to the Response.Redirect method.

EXAMPLE

Listing 11.3: The Session Object and Authentication Information

```
<%If Session("IsGoodUser") = False Then
    str = Application("SiteURL") & "/"
    str = str & "ari/breach.asp"
    Response.Redirect str
  End If
%>
```

CAUTION

If you are writing script that uses the Response.Redirect method, redirection must occur before any other HTML is sent to the client. Redirection code is best placed before the <HTML> tag in your Active Server Page. If you try to redirect a response after the server starts sending data to the browser, your code will cause an error.

The code in Listing 11.3 checks to see if the user is not authenticated. If the page senses an intrusion, the visitor is redirected to a page that informs him that he has been denied entry.

As you start working through this code on your own, you might want to extend this authentication Session variable technique to support a finer degree of access. You might use special Session variables to define which pages a visitor can and cannot visit. For example, if the user is a supervisor, you can create a Session-level variable, Session("IsSupervisor") and assign it a True value when the user logs in.

Using Certificates

Authentication, the process of making sure the people trying to enter your site are ones you want to let in, is a significant security concern. Using the UserID and password schema to secure your site is a very good way to prevent unwanted visitors from entering your site as long as each password is kept private by the person to whom it has been assigned. However, what do you do if a person's password is stolen, or a visitor distributes it freely to others? You have a problem.

A common solution to ensuring user authenticity is to issue a client-side digital certificate. A client-side certificate installs directly on the client machine. It is not randomly distributed. Client-side certificates are usually dedicated to a specific person on a specific computer. The certificate contains information such as name, location, and a unique serial number. Certificates are issued from your site. If a client has a certificate to your site, that certificate's data is part of the HTTP transfer. You can access a certificate's data by using the Request.ClientCertificate collection.

✔ For details about the members of the of the `Request.ClientCertificate` collection, see Appendix A, "ASP Object Model," page 487.

To send a certificate to a client, your site must have a digital certificate of its own from a certifying authority. In addition, you must have Certificate Server installed along with Internet Information Server. Certificate Server ships with NT 4.0 Option Pack and with Windows 2000 Server.

Encoding Data Using the Windows Script Encoder

Scripting is hard work. Some scripts really are rocket science. If you put a lot of time and thought into your scripts, you might not want to share the fruit of your labor with every Tom, Dick, and Harry who knows enough to select View, Source from the Internet Explorer menu to view your source code. You can protect your scripts from public exposure by using the Microsoft Script Encoder Utility.

NOTE

You can download the Windows Script Encoder utility from the Microsoft Developer Network Web site at `http://msdn.microsoft.com/scripting/`. It's free.

The Windows Script Encoder converts your source code into a format that can by deciphered and executed by Internet Explorer and Internet Information Server. This means you can protect your programming effort in both server-side and client-side scripts from being viewed by those people who use your scripts. Your source code is private to you (see Figure 11.13) .

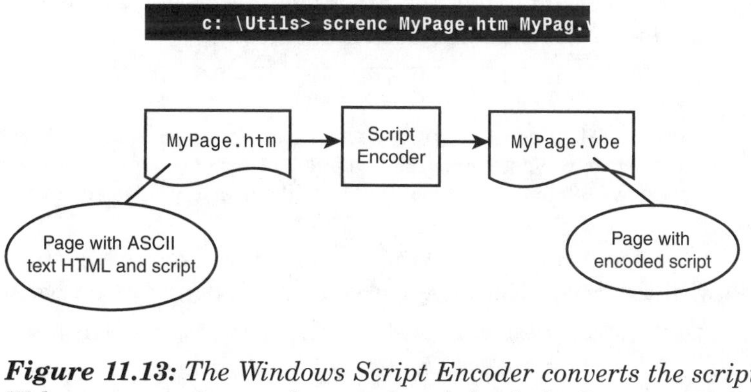

Figure 11.13: *The Windows Script Encoder converts the script in your Web pages to a format that can be read only by Internet Explorer 5.0 and IIS 5.0.*

The Script Encoder converts scripts written in either JavaScript or VBScript. However, be advised that after you encode your scripts, these scripts will run on Microsoft Internet Explorer and Internet Information Server only. Encoded scripts are not supported by Netscape at all!

Script Encoding Versus Data Encryption

Script encoding is different from data encryption. You use script encoding to transform source code into a format that can be decoded by Internet Explorer or Internet Information Server. You use the encoding utility to hide your source code. After your source is encoded, it cannot be decoded back into human-readable source code. The encoded source code is meaningful to the scripting engine only. This is a very similar dynamic to compiling text-based source code into machine language when programming in Visual Basic or C++. Only the person who created the code has a human-understandable copy of the source. All the end user gets is a compiled copy that can be used only by the computer and is not subject to the prying eyes of other people.

Encryption, on the other hand, is a back and forth process. You use your encryption key to encrypt data on your end. Then, you send it out over the Internet to another party who has an associated deciphering key that transforms the encrypted data back into human-readable form.

Using the Windows Script Encoder

The Windows Script Encoder is a *command line program*. You run it as you would an old time, character-based DOS program. You run the Script Encoder in Windows in a DOS window.

There are a few ways to open a DOS window in Windows. One way is to MS-DOS Prompt from the Start menu. Another way is to type the word `command` in the Start menu's Run dialog.

TIP

Use the Windows Explorer to select the directory in which the Script Encoder resides. Then when you enter `command` in the Run dialog, if you are running Windows 95 or Windows 98, the DOS window opens to the directory selected in Windows Explorer.

After you have a DOS Window opened, you enter a command string to work with the Script Encoder. The command string for the Script Encoder is

`Screnc Source_Unencoded_FileName Destination_Encoded_FileName`

Where

> `Screnc` is the executable file for the Script Encoder.

> `Source_Unencoded_FileName` is the location and filename of the Web page that contains the scripts you want to encode.

`Destination_Encoded_FileName` is the destination location and file-name to which the Scripting Encoder output the Web page that contains encoded script. (If you are encoding VBScript, IE 5 recognizes the file extension `vbe` as a Web page with encoded script by default.)

For example, if we have an HTML file named `11asp04.htm` ready for encoding, the command we enter at the DOS command line is

`Screnc 11asp04.htm 11asp04.vbe`

When the Script Encoder runs, it generates the file `11asp04.vbe`.

Figure 11.14 shows the source code view in Notepad for a Web page that contains script. One of the Notepad windows contains the source code before being encoded. The other window contains encoded source code. Notice that the HTML in the source code is unaffected by encoding, but that the script, after encoding, is unreadable as standard VBScript.

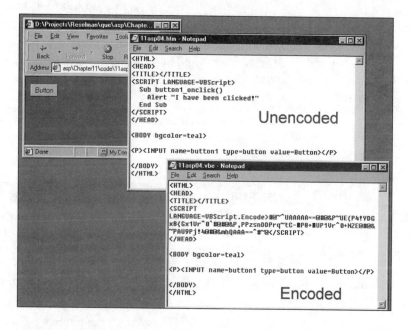

Figure 11.14: The Windows Script Encoder protects your code from being used by others.

Working with the Windows Script Encoder

There are a few extra details that you need to know concerning the Script Encoder. The first is that this technology is supported by IE 5 only. You can use it with an earlier version of Internet Explorer if you install the scripting engine version 5.

Second, there are optional switch parameters that you can use with the command line statement. Table 11.1 shows the switches and a brief description of each.

Table 11.1: Command-Line Switch Parameters for the Windows Script Encoder

Switch	Description
/s	Use this switch if you want to run without screen output.
/f	Use this switch to overwrite the source file.
/xl	Specifies that the language directive <@language> should not be added to ASP files.
/l DefLanguage	Specifies the default language to use during encoding. (Be advised that the switch is used for ASP files using the <% %> tags. If you use the <SCRIPT Language=VBScript> tag, the encoder reads the Language attribute to determine which language to encode into.)
/e ExtensionFile	Associates a file type to an input file. At the present time, the Script Encoder recognizes asp, asa, cdx, htm, html, js, sct, and vbs as valid script extensions.

Please be advised that these switches are used for advanced operations, particularly on the server side. If you want more details about them, refer to the Script Encoding documentation on the Microsoft Developer Network scripting site at msdn.microsoft.com/scripting.

For the most part, if you use the simple command line syntax and remember to set the Language attribute the <SCRIPT> tag when writing your scripts, you should have no problem encoding your work.

Working with Transactions

Way back in Chapter 1, "The Fundamentals of Distributed Computing Using ASP," we talked about the fact that a significant benefit of Active Server Page technology is that it makes it much easier to build and maintain a distributed application architecture. However, with regard to working with data writes to a database in a distributed environment, there are hurdles to overcome.

Let's imagine that we run a travel agency. Our agency provides a service that makes all the reservations needed to travel on a given day. Our customers give us their name and the day they want to travel. Our travel agency, Aristotle Travel, makes the necessary reservations on the airline, at the hotel, and with the caterer.

Airline, Hotel, and Caterer data live in separate databases. Being a modern travel agency, we are also excellent software developers. We decide to make an Active Server Page that writes the traveler's name and reservation date to the various databases within one function. Figure 11.15 illustrates our idea.

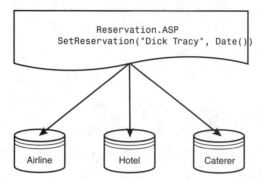

Figure 11.15: *A single transaction can write to many databases.*

When we run the code in production, we find that the Caterer database is unreliable. Sometimes it accepts a write and sometimes it fails. Needless to say, our data is all messed up. The Airline database has travelers who do not appear in the Caterer database. We have too many unhappy customers. We need a solution to our problem. It's in this type of situation that Microsoft Transaction Server comes into play.

Understanding MTS

When we combine data writes into a group, we have what we call a transaction. One transaction can have one or many data writes or deletes. With regard to our reservation transaction, we have created a mandate for ourselves that says if one reservation for a traveler cannot be made, none of the reservations can be made. It's an all or nothing scenario. You commit all the way or none of the way. This type of transaction is called a *two-phase commit*. In the eyes of our reservation system, a reservation is not successful unless all parties, Airline, Hotel, and Caterer, accept the reservation data.

Microsoft Transaction Server (MTS) is a mediation tool that sits between our code and the database. When we put it into action, MTS takes our requests to write and make deletes to a database and executes them on our behalf. If something goes wrong on a particular database, MTS performs a *rollback* on the other databases to which we have already modified data. A rollback resets all the data to the original state before we executed writes or deletes. In terms of data integrity, this is a valuable service (see Figure 11.16).

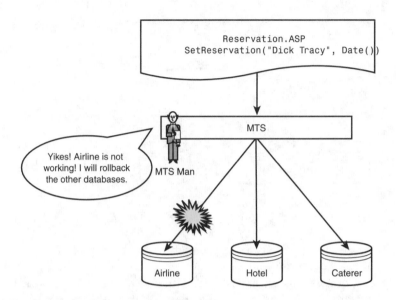

Figure 11.16: *MTS rolls back data if an error occurs in one of the data sources for a transaction.*

MTS provides other services. In a small data environment, you really don't experience many problems when multiple programs try to access the same database. However, if you have thousands of programs trying work with the same database, things get sticky. MTS acts like a traffic cop in situations such as this. It pools data connects and allocates them to the benefit of all parties needing to work with the database. This is a very valuable service, particularly in enterprises where performance time is critical.

Microsoft Transaction Server installs from the Microsoft NT 4.0 Option Pack. With regard to Windows 2000, Transaction Server has been integrated with COM as a new technology called COM+. The scope of our discussion in this chapter will use MTS under Windows NT 4.0. However, the code we use in this chapter can be used under Windows 2000.

Using Transactions in ASP

If you want your Active Server Page to be mediated by MTS, you must use the `<% @Transaction=Required %>` tag as the first line of your Active Server Page. The tag notifies MTS to keep track of any datasource connection made by the scripts in your page. If an error occurs in your script because of a datasource connection, your script uses with the `ObjectContext` object to facilitate MTS protection of the transaction. (You'll learn about the `ObjectContext` object in the next section.) Listing 11.4 shows you the Active Server Page code that writes reservations to the Airline, Hotel, and Caterer databases for our fictitious company, Aristotle Travel.

Listing 11.4: Using an ASP Script with MTS (`11asp06.asp`)

```
<% @Transaction =  Required %>
<HTML>
<HEAD>
<TITLE></TITLE>
</HEAD>
<BODY>

<%
'************************************
Function SetReservation(Traveler, TravelDate)
    Dim cn
    Dim cmd
    Dim strSQL

    'Create the data objects
    Set cn = CreateObject("ADODB.Connection")
    Set cmd = CreateObject("ADODB.Command")

    On Error Resume Next
    'Make a SQL INSERT statement in order to
    'create the reservation
    strSQL = "INSERT into Reservations (Name, TravelDate) "
    strSQL = strSQL & "VALUES ('"
    strSQL = strSQL & Traveler & "', #" & CStr(TravelDate)
    strSQL = strSQL & "#)"

    'Make a Hotel Reservation
    cn.ConnectionString = "DSN=Hotel"
    cn.Open
    cmd.CommandText = strSQL
    cmd.ActiveConnection = cn
    cmd.Execute
    cn.Close
    'Check to make sure the write was successful
    If Err Then
        SetReservation = False
        Exit Function
    End if

    'Make an Airline Reservation
    cn.ConnectionString = "DSN=AirLine"
    cn.Open
    cmd.CommandText = strSQL
    cmd.ActiveConnection = cn
    cmd.Execute
```

continues

Listing 11.4: continued

```
        cn.Close
        'Check to make sure the write was successful
        If Err Then
            SetReservation = False
            Exit Function
        End if

        'Make a Caterer Reservation
        cn.ConnectionString = "DSN=Caterer"
        cn.Open
        cmd.CommandText = strSQL
        cmd.ActiveConnection = cn
        cmd.Execute
        cn.Close
        'Check to make sure the write was successful
        If Err Then
            SetReservation = False
            Exit Function
        End if

        SetReservation = True
End Function
'*************************************

'MTS Event handlers
Sub OnTransactionCommit()
    Response.Write "Reservation Made!"
End Sub

Sub OnTransactionAbort()
    Response.Write "Reservation Failed!"
End Sub

'*******Script Entry Point******************
If SetReservation(Request.Form("Traveler"), Date) Then
    'If the write is good, tell MTS to commit it
    ObjectContext.SetComplete
Else
    'If the write is bad, tell MTS to do a rollback
    ObjectContext.SetAbort
End If

%>
</BODY>
</HTML>
```

The data access activity is isolated into a function SetReservations().
Notice that the data access is performed on three separate ODBC data-
sources, Airline, Hotel, and Caterer. (Remember that when you use only a
DSN entry in the ADO ConnectionString, the default OLE DB Provider is
ODBC.) In addition, notice that if any of the connections fail, the function
SetReservation() returns a value of False. At the entry point to the code
you'll notice that if SetReservation() returns True, the method called is
ObjectContext.SetComplete. If SetReservation() returns False,
ObjectContext.SetAbort is the method that is invoked. Let's take a moment
to look at the ObjectContext object in detail.

Working with the ObjectContext Object Methods

The ObjectContext object represents an Active Server Page under
Transaction Server. When you run an Active Server Page under Transaction
Server, MTS makes a shadow copy of the Active Server Page. This shadow
is called the context object. The *context object* keeps the original state infor-
mation about the page in case you need to do a rollback. In other words, the
ASP ObjectContext object represents the context object within MTS (see
Figure 11.17).

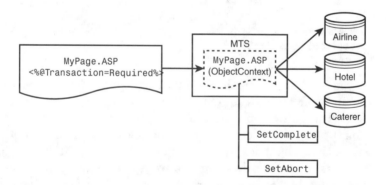

*Figure 11.17: The ObjectContext object is a shadow of your Active Server
Page under MTS.*

ObjectContext has two methods: SetComplete and SetAbort. You use the
SetComplete method to inform MTS that the data access activity in your
script was successful. MTS then commits all the data writes in the transaction to the database. Your script calls SetAbort when any of the data writes
in your script encounter an error and cannot be completed for some other
reason. For example, the Hotel database might report that there are no
vacancies and you cannot make a reservation. When you call SetAbort,
MTS performs a rollback.

Working with the `ObjectContext` Object Events

The `ObjectContext` object supports two event handlers:
`OnTransactionCommit()` and `OnTransactionAbort()`. The `OnTransactionCommit()`
event is fired when you call `ObjectContext.SetComplete`. And the event
`OnTransactionAbort` is fired when you call `ObjectContext.SetAbort`. Look
at the following code sample. It is from Listing 11.4 and shows calls
for the `SetComplete` and `SetAbort` methods as well as the use of the
`OnTransactionCommit` and `OnTransactionAbort` event handlers, which capture the method calls.

```
Sub OnTransactionCommit()
    Response.Write "Reservation Made!"
End Sub

Sub OnTransactionAbort()
    Response.Write "Reservation Failed!"
End Sub

'*******Script Entry Point*****************
If SetReservation(Request.Form("Traveler"), Date) Then
    'If the write is good, tell MTS to commit it
    ObjectContext.SetComplete
Else
    'If the write is bad, tell MTS to do a rollback
    ObjectContext.SetAbort
End If
```

As you read above, all the data writing activity for this page is isolated into
the function `SetReservation()`. If a data write fails, the function returns
`False`. If the function returns `False`, the code excerpt from Listing 11.4
calls the `ObjectContect.SetAbort` method to make MTS rollback the data
writes that took place in `SetReservation()`. In addition, the code in the
`OnTransactionAbort` event procedure is executed. In this case, a message is
sent using the `Response.Write` method to notify the calling client that no
reservation was made. If all the writes in `SetReservation()` were completed, the function returns `True`. Then `ObjectContect.SetComplete` is called
to commit the data writes. Also, the code in the `OnTransactionCommit` event
handler is executed.

More on Transaction Server

Transaction Server and the next generation technology COM+ are very
complex. We have just scratched the surface of its utility. Transaction
Server plays a large role in the distributed computing environment.
Transaction Server makes it possible for enterprises to have components
containing objects made in any language that supports COM, such as VB,
C++, Java, Delphi, and even ASP scripts, work together. These components

can live on any computer in the enterprise yet be unified for use by anyone, in any one program, anywhere. This means you can have different departments in an organization create COM components and let these components reside on computers in that department, but have the objects in the components used by other departments. In addition, a department can upgrade a component on a whim, yet have that upgrade be transparent to those using the component. This is serious technology for serious developers.

Transactions and COM+ really are the future of modern computing for Microsoft, particularly now that Internet development is so prevalent. Microsoft has gone to a great deal of trouble to make transaction support using COM+ a universal service under Windows 2000. In addition, Windows DNA (Distributed interNet Applications Architecture) is a major feature of the new development initiative from Microsoft. Windows DNA provides the ability to support transactions easily, transparently, and reliably. Microsoft is hard core about supporting transactions in a widely distributed environment. You might find it to your benefit to study MTS and COM+ in more detail.

What's Next

This chapter showed you technologies that help make your Web site and Web pages more secure. We demonstrated how to implement login access and authentication for your site. We demonstrated how to use the Script Encoder to protect your intellectual property in the scripts you write. Finally, we demonstrated how to use the `<% @Transaction %>` tag to enable your scripts to work with Microsoft Transaction Server.

The next chapter shows you how to use the technology we have been studying to create a Web page that contains a list of Web sites custom to each user.

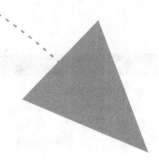

12

Creating a Custom User Page

It's time to build programs using ASP. Building real-world programs for real-world people is probably the best way to learn how to use ASP technology. Of course, you need to learn the fundamentals and theory of ASP to be able to put your knowledge to work. However, the real benefit of our labor is when we apply our knowledge to make useful, effective programs that help others and allow us to learn about those for whom we program.

In this chapter you will learn how to

- Use ASP with HTML Frames
- Use ASP to prepare client-side script
- Use Session variables to store user information
- Store user preferences in a database

Understanding the Topic Organizer

The program we are going to build is called the Topic Organizer. It is a utility that a teacher at the fictitious Aristotle Middle School can use to organize the URLs for various Web sites into a *portal* page. After these sites are organized into a common portal, he can share this page with his students and colleagues.

The Problem Domain

Even the simplest Internet technology is a challenge for a teacher unaccustomed to life in the digital age. The simple act of browsing the Net is difficult for the newcomer. However, after a teacher understands the power of having information at his fingertips, he is enthusiastic to use the Web in day-to-day classroom teaching.

Yet, there is a problem. After a teacher learns to surf, he is eager to collect Web sites to share with students. However, most times the teachers will list sites that they want to use in a classroom setting on a piece of paper. The teacher then copies the paper and distributes it to the students. The students end up typing the URLs on the list of paper into the browser for viewing.

Clearly, there is significant redundancy and waste of time in this process. The teacher types and surfs. The student types and surfs. In addition, the time it takes the teacher to create a list and distribute it to students and colleagues is too long. The teacher should be able to make a list of sites and the students should be able to access this list immediately. If the list is updated, the student should see these updates in a timely manner.

The Topic Organizer uses ASP in conjunction with the Internet Explorer browser and an ODBC datasource to implement a solution to these problems.

Features

The Topic Organizer allows an authenticated teacher to view Web site and add these Web sites to a custom list. Authentication is facilitated using a Login page into which a teacher enters a User ID and password. The UserID and Password are predefined by the Aristotle Middle School's system administrator in the ODBC datasource that the Topic Organizer uses.

An ancillary tool, the Topics Reader, allows students to select a particular teacher's Site List. Students use the Topics Reader to select and view sites from Site List. Figure 12.1 shows a screen shot of the Topic Organizer. Figure 12.2 shows a screen shot of the Topics Reader.

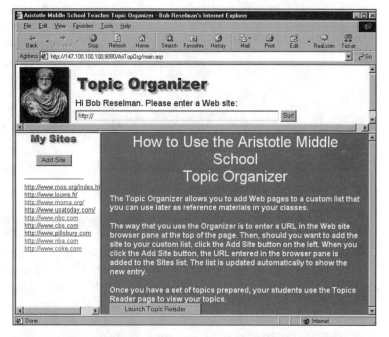

Figure 12.1: *The Aristotle Middle School Topic Organizer allows teachers to collect a list of Web sites to share with students and colleagues.*

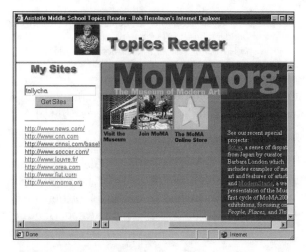

Figure 12.2: *The Topics Reader allows anyone to view the Web sites from a given teacher's list.*

A teacher uses the Topic Organizer by entering a URL into the Web site Browser Pane at the top of the page. Then, should the teacher want to add the site to his custom list, he clicks the Add Site button on the left. When the teacher clicks the Add Site button, the URL entered in the Browser Pane is added to the Sites list. The list is updated automatically to show the new entry (see Figure 12.1). The Topic Organizer requires that a teacher log in to a login page before he can gain access to the Topic Organizer.

Anyone can use the Topics Reader. A student or colleague enters the URL for the Reader page in his Web browser. Then, the user enters the Teacher Identification code for a given teacher in the TeacherID textbox on the Site List Pane on the left and clicks the Get Sites button. The Reader shows the current Site List for the designated teacher. The user clicks a URL on the Site List to view it in the Reader's Viewer Pane.

Architecture

The Topic Organizer and Topics Reader use ASP in conjunction with an Internet Explorer client and an ODBC datasource. Various Active Server Pages contain the logic that reads, writes, and graphically formats for presentation. The ODBC datasource stores the authentication data as well as the Site List information for each teacher. Internet Explorer provides presentation services and the client-side logic by which Web pages are selected from the Organizer/Reader Site List and viewed in the browser.

CAUTION

Be advised that this application uses Internet Explorer as the client browser. The client code for this application leverages the Document Object Model with Microsoft's version of JavaScript. Netscape Navigator encounters errors when running the client-side scripts for this application.

Each component of the overall application—Login, The Topic Organizer and the Topics Reader—is implemented using an associated Active Server Page (see Figure 12.3). The Login page (`default.asp`) uses component pages `default.asp` and `verify.asp`. The `default.asp` login page has the `<INPUT>` elements into which the user enters a UserID and password. The page `verify.asp` contains the validation logic that the application uses to verify UserID and password authenticity. If a user is authentic, he is given access to the Topic Organizer's component page, `main.asp`. Should the UserID and password be invalid, the user is fed an error page, `LogonErr.asp`.

Both the Topic Organizer and Topics Reader pages use HTML frames. Each page contains three frames. These frames have the HTML names `services` that correspond to the Site List Pane; `browser`, which corresponds to the Browser Pane; and `viewer`, which corresponds to the View Pane.

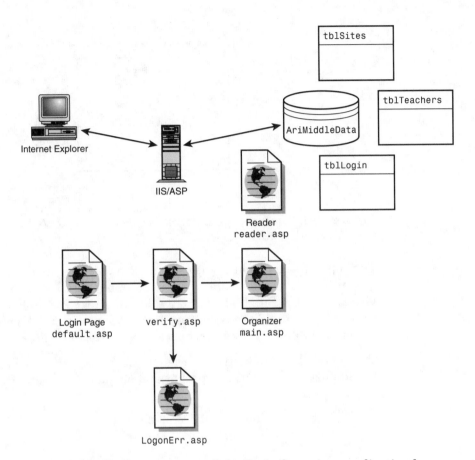

Figure 12.3: *Each component of the Topic Organizer application has a dedicated Active Server Page.*

With regard to the Topic Organizer component, the Site List Pane allows the teacher to add sites to his list and view sites already on the list. The Browser Pane contains a URL textbox into which a teacher enters a URL to view. The Viewer Pane shows a Web page that a teacher enters in the Browser Pane or selects from the Sites List Pane (see Figure 12.4). The Active Server Page, addSite.asp, is associated with the Site List Pane frame. This page contains the code that adds a URL to the teacher's Web site list and updates the list. The Browser Pane has an associated Active Server Page, getURL.asp. This page contains the logic that displays into the Viewer Pane's URL textbox the Web page that's entered by the teacher.

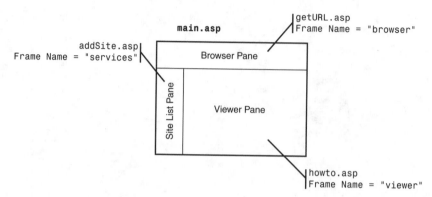

Figure 12.4: *The component pages use <FRAME> elements to divide the page into three independent regions.*

The Topics Reader component uses the Browser Pane to display a logo graphic only. The textbox in which users enter URLs is absent. Users can visit sites in the Site List Pane only. The Site List Pane allows users to select sites on the Site List to view in the Viewer Pane. The ability to add sites to the Site List is not part of the Topics Reader feature set.

The Service List Pane uses the readSite.asp Active Server Page to retrieve the site list for a particular teacher and populate the contents of the list into the pane.

Figure 12.5 shows the overall architecture, including the Login, Topic Organizer, and Topics Reader components.

Working with Frames and Frame Security

Both the Topic Organizer and Topics Reader use HTML <FRAME> elements to divide the Web page into three independent regions, each containing a component page as previously described. The reason that we use <FRAME> elements is we can view a Web page in one <FRAME> without having to refresh the Web pages in the other <FRAME> elements. This allows the Site Pane and Browser Pane to remain independent anchors. Using FRAME elements allows us to keep a portion of the Organizer Web page stationary in one FRAME as content changes in another FRAME.

Listing 12.1 shows the HTML for the Topic Organizer page, main.asp. Notice that the page uses a <FRAMESET> embedded within a <FRAMESET> to achieve the three-region <FRAME> layout. This is a common practice.

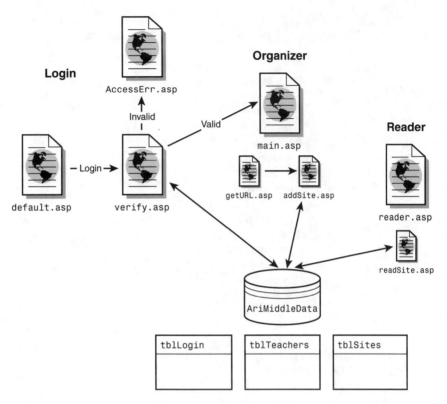

Figure 12.5: *The Topic Organizer architecture uses Active Server Pages in conjunction with an ODBC datasource.*

Listing 12.1: Using FRAME Elements (12asp01.asp/main.asp)

```
<%
'=====================================
'Page Name: main.ASP
'Purpose: Main page for the Topic
'Organizer.
'=====================================

'Security check
If Session("IsGoodUser") = False Then
    Response.Redirect Application("AccessErrFile")
  End If
%>

<HTML>
<HEAD>
```

continues

Listing 12.1: continued

```
<TITLE>Aristotle Middle School Topic Organizer</TITLE>
</HEAD>

<FRAMESET FRAMEBORDER="1"
          FRAMESPACING="0"
          ROWS="140,*">
   <FRAME MARGINWIDTH="0"
          MARGINHEIGHT="0"
          SRC="getURL.asp"
          NAME="browser">
   <FRAMESET FRAMEBORDER="1"
             FRAMESPACING="0"
             COLS="180,*">
      <FRAME MARGINWIDTH="18"
             MARGINHEIGHT="0"
             SRC="addSite.asp"
             NAME="services">
      <FRAME MARGINWIDTH="18"
             MARGINHEIGHT="0"
             SRC="howto.asp"
             NAME="viewer">
   </FRAMESET>
</FRAMESET>
<BODY>

</BODY>
</HTML>)
```

TIP

For a complete listing and discussion of all the HTML including <FRAME> and <FRAMESET> elements, visit the Microsoft Developer Network HTML Reference Web site at http://msdn.microsoft.com/workshop/author/html/reference/elements. asp#ie40_htmlref.

As you previously read, using <FRAME> elements allows us to keep a portion of the Organizer Web page stationary in one <FRAME> while content changes in another <FRAME>. This means we keep a list of Web sites in the Site List Pane and have that list call pages that will appear in the View Pane independently. You use the Target attribute of an <A HREF> tag to have content called in one <FRAME> yet appear in another <FRAME>. For example, if you want to write a hypertext jump to the Web site http://www.mcp.com from a <FRAME Name="service"> and targeted to appear in a <FRAME Name="viewer">, you write

```
<A HREF="http://www.mcp.com" TARGET="viewer"> Click me to go to MCP.COM </A>
into a Web page that is resident in <FRAME Name="service">.
```

The good news about using <FRAME> elements in our page is that it's going to allow us to keep a stationary Site List to which we can add sites or select sites. The bad news about using <FRAME> elements is that they add a level of coding difficulty in terms of being able to keep track of the Web page that is in a <FRAME> at any given time. The problem is the security structure built into the Document Object Model. The DOM does not permit you to write a script that can determine the URL of a Web page in another <FRAME> element, unless the pages in both <FRAME> elements are from the same Web site. This means that if the teacher loads a Web page for PBS.org into the Viewer Pane, script in the Site List Pane cannot determine the URL in the Viewer Pane. This is because the Web Page in the Site List Pane is from our Web site, the Aristotle Middle School Web site, and the page in the Viewer Pane is from PBS.org. These are two different sites and PBS.org is considered outside our domain.

The code in Listing 12.2 shows you client-side JavaScript that uses the DOM to access the location.href property of the document object to report the URL of a page. Figure 12.5 shows the output of the code.

EXAMPLE

Listing 12.2: Using the location.href Property of the Document Object (12asp02.asp)

```
<HTML>
<HEAD>
<TITLE></TITLE>
<SCRIPT ID=clientEventHandlersJS LANGUAGE=javascript>
<!—

function btnURL_onclick() {
    alert(document.location.href);
}

//—>
</SCRIPT>
</HEAD>
<BODY>
<INPUT type="button"
       value="Click Me to Find the URL"
       name=btnURL
       LANGUAGE=javascript
       onclick="return btnURL_onclick()">
<P> </P>

</BODY>
</HTML>
```

OUTPUT

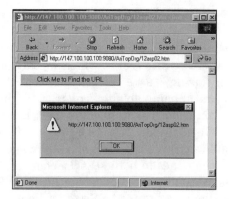

Figure 12.6: *You can use the DOM to report the URL of your Web page.*

As you read previously, the DOM will not let you go peeking from one
<FRAME> into another <FRAME> element to get a URL. Listing 12.3 shows you
a page that has two <FRAME> elements displayed horizontally. The top FRAME
contains Listing 12.4. Listing 12.4 shows you the code that you would use
to try to determine the URL of a page in another <FRAME> element. Figure
12.7 shows you the error the DOM fires.

EXAMPLE

Listing 12.3: Displaying a FRAMESET Horizontally by Using the ROWS Attribute (12asp03.asp)

```
<HTML>
<HEAD>
<TITLE>Things the DOM won't let you do</TITLE>
</HEAD>

    <FRAMESET FRAMEBORDER="1"
              FRAMESPACING="0"
              ROWS="60,*">
        <FRAME MARGINWIDTH="18"
               MARGINHEIGHT="0"
               SRC="12asp04.htm"
               NAME="services">
        <FRAME MARGINWIDTH="18"
               MARGINHEIGHT="0"
               SRC="http://www.mcp.com"
               NAME="viewer">
    </FRAMESET>
<BODY>
</BODY>
</HTML>
```

EXAMPLE

Listing 12.4: Using the `frames` Collection of the `parent` Object (12asp04.asp)

```
<HTML>
<HEAD>
<TITLE></TITLE>
<SCRIPT ID=clientEventHandlersJS LANGUAGE=javascript>
<!--

function btnURL_onclick() {
    alert(parent.frames("viewer").location.href);
}
//-->
</SCRIPT>
</HEAD>
<BODY bgcolor=RED>
<INPUT type="button"
        value="Click Me to Find the URL in another <FRAME>"
        name=btnURL
        LANGUAGE=javascript
        onclick="return btnURL_onclick()">
<BR>
<FONT color=white size=4 face=Arial>
I AM NOT MCP
</FONT>
</BODY>
</HTML>
```

OUTPUT

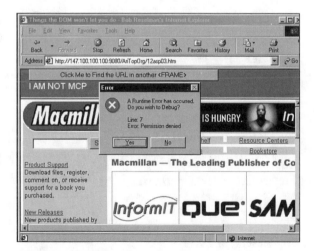

Figure 12.7: *You cannot access the URL of a* `<FRAME>` *element's page from within another* `<FRAME>` *element.*

So why are we trying to determine URLs between <FRAME> elements? Remember that the idea behind the Topic Organizer is that a teacher enters a URL in the text box of the Browser Pane to have a Web site displayed in the Viewer Pane. Having the Browser Pane request a page and having that page be displayed in the Viewer Pane is not a problem. However, after the Web page is in the Viewer Pane, the Site List pane cannot take a peek in the <FRAME> of the Viewer Pane to determine the URL of the page it is displaying. The Site List Pane needs to know the URL of the page in the Viewer Pane to add the URL to the teacher's Site List. There are a few ways to solve this problem. We will look at one of them later in this chapter. First let's review the data structures that the Login, Organizer, and Reader component pages use.

Structuring Data

All the component pages of the Topic Organizer use tables in the ODBC datasource `AriMiddleData`. The datasource for the entire application is defined as an Application-level variable in the `Global.ASA` (see Listing 12.5). The datasource is an Access database configured to run under ODBC. The Access database file resides on the same computer as Internet Information Server.

EXAMPLE

Listing 12.5: `Global.ASA` with Application-Level Variables (`12asp05.asp/Global.ASA`)

```
<SCRIPT LANGUAGE=vbscript RUNAT=Server>
'*********************
'Filename: Global.ASA
'Application: Aristotle Topic Organizer
'
'Programmer: Bob Reselman
'
'Copyright 2000 Macmillan Computer Publishing
'*********************
Sub Application_OnStart()
    Application("SiteURL") = "http://www.mySite.com/AriTopOrg"
    Application("DBSource") = "AriMiddleData"
    Application("LogonErrFile") = "LogonErr.asp"
    Application("AccessErrFile") = "AccessErr.asp"
End Sub

Sub Session_OnStart()
    Session("IsGoodUser") = False
    Session("FirstName") = ""
    Session("LastName") = ""
    Session("UserID") = ""
End Sub
```

```
Sub Application_OnEnd()

End Sub
Sub Session_OnEnd()
    Session.Abandon
End Sub
</SCRIPT>
```

The tables in the datasource that the component pages use are tblLogin, tblTeachers, and tblSites (see Figure 12.8). The Login page (*default.asp*) uses the tblLogin table for authentication. The tblLogin table contains the TeacherID—which in this case is the same as LoginID—and the password information. The table, tblTeachers—which is used to populate session-level variables Session("FirstName) and Session("LastName")—contains a list of TeacherID's with the first name and last name of a given teacher. The table tblSites keeps a list of the TeacherIDs and URLs for each site selection. This table is used by the pages addSite.asp and readSite.asp. Figure 12.8 shows these tables with fields.

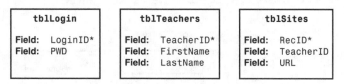

Figure 12.8: The tables and fields used by the component pages of the Topic Organizer relate to each other using key fields. Key fields are noted with an asterisk.

Reading Data Between <FRAME> Elements

The solution to the problem of determining the current URL in the Viewer Pane from the Site List pane is to use the data in the Browser Pane's URL text box. As you read previously, the DOM does not allow us to determine the current URL of a page in the Viewer Pane frame by peeking into the document object's location.href property from the Site List Pane. However, the DOM does permit us to peek into the Browser Pane's text box from another <FRAME> element, provided both pages come from the same ASP Application or Web Site. The Browser Pane's text box, named MyURL, contains the URL of the page that is displayed in the Viewer Pane. (Remember that the user enters the URL in the Browser Pane and then clicks the Surf button to display the requested Web page in the Viewer Pane.) If we want to know the contents of the Viewer Pane, all we need to do is query the MyUrl text box in the Browser Pane for its value.

To work between <FRAME> elements to determine the value entered in a textbox of a Web page, we write the following code in the <FRAME> element, making the query to the other <FRAME>.

```
str = parent.frames.item(0).MyForm.MyURL.value
```

Where

parent is the object that contains all the frames, in this case the window object.

frames is the collection of <FRAME> elements in a given window.

item (indexNum) is the a given frame/document in the frames collection.

MyForm is the form object that contains the text box element.

MyURL is the name of a given text box element.

value is the text entered in the text box element.

We invoke this code in a piece of client script that's in the Web page of the Site List Pane. Figure 12.9 illustrates this concept.

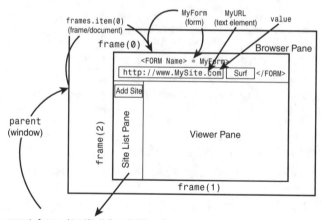

```
str = parent.frames.item(0).MyForm.MyURL.value
The value of str is http://www.MySite.com.
```

Figure 12.9: *The script in the Web page in the Topic Organizer's Site List Pane looks in the text element in the Browser Pane frame for the current URL value.*

Implementing the Topic Organizer

Now that we've discussed the architecture we are going to use to make the application, let's create the site. The first thing we need to create is the Login Page.

Creating the Login Page

The Login page as shown in Figure 12.10 allows a teacher access the Topic Organizer. The UserID and password have been entered in the AriMiddleData datasource previously by the system administrator. Listing 12.6 shows the Active Server Page (default.asp) for the Login page. Note that illustration of the Login page in Figure 12.10 exposes the borders of the tables in the Login page. Showing the borders is done to make the HTML in Listing 12.6 easier to understand. The code within the listing has the tables' Border attribute set to zero, which means show no borders.

EXAMPLE

Listing 12.6: The Login Page that Submits Verification Data (12asp06.asp/default.asp)

```
<%
'======================================
'Page Name: default.ASP
'Purpose: Allows a user to login
'          to the site. The ASP
'          verify.asp contains the
'          verification logic.
'======================================


'Clean out the session
'A new login indicates a new user
Session.Abandon %>

<HTML>
<HEAD>
<TITLE></TITLE>
</HEAD>
<BODY>
<FORM NAME=MyForm
      Method=Post
      Action=<%=Application("SiteURL")& "/verify.asp"%>>
<TABLE Border=0>
<TR><TD><IMG SRC="smbustb.gif"></TD>
<TD><IMG SRC="title.gif"><BR>
<TABLE Border=0>


<TR>
<TD><FONT SIZE=4 Face=ARIAL Color=#000080>
UserID: </FONT></TD>
<TD><FONT SIZE=4 Face=ARIAL Color=#000080>
Password:</FONT></TD></TR>
  <TR><TD><INPUT   Name=LoginID></TD>
```

continues

Listing 12.6: continued

```
<TD><INPUT Type=Password Name=PWD></TD>
</TR>
<TR><TD>
<INPUT type="submit" value="Logon"   name=submit1>
</TD></TR>
</TABLE>
</TD>
</TR>
</TABLE>
</FORM>
</BODY>
</HTML>
```

OUTPUT

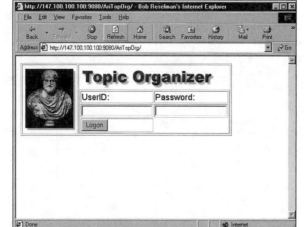

Figure 12.10: *The default page for the site requires that the user login.*

Verifying a Login

After the user logs in, the data in the Login page is submitted to the Active Server Page, `verify.asp`, which contains the logic that confirms whether the password provided by the user matches the one stored in the application's database. The logic and the data access code in this page are very similar to the logic you saw in the Login page developed in Chapter 11, "Working with Security and Transactions."

✔ For information about creating Login pages, see the section in Chapter 11 titled, "Creating a Simple Login Page," page 283.

Listing 12.7 shows the Active Server Page, `verify.asp`.

EXAMPLE

Listing 12.7: Using the Application's Database to Authenticate Users (12asp07.asp/verify.asp)

```
<%
'=======================================
'Page Name: verify.ASP
'Purpose: Checks to make sure that user
'          has submitted a valid UserID]
'          and password. If the user is
'          authenticated, then this page
'          redirects to the Main page,
'          Main.ASP.
'=======================================


Sub GetNames(LoginID, FirstName, LastName)
'**************************
'
'Parameters: LoginID, A string that indicates the
'                       LoginID of the User
'
'            FirstName, The teacher's first name, a retuned value
'
'            Last Name, The teacher's last name, a retuned
'                        value
'
'Return:    None
'
'Remarks:   This method sub returns back the a teacher's
'            First Name and Last name from the Ari Middle
'            School datasource. The sub passes in the
'            LoginID.
'            The LoginID corresponds to the TeacherID field in
'            the datasource. The datasource fields are
'            FirstName and LastName. The field values
'            are passed out through the FirstName
'            and LastName parameters of the Sub.
'
'
'Programmer: Bob Reselman
'Copyright: 2000
'
'History: Created 1/7/2000
'
'**************************
        Dim cn 'Connection var
        Dim rs 'Recordset var
        Dim strSQL 'SQL Statement var
        Dim strCn 'Connection String var
```

continues

Listing 12.7: continued

```
    'Create a Connection Object
    Set cn = CreateObject("ADODB.Connection")
    Set rs = CreateObject("ADODB.Recordset")
    'Make the SQL statement that returns
    'the user with password, should one exist
    strSQL = "SELECT * FROM tblTeachers WHERE TeacherID = '"
    strSQL = strSQL & LoginID & "'"

    'Set error trappong
  'On Error Resume Next
    'Open the Connection
    cn.ConnectionString = "DSN=" & Application("DBSource")
    cn.Open
    If Err Then Exit Sub

    'Get the user from the DB
    rs.Open strSQL, cn
    If Err Then Exit Sub

    'This checks to make sure if no
    'recordset was returned
    MyErr = rs("FirstName")
    If err then
        Exit Sub
    End if
    'Wire up the return fields
    FirstName = rs("FirstName")
    LastName = rs("LastName")

    'Leave town
    rs.Close
    cn.Close
End Sub


Function Login(LoginID, Password)
'***************************
'
'Parameters: LoginID  A String that indicates the
'                        LoginID of the User
'
'            Password A String that indicates the
'                        the password to be validated agains
'                        the LoginID
'
'Return:    True,  if the LoginID and Password coincide
'
```

```
'Remarks:    This method uses data kept in an external
'            database to do LoginID/Password validation.
'            The function retrieves a record from the
'            Access file, indicated by the application
'            variable, Application("DBSource").
'            The record is retrieved according to the
'            LoginID. If a record is retrieved and if
'            the Login ID and Password match up, the
'            method returns True.
'
'Programmer: Bob Reselman
'Copyright: 1999
'
'History: Created 11/28/1999
'
'***************************


    Dim cn 'Connection var
    Dim rs 'Recordset var
    Dim strSQL 'SQL Statement var
    Dim strCn 'Connection String var

    'Create a Connection Object
    Set cn = CreateObject("ADODB.Connection")
    Set rs = CreateObject("ADODB.Recordset")
    'Make the SQL statement that returns
    'the user with password, should one exist
    strSQL = "SELECT * FROM tblLogin WHERE LoginName = '"
    strSQL = strSQL & LoginID & "'"

    'Set error trappong
    On Error Resume Next
    'Open the Connection
    cn.ConnectionString = "DSN=" & Application("DBSource")

    cn.Open
    If Err Then Exit Function

    'Get the user from the DB
    rs.Open strSQL, cn
    If Err Then Exit Function

    'This checks to make sure if no
    'recordset was returned
    MyErr = rs("PWD")
    If err then
```

continues

Listing 12.7: continued

```
        Exit Function
    End if

    'If the passwords match up, return TRUE
    If rs("PWD") = Password Then
        Login = True
    Else
        Login = False
    End If
    'Leave town
    rs.Close
    cn.Close
End Function
'=========Entry Point============
If Login(Request.Form("LoginID"), Request.Form("PWD")) Then
    'Set a session level var for the UserID
    Session("UserID") = Request.Form("LoginID")

    Dim FirstName
    Dim LastName
    'Get the teachers First Name and Last Name
    GetNames Session("UserID"), FirstName, LastName

    'Set a session level var for the FirstName and LastName
    If FirstName <> "" Then Session("FirstName") = FirstName
    If LastName <> "" Then Session("LastName") = LastName
    'If the login data is good, redirect the visitor
    'to the site's content directory
    Session("IsGoodUser") = True
    Response.Redirect "main.asp"
Else
    'Report a logon error.
    Response.Redirect Application("LogonErrFile")
End If
%>
```

The overall logic for the page is that if the user is authentic, he is allowed access to the Topic Organizer page. However, if the user's UserID or password are not valid, he is redirected to the page indicated by the Application-level variable, Application("LogonErrFile"). In addition, if the user is valid, a return trip is made to the database using the GetNames() function. The purpose of the return trip is to get the first and last name of the teacher and assign this information to the Session-level variables, Session("FirstName") and Session("Last Name"). These Session-level variables are used in the Browser Pane page (getURL.asp) to provide acknowledgement to the teacher that the Topic Organizer is indeed displaying his custom data (refer to Figure 12.1).

Getting and Displaying a URL

The Topic Organizer allows the user to enter a URL in the text element of the Browser Pane. After a URL is entered in the text element, the user clicks the Surf button to have the page displayed. The Active Server Page associated with the Browser Pane is getURL.asp. The Active Server Page getURL.asp contains the HTML that displays the URL text element, MyURL, and the Surf button. Also, the Active Server Page contains the event handler code for the onclick() event for the Surf button. The code is written in client-side JavaScript. When the user clicks the Surf button, the onclick() event handler is called. The code in the onclick() event handler displays in the Viewer Pane the Web page that corresponds to the URL entered in the text element. Listing 12.8 shows the HTML and client side JavaScript for the Active Server Page, getURL.asp.

EXAMPLE

Listing 12.8: Displaying the Browser Pane's URL Entry in the Viewer Pane (12asp8.asp/getURL.asp)

```
<%
'=====================================
'Page Name: getURL.asp
'Purpose: Reads the URL in the text element,
'         then asks the View Pane to
'         display the URL contents in
'         its window.
'=====================================


'Security check
If Session("IsGoodUser") = False Then
    Response.Redirect Application("AccessErrFile")
  End If
%>


<HTML>
<HEAD>
<TITLE>Aristotle Middle School Topic Organizer</TITLE>

<SCRIPT ID=clientEventHandlersJS LANGUAGE=javascript>
<!—
//Enter the new Web site
function btnSurf_onclick() {
    //Get the URL from textbox
    TheURL = document.MyForm.MyURL.value
    //Make sure it is not empty
    if(TheURL==""){
        alert("You must enter a valid URL: http://www.sitename.com");
        return false;
        }
```

continues

Listing 12.8: continued

```
      //Make sure that it is not the init phrase
      if (TheURL=="Enter a Web Site"){
        alert("You must enter a valid URL: http://www.sitename.com");
        return false;
        }
      //If all is good, go tell the viewer pane to
      //display the URL
      parent.frames("viewer").location.href=TheURL
}
//-->
</SCRIPT>
</HEAD>

<BODY>
<TABLE Border=0>
<TR><TD><IMG SRC="smbustb.gif"></TD>
<TD><IMG SRC="title.gif"><BR>
<TABLE Border=0>
<FORM NAME=MyForm>
<TR>
<TD><FONT SIZE=4 Face=ARIAL Color=#000080>
Please enter a Web site: </FONT></TD></TR>
<TR><TD><INPUT Size=60 Name=MyURL Value="Enter a Web Site"></TD>
<TD>

</TD>
<TD><INPUT type="button"
          value="Surf"
          name=btnSurf
          LANGUAGE=javascript
          onclick="return btnSurf_onclick()">
</TR>
</FORM>
</TABLE>
</TD>
</TR>
</TABLE>

</BODY>
</HTML>
```

The important piece of code is shown below. This client-side code asks the View Pane to display the Web page associated with the URL entered. This code is from the onclick() event handler listed previously. The code works with the location.href property to assign the requested URL as the document object in <FRAME Name="viewer" element. These objects are part of the DOM.

```
TheURL = document.MyForm.MyURL.value
    .
    .
    .

//display the URL
parent.frames("viewer").location.href=TheURL
```

Adding a Site to the Site List

Now that we have the URL entry and viewing features for the Topic Organizer implemented, lets look at how we add a site to a teacher's Site List. Adding a site to the Site List is where we really put ASP to use.

The way the Site List Pane works is that the Pane's <FRAME> element loads in the addSite.asp Active Server Page upon initialization. The addSite.asp page has server-side script that executes a database lookup for existing sites for a given teacher. The lookup is done using UserID, (the LoginID field in the table, tblLogin), as the lookup criteria. The script gets the value of the UserID from the Session-level variable, Session("UserID"). (The Session-level variable, Session("UserID") is assigned a value during the login process.) After the lookup takes place, the list of sites is returned as an ADO Recordset object. The server-side code traverses the Recordset object and wraps each URL in a teacher's list in a set of <A HREF=…></A> tags. Each of these tags has the Viewer Pane's <FRAME> element, viewer assigned as the Target= attribute. Wrapping the list items in these hyper-text tags causes the URL to be displayed in the Viewer Pane when the user clicks on the list item in the Site List Pane. In addition, the page contains an HTML <FORM>, an <INPUT> element of type Hidden and a Submit button with associated client-side script that traps the Submit event. The Hidden element is named TheURL. The Hidden element plays a very important role in the data submission process.

Before we go on with more details, please look at the contents of the addSite.asp page in Listing 12.9.

EXAMPLE

Listing 12.9: Server-Side Code Adding a Site to a Database (12asp9.asp/addSite.asp)

```
<%
'=====================================
'Page Name: addSite.ASP
'Purpose: Adds the site that is entered
'         in the browser pane text box
'         to the the application's
'         datasources.
'=====================================
%>
<%
```

continues

Listing 12.9: continued

```
'Security Check
If Session("IsGoodUser") = False Then
    Response.Redirect Application("AccessErrFile")
End If
%>


<%


Function GetSites(UserID)
'**************************
'
'Parameters: UserID A String that corresponds to the
'                   TeacherID of the User


'Return:     A string of HTML that contains a list of HREFs
'                for the teachers's selected sites
'
'Remarks:    This function returns a string of HTML that
'                contains valud <A HREF> tags. The tags are a
'                list of URLS that the teachers added to his or
'                her organizer previously.
'
'Programmer: Bob Reselman
'Copyright: 2000
'
'History: Created 1/7/2000
'
'**************************
    Dim cn 'Connection var
    Dim rs 'Recordset var
    Dim strSQL 'SQL Statement var
    Dim strHRef 'HRef string var
    Dim strBuffer 'Buffer var
    Dim dq

    dq = chr(34) 'quote mark for HTML emulation purposes

    'Create a Connection Object
    Set cn = CreateObject("ADODB.Connection")
    Set rs = CreateObject("ADODB.Recordset")
    'Make the SQL statement that returns
    'the user with password, should one exist
    strSQL = "SELECT * FROM tblSites WHERE TeacherID = '"
    strSQL = strSQL & UserID & "'"
```

```
        'Set error trappong
        On Error Resume Next
        'Open the Connection
        cn.ConnectionString = "DSN=" & Application("DBSource")
        cn.Open
        If Err Then Exit Function
        'Get the user from the DB
        rs.ActiveConnection = cn
        rs.Open strSQL

        If Err Then Exit Function

        'This checks to make sure if no
        'recordset was returned
        MyErr = rs("TeacherID")
        If err then
            Exit Function
        End if
        'Let's make the <HRrefs> containing all the
        'records in the recordset.
        While Not rs.EOF
            'Make a string of the format
            '<A HREF="HTTP://www.site.com">http://www.site.com</A>
            strBuffer = "<A HREF=" & dq & rs("URL") & dq
            strBuffer = strBuffer & " Target=" & dq & "viewer" & dq & ">"
            strBuffer = strBuffer & rs("URL") & "</A><BR>" & vbCrlf
            'Contatenate the buffer onto the HRef var
            strHRef = strHRef & strBuffer
            rs.MoveNext
        Wend

        'Leave town
        rs.Close
        cn.Close
        GetSites = strHRef
End Function

Function AddSite(UserID, URL)
'**************************
'
'Parameters: UserID, A String that corresponds to the
'              TeacherID of the User
'
'              URL, The URL to add to the teacher's list
'
```

continues

Listing 12.9: continued

```
'Return:     True if successful
'
'Remarks:    The function adds a URL to the table,
'            tblSites in the Ari Middle School datasource
'
'Programmer: Bob Reselman
'Copyright: 2000
'
'History: Created 1/7/2000
'
'***************************
    Dim cn 'Connection var
    Dim cmd 'Command object
    Dim strSQL 'SQL Statement var

    'Create a Connection Object
    Set cn = CreateObject("ADODB.Connection")
    Set cmd = CreateObject("ADODB.Command")
    'Use the SQL INSERT clause to create a
    'record.
    strSQL = "INSERT INTO tblSites (TeacherID, URL)"
    strSQL = strSQL & " VALUES"
    strSQL = strSQL & " ('" & UserID & "', '" & URL & "')"
    'Set the SQL statement to the Command object.
    cmd.CommandText = strSQL
    'Set error trapping
    On Error Resume Next
    'Open the Connection
    cn.ConnectionString = "DSN=" & Application("DBSource")
    cn.Open
    If Err then Exit Function
    'Set an connection to the Command object
    cmd.ActiveConnection = cn
    'Run the command
    cmd.Execute
    If Err then Exit Function
    'Close up shop
    cn.close
    'If you get to here, life is good!
    AddSite = True
End Function


'===========ENTRY POINT================
%>
<HTML>
```

```
<HEAD></HEAD>
<TITLE></TITLE>
<SCRIPT ID=clientEventHandlersJS LANGUAGE=javascript>
<!—
function MyForm_onsubmit() {
    if (parent.frames.item(0).MyForm.MyURL.value==
        "Enter a Web Site"){
        return false;
    }
    //Get the value from the Browser <FRAME> text element
    //and assign it to the hidden element
    document.MyForm.TheURL.value =
            parent.frames.item(0).MyForm.MyURL.value;
}

//—>
</SCRIPT>
<BODY>


<FONT Face=Arial size=3 color=navy>
</FONT>
<CENTER>
<P>
<Img Src=sites.gif><BR>

<Form name=MyForm
      method="post"
      action="<%=Application("SiteURL") & "/addSite.asp"%>"
      LANGUAGE=javascript
      onsubmit="return MyForm_onsubmit()">

<INPUT Type=Hidden Name=TheURL value="">
<INPUT type="submit" value="Add Site" id=submit1 name=submit1>
</FORM>

</CENTER>
<HR>
<FONT Face=Arial size=2 color=navy>
<%

'Make sure that there is a URL form field.
'Also, make sure that if there is a URL, it is a
'viable URL. (Use the VBScript Instr() function.)
'If it doesn't have at least an "HTTP://,
'you know that you have a problem.
```

continues

Listing 12.9: continued

```
  If Request.Form("TheURL") <> "" _
  AND Instr(1, Request.Form("TheURL"), "http://", 1) <> 0 Then
  'Call the addSite method to add a site
   If addSite(Session("UserID"), Request.Form("TheURL")) then
        Response.Write GetSites(Session("UserID"))
   Else
        'Send an error message if the addSite
        'function fails.
        Response.Write "Loading Error"
   End If
Else
   'If there in no URL form field, this means this
   'Is a brand new session. Don't add any sites.
   Response.Write GetSites(Session("UserID"))
End If

%>
</FONT></BODY></HTML>
```

Let's examine the client-side scripting first. When a teacher wants to add a site to his list, he clicks the Add Site button. The Add Site button is a Submit button in disguise. When the teacher clicks the Submit button, a Submit event is fired. This event is captured by the onsubmit() event procedure. The reason we are capturing the Submit event is that we need to assign the URL in the Browser Pane to the Hidden element, TheURL, so that it might be submitted on to the Internet Server, too.

Let's look at the onsubmit() event procedure.

```
<SCRIPT ID=clientEventHandlersJS LANGUAGE=javascript>
<!--
function MyForm_onsubmit() {
    if (parent.frames.item(0).MyForm.MyURL.value==
        "Enter a Web Site"){
        return false;
    }
    //Get the value from the Browser <FRAME> text element
    //and assign it to the hidden element
    document.MyForm.TheURL.value =
            parent.frames.item(0).MyForm.MyURL.value;
}
//-->
</SCRIPT>
```

The line

```
document.MyForm.TheURL.value
```

refers to the Hidden element named, TheURL, which is a child element of the <FORM> named MyForm.

The line

```
parent.frames.item(0).MyForm.MyURL.value
```

refers to the text element in the Browser Pane <FRAME>. In this instance, we are referring to the <FRAME> element by its index number with the DOM frames collection and not its string name.

Thus, when the teacher clicks the Add Site (Submit) button, the code looks into the text element in the Browser Pane to get the current URL. This value is then assigned to the Hidden element. The reason we use an HTML Hidden element is that it is an easy way to create a value that is sent on to the Internet Server during a form submission. When the Submit button is clicked, the data in the Hidden element is submitted to the Internet Server by default. On the server side, the Hidden element shows in the Request object's form collection as Request.Form("TheURL").

NOTE

If you want to abort a form submission using the onsubmit() event procedure under JavaScript, have the onsubmit() event procedure return False.

CAUTION

Remember, JavaScript is case sensitive. VBScript is not.

The onsubmit() event procedure traps the form submission right before data gets sent to the server, which is why we tack on value to the Hidden element at that point. After the onsubmit() event procedure code runs its course, the browser submits the data to the addSite.asp page on the server. If you think this process looks like a recursive call in that the page on the client side is calling itself back on the server, you are right. The addSite.asp page holds both the client-side and server-side processing for the overall interaction.

Let's move back over to the server side to see how a site is added to the Site List and how the Site List retrieval is performed. The server-side script contains two functions. The function AddSite(UserID, URL) encapsulates the process of adding a site to the table in the datasource that stores the site lists for given teachers. The function GetSites(UserID) retrieves the sites for a given teacher from the datasource and returns these sites as a string of HTML in which each site is wrapped in a set of <A HREF></A> tags, as we discussed previously.

The server-side logic from the entry point for the page is straightforward. The script checks to see if there is an element MyURL in the Request.Form collection. If there is, and if the collection element contains at least the characters http:// indicating a reasonable probability that the string is a viable URL, the functions AddSite and GetSites are called. If there is no URL present in the MyURL element, or one that is poorly formed, this means that this is either the initial call to the page or that the URL that was submitted is not valid. In this case, the function AddSite is not called. Figure 12.11 illustrates this logic.

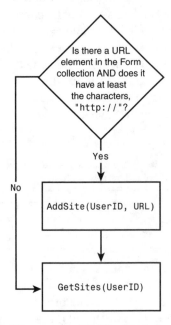

Figure 12.11: The high-level logic of the addSite.asp server-side script.

Providing a Simple Help System

With regard to the Organizer, we have implemented the functionality to display a URL and to list and select a teacher's implemented sites. The last thing we need to provide is a help system that teaches the user how to use the application. Good programs provide good help systems. Not all help systems need to be long and utterly exhaustive. For an application with this small a scope, all a good help system needs to provide is enough information to get the user up and comfortably productive. The Topic Organizer provides such a help system.

The help system is a simple page of HTML that appears in the Viewer Pane upon startup. The help system describes how to use the application in a simple manner. In addition, the help system refers to the Topics Reader component and provides a button the user can click to launch the Topics Reader in a separate browser window. Listing 12.10 shows the code for the onscreen help page, howto.asp. (See Figure 12.1 to view the page in a browser.) Notice that the page contains client-side script that has an onclick() event procedure for the button element, btnReader. This button element opens a Topics Reader in a new browser window. Also, notice that the window object's open method is used to open the new browser window.

EXAMPLE

Listing 12.10: A Simple, Effective Help System (12asp10.asp/howto.asp)

```
<%
'=====================================
'Page Name: howto.ASP
'Purpose: Provides instructions
'         about how to use the
'         topic organizer
'=====================================
%>
<HTML>
<HEAD>
<TITLE></TITLE>
<SCRIPT ID=clientEventHandlersJS LANGUAGE=javascript>
<!--

function btnReader_onclick() {
    window.open("http://www.mySite.com/AriTopOrg/reader.asp",
              "ReaderWin",
              "status=yes,toolbar=no,menubar=no,location=no,resizable=yes");
}

//-->
</SCRIPT>
</HEAD>
<BODY bgcolor= red>

<P Align=Center><FONT color=lightyellow face=Arial
size=6>How to Use the Aristotle Middle School<BR>
Topic Organizer</FONT></P>

<P><FONT color=lightyellow face=Arial size=3>

<B>The Topic Organizer allows you to add Web pages
to a custom list that you can  use later as reference
materials in your classes.
<P>
The way that you use the Organizer is to enter
a URL in the Web site browser pane at the top of the
```

continues

Listing 12.10: continued

```
page. Then, should you want to add the site to
your custom list, click the Add Site button on the
left. When you click the Add Site button, the URL
entered in the browser pane is added to the Sites list.
The list is updated automatically to show the new
entry.
<P>
Once you have a set of topics prepared, your students
use the Topics Reader page to view your topics.</B><BR>
<INPUT type="button"
       value="Launch Topics Reader"
       name=btnReader
       LANGUAGE=javascript
       onclick="return btnReader_onclick()">

</FONT></P>

</BODY>
</HTML>
```

Previously you read that the help system provides a button that uses the `window.open` method to display a new browser window that contains the Topics Reader page. Let's take a moment to learn about the `window.open` method.

Using the `window.open` Method

The `window.open` method allows you to create, configure, and display a new browser window. The syntax for the `window.open` method is

```
objWin=window.open(strURLToLoad, strWindowName, strFeatures, bReplaceHistory)
```

Where

`strURLToLoad` is an optional string that indicates the URL of a Web page to load into the window. If no URL is indicated, the `blank:about` page is displayed.

`strWindowName` is an optional string that you can use to conform to the `Target` attribute of a `<A>` or `<FORM>`. For example, if you have a page with a `<FRAME name="services">` element and you set the `strWindowName` attribute to services, the window opens in that `<FRAME>`.

`strFeatures` is an optional string that indicates the configuration setting for window. The details are as follows:

channelmode expected value: yes | no | 1 | 0 Indicates whether to display the window in theater mode and show the channel band. Default value is no.

directories expected value: yes | no | 1 | 0 Indicates whether to add directory buttons. The default value is yes.

fullscreen expected value: yes | no | 1 | 0 Indicates whether to display the browser in a fullscreen or normal window. The default value is no. The value no displays the browser in a normal window. Be advised that fullscreen hides the browser's title bar and menus. Be careful how you use it.

height is an integer that specifies the height of the window, in pixels. The minimum value is 100.

left is an integer that specifies the left position, in pixels. This value is relative to the upper-left corner of the screen.

location, expected value: yes | no | 1 | 0 indicates whether to display the input field for entering URLs directly into the browser. The default value is yes.

menubar, expected value: yes | no | 1 | 0 indicates whether to display the menu bar. The default is yes.

resizable, expected value: yes | no | 1 | 0 indicates whether to display resize handles at the corners of the window. The default value is yes.

scrollbars, expected value: yes | no | 1 | 0 indicates whether to display horizontal and vertical scrollbars. The default value is yes.

status, expected value: yes | no | 1 | 0 indicates whether to add a status bar at the bottom of the window. The default value is yes.

titlebar, expected value: yes | no | 1 | 0 indicates whether to display a title bar for the window. This parameter is ignored unless you are opening a window using an HTML Application or a trusted dialog box. The default value is yes.

toolbar, expected value: yes | no | 1 | 0 indicates whether to display the browser toolbar. The default value is yes.

top is an integer that specifies the top position in pixels. This value is relative to the upper-left corner of the screen.

width is an integer that specifies the width of the window in pixels. The minimum value is 100.

bReplaceHistory is a boolean value indicating whether the new window should replace the calling window in the history list. If the value is True, the window is not added to the history list.

The trick to working with the window.open method is to master configuring the various parameters of the method. Once you get the hang of things, you can create browser windows that emulate dialog boxes, occupy a specific location on your computer screen, or present pages in a full screen mode, as you see in a trade show or department store kiosk.

Coding the Topics Reader

The Topics Reader component, reader.asp, is similar to the Topic Organizer except that it lacks URL entry and site addition features. The Topics Reader is accessible to anybody who wants to select and view sites from the Site List for a given instructor.

As you read at the beginning of the chapter, the Topics Reader presents the user with a Web page containing three frames. The top frame, which was the Browser Pane in the Topic Organizer, contains an identifying logo. The left frame, which is the Site List Pane, contains a text element into which a user enters a TeacherID (LoginID) to view a site list dedicated to the teacher. The left frame is still the Viewer Pane. The only dynamic activity is in the Site List Pane. The Get Sites button in the Site List Pane is a Submit button in disguise. When the user clicks the Get Sites button, the form to which the button is attached makes a recursive call to the Active Server Page, readSite.asp. The Active Server Page readSite.asp contains the GetSites(TeacherID) function that you saw previously in the addSite.asp component page of the Topic Organizer. The function GetSites(TeacherID) returns the string of sites embedded in HTML <A HREF></A> tags. The TeacherID value is the value passed from the client to the server from the text element in the Site List Pane. Listing 12.11 shows the code for the Site List Pane of the Topics Reader. Figure 12.12 shows the output of Listing 12.11.

EXAMPLE

Listing 12.11: The Code for the Topics Reader (12asp11.asp/readSite.asp)

```
<%
'=====================================
'Page Name: readSite.ASP
'Purpose: To provide a list of the sites
'          that a teacher has selected for
'          a class.
'=====================================

Function GetSites(UserID)
'***************************
'
```

```
'Parameters: UserID A String that corresponds to the
'                TeacherID of the User
'

'Return:    A string of HTML that contains a list of HREFs
'                for the teachers's selected sites
'

'Remarks:   This function returns a string of HTML that
'                contains valud <A HREF> tags. The tags are a
'                list of URLS that the teachers added to his or
'                her Organizer previously.
'

'Programmer: Bob Reselman
'Copyright: 2000
'

'History: Created 1/7/2000
'

'**************************
    Dim cn 'Connection var
    Dim rs 'Recordset var
    Dim strSQL 'SQL Statement var
    Dim strHRef 'HRef string var
    Dim strBuffer 'Buffer var
    Dim dq

    dq = chr(34) 'quote mark

    'Create a Connection Object
    Set cn = CreateObject("ADODB.Connection")
    Set rs = CreateObject("ADODB.Recordset")
    'Make the SQL statement that returns
    'the user with password, should one exist
    strSQL = "SELECT * FROM tblSites WHERE TeacherID = '"
    strSQL = strSQL & UserID & "'"

    'Set error trappong
    On Error Resume Next
    'Open the Connection
    cn.ConnectionString = "DSN=" & Application("DBSource")
    cn.Open
    If Err Then Exit Function
    'Get the user from the DB
    rs.ActiveConnection = cn
    rs.Open strSQL

    If Err Then Exit Function
```

continues

Listing 12.11: continued

```
    'This checks to make sure if no
    'recordset was returned
    MyErr = rs("TeacherID")
    If err then
        Exit Function
    End if
    'Let's make the <HRrefs> containing all the
    'records in the recordset.
    While Not rs.EOF
        'Make a string of the format
        '<A HREF="HTTP://www.site.com">http://www.site.com</A>
        strBuffer = "<A HREF=" & dq & rs("URL") & dq
        strBuffer = strBuffer & " Target=" & dq & "viewer" & dq & ">"
        strBuffer = strBuffer & rs("URL") & "</A><BR>" & vbCrlf
        'Contatenate the buffer onto the HRef var
        strHRef = strHRef & strBuffer
        rs.MoveNext
    Wend

    'Leave town
    rs.Close
    cn.Close
    GetSites = strHRef
End Function

%>
<HTML>
<HEAD>
<TITLE></TITLE>
<BODY>
<FONT Face=Arial size=3 color=navy>
</FONT>
<CENTER>
<P>
<Img Src=sites.gif><BR>
<Form name=MyForm
        method="post"
        action="<%=Application("SiteURL") & "/readSite.asp"%>">
<INPUT value="
<%
Session("TeacherID") = Request.Form("TeacherID")
If Session("TeacherID") = "" then
    Response.Write "Enter TeacherID"
Else
    Response.Write Session("TeacherID")
End If
%>
```

```
" name=TeacherID><BR>
<INPUT type="submit" value="Get Sites" id=submit1 name=submit1>
</FORM>
</CENTER>
<HR>
<FONT Face=Arial size=2 color=navy>
<%
'If this is not the first time the URL list
'page has been called, then go get all the lists
If Session("TeacherID") <> "" Then
    Response.Write GetSites(Session("TeacherID"))
End if
%>
</FONT></BODY></HTML>
```

OUTPUT

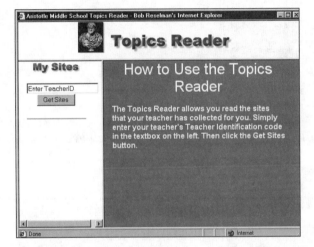

Figure 12.12: *The Topics Reader allows anyone to view a Site List for a given teacher.*

Installing the Application

The final item we need to cover is how to create the ASP Application on the IIS computer and add the Active Server Pages that make up the Topic Organizer to the application.

Creating the Application Directory

The first thing we need to create is a directory in the wwwroot subdirectory of Inetpubs. After you have the directory created, go to the MCP Web site dedicated to this book (http://www.quecorp.com/series/by_example/) and download the files for this chapter. Copy the files into the directory you have just created.

As an example, in Figure 12.13 we have created a directory \QueASP\chp12 and put the pages for this application in that directory.

Table 12.1 shows a list of the necessary files with a short description of each.

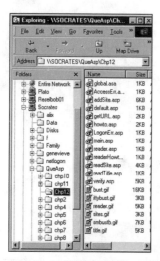

Figure 12.13: *All of the Active Server Pages,* Global.ASA, *and supporting graphics files for the Topic Organizer application are copied into the same directory.*

Table 12.1: The Files for the Topic Organizer

Filename	Description
Global.ASA	Application global file
accessErr.asp	Shown when unauthorized access is attempted
addSite.asp	Site List Pane component page for Topic Organizer
default.asp	Login Page
getURL.asp	Browser Pane component page for Topic Organizer
howto.asp	Topic Organizer Help Page
logonErr.asp	Error page displayed for invalid login
main.asp	Topic Organizer main page with three frames
reader.asp	Topics Reader main page with three frames
readerHowTo.asp	Topics Reader Help page
readSite.asp	Site List Pane component page for Topics Reader
readTitle.asp	Browser Pane component page for Topics Reader
bust.gif	Graphic for LogonErr.ASP
smbustb.gif	Graphic for Login page
ittybust.gif	Graphic for getURL.asp and ReadTitle.asp
reader.gif	Title graphic for ReadTitle.asp
sites.gif	Graphic for addSite.asp and readSite.asp
title.gif	Title graphic for getURL.asp

Creating the Virtual Directory

After you have created the application directory and copied the application files into the directory, you need to create the virtual directory that provides the application with a name and scope. If you are running Personal Web Server, you create the Virtual Directory using Personal Web Server Manager. If you are running Internet Information Server 4.0 under Windows NT 4.0, you use the Information Management Console. Windows 2000 users use the Information Services Manager. Figure 12.14 show the Properties Page that you use to create a virtual directory under IIS 4.0 and Windows NT 4.0. The Topic Organizer's virtual directory and application is named `AriTopOrg`.

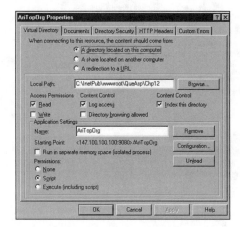

Figure 12.14: The virtual directory and application name used in this chapter for the Topic Organizer is `AriTopOrg`.

Make sure you add a default page, `default.asp`, to the Documents tab of the Windows NT/IIS Directory Properties tab. This allows users to type in the site URL and the virtual directory name without having to type a complete filename for the default Active Server Page. In addition, creating and adding `default.asp` as the default document list creates a level of security that is useful.

✔ For a review of working with virtual directories on Personal Web Server and Internet Information Server, see the section in Chapter 2, titled "The ASP Application and Virtual Directories," page 39.

Configuring the ODBC Datasource

The Active Server Pages for the Topic Organizer application require that the application's MS Access database (`AriMiddle.mdb`) be registered as an ODBC datasource under the name `AriMiddleData`.

First, you need to copy the database file onto the same computer upon which IIS or PWD is installed. Then, you register it as an ODBC data-source by using the ODBC Data Source Administrator. You access the Data Source Administrator by clicking the ODBC Data Sources (32bit) icon in the Windows Control Panel. Figure 12.15 shows the Data Source Administrator dialog box. Click the Help button on the Data Source Administrator to learn the details of how to configure the installation. Also, be advised that it is very important that you register the database under the System DSN tab. It is the only way that the ASP engine will be granted access to the file by Window NT.

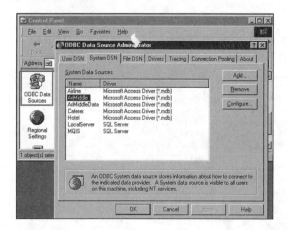

Figure 12.15: Make sure when using the ODBC Data Source Administrator to configure the application database, you make it a System database.

Initializing the Application-Level Variables

The last thing you need to do is set the global Application variables for the Site URL and the application's datasource. The site URL that was used for this chapter is

`http://147.100.100.100:9080/AriTopOrg`

Where

`http://147.100.100.100` is the IP address of the server.

`9080` is the port to which the server has been configured to accept HTTP (Web page) requests. You can think of a port as a specific entryway that is defined for the server. The server for a specific protocol then looks to the port for its data. For example, the conventional port for the FTP protocol is 21. The FTP server is always listening to Port 21 for any data sent using the FTP protocol. Using a port number of 9080 for the HTTP server is unusual. Usually port 80 is assigned to accept HTTP protocol data.

However, this particular server was given this unconventional port setting because of the limitations imposed by the network *firewall*.

AriTopOrg is the virtual directory and application name for the Topic Organizer.

Listing 12.5, previously in this chapter, shows the Global.asa file in which Application-level variables have been set.

You should change the URL assigned to the Application("SiteURL") variable in the Global.ASA file to be the URL of your Web server. You can use either an IP addressing scheme or a Domain Name, should your server have one. Don't forget to include the virtual directory as part of the URL. After all these installation and configuration tasks are completed, you are ready to go.

What's Next

This chapter gave you a first real look at a full-scale application made using Active Server Page technology in conjunction with client-side script. We made an application that has data and presentation customized to a given user. You learned how to design and implement an ASP application that used multiple pages. You learned how to work with HTML <FRAME> elements. In addition, you learned how to manipulate the DOM to access data in elements between frames and to create new windows. Finally, you learned how to configure a server to run the application.

The next chapter shows you how to create a Web-based, online address book. You'll learn how to make an application that allows you to create and organize lists of your friends and associates. You'll use the skills you have acquired thus far as well as learn some new techniques that will enhance your mastery of Active Server Page programming.

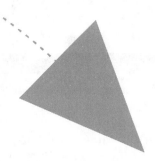

Creating a Personal Address Book

Providing a Personal Information Management (PIM) service is a growing trend among many companies and organizations that maintain Web sites. Usually, PIM pages are offered by companies and organization to encourage users to revisit the site often. Visitation volume is important to companies doing business on the Web. In some cases, the true worth of a site is often determined not so much by its sales volume, but rather by its visitation rate. Having a high rate of visitation is referred to in the industry as "getting the eyeballs."

The Personal Address Book that we are going to make in this chapter is a scaled-back PIM. It's part of the Aristotle Middle School Web site that we have been developing throughout the last part of this book. The Personal Address Book allows a teacher to keep a custom list of addresses, each with an associated telephone number.

In this chapter you will

- Learn how to use the HTML Hidden element to maintain state information
- Learn to use client-side script to control an HTML <FORM>
- Learn how to validate data
- Learn how to edit and delete data in a database using SQL
- Learn how to relate data in a query string to the Request.Form() collection

Planning the Personal Address Book

The Aristotle Middle School Personal Address Book is a Web-based address book that keeps and presents a list of addresses for a given teacher. Each teacher in the school has the ability to create his or her own address book. The data for the address books is stored in an ODBC datasource that resides on the server side. Figure 13.1 shows an instance of the Personal Address Book address list page.

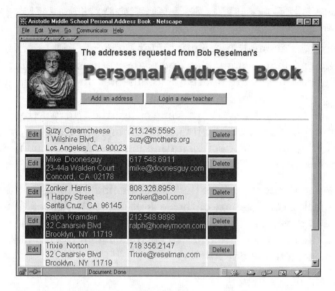

Figure 13.1: *The Aristotle Middle School Personal Address Book keeps a list of addresses for a teacher.*

Features

The Personal Address Book allows a user to display a dedicated list of addresses. The user can add an address to the Personal Address Book. Also, the user can edit or delete an existing address in the book.

The Personal Address Book is secure. Each user accesses his or her book by logging on through a login page. Figure 13.2 shows the login page.

Application Architecture

The Personal Address Book application architecture uses a series of related Active Server Pages to retrieve, display, and manipulate address book data. Figure 13.3 illustrates the relationship of the Active Server Pages of the Personal Address Book application to one another.

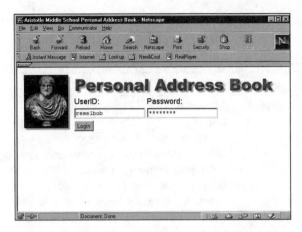

Figure 13.2: *The Aristotle Middle School Personal Address Book requires that a user is authenticated before he is granted access to his address book.*

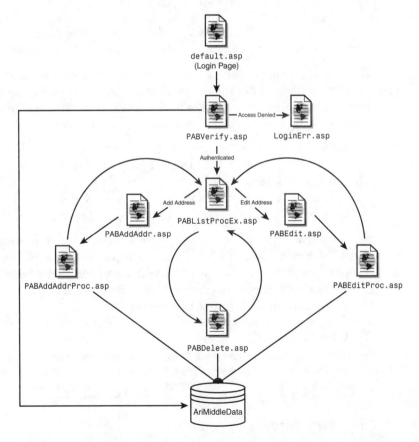

Figure 13.3: *Features of the Personal Address Book are encapsulated into a set of related Active Server Pages.*

Table 13.1 lists and describes each page within the Personal Address Book architecture.

Table 13.1: The Files for the Topic Organizer

Filename	Description
global.ASA (not shown)	Application global file
default.asp	Login Page
PABVerify.asp	Contains authentication logic
AccessErr.asp	Displays unauthenticated page access error
LoginErr.asp	Displays a login error message
PABListProcEx.asp	Displays a teacher's address book
PABAddAddr.asp	Displays a form page into which a teacher adds a new address
PABAddAddrProc.asp	Takes address data from PABAddAddr.asp and adds it to the address book
PABEdit.asp	Displays a populated form page that a teacher uses to edit an existing address
PABEditProc.asp	Takes edited address data from PABEdit.asp and updates the data in the teacher's address book
PABDelete.asp	Deletes a chosen address from the address book

The way the address book application works is that first a user logs in. If the login data is valid, the Active Server Page PABListProcEx.asp is called. This page displays the address book for the authenticated teacher. If the user is not authentic, the page LoginErr.asp is called.

The page displayed by PABListProcEx.asp shows a list of addresses for the teacher. To the left of each address is an Edit button. To the right of each address is a Delete button. The user clicks the Edit button if he wants to change data in the existing address. The user clicks the Delete button if he wants to remove the address from the book (refer to Figure 13.1).

Should a teacher want to add an address to the Personal Address Book, he clicks the Add an address button at the top of the page. If the teacher wants to log out and allow another teacher to access his book, the teacher clicks the Login a new teacher button. Clicking this button returns control of the application back to the Login page.

NOTE

This ASP Application name for the Personal Address Book is AriAddressBook. When you install the application, you need to create a virtual directory named AriAddressBook under Internet Information Server for this application.

Data Structure

The Personal Address Book data is stored in an MS Access database that is registered as an ODBC datasource on the Web server computer. The name of the datasource is `AriMiddleData`. The name of the MS Access filename is `AriMiddle.mdb`. The application references the datasource through an Application level variable, `Application("DBSource")`. This variable is defined and initialized in the `global.ASA` file for the application. Listing 13.1 shows the contents of `global.ASA` for the Personal Address Book Application.

EXAMPLE

Listing 13.1: Storing Datasource and Site URL Information in `Global.ASA` (13asp01.asp/Global.ASA)

```
<SCRIPT LANGUAGE=vbscript RUNAT=Server>
'*********************
'Filename: Global.ASA
'Application: Personal Address Book
'
'Programmer: Bob Reselman
'
'Copyright 2000 Macmillan Computer Publishing
'*********************
    Sub Application_OnStart()
        Application("SiteURL") = _
            "http://147.100.100.100:9080/AriAddressBook"
        Application("DBSource") = "AriMiddleData"
        Application("LogonErrFile") = "LogonErr.asp"
        Application("AccessErrFile") = "AccessErr.asp"
    End Sub

    Sub Session_OnStart()
        Session("IsGoodUser") = False
    End Sub

    Sub Application_OnEnd()
    End Sub

    Sub Session_OnEnd()
        Session.Abandon
    End Sub
</SCRIPT>
```

Login authentication data is stored in the table, `tblLogin`. The data specific to the Personal Address Book is stored in the table, `tblAddresses`. In addition, the table, `tblTeacher` is used to resolve the `LoginID` to the First Name and Last Name for a given teacher. Figure 13.4 shows the fields for each table the application uses.

NOTE

Please be advised that the `AriMiddleData` datasource is the same one that has been used for all application examples within this book under the theme of the Aristotle Middle School.

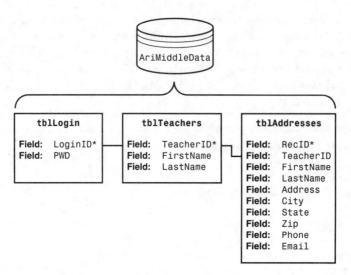

Figure 13.4: The Personal Address Book uses three tables in the `AriMiddleData` *datasource. Key fields are indicated with an asterisk.*

As you read previously, the `tblAddresses` table stores all the addresses for all the teachers in the Aristotle Middle School. When the program needs to determine the addresses for a particular teacher, it does a query on the table, asking it to return all the addresses that correspond to a given teacher's `TeacherID`. You'll learn more about querying the addresses table later in this chapter. Figure 13.5 shows the contents of the `tblAddresses` table.

RecID	TeacherID	FirstName	LastName	Address	City	State	Zip	Phone	Email
12	reselbob	Ralph	Kramden	32 Canarsie Blvd	Brooklyn	NY	11719	212.548.9898	ralph@honeymoon.com
16	reselbob	Ed	Norton	32 Canarsie Blvd	Brooklyn	NY	11789	212.524.6598	Ed@honeymoon.com
18	reselbob	Trixie	Norton	32 Canarsie Blvd	Brooklyn	NY	11789	718.356.2147	Trixie@reselman.com
23	reselbob	Mike	Doonesguy	23-44a Walden Court	Concord	CA	02178	213.548.6911	mike@doonesguy.com
43	tallycha	Lois	Lane	The Daily Planet	Metropolis	MN	65451	312.254.7849	lois@planet.com
48	tallycha	Perry	White	The Daily Planet	Metropolis	MN	65451	312.214.2452	perry@planet.com
52	tallycha	Jimmy	Olson	The Daily Planet	Metropolis	MN	65451	312.215.2153	jimmy@planet.com
53	tallycha	Clark	Kent	The Daily Planet	Metropolis	MN	65451	312.254.8978	clark@planet.com
54	tallycha	George	Washington	1 President Way	Mt.Vernon	VA	45213	712.214.2567	geoge@usa.gov
55	tallycha	Alexander	Hamilton	22 Murray Street	NY	NY	10003	212.248.8978	alexander@usa.gov
57	tallycha	Aaron	Burr	45 LaFayette Street	NY	NY	10002	212.557.3265	aaron@usa.gov
60	reselbob	Motorhead	Sherwood	3 Vine Street	Los Angeles	CA	90015	213.256.6666	motorhead@mother.org
62	reselbob	Suzy	Creamcheese	1 Wilshire Blvd.	Los Angeles	CA	90023	213.245.5595	suzy@mothers.org

Figure 13.5: This list is a query for all occurrences of teacher identification codes in the `TeacherID` *field of the addresses table.*

Building the Login Pages

The login process requires the use of three Active Server Pages. The entry page, `default.asp`, provides the login form into which a teacher enters his or her LoginID and Password. The Active Server Page, `PABVerify.asp`, contains the authentication logic. If the teacher enters a valid UserID and password, he is given access to the page that displays the teacher's address book. Otherwise, control of the application is passed to a Login Error page, `LoginErr.asp` (refer to Figure 13.3).

> **NOTE**
>
> The mechanics for this login scheme are identical to the one described in Chapter 12, "Creating a Custom User Page."

Listing 13.2 shows the code for the Login page, `default.asp`. The output of the code is what you saw in Figure 13.2

EXAMPLE

Listing 13.2: The Default Authentication Page (`13asp02.asp/default.asp`)

```
<%
'=======================================
'Page Name: default.ASP
'Purpose: Allows a user to login
'          to the site. The related ASP
'          PADverify.asp contains the
'          verification and display logic.
'=======================================
%>
<HTML>
<HEAD>
<TITLE>Aristotle Middle School Personal Address Book</TITLE>
</HEAD>
<BODY>
<FORM NAME=MyForm
      Method=Post
      Action="<%=Application("SiteURL")& "/PABverify.asp"%>">
<TABLE Border=0>
<TR><TD><IMG SRC="smbustb.gif"></TD>
<TD><IMG SRC="logo.gif"><BR>
<TABLE Border=0>


<TR>
<TD><FONT SIZE=4 Face=ARIAL Color=#000080>
UserID:  </FONT></TD>
<TD><FONT SIZE=4 Face=ARIAL Color=#000080>
Password:</FONT></TD></TR>
 <TR><TD><INPUT   Name=LoginID></TD>
 <TD><INPUT Type=Password Name=PWD></TD>
</TR>
<TR><TD>
<INPUT type="submit" value="Logon"  name=submit1>
</TD></TR>
</TABLE>
```

continues

Listing 13.2: continued

```
</TD>
</TR>
</TABLE>
</FORM>
</BODY>
</HTML>
```

Listing 13.2 is a simple Active Server Page that displays a login page with cosmetic graphics. The reason an Active Server Page is used instead of a standard HTML page is that the page Action attribute of the <FORM> element retrieves a reference to this site's URL from the Application("SiteURL") variable that is initialized in global.ASA. A standard HTML page does not offer the dynamic programming capabilities needed to access application-level variables stored in global.ASA. All the pages of this application refer to the Application("SiteURL") value when a reference for the site's URL is required. Centralizing the URL for the site in global.ASA allows us to change the site's URL easily should we want to use the Personal Address Book in other ASP applications.

Listing 13.3 shows the code for PABVerify.asp. The Active Server Page PABVerify.asp contains the data-access mechanics and authentication logic the application needs to allow a teacher access to his or her address book.

EXAMPLE

Listing 13.3: Authenticating Users (13asp03.asp/PABVerify.asp)

```
<%
'=====================================
'Page Name: PABverify.ASP
'Purpose: Checks to make sure that user
'          has submitted a valid LoginID
'          and password. If the user is
'          authenticated, then this page
'          redirects to the address list page,
'          PABListProcEx.ASP.
'=====================================


Sub GetNames(LoginID, FirstName, LastName)
'*************************
'
'Parameters: LoginID, A string that indicates the
'                       LoginID of the User
'
'           FirstName, The teacher's first name, a returned value
'
'           Last Name, The teacher's last name, a returned' value
'
'Return:    See the parameter values.
```

```
'
'Remarks:    This sub returns a teacher's First Name
'               and Last Name from the Ari Middle
'               School datasource. The sub passes in the
'               LoginID and passes the retrieved value out
'               'through the FirstName and LastName arguments.
'
'               The LoginID corresponds to the TeacherID field
'               and LoginID fields in the datasource. .
'
'Programmer: Bob Reselman
'Copyright: 2000
'
'History: Created 1/7/2000
'
'***************************
        Dim cn 'Connection var
        Dim rs 'Recordset var
        Dim strSQL 'SQL Statement var

        'Create a Connection and Recorset Object
        Set cn = CreateObject("ADODB.Connection")
        Set rs = CreateObject("ADODB.Recordset")
        'Make the SQL statement that returns
        'the user with password, should one exist
        strSQL = "SELECT * FROM tblTeachers WHERE TeacherID = '"
        strSQL = strSQL & LoginID & "'"

        'Set error trapping
        On Error Resume Next
        'Open the Connection
        cn.ConnectionString = "DSN=" & Application("DBSource")
        cn.Open
        If Err Then Exit Sub

        'Get the user from the DB
        rs.Open strSQL, cn
        If Err Then Exit Sub

        'This checks to make sure if no
        'recordset was returned
        MyErr = rs("FirstName")
        If err then
            Exit Sub
        End if
        'Wire up the return fields
```

continues

Listing 13.3: continued

```
        FirstName = rs("FirstName")
        LastName = rs("LastName")

        'Leave town
        rs.Close
        cn.Close
End Sub


Function Login(LoginID, Password)
'**************************
'
'Parameters: LoginID  A String that indicates the
'                     LoginID of the User
'
'            Password A String that indicates the
'                     the password to be validated against
'                     the LoginID
'
'Return:     True,  if the LoginID and Password coincide
'
'Remarks:    This method uses data kept in an external
'            database to do LoginID/Password validation.
'            The function retrieves a record from the
'            Access file, indicated by the application
'            variable, Application("DBSource").
'            The record is retrieved according to the
'            LoginID. If a record is retrieved and if
'            the Login ID and Password match up, the
'            method returns True.
'
'Programmer: Bob Reselman
'Copyright: 1999
'
'History: Created 11/28/1999
'
'**************************


        Dim cn 'Connection var
        Dim rs 'Recordset var
        Dim strSQL 'SQL Statement var
        Dim strCn 'Connection String var

        'Create a Connection Object
        Set cn = CreateObject("ADODB.Connection")
```

```
        Set rs = CreateObject("ADODB.Recordset")
        'Make the SQL statement that returns
        'the user with password, should one exist
        strSQL = "SELECT * FROM tblLogin WHERE LoginName = '"
        strSQL = strSQL & LoginID & "'"

        'Set error trapping
        On Error Resume Next
        'Open the Connection
        cn.ConnectionString = "DSN=" & Application("DBSource")

        cn.Open
        If Err Then Exit Function

        'Get the user from the DB
        rs.Open strSQL, cn
        If Err Then Exit Function

        'This checks to make sure if no
        'recordset was returned
        MyErr = rs("PWD")
        If err then
            Exit Function
        End if

        'If the passwords match up, return TRUE
        If rs("PWD") = Password Then
            Login = True
        Else
            Login = False
        End If
        'Leave town
        rs.Close
        cn.Close
End Function
'================================
'=========Entry Point============
'================================
If Login(Request.Form("LoginID"), Request.Form("PWD")) Then
   Dim FirstName
   Dim LastName
   'Get the teacher's name from the GetName Sub
   GetNames Request.Form("LoginID"), FirstName, LastName
   Dim URL 'Buffer for URL
   Dim QS 'Query String variable
   'Emulate a form submission for the LoginID by
```

continues

Listing 13.3: continued

```
'creating the query string that the would be passed
'for the form by the browser.
QS = "/PABListProcEx.asp?LoginID=" & Request.Form("LoginID")
QS = QS & "&FName=" & FirstName
QS = QS & "&LName=" & LastName

URL = Application("SiteURL") & QS
'Redisplay the list
Response.Redirect URL
Else
    'Report a logon error.
    Response.Redirect Application("LogonErrFile")
End If
%>
```

Figure 13.6 shows a flow chart illustrating the logic of PABVerify.asp as shown in Listing 13.2. The flow chart corresponds to the activity starting from the line commented =========Entry Point============ in the listing. This code is straightforward. It's been used in other places in this book. However, notice that PABVerify.asp constructs a query string to pass data onto another page. We haven't seen this technique before.

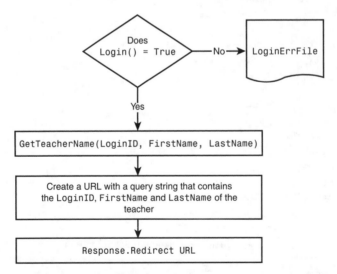

Figure 13.6: *The Active Server Page for authentication constructs a query string to pass data on to other pages.*

Persisting State Using Query Strings

In previous chapters, we have used Session variables to maintain state information between pages. This application is going to take a different track. We are going to use query strings to pass information between pages.

A query string is data that is packaged in `name=value` pairs, tacked onto a URL, and then passed on to the page indicated by the Web address in the URL. The following line of code shows a URL with a query string for the `name=value` pairs `FirstName=Bob` and `LastName=Reselman`.

`http://www.mysite.com/mypage.htm?FirstName=Bob&LastName=Reselman`

Notice that in the URL, the query string follows the question mark character (?) after the Web address. This construction is part of the HTTP standard.

Query strings have been around for awhile. In fact, the collection `Request.QueryString` is nothing more than a fancy repackaging of query strings as they exist in the standard to the HTTP protocol.

✔ For a review of the `Request.QueryString` collection, see the section "Using the Request Object" in Chapter 6, "Beginning ASP: Client-Server Communication," p. 141.

As you learned previously in this chapter, the Active Server Page `PABVerify.asp` constructs a query string to pass the login data on to the Active Server Page that displays the address book for a given teacher. The following code sample is extracted from Listing 13.3. This code constructs the query string that contains the `LoginID`, `FirstName`, and `LastName` for a teacher, and then passes the information on to the Active Server Page that displays the teacher's address book, `PABListProcEx.asp`.

```
QS = "/PABListProcEx.asp?LoginID=" & Request.Form("LoginID")
QS = QS & "&FName=" & FirstName
QS = QS & "&LName=" & LastName

URL = Application("SiteURL") & QS
'Redisplay the list
Response.Redirect URL
```

The query string structure represents the same data a user would manually enter into `Text` elements in an HTML `<FORM>` element and then submit to a server if the `<FORM>` element's `Method` attribute were assigned the value `"Get"`.

Let's move on to see how the Active Server Page, `PABListProcEx.asp` processes the data submitted in the query string.

Displaying a Teacher's List

The Active Server Page, `PABListProcEx.asp`, retrieves and displays the list of addresses for a given teacher's Personal Address Book. Listing 13.4 shows the code for the Active Server Page. The sections that follow provide a detailed discussion of the code. See Figure 13.1 for the output of this Active Server Page.

Listing 13.4: Listing a Personal Address Book (13asp04.asp/PABListProcEx.asp)

```
<%
'Security Check
If Session("IsGoodUser") = False Then
    Response.Redirect Application("AccessErrFile")
End If


'======================================
'Page Name: PABListProcEx.ASP
'Purpose: Returns a list all the entries
'         in a teacher's address book
'
'Created: 1/15/2000
'Programmer: Bob Reselman
'======================================
'***************************
Sub GetAddresses(TeacherID)
'
'Parameters: TeacherID, the LoginID of the teacher
'
'Return: None
'Remarks:'  This Sub outputs HTML string that contains
'           a list of all the entries in a given teachers
'           Address Book. Each entry contains a two
'           buttons. One for editing an entry and
'           one for deleting an entry.
'
'           Use the this function to add an entry
'           to the address table in the Aristotle
'           Middle School Datasource. The datasource is
'           stored in the Application variable,
'           Application("DBSource")
'
'Programmer: Bob Reselman
'Copyright: 2000
'
'History: Created 1/15/2000
'
'***************************
    Dim cn 'Connection var
    Dim rs 'recordset object
    Dim strSQL 'SQL Statement var

    'Create a Connection Object
    Set cn = CreateObject("ADODB.Connection")
    Set rs = CreateObject("ADODB.Recordset")
    'Use the SQL SELECT clause to retreive a
```

```
'record.
strSQL = "SELECT RecID, FirstName, LastName, "
strSQL = strSQL & "Address, City, State, Zip, "
strSQL = strSQL & "Phone, Email "
strSQL = strSQL & "FROM tblAddresses WHERE "
strSQL = strSQL & "TeacherID='"
strSQL = strSQL & TeacherID & "' "
'Sort of the last name
strSQL = strSQL & "ORDER By LastName"
'Set the SQL statement to the Command object.
'Open the Connection
cn.ConnectionString = "DSN=" & Application("DBSource")
cn.Open
If Err then Exit Sub
'Open the recordset
rs.ActiveConnection = cn
rs.Open strSQL
If Err then Exit Sub
'Traverse the recordset and make
'a list of phone entries

Dim i 'increment suffix that gets added
       'onto the end of each form name for
       'the edit and delete forms.
Dim dq 'Quotation mark
Dim FontClr        'var to hold fore color info
Dim BckClr      'var to hold background color

Foreclr = "White"
BckClr = "#000080"
i = 1
While not rs.EOF
    'Make an Edit button, which is a Submit button
    'in disguise. Each Submit button belongs to
    'a unique form . This form contains the record
    'number and other fields of the entry. The form's
    'data is submitted to a page PABEdit.asp. This
    'page contains editing display and processing code.

    'Check to see if the variable i is even
    'or odd. If it is even make the background
    'color of the row blue and the font color beige.
    'If it is odd make the font blue and the back-
    'ground beige. This makes rows with alternating color
    'that are much easier to read and understand.
    If CInt(i) mod 2 = 0 then
```

continues

Listing 13.4: continued

```
                    Foreclr = "#ffefd5"
                    BckClr = "#000080"
              Else
                    Foreclr = "#000080"
                    BckClr = "#ffefd5"
              End If


'==================EDIT BUTTON======================%>
<TR><TD VAlign=Center bgcolor=<%=BckClr%>>
<FORM name=MyFormE<%=Cstr(i)%>
method=post
action="<%=Application("SiteURL") & "/PABEdit.asp"%>">
<INPUT type=Submit value="Edit" name=submit1>
<INPUT type=HIDDEN name=RecID value="<%=rs("RecID")%>">
<INPUT type=HIDDEN name=edFName value="<%=rs("FirstName")%>">
<INPUT type=HIDDEN name=edLName value="<%=rs("LastName")%>">
<INPUT type=HIDDEN name=Address value="<%=rs("Address")%>">
<INPUT type=HIDDEN name=City value="<%=rs("City")%>">
<INPUT type=HIDDEN name=State value="<%=rs("State")%>">
<INPUT type=HIDDEN name=Zip value="<%=rs("Zip")%>">
<INPUT type=HIDDEN name=Phone value="<%=rs("Phone")%>">
<INPUT type=HIDDEN name=Email value="<%=rs("Email")%>">

<INPUT type=Hidden
        name=LoginID
        value="<%=Request.QueryString("LoginID")%>">
<INPUT type=Hidden
        name=FName
        value="<%=Request.QueryString("FName")%>">
<INPUT type=Hidden
        name=LName
        value="<%=Request.QueryString("LName")%>">
</FORM></TD>
<TD VAlign=Top bgcolor=<%=BckClr%>>

<%'==================ADDRESS LISTING====================%>
<FONT Face=Arial Size=3 Color=<%=ForeClr%>>
<%=rs("FirstName")%> 
<%=rs("LastName")%><BR>
<%=rs("Address")%><BR>
<%=rs("City")%>, 
<%=rs("State")%> 
<%=rs("Zip")%>></FONT></TD>
<TD VAlign=Top bgcolor=<%=BckClr%>>
<FONT Face=Arial Size=3 Color=<%=ForeClr%>>
<%=rs("Phone")%><BR>
```

```
<%=rs("Email")%></FONT></TD>
<%
'Make a Delete button in the same manner as you made
'the Edit buttons. Except the submission page for the
'Delete button is PABDelete.asp

'====================DELETE Button====================%>
<TD VAlign=Center bgcolor=<%=BckClr%>>
<FORM name=MyFormD<%=Cstr(i)%>
method=post
action="<%=Application("SiteURL") & "/PABDelete.asp"%>">
<INPUT type=Submit value="Delete" name=submit1>
<INPUT type=HIDDEN name=RecID value="<%=rs("RecID")%>">
<INPUT type=HIDDEN name=delFName value="<%=rs("FirstName")%>">
<INPUT type=HIDDEN name=delLName value="<%=rs("LastName")%>">
<INPUT type=HIDDEN name=Address value="<%=rs("Address")%>">
<INPUT type=HIDDEN name=City value="<%=rs("City")%>">
<INPUT type=HIDDEN name=State value="<%=rs("State")%>">
<INPUT type=HIDDEN name=Zip value="<%=rs("Zip")%>">
<INPUT type=HIDDEN name=Phone value="<%=rs("Phone")%>">
<INPUT type=HIDDEN name=Email value="<%=rs("Email")%>">

<INPUT type=Hidden
       name=LoginID
       value="<%=Request.QueryString("LoginID")%>">
<INPUT type=Hidden
       name=FName
       value="<%=Request.QueryString("FName")%>">
<INPUT type=Hidden
       name=LName
       value="<%=Request.QueryString("LName")%>">
</FORM></TD>
        <%
        i = i + 1
        rs.MoveNext
    Wend
    'Close up shop
    cn.close
End Sub
'===============================================
'================Entry Point====================
'===============================================
%>
<HTML>
<HEAD>
<TITLE>Aristotle Middle School Personal Address Book</TITLE>
```

continues

Listing 13.4: continued

```
</HEAD>
<SCRIPT LANGUAGE=javascript>
<!--
    function btnNewTeacher_onclick(){
        //get the URL from the HIDDEN element name SiteURL
        //and assign it as the form ACTION, thus diverting
        //the default Submit behavior
        document.MyForm.action =
            document.MyForm.SiteURL.value +
                "/default.asp";
        //Submit the data, which in this case is a call
        //to the default login page
        document.MyForm.submit();
    }
//-->
</SCRIPT>

<BODY>
<TABLE Border=0>
<TR>
<TD><IMG SRC="smbustb.gif"></TD>
<TD><FONT SIZE=4 Face=ARIAL Color=#000080>
The addresses requested from <%=Request.QueryString("FName")%>
 <%=Request.QueryString("LName")%>'s
<BR><IMG SRC="logo.gif"><BR>
</FONT>
<FORM name=MyForm
  method=Post
  action="<%=Application("SiteURL") & "/PABAddAddr.asp"%>">
<INPUT type=Hidden
  name=LoginID
  value="<%=Request.QueryString("LoginID")%>">
<INPUT type=Hidden
  name=FName
  value="<%=Request.QueryString("FName")%>">
<INPUT type=Hidden
  name=LName
  value="<%=Request.QueryString("LName")%>">
<INPUT type=Hidden
  name=SiteURL
  value="<%=Application("SiteURL")%>">
<INPUT type="Submit"
  value="Add an address"
  name=submit1>
<INPUT type="button"
        value="Login a new teacher"
```

```
            name=btnNewTeacher
            Language=JavaScript
            onclick=btnNewTeacher_onclick()>
</FORM>
</TD></TR>
</TABLE>
<HR>
<TABLE>
<%
'Get address output the list of addresses with
'Edit and Delete buttons within an HTML as rows
'of an HTML <TABLE>
Call GetAddresses(Request.QueryString("LoginID"))%>
</TABLE>
</BODY>
</HTML>
```

Data Persistence

The `PABListProcEx.asp` Active Server Page uses the `<INPUT type=
Hidden...>` element to store information that is going to be passed on to
other pages later. The `Hidden` element allows you to name and store data in
a page without having that data displayed. When you use a `Hidden` element,
it's similar to having an initialized variable hard coded in your page. The
following code shows a `Hidden` element named `FName` that stores the value
"Bob".

```
<INPUT type=Hidden name=FName value=Bob>
```

The benefit of using a `Hidden` element is that when the data in the `<INPUT
type=Hidden>` element's parent `<FORM>` is submitted to the server, the data
in the `Hidden` element is passed along too. It's an easy, free way to pass data
between pages. In addition, data in `Hidden` elements is visible to client-side
script. The Document Object Model considers the `Hidden` element to be a
child object of the `form` object. Thus, if you wanted to access the value of the
following `Hidden` element through the Document Object Model

```
<FORM name=MyForm
      method=Post
      action=www.mysite.com/mypage.asp>
<INPUT type=Hidden name=FName value="Bob">
</FORM>
```

you would write

```
str = document.MyForm.FName.value
```

The code that follows is an extract from Listing 13.4. It shows how the
`Hidden` elements in the page are populated using the `Request.QueryString`
collection.

```
<FORM name=MyForm
  method=Post
  action="<%=Application("SiteURL") & "/PABAddAddr.asp"%>">
<INPUT type=Hidden
  name=LoginID
  value="<%=Request.QueryString("LoginID")%>">
<INPUT type=Hidden
  name=FName
  value="<%=Request.QueryString("FName")%>">
<INPUT type=Hidden
  name=LName
  value="<%=Request.QueryString("LName")%>">
<INPUT type=Hidden
  name=SiteURL
  value="<%=Application("SiteURL")%>">
<INPUT type="Submit"
  value="Add an address"
  name=submit1>
<INPUT type="button"
        value="Logon a new teacher"
        name=btnNewTeacher
        Language=JavaScript
        onclick=btnNewTeacher_onclick()>
</FORM>
```

The `Request.QueryString` collection represents the values in the HTTP `QueryString` that are sent to the server from the previous calling page. In this case, `PABVerify.asp`—the authentication page—is the calling page. `PABVerify.asp` packed name=value pairs representing the `LoginID`, `FirstName`, and `LastName` values into a query string and passed them on to this page.

We use the `Request.QueryString` collection to unpack the data in each name=value pair in a submitted query string. The `Request.QueryString` collection takes one parameter, the name of the name=value pair from which you want to determine the value. For example, if you have a name=value pair FName=Bob and you want to use the `Request.QueryString` collection to determine the value in that pair, you would write

str = Request.QueryString("FName")

You will find that the `Hidden` element is used in conjunction with the `Request.QueryString` collection throughout this application. Now that you have an understanding as to how we use the `Hidden` element to store data and pass the stored data between pages using query strings, let's look at the mechanics of retrieving and displaying the addresses from a given teacher's address book.

Retrieving a List of Addresses Using SQL

The process of retrieving and displaying the list of addresses for a given teacher is encapsulated in the Sub GetAddresses(TeacherID). GetAddresses() opens the datasource and retrieves the addresses for a teacher using an SQL SELECT statement. The Sub wraps the addresses in HTML table row (<TR><TD></TD></TR>) tags and creates the Submit buttons in the guise of Edit and Delete buttons. You can find the Sub GetAddresses(TeacherID) at the top of Listing 13.3.

✔ For a review of the SELECT statement see the section, "Understanding SQL" in Chapter 8, "Moving Forward with ASP: Working Data Access," p. 192.

Understanding the Edit and Delete Button Architecture

As you read previously in this chapter, a teacher can change the information in an address by clicking the Edit button on the Address List page. In addition, he can remove an address by clicking the Delete button associated with the address. Let's look in more detail at the editing and deletion programming.

Edit and delete functionality is implemented on an address-by-address basis. Each Edit and Delete button is associated with an address. The buttons are really Submit buttons in which the value attributes have been set to either "Edit" or "Delete", depending on the function the button is to implement. As the GetAddresses() procedure traverses the returned ADO Recordset object that contains a teacher's addresses wrapping HTML row and table cell tags around each address, it embeds each Edit and Delete button in a distinct <FORM> element. The <FORM> element in which the Edit button (née Submit button) resides contains all the data for the given address. This data is assigned to Hidden elements. This <FORM> element has its Action attribute set to the Active Server Page, PABEditProc.asp. PABEditProc.asp contains the display form the teacher uses to modify an existing address. The <FORM> element in which the Delete button resides contains all the data for the associated address in Hidden elements too. However, the Action attribute for the <FORM> element is set to the Active Server Page PABDelete.asp. The Active Server Page, PABDelete.asp, contains the logic and data access functionality that deletes the submitted address.

When the teacher clicks the Edit button, the address data assigned to the Hidden elements in the button's parent form is passed on to the PABEditProc.asp Active Server Page. When the teacher clicks the Delete button, the address data in the button's parent form is passed to the PABDelete.asp Active Server Page.

Figure 13.7 illustrates this design concept.

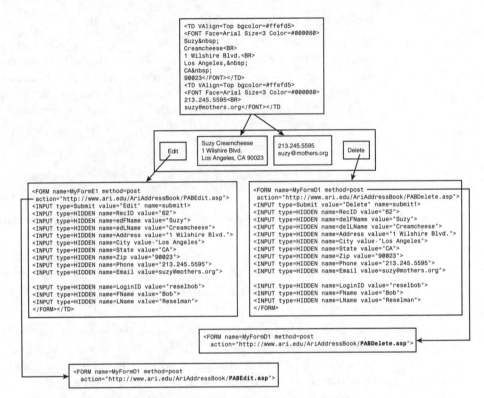

Figure 13.7: *The parent* <FORM> *for each Edit and Delete button contains all the data for a given address.*

Making the Address List Easy to Read

You'll notice that the rows in the Personal Address Book shown in Figure 13.1 use alternate background and font colors. The list is presented in this manner to make the addresses easier to read. Alternating the colors allows the teacher to differentiate between rows quite easily.

Creating rows with alternating color is achieved by using the MOD operator to determine even and odd numbered rows. The following code is executed within the While...Wend of Listing 13.4. The code uses the MOD operator to determine even and odd numbers.

```
If CInt(i) mod 2 = 0 then
    Foreclr = "#ffefd5"
    BckClr = "#000080"
Else
    Foreclr = "#000080"
    BckClr = "#ffefd5"
End If
```

The MOD operator returns the remainder when one number is divided by another. For example:

3 MOD 2 evaluates to 1

15 MOD 6 evaluates to 3

4 MOD 2 evaluates to 0

If you want to find out whether a number is even, use the number in an expression with the MOD operator and the value two. If the expression evaluates to zero (no remainder), you know the number is even.

For example

```
Dim x as Integer
'assign x some value
 .
 .
If x MOD 2 = 0 then
    Alert "X is even"
End If
```

The code this example is excerpted from contains a programmer-defined counter variable, i. One of the roles of this counter variable is to keep track of the row number for each item in the address list. Every time the GetAddresses() procedure makes a trip through the While...Wend loop, the counter variable increases by one. As the loop runs, GetAddresses checks to see whether a row is even or odd. If it is even, it sets the background color variables, BckClr, to the hexadecimal value for the color dark blue and the foreground color variable, ForeClr, to the color value for beige. If the row is odd, the color assignment is reversed. The ForeClr variable is assigned to the Color attribute of the <FONT> tags for data within the cells of a table row. The BckClr variable is assigned to the bgcolor attribute of each table cell (<TD>) in a given row. The following code shows the color assignment:

```
<TR><TD VAlign=Center bgcolor=<%=BckClr%>>
 .
 .
<FONT Face=Arial Size=3 Color=<%=ForeClr%>>
```

Editing an Address

When a teacher clicks the Edit button for an address in the Personal Address Book, the parent <FORM> element submits that address to the PABEdit.asp Active Server Page. Listing 13.5 shows the code for PABEdit.asp. Figure 13.8 shows the ASP code output in a browser.

EXAMPLE

Listing 13.5: ASP Code for the Address Book Edit Page (`13asp05.asp`/`PABEdit.asp`)

```
<%
'======================================
'Page Name: PABEdit.ASP
'Purpose: Displays the data address that the
'          teacher wants to edit in the
'          address book.
'
'
'Created: 1/15/2000
'Programmer: Bob Reselman
'======================================
%>
<HTML>
<HEAD>

<TITLE></TITLE>
</HEAD>
<BODY>

<HTML>
<HEAD>
<TITLE>Aristotle Middle School Personal Address Book</TITLE>
</HEAD>
<BODY>
<TABLE Border=0>
<TR>
<TD><IMG SRC="smbustb.gif"></TD>
<TD><FONT SIZE=4 Face=ARIAL Color=#000080>
Editing an address from <%=Request.Form("FName")%> 
<%=Request.Form("LName")%>'s
<BR><IMG SRC="logo.gif"><BR>
</FONT>
<FORM name=MyForm
      method=Post
      action= "<%=Application("SiteURL") & "/PABEditProc.asp"%>">

<INPUT type=Hidden
       name=LoginID value="<%=Request.Form("LoginID")%>">
<INPUT type=Hidden
       name=FName value="<%=Request.Form("FName")%>">
<INPUT type=Hidden
       name=LName value="<%=Request.Form("LName")%>">

</TABLE>
<TABLE>
<%
```

```
'The HIDDEN element is used to persist the record number
'(RecID) for the selected address to edit.
%>
<INPUT Type=HIDDEN
        name=RecID
        value="<%=Request.Form("RecID")%>">
<%'Text elements that contain the fields to edited. The
  'address data for each field is assigned to the VALUE
  'attribute of each text element.%>
<TR><TD><FONT SIZE=3 Face=ARIAL Color=#000080>
First Name: </FONT></TD>
<TD><INPUT
      name=edFName
      value="<%=Request.Form("edFName")%>"></TD></TR>
<TR><TD><FONT SIZE=3 Face=ARIAL Color=#000080>
Last Name</FONT></TD>
<TD><INPUT
      name=edLName
      value="<%=Request.Form("edLName")%>"></TD></TR>
<TR><TD><FONT SIZE=3 Face=ARIAL Color=#000080>
Street:</FONT></TD>
<TD><INPUT
      name=Address
      value="<%=Request.Form("Address")%>"></TD></TR>
<TR><TD><FONT SIZE=3 Face=ARIAL Color=#000080>
City:</FONT></TD>
<TD><INPUT
      name=City
      value="<%=Request.Form("City")%>"></TD></TR>
<TR><TD><FONT SIZE=3 Face=ARIAL Color=#000080>
State:</FONT></TD>
<TD><INPUT
      name=State
      value="<%=Request.Form("State")%>"></TD></TR>
<TR><TD><FONT SIZE=3 Face=ARIAL Color=#000080>
Zip:</FONT></TD>
<TD><INPUT
      name=Zip
      value="<%=Request.Form("Zip")%>"></TD></TR>
<TR><TD><FONT SIZE=3 Face=ARIAL Color=#000080>
Phone:</FONT></TD>
<TD><INPUT
      name=Phone
      value="<%=Request.Form("Phone")%>"></TD></TR>
<TR><TD><FONT SIZE=3 Face=ARIAL Color=#000080>
Email:</FONT></TD>
```

continues

Listing 13.5: continued

```
<TD><INPUT
     name=Email
     value="<%=Request.Form("Email")%>"></TD></TR>
<TR><TD></TD><TD><INPUT type="submit"
                  value="Edit this address"
                  name=submit1></TD></TR>
</TABLE>
</FORM>
</TD></TR>
<TD>
</TABLE>

</BODY>
</HTML>
```

OUTPUT

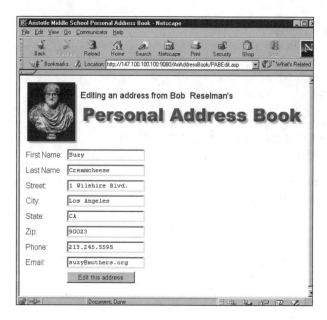

Figure 13.8: *The user makes modifications to an address from the edit page,* `PABEdit.asp`.

Using `PABEdit.asp` and `PABEditProc.asp`

When the teacher clicks the Edit button, he is presented with the Edit page, `PABEdit.asp`. When `PABEdit.asp` is called on the server side, it inspects the `Request.Form` collection to determine the values that were assigned to the `Hidden` elements of the previous calling page, `PABListProcEx.asp`. These values are used to populate the `Text` elements on the Edit page. The teacher modifies these `Text` element values. Also, behind the scenes the LoginID, FirstName (FName), and LastName (LName) of the teacher were passed from the Address Book Page in Hidden elements. These values are reassigned to the Hidden elements in this Edit page.

When the modifications are complete, the teacher clicks the Edit this address button. Clicking this button submits the edited data to PABEditProc.asp. As you read above, PABEditProc.asp contains the data access and update logic that modifies the address within the application's datasource.

Listing 13.6 shows the contents of the Active Server Page, PABEditProc.asp.

EXAMPLE

Listing 13.6: ASP Code That Processes Address Edits (13asp06.asp/PABEditProc.asp)

```
<%
If Session("IsGoodUser") = False Then
    Response.Redirect Application("AccessErrFile")
End If


'======================================
'Page Name: PABEditProc.ASP
'Purpose: Contains the functions and
'         logic that allows a teacher
'         to edit an existing address
'         in the address book.
'
'Created: 1/15/2000
'Programmer: Bob Reselman
'======================================
'**************************************


Function EditRecord(RecID)
'
'Parameters: RedID, the record identifier of the
'               record to modify
'
'Return: True, if successful
'
'Remarks:  Use the this function to modify an address
'          from the address table in the Aristotle
'          Middle School Datasource. The datasource is
'          define as the Application variable,
'          Application("DBSource")
'
'Programmer: Bob Reselman
'Copyright: 2000
'
'History: Created 1/15/2000
```

continues

Listing 13.6: continued

```
'****************************************
      Dim cn 'Connection var
      Dim cmd 'Comamnd object
      Dim strSQL 'SQL Statement var
      On Error Resume Next
      'Create a Connection Object
      Set cn = CreateObject("ADODB.Connection")
      Set cmd = CreateObject("ADODB.Command")
      'Use the SQL UPDATE clause to edit a
      'record.
      strSQL = "UPDATE tblAddresses SET "
      strSQL = strSQL & "FirstName='" & Request.Form("edFName") & "'"
      strSQL = strSQL & ", " & "LastName='" & Request.Form("edLName") & "'"
      strSQL = strSQL & ", " & "Address='" & Request.Form("Address") & "'"
      strSQL = strSQL & ", " & "City='" & Request.Form("City") & "'"
      strSQL = strSQL & ", " & "State='" & Request.Form("State") & "'"
      strSQL = strSQL & ", " & "Zip='" & Request.Form("Zip") & "'"
      strSQL = strSQL & ", " & "Phone='" & Request.Form("Phone") & "'"
      strSQL = strSQL & ", " & "Email='" & Request.Form("Email") & "'"
      strSQL = strSQL & " WHERE RecID =" & CInt(RecID)
      'Set the SQL statement to the Command object.
      'Open the Connection
      cn.ConnectionString = "DSN=" & Application("DBSource")
      cn.Open
      If Err then Exit Function
      'Open the recordset
      cmd.ActiveConnection = cn
       'Set the SQL statement to the Command object.
      cmd.CommandText = strSQL
      cmd.Execute
      If Err then Exit Function
      'Life is good at this point
      cn.Close
      'Return True to show success
      EditRecord = True
End Function
'=============================================
'====================Entry point===============
'=============================================
'Delete the record passed to the page
if EditRecord(Request.Form("RecID")) then
   Dim URL 'Buffer for URL
   Dim QS 'Query String variable
   'Emulate a form submission for the LoginID by
   'creating the query string that the would be passed
   'for the form by the browser
   QS = "/PABListProcEx.asp?LoginID=" & Request.Form("LoginID")
```

```
    QS = QS & "&FName=" & Request.Form("FName")
    QS = QS & "&LName=" & Request.Form("LName")

    URL = Application("SiteURL") & QS
    'Redisplay the list
    Response.Redirect URL
Else
%>


<HTML>
<HEAD>
<TITLE></TITLE>
</HEAD>
<BODY>

<TABLE Border=0>
<TR>
<TD><IMG SRC="smbustb.gif"></TD>
<TD><FONT SIZE=4 Face=ARIAL Color=#000080>
Error editing the address submitted for <%=Request.Form("FName")%> 
<%=Request.Form("LName")%>'s
<BR><IMG SRC="logo.gif"><BR>
</FONT>
<FORM name=MyForm
      method=Post>

<INPUT type=Hidden
       name=LoginID
       value="<%=Request.Form("LoginID")%>">
<INPUT type=Hidden
       name=FName
       value="<%=Request.Form("FName")%>">
<INPUT type=Hidden
       name=LName
       value="<%=Request.Form("LName")%>">
</TABLE>

</FORM>
</TD></TR>
</TABLE>
<HR>
<FONT SIZE=4 Face=ARIAL Color=Red>
There has been an error editing the address you submitted.
</FONT>
</BODY>
</HTML>
<%End If%>
```

The bulk of the work of the `PABEditProc.asp` takes place in the function `EditRecord(RedID)`. `EditRecord(RedID)` uses the SQL `UPDATE` command to write the changes made in the modified address to the application's datasource. (You'll learn how to use the `UPDATE` command in the next section.) If the function returns `True`, a query string is constructed in the same manner that you learned about in the authentication page, `PABVerify.asp`. The query string is passed to the central Active Server Page, `PABListProc.asp`, that displays a list of addresses for teacher. Calling `PABListProc.asp` displays a refreshed address book in browser. If the function returns `False`, an error message is displayed.

The SQL `UPDATE` Command

You use the ADO `Command` object in conjunction with the SQL `UPDATE` command to modify a record in an ODBC database. The `UPDATE` command takes the syntax

```
UPDATE tblName SET FieldName1='Field1strData',
FieldName2=Field2numData, FieldName_n=#FieldnDateData#
WHERE FieldName=SomeCriteriaValue
```

Where

> `UPDATE` is the SQL Command.
>
> `tblName` is the name of the table in which the record(s) to be modified reside.
>
> `SET` is a SQL keyword indicating the fields to modify.
>
> `FieldName1`, `FieldName2`, and `FieldName_n` are the names of the fields to modify.
>
> `WHERE` is a SQL keyword indicating condition criteria.
>
> `FieldName=SomeCriteriaValue` is a criteria to satisfy.

NOTE

When assigning a string value to a field, don't forget to use the single quotation mark (`'`) at the beginning and end of the string.

When assigning a data value to a field, don't forget to use the pound sign character (#) before and after the date notation.

For example, if you want to create a SQL statement that updates the `FirstName` and `LastName` fields of a table name `tblTeachers`, for a teacher with the `TeacherID` bunnybug, you would write

```
UPDATE tblTeachers SET FirstName='Bugglesworth', LastName='Bunny'
WHERE TeacherID='bunnybug'
```

You can use the UPDATE command to modify many records in a table. For example, if you wanted to change the tblTeachers table so all occurrences of "Bob" in the field FirstName are changed to "Robert", you would write

```
UPDATE tblTeachers SET FirstName='Robert'
WHERE FirstName='Bob'
```

After you have a SQL statement created that uses the UPDATE command to modify an address, you assign the SQL statement to the CommandText property of Command object. Then you call the Command.Execute method to invoke the modification on the datasource. The following code is an extract from Listing 13.6 that illustrates how you use the Command object to modify address data on the datasource.

```
.
.
cn.ConnectionString = "DSN=" & Application("DBSource")
n.Open
If Err then Exit Function
'Open the recordset
cmd.ActiveConnection = cn
cmd.CommandText = strSQL
cmd.Execute
If Err then Exit Function
'Life is good at this point
cn.Close
```

Deleting an Address

If the teacher clicks the Delete button to the left of an address listing, the button's parent <FORM> element submits the address data to the Active Server Page, PABDelete.asp. (Remember that the Delete button is really a Submit button in disguise.) PABDelete.asp contains the logic and data access functionality that removes an address from the application's datasource. Listing 13.7 shows the contents of the Active Server Page, PABDelete.asp.

EXAMPLE

Listing 13.7: ASP Code That Deletes Addresses (13asp07.asp/PABDelete.asp)

```
<%
If Session("IsGoodUser") = False Then
    Response.Redirect Application("AccessErrFile")
End If

'=====================================
'Page Name: PABDelete.ASP
'Purpose: Deletes an address from a
'         teacher's address book.
'
```

continues

Listing 13.7: continued

```
'Created: 1/15/2000
'Programmer: Bob Reselman
'====================================
'************************************
Function DeleteRecord(RecID)
'
'Parameters: RedID, the record identifier of the
'            record to delete
'
'Return: True, if successful
'
'Remarks:  Use this function to delete an address
'          from the address table in the Aristotle
'          Middle School Datasource. The datasource is
'          defined in the Application variable,
'          Application("DBSource")
'
'Programmer: Bob Reselman
'Copyright: 2000
'
'History: Created 1/15/2000
'
'***************************
    Dim cn 'Connection var
    Dim cmd 'Command object var
    Dim strSQL 'SQL Statement var
    On Error Resume Next
    'Create a Connection Object
    Set cn = CreateObject("ADODB.Connection")
    Set cmd = CreateObject("ADODB.Command")
    'Use the SQL DELETE clause to create a
    'record.
    strSQL = "DELETE * FROM tblAddresses"
    strSQL = strSQL & " WHERE RecID =" & CInt(RecID)
    'Open the Connection
    cn.ConnectionString = "DSN=" & Application("DBSource")
    cn.Open
    If Err then Exit Function
    'Open the recordset
    cmd.ActiveConnection = cn
    'Set the SQL statement to the Command object
    cmd.CommandText = strSQL
    cmd.Execute
    If Err then Exit Function
    'Life is good at this point
    cn.Close
```

```
        DeleteRecord = True
End Function
'**************************************
'================================================
'=================Entry Point===================
'================================================
'Delete the record passed to the page
if DeleteRecord(Request.Form("RecID")) then
  Dim URL 'Buffer for URL
  Dim QS 'Query String variable
  'Emulate a form submission for the LoginID by
  'creating the query string that the would be passed
  'for the form by the browser. Then when you need to
  'get the values from the query string use to
  'Request.QueryString() Collection.
  QS = "/PABListProcEx.asp?LoginID=" & Request.Form("LoginID")
  QS = QS & "&FName=" & Request.Form("FName")
  QS = QS & "&LName=" & Request.Form("LName")

  URL = Application("SiteURL") & QS
  'Redisplay the list
  Response.Redirect URL
  Response.End
Else
%>
<HTML>
<HEAD>
<TITLE></TITLE>
</HEAD>
<BODY>

<TABLE Border=0>
<TR>
<TD><IMG SRC="smbustb.gif"></TD>
<TD><FONT SIZE=4 Face=ARIAL Color=#000080>
Error deleting the address submitted for <%=Request.Form("FName")%> 
<%=Request.Form("LName")%>'s
<BR><IMG SRC="logo.gif"><BR>
</FONT>
<FORM name=MyForm
      method=Post>

<INPUT type=Hidden name=LoginID value="<%=Request.Form("LoginID")%>">
<INPUT type=Hidden name=FName value="<%=Request.Form("FName")%>">
<INPUT type=Hidden name=LName value="<%=Request.Form("LName")%>">
</TABLE>
```

continues

Listing 13.7: continued

```
</FORM>
</TD></TR>
</TABLE>
<HR>
<FONT SIZE=4 Face=ARIAL Color=Red>
There has been an error deleting the address you submitted.
</FONT>
</BODY>
</HTML>
<%End If%>
```

The PABDelete.asp Active Server Page is one big If...Then...Else statement. The first thing the page does is call the page's DeleteRecord(RecID) function. If the function returns True, a query string containing the teacher's LoginID, FirstName, and LastName is constructed. The LoginID, FirstName, and LastName data is passed from the Hidden elements of the previous page. (Using Hidden elements to store inter-page data and then constructing a query string to pass teacher this information between pages has been used repeatedly throughout this chapter.) The query string is attached to the URL for the Active Server Page, PABListProcEx.asp. Then the code calls Request.Redirect on the newly constructed URL. PABListProcEx.asp displays a refreshed list of addresses for the given teacher's Personal Address Book.

If the function DeleteRecord() returns False, the body of the Active Server Page is passed back to the calling client. The body of the Active Server Page contains an error message.

The SQL DELETE Command

As you read above, the work of removing an address from the application's datasource is encapsulated in the function, DeleteRecord(RecID). The function is a wrapper for the SQL DELETE statement.

The SQL DELETE statement removes a record or records from a datasource. The syntax for the DELETE statement is

DELETE * FROM tableName WHERE condition1 AND condition_n

Where

   DELETE is the SQL command.

   * denotes all files.

   FROM is the SQL keyword indicating the tablename.

   tablename is the name of the table from which to remove records.

WHERE is the SQL keyword indicating a condition or set of conditions.

condition1 is a condition, usually a value associate with a field name.

condition_n is the last condition in a series of conditions.

EXAMPLE

For example, if you want to remove a record with the record ID of 302 from the table, tblAddresses, you would write

```
DELETE * FROM tblAddresses WHERE RecID=302
```

You use the DELETE command with the ADO Command object just as you use the UPDATE command. You create the Command object, attach the SQL statement to the Command object's CommandText property, and then call the Command object's Execute method to invoke the SQL command. Review the DeleteRecord() function to get a sense of how the DELETE command is used with the Command object in the Active Server Page, PABDelete.asp.

Adding an Address

The last feature we need to satisfy is the ability for a teacher to add an address to his Personal Address Book. At the top of the page in the Personal Address Book listing the addresses for a teacher is a button labeled Add an address (refer to Figure 13.1). When a teacher clicks the button to add an address, the PABAddAddr.asp page is called. The Active Server Page displays a set of Text elements into which a teacher enters the data for a new address. Listing 13.8 shows the code for PABAddAddr.asp. Figure 13.9 shows the output of the page in a browser.

EXAMPLE

Listing 13.8: Validating User Input (13asp08.asp/PABAddAddr.asp)

```
<%
If Session("IsGoodUser") = False Then
    Response.Redirect Application("AccessErrFile")
End If


'=======================================
'Page Name: PABAddAddr.ASP
'Purpose: Contains the display and
'         data collection functionality
'         that a teacher uses create a
'         address to add to the book
'
'Related file: PABAddAddrProc.ASP, this file is
'              called when the user wants to submit
'              data to be added to the database
'
'Created: 1/15/2000
```

continues

Listing 13.8: continued

```
'Programmer: Bob Reselman
'======================================
%>
<HTML>
<HEAD>

<TITLE>Aristotle Middle School Personal Address Book</TITLE>
</HEAD>
<SCRIPT ID=clientEventHandlersJS LANGUAGE=javascript>
<!--

function MyForm_onsubmit() {
   //Let's validate the form before
   //we send it in.
   //First Name
   if (document.MyForm.addFName.value==""){
        alert("You must provide a First Name");
        return false;
      }
   //Last Name
   if (document.MyForm.addLName.value==""){
        alert("You must provide a Last Name");
        return false;
      }
   //Address
   if (document.MyForm.addStreet.value==""){
        alert("You must provide a Street entry");
        return false;
        }
   //City
   if (document.MyForm.addCity.value==""){
        alert("You must provide a City");
        return false;
        }
   //State
   if (document.MyForm.addState.value==""){
        alert("You must provide a State");
        return false;
        }
   //Zip
   if (document.MyForm.addZip.value==""){
        alert("You must provide a Zip Code");
        return false;
        }
   //Phone
   if (document.MyForm.addPhone.value==""){
```

```
            alert("You must provide a Phone Number");
            return false;
        }
    //Email
    if (document.MyForm.addEmail.value==""){
            alert("You must provide an Email address");
            return false;
        }
    //If you get this far, life is good. You can
    //do a submit.
    document.MyForm.submit()
    return true
}
//-->
</SCRIPT>
<BODY>
<HTML>
<HEAD>
<TITLE>Aristotle Middle School Personal Address Book</TITLE>
</HEAD>
<BODY>
<TABLE Border=0>
<TR>
<TD><IMG SRC="smbustb.gif"></TD>
<TD><FONT SIZE=4 Face=ARIAL Color=#000080>
Add an address to <%=Request.Form("FName")%> <%=Request.Form("LName")%>'s
<BR><IMG SRC="logo.gif"><BR>
</FONT>
<FORM name=MyForm
 method=Post
 action= "<%=Application("SiteURL") & "/PABAddAddrProc.asp"%>"
 LANGUAGE=javascript
 onsubmit="return MyForm_onsubmit()">
<%'Hidden elements are used to persist the LoginID,
  'the Teacher's first name and last name from
  'page to page.%>
<INPUT type=Hidden
        name=LoginID value="<%=Request.Form("LoginID")%>">
<INPUT type=Hidden
        name=FName value="<%=Request.Form("FName")%>">
<INPUT type=Hidden
        name=LName value="<%=Request.Form("LName")%>">
</TABLE>
<%'Text elements for the address fields%>
<TABLE>
<TR><TD><FONT SIZE=3 Face=ARIAL Color=#000080>
First Name: </FONT></TD>
```

continues

Listing 13.8: continued

```
<TD><INPUT name=addFName></TD></TR>
<TR><TD><FONT SIZE=3 Face=ARIAL Color=#000080>
Last Name</FONT></TD>
<TD><INPUT name=addLName></TD></TR>
<TR><TD><FONT SIZE=3 Face=ARIAL Color=#000080>
Street:</FONT></TD>
<TD><INPUT name=addStreet></TD></TR>
<TR><TD><FONT SIZE=3 Face=ARIAL Color=#000080>
City:</FONT></TD>
<TD><INPUT name=addCity></TD></TR>
<TR><TD><FONT SIZE=3 Face=ARIAL Color=#000080>
State:</FONT></TD>
<TD><INPUT name=addState></TD></TR>
<TR><TD><FONT SIZE=3 Face=ARIAL Color=#000080>
Zip:</FONT></TD>
<TD><INPUT name=addZip></TD></TR>
<TR><TD><FONT SIZE=3 Face=ARIAL Color=#000080>
Phone:</FONT></TD>
<TD><INPUT name=addPhone></TD></TR>
<TR><TD><FONT SIZE=3 Face=ARIAL Color=#000080>
Email:</FONT></TD>
<TD><INPUT name=addEmail></TD></TR>
<TR><TD></TD><TD><INPUT type="submit"
                        value="Add to address book"
                        name=submit1></TD></TR>
</TABLE>
</FORM>
</TD></TR>
</TABLE>

</BODY>
</HTML>
```

Using `PABAddAddr.asp` and `PABAddAddrProc.asp`

When the teacher wants to add an address to the Personal Address Book, he enters the address data into the form on the Active Server Page, `PABAddAddr.asp`. Then the teacher clicks the Add to address book button at the bottom of the form to submit the form data to another Active Server Page, `PABAddAddrProc.asp`, for processing. (The Add to address book button is a Submit button in disguise.) However, before the processing page is called, the data in the form page is validated by client-side JavaScript. The JavaScript captures the form submission using the `<FORM>` element's `onsubmit` event procedure, `MyForm_onsubmit()`. The internals of the event procedure check each Text element in the form to make sure a string has been entered. If any Text element does not contain a string, an error message is displayed in an alert dialog box and the function is aborted by returning False (refer to Figure 13.9). The following code is an extract from the MyForm_onsubmit() event procedure in Listing 13.8. The code checks to make sure there is data in the Text element for the First Name:

```
//First Name
  if (document.MyForm.addFName.value==""){
        alert("You must provide a First Name");
        return false;
    }
```

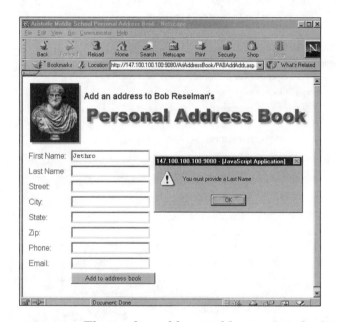

Figure 13.9: *The teacher adds an address using the Active Server Page,* PABAddAddr.asp.

The SQL INSERT Command

After the data for a new address is validated, the data is submitted to the Active Server Page, PABAddAddrProc.asp, for processing. The page PABAddAddrProc.asp contains writes the new data to the application's datasource. Listing 13.9 shows the code for the Active Server Page PABAddAddrProc.asp.

Listing 13.9: Adding Addresses to the Datasource (13asp09.asp/PABAddAddrProc.asp)

```
<%
If Session("IsGoodUser") = False Then
    Response.Redirect Application("AccessErrFile")
End If

Response.Buffer = True
'Security Check


'=====================================
'Page Name: PABAddAddrPoc.ASP
'Purpose: Contains the functions and
'         logic that adds an address
'         to a teacher's address book
'
'Created: 1/15/2000
'Programmer: Bob Reselman
'=====================================
'**************************
Function AddAddress(TeacherID, _
                    FirstName, _
                    LastName, _
                    Street, _
                    City, _
                    State, _
                    Zip, _
                    Phone, _
                    Email)
'Parameters: TeacherID, teacher LoginID
'             FirstName, An addressee's first name
'            LastName, An addressee's last name
'            Street, An addressee's street address
'            City, An addressee's city
'            State, An addressee's state
'            Zip, An addressee's zip
'            Phone, An addressee's phone number
'            Email, An addressee's email address
'
'Return:    True, if the add to the datasource is
'             successful
'
'Remarks:   Use the this function to add an entry
'            to the address table in the Aristotle
'            Middle School Datasource. The datasource is
'            define as the Application variable,
'            Application("DBSource")
```

```
'Programmer: Bob Reselman
'Copyright: 2000
'
'History: Created 1/15/2000
'
'*************************
    Dim cn  'Connection var
    Dim cmd 'Command object
    Dim strSQL 'SQL Statement var

    'Create a Connection Object
    Set cn = CreateObject("ADODB.Connection")
    Set cmd = CreateObject("ADODB.Command")
    'Use the SQL INSERT clause to create a
    'record.
    strSQL = "INSERT INTO tblAddresses (TeacherID, FirstName, "
    strSQL = strSQL & "LastName, Address, City, "
    strSQL = strSQL & "State, Zip, Phone, Email)"
    strSQL = strSQL & " VALUES"
    strSQL = strSQL & " ('" & TeacherID
    strSQL = strSQL & "', '" & FirstName& "', '" & LastName
    strSQL = strSQL & "', '" & Address & "', '" & City
    strSQL = strSQL & "', '" & State & "', '" & Zip
    strSQL = strSQL & "', '" & Phone & "', '" & Email & "')"
    'Set the SQL statement to the Command object.
    cmd.CommandText = strSQL
    'Set error trapping
    On Error Resume Next
    'Open the Connection
    cn.ConnectionString = "DSN=" & Application("DBSource")
    cn.Open
    If Err then Exit Function
    'Set an connection to the Command object
    cmd.ActiveConnection = cn
    'Run the command
    cmd.Execute
    If Err then Exit Function
    'Close up shop
    cn.close
    'If you get to here, life is good!
    AddAddress = True
End Function
%>


<%
```

Listing 13.9: continued

```
'================================================
'===============Entry Point====================
'================================================

Dim FirstName
Dim LastName
Dim Address
Dim City
Dim State
Dim Zip
Dim Phone
Dim Email
Dim b 'Boolean buffer for function returns

'Populate the variables with the
'data sent from the previous page
TeacherID = Request.Form("LoginID")
FirstName = Request.Form("addFName")
LastName = Request.Form("addLName")
Address = Request.Form("addStreet")
City = Request.Form("addCity")
State = Request.Form("addState")
Zip = Request.Form("addZip")
Phone = Request.Form("addPhone")
Email = Request.Form("addEmail")

'Add this data to the Address book using
'the AddAddress() function
b = AddAddress(TeacherID, FirstName, LastName, Address, _
               City, State, Zip, Phone, Email)
%>
<HTML>
<HEAD>
<TITLE>Aristotle Middle School Personal Address Book</TITLE>
</HEAD>
<BODY>
<TABLE Border=0>
<TR>
<TD><IMG SRC="smbustb.gif"></TD>
<TD><FONT SIZE=4 Face=ARIAL Color=#000080>
Address
<%If b = False then
'Make the word, "not" in red font
Response.Write "<FONT SIZE=4 Face=ARIAL Color=Red>"
Response.Write "not "
Response.Write "</FONT>"
```

```
End if%>
added to
<%=Request.Form("FName")%>
<%=Request.Form("LName")%>'s
<BR><IMG SRC="logo.gif"><BR>
</FONT>
<FORM name=MyForm
        method=get
        action="<%=Application("SiteURL") & "/PABListProcEx.asp"%>">

<INPUT type=Hidden
        name=LoginID value="<%=Request.Form("LoginID")%>">
<INPUT type=Hidden
        name=FName value="<%=Request.Form("FName")%>">
<INPUT type=Hidden
        name=LName value="<%=Request.Form("LName")%>">

<INPUT type="submit"
        value="Show address list for
        ➥<%=Request.Form("FName") & " "%><%=Request.Form("LName")%>"
name=submit1></FORM>
</TD></TR>
</TABLE>
<HR>
<%If b = True Then%>
<FONT SIZE=4 Face=ARIAL Color=Black>
The address:</FONT>
<P>
<FONT SIZE=4 Face=ARIAL Color=#000080>
<%=Firstname%> <%=Lastname%><BR>
<%=Address%><BR>
<%=City%>, <%=State%><BR>
<%=Zip%><BR>
<%=Phone%><BR>
<%=Email%><BR>
</FONT>
<P>
<FONT SIZE=4 Face=ARIAL Color=Black>
has been added to your address
book, <%=Request.Form("FName")%>.</FONT>
<%Else%>
<FONT SIZE=4 Face=ARIAL Color=Red>
There has been an error encounter when the
program tried to add an address to the Address
Book.
<P>
```

continues

Listing 13.9: continued

```
The error seems to be due to internal communication
with the application's database.
<P>
Please accept our apologizes. There error is not
your fault. Please notify the system administrator
that there is an error. The system administrator can be
reached at:<P>

Extension 4511
</FONT>
<%End If%>
<%Response.End%>
</BODY>
</HTML>
```

The `PABAddAddrProc.asp` Active Server Page assigns the data passed from the `Hidden` elements in `PABAddAddr.asp` to local variables using the `Request.Form()` collection. After the values are assigned to local variables, the page calls the `AddAddress()` function to add the data in these variables to the application's datasource. The `AddAddress()` function uses the SQL `INSERT` statement to the address data to the application's datasource. You learned how to use the `INSERT` statement in a previous chapter.

> ✔ For a review of the `INSERT` statement see the section, "Inserting Data into a Table Using SQL," in Chapter 8, p. 205.

If `AddAddress` is successful, it returns `True`. The `LoginID`, `FirstName`, and `LastName` of the teacher are packed up into the query string and attached to the URL for `PABListProcEx.asp`. This is pretty common business by now. Then the Active Server Page `PABListProcEx.asp` is again called to display a refreshed list of addresses for the given teacher.

NOTE

Note that at the beginning of the page, the `Response.Buffer` property is set to `True`. This is done to make sure all the processing on the server side is performed before any data is sent to the client.

Logging in a New Teacher

At the top of the Address List page, `PABListProcEx.asp`, is a button that returns control back to the login page when clicked by the teacher(refer to Figure 13.1). The following code is an extract from Listing 13.3:

EXAMPLE

```
<SCRIPT LANGUAGE=javascript>
<!—
    function btnNewTeacher_onclick(){
        //get the URL from the HIDDEN element name SiteURL
        //and assign it as the form ACTION, thus diverting
        //the default Submit behavior
        document.MyForm.action =
            document.MyForm.SiteURL.value +
                "/default.asp";
        //Submit the data, which in this case is a call
        //to the default login page
        document.MyForm.submit();
    }
//—>
</SCRIPT>
.
.
.
.
<INPUT type=Hidden
  name=SiteURL
  value="<%=Application("SiteURL")%>">
.
.
```

The code shown above is the btnNewTeacher_onclick() event procedure that is called when the user clicks the Logon a new teacher button. The interesting thing about this code snippet is that it causes control to pass to the login page, default.asp, by redefining the string assigned to Action attribute of the <FORM> element, MyForm. The new value of the Action attribute is the value of the Hidden element, SiteURL. This Hidden element's value is defined within the <FORM> element and gets its value on the server side from the Application variable that stores the site's URL. After the Action attribute is redefined, the JavaScript emulates the clicking of a Submit button by calling the document.MyForm.Submit() method. Thus, the default login page is called.

We use the technique of redefining the Action attribute of a <FORM> element in script using Hidden elements because it allows us to provide the data in the Application("SiteURL") variable at run time without having to generate the client-side JavaScript on the server side. If this seems confusing, remember that in an Active Server Page, you cannot embed server-side script within client-side script. The following code demonstrates the error:

EXAMPLE

```
<SCRIPT LANGUAGE=javascript>
<!—
function btnNewTeacher_onclick(){
//BIG ERROR BELOW
//You cannot embed server-side script in
//client-side script
document.MyForm.action =
  document.MyForm.SiteURL.value + <%Application("SiteURL")%>

document.MyForm.submit();
}
//—>
</SCRIPT>
```

As you can see, we cannot provide the Application's site URL on the server side using inline, server-side script. Of course, we could hard code the URL to the client-side script. However, that would defeat the purpose of using the Application-level variable as a central storage point for the site's URL. If we want to change the site URL, we need to remember to go back to this client-side function and make the change. Given the volume of code we have written, we might easily forget. The best thing to do is to be consistent with the application's architectural principles. And one of these principles is to keep the site's URL in an Application-level variable.

We can, however, use the `Application("SiteURL")` variable to assign the site's URL to a `Hidden` element on the server side. Then, all the client-side code needs to do is consult the particular `Hidden` element's value to get the site's URL.

What's Next

You've just learned a lot about programming by implementing a very limited set of application features. You've learned how to use HTML `Hidden` elements to persist data from page to page. You've learned how to pass data between pages using query strings. In addition, you've learned how to use the `Request.QueryString` collection to work with data in a submitted query string.

You've learned how to use client-side event procedures to do data validation. You've learned how to use the SQL `UPDATE` and `DELETE` command.

To this point, except for the use of ADO, all of the functionality in your Active Server Page Applications has been implemented using VBScript, JavaScript, and HTML. The next chapter is going to show you how to use create Active Server Pages that use functionality in objects that reside in custom made ActiveX components.

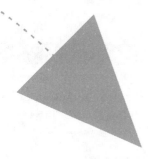

14

Creating a Class Attendance Page

One of the benefits of ASP technology is the ability to access functionality within custom made ActiveX Components using server-side script. ActiveX Components are created using programming languages, such as Visual Basic or C++, and are run on 32-bit Windows operating systems. If you know Visual Basic or C++ and are familiar with the details of ActiveX technology, you can create custom ActiveX Components for use in your Active Server Pages. ActiveX Components allow you to overcome some of the shortcomings of ASP technology. ActiveX Components allow you to exercise a greater degree of type control and error checking. ActiveX Components are more efficient. In addition, putting programming logic in ActiveX Components protects your work. Code in ActiveX Components is compiled and not exposed in open VBScript.

In this chapter you will

- Learn how to install an ActiveX DLL on your Web server

- Use `CreateObject()` to work with objects in ActiveX Components

- Work with `Collection` classes

- Learn how to use a `For...Each` Loop to iterate through `Collection` classes

- How to use the HTML `<SELECT>` to provide choices to users

Working with a Custom ActiveX DLL

ActiveX components are stored in an ActiveX Object Library. There are two kinds of ActiveX Object Libraries, the ActiveX DLL and the ActiveX EXE. An ActiveX DLL is an object library that runs in the same process space as the program using it. An ActiveX EXE runs in its own *process space*. A process space is a portion of memory that a program owns. In most cases, an ActiveX EXE runs slower than an ActiveX DLL. However, keep in mind that slow compared to fast in this technological arena is a matter of tenths of a second.

ActiveX Object Libraries are created according to the Component Object Model (COM) specification created by Microsoft. COM is a low-level standard that is independent of any given language. Therefore, you can create an ActiveX Object Library using any language that allows you to support the COM standard. Presently, Visual Basic, C++, Delphi, and Java allow you to write ActiveX Object Libraries. Visual Basic allows you to do so with the most ease. VB does a lot of the hard work involved in COM programming behind the scenes.

✔ For a review of the ActiveX Libraries see "Working with ActiveX Components" in Chapter 5, "Fundamentals of Object-Oriented Programming," p. 111.

The benefit of language independence is that you can use any ActiveX Component in your Active Server Pages, regardless of the language in which it was written. All ActiveX Components are wired together in the same manner.

Working with Custom Objects

As you read previously, using an object in a custom ActiveX Object Library allows you to overcome the shortcomings that exist in ASP technology. When you use an object in your Active Server Page, you do not need to know anything about the internals of the object. All you need to know is how to work with the properties, methods, and events of the object. Using an ActiveX Object Library allows you to program faster with more power and ease.

Usually programmers who make ActiveX Components are a separate group within a development team. These programmers have the ability to abstract the logic and data access functions of an application into an ActiveX Object Library. If you remember Chapter 1, "The Fundamentals of Distributed Computing Using ASP," this sort of programming is what we call Mid-Tier or Logic Tier programming. After an application has been abstracted into an ActiveX DLL or ActiveX EXE, the way in which an end user interacts with the program in the Presentation tier is open to a variety of techniques.

You might decide to use Active Server Pages to provide a user interface to the ActiveX Object Library, or you might create a dedicated client program written in Visual Basic or C++. Because this is a book about ASP, we are going to use Active Server Pages to work with a custom ActiveX DLL that was created especially for this chapter.

The ActiveX DLL that we use in this chapter contains logic and data access functionality that allows a user to take attendance for a class of students at a fictitious school, The Socrates Alternative School. This ActiveX DLL was created in Visual Basic. The source code and compiled ActiveX DLL are available for download along with the listing examples for this chapter.

Installing an ActiveX DLL on an IIS Computer Using `Regsvr32.EXE`

Before you can use an ActiveX DLL within your Active Server Page, you must have it installed on the system on which the DLL is going to run. ActiveX/COM technology requires that a lot of information about the objects in the DLL be entered into the System Registry of the computer hosting the component. If the DLL ships within a Setup program, usually the Setup program does the registration process when it runs. However, many ActiveX DLL's ship as a single file. In cases such as this, you must use the `Regsvr32.exe` utility to register the DLL. You can copy `Regsvr32.exe` from the Windows System directory into the directory in which you want to store and run the DLL on your Internet server, or you can copy the DLL directly into your Windows System directory. If you have trouble locating `Regsvr32.exe`, run the Find File utility that ships with Windows to locate the file.

`Regsvr32.exe` is a command line utility that you run from within a DOS Command Prompt Window. The utility knows how to look into the ActiveX DLL to retrieve and enter information about the ActiveX Components stored within it into the System Registry. The syntax for running `Regsvr32.exe` is

`Regsvr32  DLLName.DLL.`

Where `DLLName.DLL` is the name of the ActiveX DLL.

Figure 14.1 shows you `Regsvr32.exe` run from a command line in a DOS Command Prompt Window.

If you want to remove (or as we say in the trade, unregister) the information about the ActiveX DLL from the System Registry, use `Regsvr32.exe` with its `/u` flag parameter like so:

`Regsvr32  /u  DLLName.DLL.`

Figure 14.2 shows the DOS command line used to unregister an ActiveX DLL.

CAUTION

Never delete an ActiveX DLL without first unregistering it using `Regsvr32.exe`.

OUTPUT

Figure 14.1: If the DLL registration goes smoothly, `Regsvr32.exe` displays a special dialog box indicating a successful registration.

OUTPUT

Figure 14.2: A special dialog box appears when `Regsvr32.exe` successfully unregisters an ActiveX DLL.

NOTE

All you need to do to register an ActiveX EXE is run the executable from the command line, like so:

```
ExeName.exe
```

ActiveX EXEs have a registration facility built right in. The first time you run the EXE, the registration process takes place.

If you want to unregister the ActiveX EXE, enter the ActiveX EXE filename at the command line followed by the flag parameter `/UnregServer`:

```
ExeName.exe /UnregServer
```

After you have an ActiveX DLL registered on the Internet Server, you are ready to use it in your Active Server Pages.

Accessing an ActiveX Object library

You create objects from a custom ActiveX Object Library using the
CreateObject() function. (You've seen the CreateObject function before in
this book. We've used it when working with ADO.) For example, if we have
a custom object library, MyCustLib, that contains a class, CoolObj, we would
write

```
Dim obj
Set obj = CreateObject("MyCustLib.CoolObj")
```

Be advised that the name of an Object Library might or might not be the
same as that of the DLL in which the Object Library ships. Development
environments such as Visual Basic and Visual InterDev provide tools that
allow you to determine the name of an Object Library and classes within
the library.

> ✔ For details about working with Visual InterDev, download the tutorial "Visual InterDev 101"
> from the companion Web site for this book.

Working with Collection Objects

Before you move on to the details of working with the ActiveX Object
Library for our fictitious alternative school, you need to understand
Collection classes. A Collection class is a special type of class and is used
extensively in the Socrates Alternative School Object Library.

A Collection class is a class that is custom-made to contain a collection of a
specific object. For example, in ADO, the Fields collection is a collection
that contains a collection of Field objects.

ActiveX programmers have the ability to create custom Collection classes
in languages such as Visual Basic or C++.

Collection classes must expose the following properties and methods:

Table 14.1: **Collection** *Class Properties and Methods*

Property/Method	Description
.Add(Prop1Val, Prop2Val, Prop3Val, PropnVal, sKey)	Creates and adds an object to the Collection class. You create an object within the Collection class by entering the property values for the collected object as arguments to the Add method.
.Count	Returns the number of objects in the Collection class. Read only.
Item(index|keyName)	Returns a specific object from a Collection class either by index number or keyName. Read only.
Remove(index|keyName)	Removes a specific object from a collection class either by index number or keyName. Read only.

The benefit of using a `Collection` class is that you can create an object within the collection by just adding the data, without having to create and add the object explicitly.

For example, imagine we have a class, `clsPersons`, which is a `Collection` class for the class, `clsPerson`. (In other words, the `Collection` class `clsPersons` is designed to hold a bunch of `clsPerson` objects.) The `clsPerson` class supports three properties:

```
clsPerson.FirstName As String
clsPerson.LastName As String
clsPerson.DateOfBirth As Date
```

If we want to create a new `clsPerson` object within the `Collection` class, we would write the code shown in Listing 14.1. A `Collection` class allows you to create objects implicitly.

EXAMPLE

Listing 14.1: Creating Objects with a `Collection` Class

```
'Create a variable to hold the Collection class
Dim pns
'Create the Collection class
Set pns= CreateObject("MyLib.clsPersons")
'Create a clsPerson in the Collection class by
'adding values for the FirstName, LastName and DateOfBirth.
'Also, give the newly created clsPerson object
'the keyname, "Bob"
pns.Add CStr("Robert"), CStr("Reselman") , _
            CDate("7/4/1776"), "Bob"
'Write out the FirstName and LastName of the object that is
'with the keyname, "Bob"
Response.Write pns("Bob").FirstName & " " & _
                pns("Bob").LastName
```

The output of the code shown in Listing 14.1 is as follows:

```
Robert Reselman
```

OUTPUT

Notice in Listing 14.1 that we used the `Add` method of `Collection` class object pns to create a new `clsPerson` object. This new class in created within the `Collection` class object. The `Collection` class does all the work. All we needed to do was provide the values for the `FirstName`, `LastName`, and `DateOfBirth` properties. In addition, we added an `sKey` value that we can use to identify the object within the `Collection` class. How did we know to use the `FirstName`, `LastName`, and `DateOfBirth` properties? The answer is that `FirstName`, `LastName`, and `DateOfBirth` are the properties of the `clsPerson` object. The `Collection` class, `clsPersons`, knows enough to look for these properties as parameters of its `Add` property. It's as if the `Collection` class says to itself, "I am a `Collection` class for `clsPerson` objects.

If a programmer calls my Add method and provides me with the values for FirstName, LastName, DateOfBirth, and an sKey, I will make a clsPerson object inside of me. Also, I will refer to this newly made clsPerson object by the value of the sKey. If a programmer uses my Item property and passes me the sKey as an argument, I will return to him or her the clsPerson object that corresponds to that sKey."

NOTE

ActiveX programming convention relates a Collection class to the collected class by the using the suffix "s". For example, if you want to make a Collection class for a class, clsDog, you name the Collection class, clsDogs. If you have a class, clsStudent, when you create or instantiate its Collection class, you name the Collection class clsStudents.

CAUTION

Remember that in VBScript all variables are Variants. Not all Collection classes support Variants for Add method parameter types. When you pass parameters to the Add method of a Collection class, make sure the type of each parameter corresponds to the type the Add method is expecting. For example, if your Collection class expects Integer types for its parameters and you pass the default Variant type, you will get an error. You might have to use the VBScript conversion functions to ensure type consistency.

How do we know how to order the parameters for the Add method? One way is to use Intelli-sense if you are programming under Visual InterDev or Visual Basic. The programming environment shows you the parameter order of a particular Collection class as you are writing the code. Another way is to use *named arguments*. Named arguments allow you to assign the parameter name to the value you are providing to a method. However, at this time VBScript does not support named parameters, which is unfortunate. Therefore, unless you have a good set of documentation for the Collection class you are using or a robust development environment such as Visual InterDev, you might have trouble.

NOTE

The sKey value is the last parameter in any Add method for a Collection object. It is an optional value that you can use or not use.

Using For...Each with Collection Classes

An added benefit of working with the Collection class is that you can use a For...Each loop to traverse all the objects within the Collection class. For...Each loops have the smarts to say to a Collection class, "Show me each object in your collection." As each object is presented, you can work its properties and methods.

The syntax for a Collection class is

```
For Each obj In objs
    'Do something with obj.someProperty
Next
```

Where

>   For Each is a keyword that indicates a loop
>
>   *obj* is an object in the collection
>
>   In is a keyword that indicates the Collection class being referenced
>
>   *objs* is a given Collection class
>
>   Next is a keyword for the loop iterator

Listing 14.2 shows you an Active Server Page that creates objects within a Collection class and then uses the For...Each loop to display a list the values of two of the object's properties. The output of Listing 14.2 is shown in Figure 14.3.

EXAMPLE

Listing 14.2: For...Each Loops and the Collection Class

```
<HTML>
<HEAD>
<TITLE></TITLE>
</HEAD>
<BODY>
<FONT Color=Blue Face=Arial Size=5>
<%
Dim pns
Dim pn
'Create a Collection class of type clsPersons
Set pns = CreateObject("MyLib.clsPersons ")
'Create some clsPerson objects
pns.Add CDate("7/4/1776"), "Robert", "Reselman"
pns.Add CDate("10/12/1492"), "Bugglesworth", "Bunny"
pns.Add CDate("7/17/1969"), "Daffrondo", "Duck"
pns.Add CDate("8/7/1969"), "Porkensington", "Pig"

'Traverse the Collection class and report the
'First and Last Name of each clsPerson object
'in the Collection class.
For Each pn In pns
  Response.Write pn.FirstName & " " & pn.LastName & "<BR>"
Next
%>
</FONT>
</BODY>
</HTML>
```

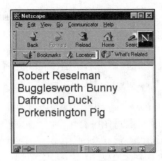

OUTPUT

Robert Reselman
Bugglesworth Bunny
Daffrondo Duck
Porkensington Pig

Figure 14.3: *Collection classes allow you to work with objects on the fly.*

Being able to work with a Collection class is an important skill to have. The code you are going to see in the Socrates Alternative School Application in the next section uses Collection classes extensively.

The Socrates Alternative School Application

The Socrates Alternative School Application is an ASP Application that has a feature allowing a teacher to login, select a class he teaches, and then take attendance for that class. After the teacher takes attendance, the application presents the teacher with a report that summarizes the attendance activity of all the students within the class. Figure 14.4 shows the attendance report the application makes after the teacher takes attendance.

OUTPUT

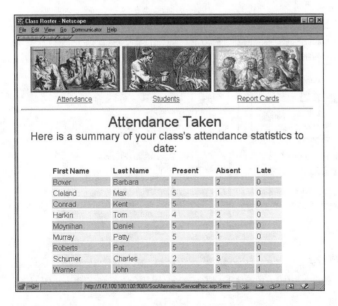

Figure 14.4: *The Socrates Alternative School application allows the teacher to take attendance and keep track of overall attendance activity.*

The Socrates Alternative School is different from any ASP application we have yet to create in that all the logic and data access functionality for the application is contained in a server-side ActiveX DLL. The Active Server Pages we make act as nothing more than a Graphical User Interface (GUI) for the objects contained within the ActiveX DLL.

The object that is central to the Socrates Alternative School application is the clsSocApp object. The clsSocApp object abstracts the login, class display, attendance taking, and reporting features of the application. Whenever an Active Server Page needs to access a feature of the application, it creates an instance of the clsSocApp object and invokes one of its methods. Throughout this chapter we'll refer to the clsSocApp object as the custom Application object. Figure 14.5 shows a diagram of the object model Socrates Alternative School Object Library.

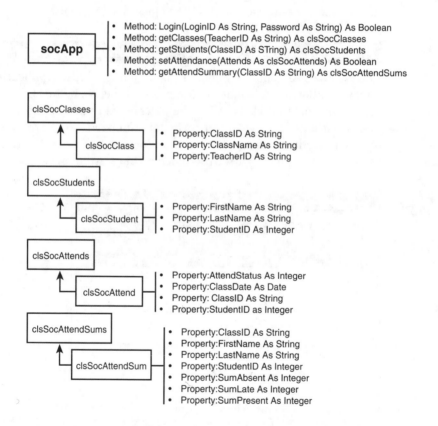

Figure 14.5: *The* clsSocApp *object is an abstraction of all the logic and data access functions for the Socrates Alternative School Application.*

Notice that the Object Model gives no indication of the existence of a data-source. Notice, too, that none of the logic is exposed. These features are hidden within the class. All an ASP programmer needs to do is call the custom App object's (`clsSocApp`) methods and work with the objects that the methods return. In addition, you will need to create one `Collection` object by which to submit attendance data to the application object for processing. You'll cover this later in the section.

Figure 14.6 shows the program flow between the various Active Server Pages of the Socrates Alternative School Application.

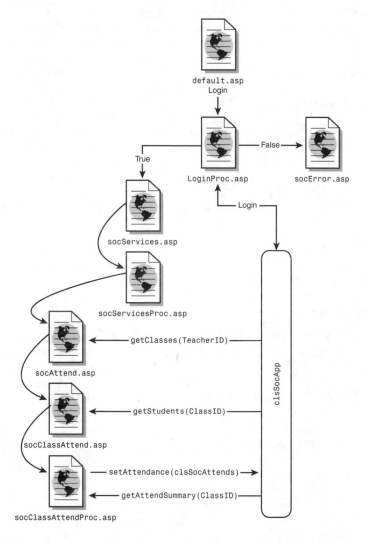

Figure 14.6: *If an Active Server Page needs to access application logic, it creates an instance of the application* `clsSocApp` *object.*

The application consists of eight Active Server Pages. Table 14.2 lists and describes each page.

Table 14.2: Socrates Alternative School Application Pages

Active Server Page	Description
Global.ASA	Contains systemwide data for the application.
Default.asp	Presents a logic page.
LoginProc.asp	Process login data. If the login is valid, control is passed to socServices.asp. Otherwise control is passed to socError.asp.
socError.asp	Reports a login error.
socServices.asp	Provides a menu of services that a teacher at Socrates Alternative School can access. At the present time, only attendance taking services are in force.
socAttend.asp	Presents a list of classes a given teacher teaches. The teacher selects a class from an HTML <SELECT> element.
socClassAttend.asp	Presents a class roster of the students in the chosen class. A student can be marked Present, Late, or Absent. The teacher chooses an attendance status for each student from a set of HTML <SELECT> elements, one dedicated to each student.
socClassAttendProc.asp	Writes the attendance data for the class to the application object's datasource and returns a summary report of attendance statistics for the entire class on a student by student basis.

Now that you have an overview of the structure of the application and understand the flow of the application between Active Server Pages, let's take a detailed look at each page.

Logging in

Listing 14.3 shows the code for the default Login page for the Socrates Alternative School application. Figure 14.7 shows the page displayed in a Web browser.

EXAMPLE

Listing 14.3: The Default Login Page (default.asp/14asp03.asp)

```
<%
'====================================
'Page: default.asp
'
'Provides login functionality
'
'Programmer: Bob Reselman
'
'Created 1/15/99
'====================================
%>
<HTML>
```

```
<HEAD>

<TITLE>Socrates Alternative School Login</TITLE>
</HEAD>

<BODY>
<P>
<CENTER>
<P><FONT SIZE = 5 FACE=ARIAL COLOR=BLUE>
Welcome to The Socrates Alternative School
</FONT>
<BR><FONT SIZE = 3 FACE=ARIAL><B>
No idea is too big. No thought is too small.</B>
<P> <Img src="./images/soclogo.jpg">
<FORM Name=frmLogin
      Method=POST
      Action="<%=Application("SiteURL") & "/LoginProc.asp"%>">
<P>
<CENTER>
<TABLE>
<TR><TD>
<FONT SIZE = 3 FACE=ARIAL COLOR=BLUE>
Login Name:</FONT></TD></TR>
<TR><TD><INPUT name=LoginID></TD></TR>
<TR><TD>
<FONT SIZE = 3 FACE=ARIAL COLOR=BLUE>
Password:</FONT></TD></TR>
<TR><TD><INPUT name=PWD
        type=Password></P></TD></TR>
<TR><TD><INPUT type="submit"
                  value="Login"
                  name=submit1></TD></TR>
 </TABLE>
 </CENTER>
</FORM>

</CENTER>
</BODY>
</HTML>
```

The login page is unremarkable except that the call is made to the
LoginProc.asp Active Server Page using a Submit button within an HTML
<FORM>. You've seen this technique used in other chapters in this book.

Listing 14.4 shows the code for the LoginProc.asp Active Server Page. This
page contains the login logic for the application. Figure 14.8 shows the
socError.asp Active Server Page. This page is called if the user submits an
invalid LoginID and password.

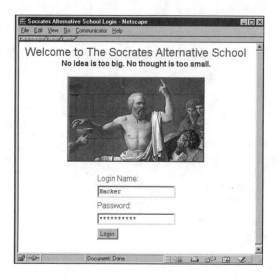

Figure 14.7: *A teacher must provide a predetermined LoginID and Password to access services within the Application.*

Listing 14.4: Using An ActiveX Component to Login (LoginProc.asp/14asp04.asp)

```
<%
'=====================================
'Page: LoginProc.asp
'
'Provides login logic functionality
'
'Programmer: Bob Reselman
'
'Created 1/15/99
'=====================================

    Dim socApp
    Dim URL

    'Keep the LoginID in a Session variable. We'll need
    'to use it throughout the session.
    Session("LoginID") = Request.Form("LoginID")

    'Create an instance of the custom App object. Remember
    'this App object is an abstraction of the entire application
    Set socApp = CreateObject("SocNewAlternate.clsSocApp")
```

```
'Use the App object's Login method to validate the user
If socApp.Login(Request.Form("LoginID"), _
                    Request.Form("PWD")) Then
    'Set a URL to the services page, if the login is valid
    URL = Application("SiteURL") & "/SocServices.asp"
        'Go to the services page
    Response.Redirect URL
Else
    'If this is an invalid error, redirect to the
    'error page.
    Response.Redirect Application("SiteURL")_
        & "/SocError.ASP"
End If

Set socApp = Nothing
%>
```

OUTPUT

Figure 14.8: *A teacher must provide a predetermined LoginID and Password to access services within the application.*

The LoginProc.asp Active Server Page creates an instance of clsSocApp. As you read previously, clsSocApp is the class that is an abstraction of the application. The page uses the object's Login(LoginID, PWD) method to validate the login data. If the method returns True, the response is redirected to an Active Server Page containing the Graphical User Interface and allowing the user to select an application service. (The application is designed to provide various services, of which attendance taking is but one.) If the clsSocApp.Login() method returns False, the response is redirected to a page reporting an error. The Response.Redirect method is used to redirect the responses.

Choosing a Service

If a login proves to be valid, response within the Socrates Alternative School application is redirected to an Active Server Page that allows a teacher to choose a service. This page is named `SocService.asp`. At the present time, only the Attendance service is implemented. The user can click the word Attendance or an illustrated button to select the Attendance service.

Listing 14.5 shows the code for the `SocServices.asp` Active Server Page. Notice that the page uses HTML anchor elements `<A HREF>` to call the Active Server Page that processes a service request. Service requests are numbered 1, 2, and 3 for Attendance, Students, and Report Cards services, respectively. Each variable is assigned to the `QueryString` variable `Serv`. The value of the `Serv` variable corresponds to the service. `Serv=1` is assigned to the `HREF` for Attendance, for example.

The `QueryString` is attached to the URL of the `HREF`. When a user click an `<A HREF...>` anchor, a call is made to the `SocServicesProc.asp` Active Server Page.

EXAMPLE

Listing 14.5: Simple HTML Produces an Effective Menu (`SocService.asp`/`14asp05.asp`)

```
<%
'======================================
'Page: SocServices.asp
'
'Presents a menu from which
'a teacher can select a service.
'NOTE: At the present time only Attendance is
'in force.
'
'Programmer: Bob Reselman
'
'Created 1/15/99
'======================================%>
<HTML>
<HEAD>
<TITLE>Socrates Alternative School Services Menu</TITLE>
</HEAD>

<BODY>
<P>
<CENTER>
<FONT SIZE = 5 FACE=ARIAL COLOR=Blue>
<P>Welcome

<%
'Use the Session Variable to find the
'value of the Login value passed from the
```

```
'page that called the redirection.
Response.write Session("LoginID")%> to
<BR>The Socrates Alternative School
<BR>Services
</FONT>

<P> <Image src="./images/soclogo.jpg">
<BR><FONT SIZE=3 FACE=ARIAL><B>
No idea is too big. No thought is too small.</B></FONT>
<P>

<TABLE>
<TR>
<TD>
<%
'Create HREF text and buttons so a teacher can
'select a service.
'Serv=1: Attendance
'Serv=2: Students
'Serv=3: Report Cards
'NOTE: At the present time only Attendance is in force!
%>
<%'===BUTTONS=========%>
<A HREF="<%Response.Write Application("SiteURL") & _
                    "/SocServicesProc.asp?Serv=1"%>">
<Img src="./images/attendance.jpg" border=0></A></TD>

<TD>
<A HREF="<%Response.Write Application("SiteURL") & _
                    "/SocServicesProc.asp?Serv=2"%>">
<Img src="./images/students.jpg" border=0></A></TD>

<TD>
<A HREF="/<%Response.Write Application("SiteURL") & _
                    "/SocServicesProc.asp?Serv=3"%>">
<Img src="./images/reportcards.jpg" border=0></A></TD>
</TR>

<TR>
<%'===TEXT=========%>
<TD Align=Center>
<A HREF="<%Response.Write Application("SiteURL") & _
                    "/SocServicesProc.asp?Serv=1"%>">
<FONT FACE=Arial>Attendance</FONT></A></TD>

<TD Align=Center>
```

continues

Listing 14.5: continued

```
<A HREF="<%Response.Write Application("SiteURL") & _
                    "/SocServicesProc.asp?Serv=2"%>">
<FONT FACE=Arial>Students</FONT></A></TD>

<TD Align=Center>
<A HREF="<%Response.Write Application("SiteURL") & _
                    "/SocServicesProc.asp?Serv=3"%>">
<FONT FACE=Arial>Report Cards</FONT></A></TD>
</TR>
</TABLE>

</CENTER>
</BODY>
</HTML>
```

Figure 14.9 shows the output of the page.

OUTPUT

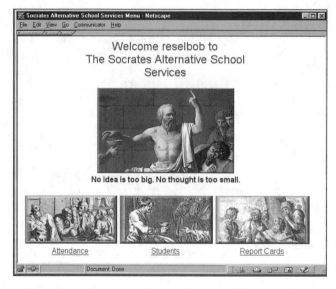

Figure 14.9: The Services page allows the teacher to choose a service.

Listing 14.7 shows the SocServicesProc,asp page. Notice the code uses a Select Case statement to determine which service the teacher chose in the previous page. The previous page is SocServices.asp, which was shown in Listing 14.5.

The `Request.QueryString` collection is examined to determine which service the teacher selected. If the teacher chose the Attendance service, response is redirected to `SocAttend.asp`. This Active Server Page presents a list of classes that the teacher teaches. The other services are not implemented. Therefore, a simple message is sent back to the teacher when these services are selected. Listing 14.6 shows the code `SocServicesProc.asp`.

✔ For a review of the `Request.QueryString` collection see "Introduction to the Request Object" in Chapter 6, "Beginning ASP: Client-Server Communication," page 140.

EXAMPLE

Listing 14.6: Filtering `QueryString` Values with a `Select Case` Statement (`SocServicesProc.asp/14asp06.asp`)

```
<%
'====================================
'Page: SocServicesProc.asp
'
'Process a request for a service
'
'NOTE: At the present time only Attendance is
'in force.
'
'Programmer: Bob Reselman
'
'Created 1/15/99
'====================================
    Dim strReturn
    Dim URL
    'Get the value of the Serv variable from the previous
    'page, SocServices.asp.
    Select Case Request.QueryString("Serv")
        Case 1:
            'Attendance is implemented, so call the page
            URL = Application("SiteURL") & "/SocAttend.asp"
            Response.Redirect URL
        Case 2:
            'The Students service is not implemented.
            'Send back a simple message
            strReturn = "Here are the Students"
            Response.write strReturn
        Case 3:
            'The Report Card service is not implemented.
            'Send back a simple message
            strReturn = "Here are the Report Cards"
            Response.write strReturn
    End Select
%>
```

Choosing a Class

The code for the Attendance feature is where we really begin to use the power of the Socrates Alternative School Object Library.

Listing 14.7 shows the code for the `socAttends.asp` Active Server Page.

EXAMPLE

Listing 14.7: Using a Custom ActiveX Component to Retrieve Data (`SocAttend.asp/14asp07.asp`)

```
<%
'====================================
'Page: SocAttend.asp
'
'Presents a list of classes that the teacher
'teaches.
'
'Programmer: Bob Reselman
'
'Created 1/15/99
'====================================%>
<HTML>
<HEAD>
<TITLE>Socrates Alternative School Attendance</TITLE>
</HEAD>
<BODY>
<CENTER>
<%'=======Beginning of Services Buttons========%>
<TABLE>
<TR>
<TD>
<A HREF="<%Response.Write Application("SiteURL") & _
                    "/ServiceProc.asp?Serv=1"%>">
<Img src="./images/attendance.jpg" border=0></A></TD>

<TD>
<A HREF="<%Response.Write Application("SiteURL") & _
                    "/ServiceProc.asp?Serv=2"%>">
<Img src="./images/students.jpg" border=0></A></TD>

<TD>
<A HREF="/<%Response.Write Application("SiteURL") & _
                    "/ServiceProc.asp?Serv=3"%>">
<Img src="./images/reportcards.jpg" border=0></A></TD>
</TR>

<TR>

<TD Align=Center>
```

```
<A HREF="<%Response.Write Application("SiteURL") & _
                      "/ServiceProc.asp?Serv=1"%>">
<FONT FACE=Arial>Attendance</FONT></A></TD>

<TD Align=Center>
<A HREF="<%Response.Write Application("SiteURL") & _
                      "/ServiceProc.asp?Serv=2"%>">
<FONT FACE=Arial>Students</FONT></A></TD>

<TD Align=Center>
<A HREF="<%Response.Write Application("SiteURL") & _
                      "/ServiceProc.asp?Serv=3"%>">
<FONT FACE=Arial>Report Cards</FONT></A></TD>
</TR>
</TABLE>
<%'=======End of Services Buttons========%>


<FONT SIZE = 5 FACE=ARIAL COLOR=blue>
<P>Socrates Alternative School Class Attendance</FONT>

<FONT SIZE = 4 FACE=ARIAL COLOR=Purple>
<P>Choose a class:<BR></FONT>
<!— Let's use an HTML form to submit
     the class request data—>
<FONT SIZE=3 FACE=ARIAL>
<FORM Method=Post Action="<%=Application("SiteURL") & _
                          "/SocClassAttend.asp"%>">

<%'Create a <SELECT> element into which you put
'the classes that a teacher teaches.%>
<SELECT name=ClassID>
<%
    Dim socApp 'a variant the stores the App object
    Dim socClasses 'a variant the stores the Collection class
                    'of courses that the teacher teaches
    Dim socClass 'a variant for a course at the Socrates
                  'Alternative School/

    'Create a custom APP object
    Set socApp = CreateObject("SocNewAlternate.clsSocApp")

    'Pass in the LoginID into the App objects's
    'getClasses methods. The method returns a Collection class
    'that contains socClass objects. Each socClass object
    'has a ClassID, ClassName and TeacherID property
    Set socClasses = socApp.getClasses(Session("LoginID"))
```

continues

Listing 14.7: continued

```
    'Traverse the Collection class and get the ClassName
    'and ClassID property from each
    'socClass object in the Collection class, socClasses.
    For Each socClass in socClasses
        'Create an <OPTION value=ClassID> tag
        Response.Write "<" + "OPTION value= " & socClass.ClassID & ">"
        'And then embed the class name in the tag.
        Response.Write socClass.ClassName & vbCrLf
    Next
    %>
</SELECT>
 <Input type=Submit value="Get class roster >>" Name=Submit>
</FORM>
</FONT>
</CENTER>
</BODY>
</HTML>
```

Figure 14.10 shows the output of the code.

OUTPUT

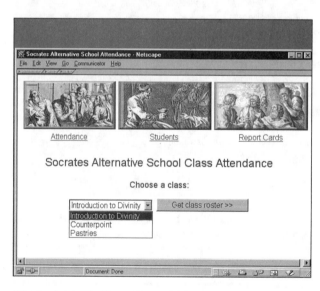

Figure 14.10: *You use an HTML <SELECT> element to provide a list of choices to a user.*

The following two lines of code from Listing 14.7 are the most powerful statements in the page.

```
Set socApp = CreateObject("SocNewAlternate.clsSocApp")
    .

    .

    .
Set socClasses = socApp.getClasses(Session("LoginID"))
```

One line of code creates the custom App object, socApp. The other line of code uses the App object's getClassses method to retrieve a Collection class of socClass objects. The socClass object contains ClassID, ClassName, and TeacherID properties. The code then uses a For...Each to traverse the Collection class. The ClassID and ClassName data is extracted from each socClass object in the collection and embedded in an HTML <SELECT> element to create a list of classes the teacher teaches.

There is a lot of work going on inside the custom App object in terms of data access and object construction. However, it's all hidden from you. All you need to do is make the App object and ask it for a Collection class of socClass objects. What could be easier?

As a Web designer you get to focus on the User Interface design, and the ActiveX Object Library programmer focuses on programming logic and data access. Should you find that your User Interface design needs improvement, you run little risk of breaking the logic of the application when you adjust the code in your Active Server Page. This is the beauty of using Object Libraries on the server side—you get a high degree of code reuse.

Using the HTML <SELECT> Element

After the teacher selects a Class from his or her list and clicks the Get class roster button, the ClassID for the selection is passed on to the SocClassAttend.asp Active Server Page. Let's take a look at the mechanics of the interaction.

A HTML <SELECT> element is used to create a dropdown combobox from which the teacher chooses a class roster. The following is the server-side code extracted from Listing 14.7 that creates the <SELECT> element:

EXAMPLE

```
<FORM Method=Post Action="<%=Application("SiteURL") & _
                            "/SocClassAttend.asp"%>">
    .

    .
<SELECT name=ClassID>
<%
    Dim socApp 'a variant the stores the App object
    .

    .

    .
```

```
    For Each socClass in socClasses
        'Create an <OPTION value=ClassID> tag
        Response.Write "<" + "OPTION value= " & socClass.ClassID & ">"
        'And then embed the class name in the tag.
        Response.Write socClass.ClassName & vbCrLf
    Next
    %>
</SELECT>
 <Input type=Submit value="Get class roster >>" Name=Submit>
</FORM>
```

OUTPUT

The code that follows is the client-side source code that the Active Server Page outputs.

```
<FORM Method=Post
        Action="http://www.schools.com/SocAlternative/SocClassAttend.asp">
<SELECT name=ClassID>
<OPTION value=div101>Introduction to Divinity
<OPTION value=music203>Counterpoint
<OPTION value=homec212>Pastries
</SELECT>
 <Input type=Submit value="Get class roster >>" Name=Submit>
</FORM>
```

As you previously read, the <SELECT> element displays a dropdown combo-box. When the user clicks the Submit button, the value of the Option attribute for the entry the user selects is submitted onto the Internet Server. The friendly name text is nothing more than a content label. For example, when the user selects the dropdown text "Introduction to Divinity," the value div101 is passed on to the server using the name of the <SELECT> element as the variable name, like so:

```
ClassID=div101
```

Figure 14.11 illustrates the concept.

NOTE

If you do not assign a value attribute to the <OPTION> element, its content label is passed as the default value of the corresponding <SELECT> element.

USING Option Explicit

If you want to make sure that all variables in the scripts of your Active Server Page are ones that you declare using the Dim keyword, use the Option Explicit statement. You write the words Option Explicit at the top of the first script in your Active Server Page. Using Option Explicit forces you to declare variables. If you use a variable without declaring it and Option Explicit is in force, an error fires when you try to run the script.

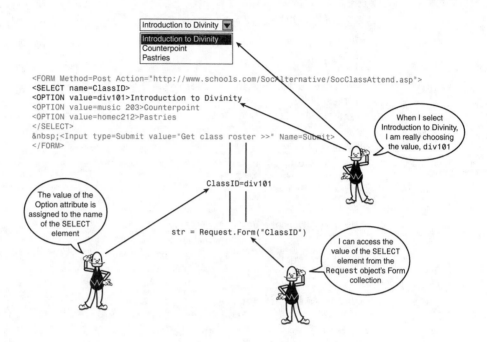

Figure 14.11: When you choose an item in a SELECT element, the value of the item's OPTION attribute is submitted to the Internet server.

Displaying a Class Roster

The SocClassAttend.asp Active Server Page displays a class roster for a class that a teacher selected in the SocAttend.asp page. Listing 14.8 shows the code for the page SocClassAttend.asp. Figure 14.12 shows the output from the listing.

EXAMPLE

Listing 14.8: Using HTML <SELECT> Elements to Determine Attendance Status (SocClassAttend.asp/14asp0.asp)

```
<%'=====================================
'Page: SocClassAttend.asp
'
'Presents a list of students in a selected class
'
'Programmer: Bob Reselman
'
'Created 1/15/99
'=====================================
Option Explicit 'Make it so we must declare variables

%>
```

continues

Listing 14.8: continued

```
<HTML>
<HEAD>
<TITLE>
<%=Request.Form("ClassID")%> Class Roster"
</TITLE>
</HEAD>
<BODY>
<CENTER>
<%'=======Beginning of Services Buttons========%>
<TABLE>
<TR>
<TD>
<A HREF="<%Response.Write Application("SiteURL") & _
                     "/ServiceProc.asp?Serv=1"%>">
<Img src="./images/attendance.jpg" border=0></A></TD>

<TD>
<A HREF="<%Response.Write Application("SiteURL") & _
                     "/ServiceProc.asp?Serv=2"%>">
<Img src="./images/students.jpg" border=0></A></TD>

<TD>
<A HREF="/<%Response.Write Application("SiteURL") & _
                     "/ServiceProc.asp?Serv=3"%>">
<Img src="./images/reportcards.jpg" border=0></A></TD>
</TR>
<%'=======Beginning of Services Text========%>
<TR>

<TD Align=Center>
<A HREF="<%Response.Write Application("SiteURL") & _
                     "/ServiceProc.asp?Serv=1"%>">
<FONT FACE=Arial>Attendance</FONT></A></TD>

<TD Align=Center>
<A HREF="<%Response.Write Application("SiteURL") & _
                     "/ServiceProc.asp?Serv=2"%>">
<FONT FACE=Arial>Students</FONT></A></TD>

<TD Align=Center>
<A HREF="<%Response.Write Application("SiteURL") & _
                     "/ServiceProc.asp?Serv=3"%>">
<FONT FACE=Arial>Report Cards</FONT></A></TD>
</TR>
</TABLE>
<%'=======End of Services menu========%>
```

```
<HR>
    <!—Let's use an HTML form to submit
    'class request data—>
<FORM Method=Post
      Action="<%=Application("SiteURL") & _
              "/SocClassAttendProc.asp"%>">
<FONT SIZE = 4 FACE=ARIAL COLOR=Purple>
<%
    Dim socApp 'a variant that stores the App object
    Dim socStudents 'a variant that stores
                        'the Students Collection object
    Dim socStudent 'a Student object
    Dim i 'counter var
    Dim clr 'color variable
    'Create an App object
    Set socApp = CreateObject("SocNewAlternate.clsSocApp")
    'Use the getStudents method to return a Collection
    'class full of student objects
    Set socStudents = socApp.getStudents(Request.Form("ClassID"))
%>

<BR>Socrates Alternative School <%=Cstr(Date())%><BR></FONT>
<TABLE WIDTH=80%>
<TR>
<TD bgcolor=#cd854f><FONT Size=4 Face=Arial>ID</FONT></TD>
<TD bgcolor=#cd854f>
<FONT Size=4 Face=Arial>Last Name</FONT></TD>
<TD bgcolor=#cd854f>
<FONT Size=4 Face=Arial>First Name</FONT></TD>
<TD bgcolor=#cd854f>
<FONT Size=4 Face=Arial>Status</FONT></TD></TR>
<%

i = 0
'Traverse the Collection class of
'Students
For Each socStudent in socStudents
    'Alternate the background color of each
    'row in the HTML <TABLE>. Use the
    'MOD operator to distinguish even rows from
    'odd rows.
    If i Mod 2 = 0 then
        clr = "#ffd700"
    Else
        clr = "#ffff88"
    End if
```

continues

Listing 14.8: continued

```
%>
<TR>
<TD bgcolor=<%=clr%>>
<FONT Face=ARIAL Size=3>
<%'Get the Student ID%>
<%=Cstr(socStudent.StudentID)%></FONT></TD>
<TD bgcolor=<%=clr%>><FONT Face=ARIAL Size=3>
<%'Get the Student's Last Name%>
<%=socStudent.LastName%></FONT></TD>
<TD bgcolor=<%=clr%>><FONT Face=ARIAL Size=3>
<%'Get the Student's First Name%>
<%=socStudent.FirstName%></FONT></TD>
<TD bgcolor=#ffffff><FONT Face=ARIAL Size=3>
<%'Construct a dedicated <SELECT> element for
'for each student. Make it so the teacher can
'select either Present, Absent or Late
'from the SELECT ComboBox%>
<SELECT Name="<%=Cstr(socStudent.StudentID)%>">
<Option value=Present>Present
<Option value=Absent>Absent
<Option value=Late>Late
</SELECT></FONT></TD></TR>
<%
          'Increment the counter integer
          'in order to keep track of the
          'number of students in the class as
          'well as the number of rows in the <TABLE>.
          i = i + 1
     Next%>
</TABLE>
<%'Persist the enrollment for the class%>
<INPUT Type=Hidden Name=Enrollment Value=<%=Cstr(i)%>>
<%'Persist the class date%>
<INPUT Type=Hidden Name=MyDate Value="<%=Cstr(Date())%>">
<%'Persist the ClassID%>
<INPUT Type=Hidden
       Name=ClassID
       Value="<%=Request.Form("ClassID")%>">
<%'Resport the class entrollment%>
<FONT Face=Arial Size=3>Enrollment: <%=Cstr(i)%> </FONT>
<BR><INPUT Type=Submit
           Name=Submit
           Value="Submit Attendance">
</FONT>
</FORM>
</BODY>
</HTML>
```

OUTPUT

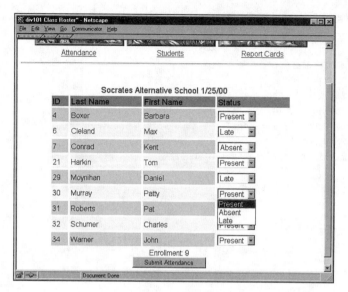

Figure 14.12: *The Attendance roster records if a student is Present, Absent, or Late.*

The code is Listing 14.8 gets a list of students in a given class at the Socrates Alternative School by using the custom App object's getClasses(ClassID) method to return a Collection class containing Student objects. The name of the Collection class is socClasses. The code uses a For...Each loop to extract the StudentID, FirstName, and LastName data from each Student socStudent object in the Collection class. (StudentID, FirstName, and LastName are properties of the Student object—refer to Figure 14.5.) These values are embedded in an HTML <TABLE>. In addition, an HTML <SELECT> element is created for each student. Each <SELECT> element gets the StudentID value as its unique name. The teacher will later use the <SELECT> element to record attendance status.

Finally, the code uses Hidden elements to *persist* enrollment, current date, and course identification data for this particular group of students. This data will be submitted to the processing page along with attendance data for each student when the teacher clicks the Submit button. The caption of the Submit button is "Submit Attendance."

Displaying an Attendance Summary

After the teacher takes attendance by selecting an attendance status for each student from the <SELECT> elements on the class roster page, he clicks the Submit Attendance button to send the attendance data on to the SocClassAttendProc.asp Active Server Page that processes the attendance data. The code for this page is shown in Listing 14.9. The output of the code is shown in Figure 14.4 that appeared previously.

EXAMPLE

Listing 14.9: Using a Custom Collection Object to Encapsulate Attendance Data
(SocClassAttenProcd.asp/14asp09.asp)

```asp
<%'====================================
'Page: SocClassAttendProc.asp
'
'Passes the Attendance data to the App
'object to writing to the data datasource.
'Also, displays a report that summarizes
'the attendance activity for a given class
'at the Socrates Alternative School
'
'Programmer: Bob Reselman
'
'Created 1/15/99
'====================================
Option Explicit 'Make it so we must declare variables

%>
<HTML>
<HEAD>
<TITLE>
<%Response.Write Request.Form("lstClassID") + " Class Roster" %>
</TITLE>
</HEAD>
<BODY>
<CENTER>
<TABLE>
<%'=======Beginning of Services menu========%>
<TR>
<TD>
<A HREF="<%Response.Write Application("SiteURL") & _
                    "/ServiceProc.asp?Serv=1"%>">
<Img src="./images/attendance.jpg" border=0></A></TD>

<TD>
<A HREF="<%Response.Write Application("SiteURL") & _
                    "/ServiceProc.asp?Serv=2"%>">
<Img src="./images/students.jpg" border=0></A></TD>

<TD>
<A HREF="/<%Response.Write Application("SiteURL") & _
                    "/ServiceProc.asp?Serv=3"%>">
<Img src="./images/reportcards.jpg" border=0></A></TD>
</TR>

<TR>
```

```
<TD Align=Center>
<A HREF="<%Response.Write Application("SiteURL") & _
                    "/ServiceProc.asp?Serv=1"%>">
<FONT FACE=Arial>Attendance</FONT></A></TD>

<TD Align=Center>
<A HREF="<%Response.Write Application("SiteURL") & _
                    "/ServiceProc.asp?Serv=2"%>">
<FONT FACE=Arial>Students</FONT></A></TD>

<TD Align=Center>
<A HREF="<%Response.Write Application("SiteURL") & _
                    "/ServiceProc.asp?Serv=3"%>">
<FONT FACE=Arial>Report Cards</FONT></A></TD>
</TR>
</TABLE>
<%'=======End of Services menu========%>
<HR>
<FONT SIZE = 4 FACE=ARIAL COLOR=Purple>
<%
Dim socApp 'Custom App object var
Dim socStudents 'Students Collection
                  'class object var
Dim socAttends 'Attendance Status Collection
                  'class object var
Dim socAttSums 'Attendance Summary Collection
                   'class object var
Dim socAttSum 'Attendance Summary object var
Dim CId 'Holds the ID for a class at the Alternative School
Dim i 'integer buffer
Dim k 'key buffer

'Create an App object
Set socApp = CreateObject("SocNewAlternate.clsSocApp")
'Create a Collection class of attendance objects
Set socAttends = CreateObject("SocNewAlternate.clsSocAttends")

'Get the classID for this submission
CId = Request.Form("ClassID")

'Go through all the elements in the form
'collection and identify the ones that have
'numeric keys. The elements are student ID's.
'These are the guys we want to add to the
'clsSocAttends collection of clsSocAttend objects
```

continues

Listing 14.9: continued

```
For Each k in Request.Form
     'Go through all the elements in the Request
     'object's Form collection. If it is a number, you
     'know that you have a studentID. Remember,
     'we named the <SELECT> elements in the previous
     'page with the StudentID. The studentID is a numeric
     'value.
     If Isnumeric(k) then
         Select Case UCase(Request.Form(k))
             Case "PRESENT": i = 1
             Case "ABSENT": i = 0
             Case "LATE": i = 2
         End Select
     'Add the data to the socAttends collection
     'Make sure you do proper typecasting or you will
     'get a type mismatch ERROR from the collection object's
     'Add method!!!!
     socAttends.Add Cstr(CId), Cint(k), Date(), Cint(i)
     End if
Next%>
</TABLE>
<%
     Dim clr 'color variable
     i = 0
'Have the App object write the attendance
If socApp.setAttendance(socAttends) then %>
   <FONT Size=6 Color=Purple Face=Arial>
Attendance Taken
   </FONT>
   <BR>
   <FONT Size=5 Color=Purple Face=Arial>
Here is a summary of your class's
attendance statistics to date:
   </FONT>
   <P>
   <CENTER>
<!—Create a TABLE —>
   <TABLE Width=80%>
<!—TABLE header————->
   <TR>
   <TD><FONT Face=Arial Color=Blue Size=3>
<B>First Name</B></FONT></TD>
   <TD><FONT Face=Arial Color=Blue Size=3>
<B>Last Name</B></FONT></TD>
   <TD><FONT Face=Arial Color=Blue Size=3>
<B>Present</B></FONT></TD>
   <TD><FONT Face=Arial Color=Blue Size=3>
```

```
<B>Absent</B></FONT></TD>
   <TD><FONT Face=Arial Color=Blue Size=3>
<B>Late</B></FONT></TD>
   </TR>
<%
'Use the App object's getAttendSummary method
'to get a Collection class of Summary objects.
'Each Summary object contains the FirstName,
'LastName, Number of Days Present, Number of Day Absent
'and Number to Days Late.
Set socAttSums = socApp.getAttendSummary(CStr(Cid))
'Traverse the Collection class
For each socAttSum in socAttSums
    'Make rows of alternating colors
    If i Mod 2 = 0 then
        clr = "#ffd700"
    Else
        clr = "#ffff88"
    End if%>
<TR>
<%'Embed the LastName, FirstName, Number of Days Present
'Number of Days Absent and Number of Days Late within
'cells of an HTML <TABLE>%>
<TD bgcolor=<%=clr%>><FONT Face=Arial Color=Blue Size=3>
<%=socAttSum.LastName%></FONT></TD>
<TD bgcolor=<%=clr%>></FONT>
<FONT Face=Arial Color=Blue Size=3>
<%=socAttSum.FirstName%></FONT></TD>
<TD bgcolor=<%=clr%>></FONT>
<FONT Face=Arial Color=Blue Size=3>
<%=socAttSum.SumPresent%></FONT></TD>
<TD bgcolor=<%=clr%>></FONT>
<FONT Face=Arial Color=Blue Size=3>
<%=socAttSum.SumAbsent%></FONT></TD>
<TD bgcolor=<%=clr%>></FONT>
<FONT Face=Arial Color=Blue Size=3>
<%=socAttSum.SumLate%></FONT></TD>
</TR>
<%
'Increase the row counter
i = i + 1
Next
%>
</FONT>
<% End If%>
</TABLE>
</CENTER>
</BODY>
</HTML>
```

This Active Server Page uses the custom socApp object as do the other pages for the ASP Application. However, this page uses the custom App object to submit data to the ActiveX DLL. To do this, the custom App object must create an instance of the Collection class that stores an attendance record for each student. This Collection class resides in the ActiveX Object Library as the clsSocAttends class. The following line of code, which is extracted from Listing 14.9, uses the CreateObject function to create a Collection class for attendance records:

```
Set socAttends = CreateObject("SocNewAlternate.clsSocAttends")
```

After the code has a Collection object for attendance in hand, it iterates through all the elements in the Request object's Form collection looking for elements with a name that is numeric, as shown below in the code extract from Listing 14.9.

```
For Each k in Request.Form
    .
    .
    .
    If Isnumeric(k) then
        Select Case UCase(Request.Form(k))
            Case "PRESENT": i = 1
            Case "ABSENT": i = 0
            Case "LATE": i = 2
        End Select
    .
    .
    .
    socAttends.Add Cstr(CId), Cint(k), Date(), Cint(i)
    End if
Next%>
```

If an element's name is numeric, the element is a <SELECT> element. (Remember that we named the <SELECT> element for each student displayed in the previous class roster page to have a name that is the same as the StudentID. StudentID is a numeric value.) After we find a <SELECT> element, we use a Select Case statement to transform the attendance status string that is assigned to the value of the <SELECT> element into an integer. Then we call the Add method of the socAttends Collection class to create a clsSocAttend object for that Student within the Collection class. The Add method takes four parameters, ClassID, StudentID, ClassDate, and StatusNumber. These correspond to the Properties of a clsSocAttend object. Remember that you can create an object within a Collection class by passing the Property values for the "object inside" the Collection class as parameters to the Collection class's Add method.

After we have the `socAttends Collection` class populated with student attendance records, we use the `socApp` object's `setAttendance(clsSocAttends)` to pass the data in the `socAttends Collection` class to the `App` object. Behind the scenes, the custom `App` object unpacks this data and writes it to the datasource. Again, this is hidden from us. Data writing is private to the custom `App` object:

```
If socApp.setAttendance(socAttends) then
```

To display the attendance summary, we invoke the `socApp` object's `getAttendSummary(CId)` method to get a `Collection` class of attendance summary objects (`clsSocAttendSums`/`clsSocAttendSum`). The name we give this `Collection` class is `socAttSums`:

```
Set socAttSums = socApp.getAttendSummary(CStr(CId))
```

The attendance summary objects in the `Collection` class contain the `StudentID`, `FirstName`, and `LastName` information about each student. In addition, each summary object provides a summary of the days present, days absent, and days late. (Refer to the object model in Figure 14.5 for review of the properties of the `clsSocAttendSum` object.)

The code traverses the `socAttendSums Collection` class extracting the `FirstName` and `LastName` data from each object in the `Collection` class. In addition, the `SumPresent`, `SumAbsent`, and `SumLate` summary information is extracted. This information is embedded in a row of an HTML `<TABLE>`. Thus, we have the Attendance summary report (see Figure 14.4) .

What's Next

This chapter has shown you how use custom-made ActiveX Object Libraries to create Active Server Pages that are powerful and easy to program. Using custom Object Libraries adds a whole new dimension to Active Server Page programming. You'll find as you move forward as an enterprise programmer that most of the functionality of the Logic tier will be encapsulated into ActiveX objects residing in ActiveX DLLs and ActiveX EXEs. You'll work with these objects in your Active Server Pages by using the `CreateObject()` function.

The next chapter is going to show you how to work with email. One of the most popular features of distributed computing is the ability to send email messages to others throughout the enterprise and on the Internet. Windows NT ships with an ActiveX Object Library that allows you to use Active Server Page technology to create and send messages to others on the Internet using nothing more than a browser.

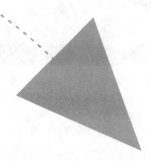

15

Creating an Email Page with the CDONTS Component

Windows NT ships with an ActiveX Component that allows you to use Internet Information Server to provide email services from your site. The name of the component is CDONTS, which is an acronym for Collaborative Data Objects for NT Server. The component is surprisingly simple to use. This chapter shows you how to get the component up and running. In addition, you'll get an overview of email technology. A fundamental understanding of email relates well to the work you will be doing with the CDONTS component.

In this chapter you will learn

- How to configure the CDONTS Component to send email

- The fundamentals of SMTP

- How to use the Instr() function in server-side scripting

- How to use the Mid() function to parse strings

Using CDONTS

The Collaborative Data Objects for NT Server is an ActiveX Component that provides, among other things, email services. You can use the CDONTS email services to enhance your IIS Web Server to be able to send and receive email messages on behalf of a visitor to your Web site.

The CDONTS ActiveX Component is available on both Windows NT 4.0 and Windows 2000 Server. For CDONTS to be operational, you must have the SMTP server that ships with both operating systems installed on the server computer. You confirm the presence of an SMTP server by checking the Microsoft Management Console in Windows NT or the Internet Services Manager in Windows 2000.

If the SMTP server is not installed on your computer or the server computer you are using to develop web sites, you or your system administrator must install it. If you are using Windows NT 4.0, the SMTP server is on the NT Option Pack CD. If you are using Windows 2000, the SMTP server should have been installed when Windows 2000 was installed. If it is not present, you should try reinstalling the operating system.

Figure 15.1 shows the Microsoft Management Console of Windows NT 4.0 with an SMTP server installed. Figure 15.2 shows the Internet Services Manager of Windows 2000 with an SMTP Server installed.

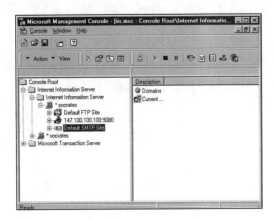

Figure 15.1: An SMTP server appears in the Microsoft Management Console in Windows NT 4.0.

Figure 15.2: *An SMTP server appears in the Internet Information Services window in Windows 2000 Server.*

Using the SMTP Protocol

When working with the CDONTS ActiveX Component, it's helpful to have an understanding about how email works under SMTP. SMTP is an acronym for Simple Mail Transfer Protocol. A protocol is nothing more than a predefined way of arranging data for transmission over the Internet. There are many protocols out there. Probably the one you use most is HTTP, the Hypertext Transfer Protocol.

Why do we need to use protocols? Remember that the only type of data that goes through the Internet is text data—characters. If you were to look at some Internet traffic, all you would see is a pile of characters as shown in Listing 15.1. Your browser has built-in intelligence that allows it to decode these characters into meaningful graphical output. When your browser decodes the characters in the listing, it displays an image of Leonardo Da Vinci's painting, the *Mona Lisa*.

Listing 15.1: A Typical Transmission of Graphical Data Over the Internet (15asp01.txt)

```
ÿØÿà&6Cc‚¸Â¸%DFSTUdtƒ'ÿÄ__<á†¡™Í¿¸»Ó®[__·¿¸¢Ä*!__-Ö¸k¸Òª<Ô®òPÆ¸|á´Ú5—
ÍÇé¸¶8\è k)'°?êI¸Ä¸ô "ÛÚô®Â·7¸ÎÀÚá‡?'_¬Œÿ<Ó®óã~ÎS¸"__+ÔMÎtÄó__·¡éN
R/?¸O__·`¯ÏŸT|¸õºaHµ""nNô|'"d'+Öé^¢A¨g-¸ÓÉY Kõ_±†\éù°-<·c<¾jì¸'mÉ¸"ùW
¯HÉF¸Ö°î·z—Ë8¥LU¸M·÷õ?¨ûç„ ûä¥GEu'|òÄ¸ü·fG„g;=¿¸M'_¯GDu1ØggááIV¬xo\
,/Ü¸"ÔÂ¸¸ëSy$¸$¸°t¸Ti¸úr¸íãÉü+Óìÿ=ŒÙºZ¸?ŸüUi„!|B»ßqjñbi<î¸ƒ{1k¥zk?Ã©7ÙV7¸ì
ùHê9Iµï©¸?z¸^¸Ï¸j¸±ËkÛ—¸5g¸[_ ZÛRH±U'Öõ- !¸è®Ï¸Ì__ç©e±¸ÿ·õãEçË.[;s*ó
ìó=îÔr';]ÿ<Ï¸*ó¸ç»?ë¸¤ÛöŸüU1Å‡e*¸&__fÆ-dÜ?~(<¸ù¸æUËìó=o¸ã¸÷âî¸*_
Of™êÛWQËb/{¿øªÌG(V¸?¸.÷-Ä1Bµ¨ùd¸,W'·/ú;ÎÅÉê¸Á-…Ï¸j¯¸Ü¶\£3›_—Æ·1L-
ú__tºÁªáHÓ¸¨_h'4]U¸Vì__øSÂ[‰1ÉÉ¸Gƒ0® ZÃôh@"Í…·c´vâ·,$¸~¸"‰
Ì(Nÿ>‹#?ptú'K.-ÉpÛ¬E=4Qø<ß¸±____@UA¸BÅ¸;`Ù"I¨_/ Jßè÷¸ÆÛ¸tL¸±,¸ÀØñDa`Pö'
E¯¶ôêH.43Œ1 ]x¸Ñ°FB¸ë°§y¸ñ¨>]=éd…X- û¸K´q^í <ö¸¥µcÑ¨fH__¸æÓá„_ XÛ¸µ¸±·.¸¢¸¸?jò
Ì¬9¸ãF¸(F`_(®°Øy_«¸_+{Úµ¸ÜHù(©P¸°]@ïéZA¸>±ÅÅãC÷WFE`4éçùÙ¸÷Úêëë)…¿ê#?uYÅM‡-
-àcFÉ°)"`ŸÆÆnGû"œàÃ¢®›^ã{ÿ<Œ¸F`ẊéÚÔ?¸‰|Ëb}ÛQ¶5=ÔªÅ«w¸ù¸µ8ã¯_›X?
```

continues

Listing 15.1: continued

```
_âÁ›‹¯#o52aH__1_NæÖ#jp\3 ;ÂÔL1¯à<÷_07Ú?H-1®h‹D_1á¸pÀ'_¤3<ß.Épjù„é_
{__ÛÒ™ºÓ¬p__àS«_'Õ@w_Eç9_azc_|Êc&ÖU"(ô_µK__¨S_ÅÎ=ª¶!]2"ØZÜ<çÿ_ÛjD'{·©ª'_
]¢¸vR1Ï(_&_«üêa"ûZ»xyÎ"…îñî_È_¨C_AøoK_1\it_ni-5è6töUÔ_"æ_Ÿ/™fZÕ moq"©Ù-k¸
__O¸Í±y.(b2ÙŒN9·=_«ëì:óÔº¯dO____ã-pG¨¨%_·Î¥DÔ#Ô_?4_ÕÕÀºØï~h·U)æ_=‡º_1=®Ú¸;
ú_DÁCcB5[MÉû+_Ã"_îê;QÍª°6Ôëï„`·'ânÛ_v_5U")é_ZÕæ,1_?Ï'¿__?_ÆúE«t…u)Óòçp0Ë_
÷_OnoH"1 ?V;÷§&"[p  ¡D_ì@#¸¥r P_Ñ_ )kßqY…^_"çæI¥ô1Bl O__<u_¬À"m&íC´$H_ÓÇz0.
°IÜ_ì¬XÁ±±"qzkb1(I+w_o·sÇµöÕÕ"?oú_ÿ<wî~¨§&2¢4h°6ì-sñùSgOÈS¸ËÙ"ØaâÕÿ=®G4dQhMWæÛ|
(oìö^¯5Cç=_9¬h"_-Øí áE_.÷_]«o¢„fm@]x§X`_õ__Í¬;P»aI¸G†p¥œ_û_{Ó?Wg_n?É§Æ0o('ìÆ_¶Â
¥X™_Q_U6_ï\ñíG?"¨óØrÌ_ë¸___Ü3zM_Ü}µb_Z1¯±__^{¨É¸¡±_ÉÀ_Iç?Rœ«Ùz}›Éx0l'Hl_
M¶ùÕËìÓÙàÃÇ_áØQ;°_ä·_-üü«ìò®·_#D"Ã_§eZ;~7ªY_¥" lQ§fA)ó'G(`_^âãË¯/"Î5_ì~ê?æ~Æ3„
·ØM_„_ìn_w8éèåR©rEÍÁµ_FÔË_ô".¬T2Øsjí?Õ_|__újk_?_gyÖZ_'_„$T_†¨ŒøI°îRhÙ-ö±__rç?-_
&a&Àít_ìïª+¬º:6g"M¯_cjÚÓë-C/>'âeGÌ{ë[ÆÄÓîg·If·"?9â™¥Räo_µ£=ËÏj?
<NS_Ñ?JÀÚ…aÍzÄ
```

The reason that text is used and not bits and bytes, is that text is very, very, very, very safe. It's very hard to send a set of text instructions over the Internet that would jump on to someone's hard drive and wreak havoc over his or her data. This use of text explains why HTML evolved as the language of the Internet. It is entirely text-based. Any computer system can use it regardless of processor type or operating system.

If everything is text-based, how does a server or browser know what to do with all that text? This is where protocols come in. A protocol says, "Hey, if you are using me to do something, this is how I expect to see this text arranged!"

Thus, as a browser using the HTTP protocol, I know that a feature of the HTTP protocol is that it can use the HTML <IMG> tag, which means that the data coming over the wire is a graphic. When a browser sees the tag set

```
<IMG SRC="../../../img/photos/collec/peint/moyen/inv0779.jpg">
```

it knows that the text coming in is encoded graphic data from the file, `inv0779.jpg`. My prior knowledge of the HTTP protocol tells me that I must decode the text stuff that's returned by the tag, `<IMG SRC="../../../img/ photos/collec/peint/moyen/inv0779>` and use my internal graphic decoding tools to display the image at hand, which in this case happens to be a photo of the *Mona Lisa.*

The protocol an Internet server uses to process incoming data is determined by the *port* from which the data comes in. Servers have these abstract software constructs, called ports, that can be conceptualized as little data-receiving docks that are identified by a standardized number. Each port has a different way to interpret and handle data according to the rules of the protocol associated with that port. There's a port that handles HTTP (port 80);

a port that handles *FTP (File Transfer Protocol*, port 21); a port that handles SMTP (Simple Mail Transport Protocol, port 25); and there are ports for other protocols as well. The server is always listening to these ports. When data comes into a port, the server says, "Ah ha, you have come in on the HTTP port, so I will apply the HTTP way of dealing with text and look in a specific directory on my hard drive for the file that you are requesting." Should a request from a client come in over the FTP protocol, the server says "Ah, you want me to interpret your incoming text according to the rules for File Transfer Protocol." The same is true of SMTP. Figure 15.3 illustrates this concept.

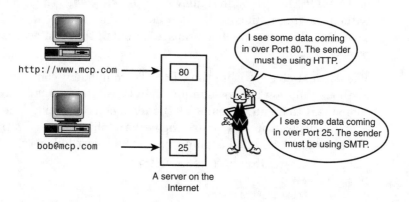

Figure 15.3: *A port is a server process that is associated with a protocol.*

The Structure of Email

SMTP is a widely-used protocol for sending email. SMTP is nowhere near as complex as HTTP. All SMTP needs to do is send data. It doesn't have to do the sort of display work that HTTP does. The SMTP protocol requires that you dedicate certain lines of text to indicate specific pieces of information required within the transmission. Minimally, a mail message using SMTP requires a From line, a To line, a Date line, a Subject line and the body of the mail message.

The following code is an example of a mail message that you can use with SMTP:

```
From: bob@cogarttech.com
To: dorothy@oz.com
Date: 1/1/2000
Subject: Dinner
Body: Interested in eating at the Vietnamese restaurant tonight?
```

As previously mentioned, SMTP is a simple protocol. However, there are still some low-level mechanics that you have to do to get a mail client to talk to the mail server using SMTP. The important thing to know is that SMTP is a text-based Internet protocol. In addition, you need to know that with regard to SMTP, the lines of text within an email message must to conform to a certain structure.

The Fundamentals of CDONTS

The CDONTS ActiveX Component acts as an intermediary between you and SMTP. The component allows you to work with the SMTP protocol without having to master the details of it. You use the `NewMail` object within the CDONTS component to prepare an email that conforms to the SMTP protocol.

The `NewMail` object within the CDONTS component contains properties and methods that you use to send mail. (In this case, you can think of the term component to mean the same as the term object library.) The following code example shows you how to use the `NewMail` object to send a message over the Internet. A detailed explanation of the object follows the example.

EXAMPLE

```
<%Set ml = CreateObject("CDONTS.NewMail")
'Prep the NewMail object
ml.From = "bob@cogarttech.com"
ml.To = "dorothy@oz.com"
ml.Subject = "Dinner"
ml.Body = "Interested in eating at the Vietnamese restaurant tonight?"
'Send the mail
ml.Send%>
```

Please notice that the code above conforms quite nicely to the basic lines of text required to comply with the SMTP protocol. Although the `Date:` line of the message is missing, this is not a problem. The `Date:` line is supplied automatically by the `NewMail` object.

Table 15.1 shows you the properties and methods of the `NewMail` object with a description of each.

Table 15.1: Properties and Methods of the **NewMail** *Object*

Property/Method	Description
Bcc	One or many email addresses that indicate the persons to whom copies of the message are to be sent. Other recipients of the message are unaware of this recipient.
Body	The content of the message
BodyFormat	Indicates the body format of the message. A value of 1 indicates that the message is sent in HTML format. A value of 0 indicates that the message is formatted as simple text.
Cc	One or many email addresses that indicate persons to whom a copy of this message is to be sent.

Property/Method	Description
ContentBase	Sets the URL from which resources are referenced. For example, if you want to make it so your message gets graphics from a Web site at the URL www.louvre.fr, you set the ContentBase property to Obj.ContentBase= "http://www/louvre.fr"
ContentLocation	Set the filepath or location from within a URL indicated in the ContentBase property. For example, to get the graphic www.lourve.fr/art/monalisa.jpg, you can set the content base to Obj.ContentBase=http://www.louvre.fr/art/ Then set the content location to Obj.ContentLocation="monalisa.jpg"
From	The email address of the person sending the message
Importance	Allows you to set the importance of a message using values 0–3
MailFormat	Indicates the encoding format of the message. A value of 0 indicates that the message is encoded in MIME format. A value of 1 indicates that the message is formatted as simple text.
Subject	The subject of the message
To	One or many email addresses that indicate the persons to whom this message is to be sent.
Value	Adds headers to the message
Version	Returns the version of the CDO Library
AttachFile(source, [ByVal Filename], [ByVal EncodingMethod])	Attaches a file to be sent along with the message
AttachURL(source, ContentLocation, [ContentBase], [EncodingMethod])	Attaches a URL to be sent along with the message
Send([From], [To], [Subject], [Body], [Importance])	Sends a mail message
SetLocaleIDs (CodePageID)	Sends information that sets text characters subject to localization—currency indicators, for example.

Understanding MIME Type?

MIME is an acronym for Multipurpose Internet Mail Extensions. MIME allows clients and servers to communicate what type of data is being sent in an email. In the early days of email, the only data type that was supported was text. However, as the Internet evolved, a method was needed to be able to support graphics and other types of non-textual data. MIME supports this need.

The way a server tells a client what type of data is in an email is by providing code in the header of the transmission indicating the type of data in the message. These lines of code are hidden from end user view and are used by the email reader or mail server. The MIME specification requires that this header take the following form:

```
Content-Type: type/subtype
```

For example, if you want to indicate that your email contains a jpeg graphic, the MIME header would be

```
Content-Type: image/jpeg
```

Where

> `Content-Type:` are reserved keywords indicating a MIME header.
>
> `image` is a MIME type.
>
> `jpeg` indicates an image subtype.

Many MIME types and subtypes are formally part of the specification. These are registered with the Internet Assigned Numbers Authority. If you want to view a list of MIME types, you can view them on the Internet at

```
http://www.isi.edu/in-notes/iana/assignments/media-types/
```

For the most part, assigning a MIME type to your email is a transparent activity. Most email readers have come a long way since the days of the "Hello World" text message. The important thing to remember is that your email can handle data other than text and that you use MIME to communicate the type of data in your email.

WHAT IS AN ENCODING METHOD?

An encoding method is an algorithm that you apply to binary data to make it appear as text characters. After these binary file formats are transformed to a textual appearance, they can be transported over the Internet. Encoding is used when you send graphics and proprietary file formats such as Word documents as email attachments. When an encoded file is received, it is then decoded into its original file format.

Two encoding methods are commonly used. One type is UUEncoding. The other is Base-64. The difference between the two is in the way each actually decodes a line, not in the final output. The mechanics of encoding are transparent when you use CDONTS. The default decoding method when you use CDONTS is UUEncoding.

Creating the Letter

To provide an email service at our Web site, we must create two Active Server Pages, one that allows a visitor to create an email and another page the sends the email that the visitor creates. Figure 15.4 illustrates this architecture.

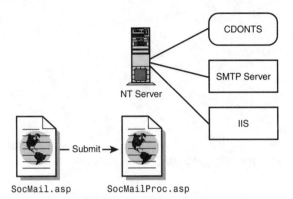

SocMail.asp — Submit → SocMailProc.asp

Figure 15.4: To use the CDONTS component, IIS and SMTP server must be installed on a NT 4.0 or Windows 2000 Server.

Preparing the User Interface

The user interface that we are going to make is very straightforward. It's an Active Server Page that contains an HTML form, which in turn contains <INPUT> elements to store the data for the From, To, Cc, and Subject properties of the CDONTS object. An HTML <TEXTAREA> element is used to store the data for the Message property. A <TEXTAREA> element is used because it allows us to enter a message with multiple lines. A Submit button is also included in the form.

Listing 15.2 shows the code for the Active Server Page that displays the email utility graphical user interface. Figure 15.5 shows the code displayed in the browser.

EXAMPLE

Listing 15.2: Creating a User Interface with Simple HTML Elements (SocMail.asp/15asp02.asp)

```
<%'=====================================
'Page: SocMail.asp
'
'Presents a form into which a user can enter
'and email message.
'
'Programmer: Bob Reselman
'
'Created 1/25/99
'=====================================
Option Explicit 'Make it so we must declare variables

%>
<HTML>
```

continues

Listing 15.2: continued

```
<HEAD>
<TITLE>Socrates Alternative School Email Utility</TITLE>

</HEAD>
<BODY>
<CENTER>
<TABLE><TR>
<TD>
<Img src=".\images\soclogo.jpg">
</TD>
<TD>
<FONT Color=Blue Size=5 Face=Arial>
The Socrates Alternative School
<BR>
Email Utility
</FONT>
</TD></TR>
</TABLE>
</CENTER>
<P>
<FORM name=MyForm
  method=post
  action="<%=Application("SiteURL") & "/socMailProc.asp"%>">
<TABLE width=100%>
<TR>
<TD>
<FONT Color=Blue Size=3 Face=Arial>
Your email address:
</FONT></TD>
<TD><INPUT Size=50 name=From></TD></TR>

<TR>
<TD>
<FONT Color=Blue Size=3 Face=Arial>
Send an email to:
</FONT></TD>
<TD><INPUT Size=50 name=To></TD></TR>

<TR>
<TD>
<FONT Color=Blue Size=3 Face=Arial>
Send a copy to these people:
</FONT></TD>
<TD><INPUT Size=50 name=Copy></TD></TR>
```

```
<TR>
<TD>
<FONT Color=Blue Size=3 Face=Arial>
What is the subject of this email?:
</FONT></TD>
<TD><INPUT Size=50 name=Subject></TD></TR>

<TR>
<TD>
<FONT Color=Blue Size=3 Face=Arial>
Message:
</FONT></TD>
<TD><TextArea name=Body
            cols=60
            rows=6></TextArea></TD></TR>

<TR><TD colspan=2 align=center>
<Input type=Submit value="Send this message" name=Submit1>
</TD></TR>
</TABLE>
</FORM>

<P>

</BODY>
</HTML>
```

OUTPUT

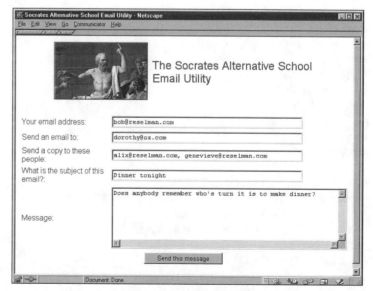

Figure 15.5: *You can use* <INPUT> *elements and* <TEXTAREA> *elements to create a user interface to send email.*

Mailing the Letter

A visitor to our Web site clicks a Submit button to send the email data to a processing page Web server. The code of this processing page is shown in Listing 15.3. The processing page validates the submitted data. Then, if the data proves to be valid, it's assigned to the respective properties of the NewMail object within the CDONTS component. After the values are assigned the properties of the NewMail object, the object's Send method is called and a confirmation message is sent back to the user.

If the data proves to be invalid, an error message is sent back to the user informing him or her that there was an error in the data that he or she submitted. Figure 15.8 shows you an illustration of the error message that the Active Server Page returns.

Listing 15.3 shows the code that processes the email data on the server side. Figure 15.6 shows the error message that is returned when the user submits invalid data.

EXAMPLE

Listing 15.3: Validating Data from the SocMail Client (SocMailProc.asp/15asp03.asp)

```
<%
'Make it so we need to declare variables
Option Explicit%>
<HTML>
<HEAD>
<TITLE>Socrates Alternative School Email Confirmation</TITLE>
</HEAD>
<BODY>
<CENTER>
<Img src=".\images\soclogo.jpg">
<BR>
<FONT Color=Blue Size=5 Face=Arial>
The Socrates Alternative School
<BR>
Email Confirmation
</FONT>
</CENTER>
<%
Function IsEmailAddrGood(EmailAddr)
'Parameters: EMailAddr, the email address to validate
'
'Return:     True, if email address is valid
'
'Remarks:    This function checks to make sure that
'            email strings are well formed. The function
'            checks that the email address conforms to
'            minimal email syntax. The function checks for
```

```
'                    the existence of the @ sign as well as the
'                    string ".com", ".net", ".org", ".edu" for each
'                    email address.
'                    Granted, other domains types can and should be
'                    supported. However, for demonstration purposes
'                    we'll confine scope to these domains types.
'
'                    In addition, the function checks to make sure
'                    that a comma is placed between each email
'                    address in the From, To, Cc fields of the
'                    email message.
'
'Programmer: Bob Reselman
'Copyright: 2000
'
'History: Created 1/27/2000
'
'***************************

Dim i 'integer buffer
Dim str 'String buffer for email address
Dim pos 'position buffer
Dim oldPos ' a secondary position buffer
Dim NumOfCommas 'Buffer to hold the number of commas
                'in the email address string
Dim NumOfAtChars 'Buffer to holds the number of @
                  'characters in the email string
Dim strTemp 'General string buffer
Dim strSngEmail 'Buffer to hold a single email address

'Intit the numeric vars
NumOfCommas = 0
NumOfAtChars = 0
pos = 0
oldPos = 0

'Convert the Email Address parameter to a
'string and set it to a variable
'local to this procedure
str = CStr(EmailAddr)

'Make sure that you do not have an empty string
If str = "" Then
    IsEmailAddrGood = False
    Exit Function
End if
```

continues

Listing 15.3: continued

```
'Find the number of commas in the string
While i <> 1
    pos = InStr(pos + 1, str, ",")
    If pos = 0 Then
        'leave the loop
        i = 1
    Else
    'Increment the number of commas
        NumOfCommas = NumOfCommas + 1
    End If
Wend
'Re init the counter vars
pos = 0
i = 0

'Check for the number of @ sign, The address must
'have at least one, if it doesn't, you have a problem.
While i <> 1
    pos = InStr(pos + 1, str, "@")
    If pos = 0 Then
        'leave the loop
        i = 1
    Else
    'Increment the number of commas
        NumOfAtChars = NumOfAtChars + 1
    End If
Wend

'Make sure that there is one more @ character
'then there are commas. For example, a well formed
'email string would be:
'bob@happy.com, bill@sad.com, tom@glad.com

'Please notice that there are 3 @ characters and
'2 commas. In a well formed email address string there
'should always be one less comma then there are
'@ characters

If NumOfCommas = NumOfAtChars -1 Then

'Now let's check to see if each email address in the email
'string contains one of the supported domains, .COM, .NET,
'.ORG or .EDU.

'Add a comma to the end of full the email string.
'Adding a comma is going to make parsing out single
'email address a lot easier.
```

```
    strTemp = str & ","
    i = 0
    LastCommaPos = 0
    NextCommaPos = 0

'Run a loop that extracts and examines
'each email address within an email string
'in order to make sure that each email address
'has a supported domain.
While i <> 1
        'Let's get the email address out one at a time.
        'Find the "next" comma
        NextCommaPos = InStr(LastCommaPos + 1, strTemp, ",")
        If NextCommaPos <> 0 Then
            'If we get a position for the next comma,
            'use the Mid function to get all characters
            'between the last comma position (oldPos) that
            'Instr used and the new position where the next
            'comma was discovered. These characters are a
            'single email address.
            strSngEmail = Trim(Mid(strTemp, LastCommaPos + 1, _
                            NextCommaPos - LastCommaPos - 1))
            'Set the position of the "next" comma to
            'be the position of the "last" comma.
            LastCommaPos = NextCommaPos

'Run an ElseIf statement to see
'if one of the supported domain types
'exists

'Use the full syntax for Instr:
'Instr(Start, LookinStr, LookForStr, ComparisonMethod)
'Setting the ComparisonMethod to 1 makes the Instr
'function do textual comparison.
'This means that Instr looks for the position of
'the LookForStr by either upper or lower case. The example
'the expression, Instr(1, "Bob", "0", 1) returns the
'value 2.
            If InStr(1, strSngEmail, ".com", 1) <> 0 Then
                IsEmailAddrGood = True
            ElseIf InStr(1, strSngEmail, ".net", 1) <> 0 Then
                IsEmailAddrGood = True
            ElseIf InStr(1, strSngEmail, ".org", 1) <> 0 Then
                IsEmailAddrGood = True
            ElseIf InStr(1, strSngEmail, ".edu", 1) <> 0 Then
                IsEmailAddrGood = True
```

continues

Listing 15.3: continued

```
                    Else
                        'If you get to here, then no supported
                        'domain is present
                        IsEmailAddrGood = False
                        'Leave the function there is no use
                        'going on
                        Exit Function
                    End if
                Else
                    'Break the loop. There email address does not
                    'conform to the supported domains
                    i = 1
                End if
        Wend
    Else
    'If you get to here, then your address is not
    'valid. It should have not made it through the
    'ElseIf above.
        IsEmailAddrGood = False
    End if

    End Function
    '==================================
    '==========Entry Point=============
    '==================================
    Dim ml 'variable for the CDO NewMail object
    Dim k 'Key buffer
    Dim IsDataOK 'Boolean buffer the confirms all
                 'the data in the email is well formed.

    'Iterate through the Request.Form keys in order
    'to validate particular fields
    For Each k in Request.Form
        Select Case k
            Case "From":
                'An email needs a From field
                IsDataOK = IsEmailAddrGood(Request.Form(k))
            Case "To":
                'An email needs a To field
                IsDataOK = IsEmailAddrGood(Request.Form(k))
            Case "Copy":
                'User does not need to copy people
                If Request.Form(k) <> "" Then
                    IsDataOK = IsEmailAddrGood(Request.Form(k))
                End If
            Case "Subject":
                'We'll allow emails without subjects to be sent.
```

```
            Case "Body":
                'An email needs a Body field
                If Request.Form(k) = "" then IsDataOK = False
        End Select
        If Not IsDataOK then
            Exit For
        End if
Next

If IsDataOK = True then
    Set ml = CreateObject("CDONTS.NewMail")
    'Prep the NewMail object
    ml.From = Request.Form("From")
    ml.To = Request.Form("To")
    ml.Subject = Request.Form("Subject")
    ml.Body = Request.Form("Body")
    ml.Cc =  Request.Form("Copy")
    'Send the mail
    'ml.Send
     'Clean Up
    Set ml = Nothing
%>
<P><FONT face="Arial" size=7 color=blue>
Mail Sent!</FONT></P>
<%Else 'send an error message%>
<FONT face="Arial" size=7 color=Red>
Mail Not Sent!</FONT>
<BR>
<FONT face="Arial" size=3 color=Red>
There is an error in the formation of one of the email
strings in your message.
<P>
Please remember that the form for an email address is:
</FONT>
<P>
<FONT face="Courier" size=3 color=Black>
person@name.com
</FONT>
<P>
<FONT face="Arial" size=3 color=Red>
You can list multiple recipients by placing a comma between
each email address, like so:
</FONT>
<P>
<FONT face="Courier" size=3 color=Black>
person@name.com, bigperson@here.net, smallperson@there.net
```

continues

Listing 15.3: continued

```
</FONT>
<P>
<FONT face="Arial" size=3 color=Red>
Also, we support the domains:
</FONT>
<FONT face="Courier" size=3 color=Black>
.com, .net, .org, .edu
</FONT>
<%End If%>
</BODY>
</HTML>
```

OUTPUT

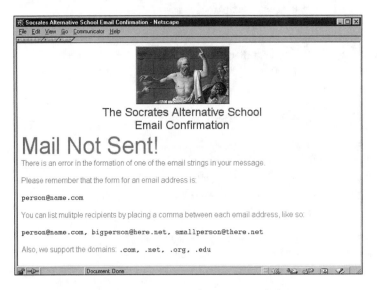

Figure 15.6: *If an email address does not contain the @ character or uses an unsupported domain, an error message is returned.*

Server-Side Versus Client-Side Validation

The SocMail application allows a user to enter one or many email address in the From, To, and Cc fields. Each address must be separated by a comma. If any of the data in these fields is not a well-formed email address or each email address is not separated by a comma, the email message will not go through. Therefore, we need to do a certain amount of validation on the server side to make sure the data is entered properly for each field.

The validation rules that we are going to enforce are provided in the following numbered list.

1. The From and To fields must contain a well-formed email address.

2. The Cc field does not need to contain an email address or addresses, but if any are provided, they must be well-formed.

3. A well-formed email address contains an @ character and a domain type of .com, .net, .org, or .edu.

4. If a line has multiple email addresses, each address is separated by a comma.

5. The Body field must contain data.

Server-side validation is used because it keeps the validation process close to the email sending routine. The validation is in the same Active Server Page as the transmission code. If validation fails on that page, the NewMail object will not send the email message. However, if validation were moved to the client side, and for some reason the client did not validate the email data properly, there is nothing to prevent the NewMail object from sending malformed data and possibly causing an error. On the other hand, the benefit of having validation on the client side is that the presence of malformed data can be reported immediately to the user and corrected before it is submitted to the server. An optimum scheme is to validate on both the client side and the server side. In this case, we are validating on the server side.

The code that determines whether an email address is well-formed is encapsulated into the function IsEmailAddrGood(). You can find this function in Listing 15.3.

Working with the Instr() Function

We use the VBScript Instr() function to determine the presence of those characters and strings that make a well-formed email address. The Instr() function detects whether a certain character or substring is contained within a string. The Instr() function takes the syntax

```
Instr(Start, LookInStr, LookForStr, ComparisonMethod)
```

Where

Start is the position within the string from which to start looking.

Instr is the name of the function.

LookInStr is the master string in which you are trying to detect the presence of any given character(s).

LookForStr is the character or substring that we are trying to detect.

ComparisonMethod indicates 0 for a Binary compare, whereas the value 1 indicates a Textual compare. A binary compare means that the character(s) we are trying to locate must match the character(s) in the master string in terms of case. For example, if we are looking for the character "a" in a string, Instr() only locates the lowercase "a" if a Binary compare is used. A text compare will locate either an "a" or an "A".

The following code shows some examples for using Instr():

EXAMPLE

InStr(1, "Bob Reselman", "b", 0) returns 3.

InStr(1, "Bob Reselman", "b", 1) returns 1. Remember that a text search using a Text compare (value of 1) is not case sensitive.

InStr(2, "Bob Reselman", "b", 0) returns 3. Remember, Instr() returns the position of the sought-after character in terms of position one of the "string to look in", even if the search starts at a character position other than position one. Thus, in this example, even though Instr() is starting its search at position 2, the first "b" it comes across from that position is at position 3 of the master string.

InStr(1, "Bob Reselman", "man", 0) returns 10.

Our code uses Instr() to do two things: To determine the number of @ characters in an email address and to determine the number of commas in an email address. All email addresses must have at least one @ character. If multiple email addresses exist, then each must be separated by a comma.

For example,

person@name.com, bigperson@here.net, smallperson@there.net

has three @ characters and two commas, and

person@name.com, bigperson@here.net, smallperson@there.net, noperson@name.com

has four @ characters and three commas.

Thus, when we check to make sure an email address string is well-formed, we are going to check to make sure there is always one more @ character than there are commas.

The code within Listing 15.3 uses Instr() within a While loop to determine the number of @ characters. The function is used also to determine the number of commas.

The code below shows the While loop that checks for the number of @ characters:

```
'Check for the number of @ sign, The address must
'have at least one, if it doesn't, you have a problem.
While i <> 1
```

```
        pos = InStr(pos + 1, str, "@")
    If pos = 0 Then
        'leave the loop
        i = 1
    Else
    'Increment the number of commas
        NumOfAtChars = NumOfAtChars + 1
    End If
Wend
```

The way the While works is that it invokes the Instr() function to return the position of an @ character. If indeed an @ character is in the str string, Instr() will return the position within the string that the character occupies. If there isn't any @ character in the string, the position will be zero. The loop is terminated. If there is an @ character in str, the loop increments the counter variable NumOfAtChars by one. Then, another trip is made through the loop. However, the start position of the Instr() function is set to the position returned in the previous trip. A new search is begun. If the return from the new position within Instr() is zero, the loop terminates. Otherwise, NumOfAtChars is again given an increment of one. This process continues until the string is completely traversed. Figure 15.7 illustrates the dynamics of this code.

```
While i <> 1
    pos = InStr(pos + 1, str, "@")
    If pos = 0 Then
        'leave the loop
        i = 1
    Else
    'Increment the number of commas
        NumOfAtChars = NumOfAtChars + 1
    End If
Wend
```

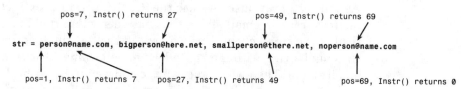

Figure 15.7: *You can use* Instr() *within a* While *loop to determine the number of occurrences of a given character.*

The same process we used to determine the number of @ characters is used to determine the number of commas. After both the number of @ characters and commas are determined, a comparison is made. If the number of @ characters is equal to the number of commas minus one, control is passed to a While loop that parses out each email in the email string. Each mail address is examined to make sure it contains the characters for the domain types that the email program supports. These domain types are .com, .net, .org, and .edu.

We parse out the individual emails within a given email string by using the Mid()function in conjunction with the Instr() function.

Working with the Mid() Function

The Mid() function returns a substring from a string at a given location. The syntax for the Mid() function is

```
Mid(StrToLookIn, StartPos, LenOfCharsToReturn)
```

Where

Mid is the function name.

StrToLookIn is the string from which the substring characters will be returned.

StartPos is the position within StrToLookIn from which Mid is to start returning characters. This value must be at least 1.

LenOfCharsToReturn is the number of characters to return starting from the position indicated by StartPos. This is an optional argument. If you do not use it, Mid() returns all the characters from the StartPos value to the end of the string.

For example,

```
Mid("Bob Reselman",3) returns b Reselman.

Mid("Bob Reselman", 3, 4) returns b Re.

Mid("Bob Reselman", 6, 2) returns es.
```

Using the Mid() Function

As you read previously, we use the Mid() function to extract a single email address from an email string that has been submitted in a From, To, or CC field of the email client. The way we extract an email address is to traverse the email string within a While loop to determine a "next" comma in the email string. Then we extract all the characters between the next comma and a "last" comma. The "last" comma position is the position of the "next" comma we found in a previous trip in the loop. If we are just starting the looping process, the position of the "last" comma is zero. Remember that multiple email addresses in an email string are separated by commas. Also, notice that we needed to create a temporary string, which is the email string with a comma tagged on at the end. We add this comma to provide consistency for the looping logic. The temporary string is created in Listing 15.3 in the line

```
strTemp = str & ","
```

First we use the `Instr()` function to locate the position of the "next" comma:

```
While i <> 1
.
.
NextCommaPos = InStr(LastCommaPos + 1, strTemp, ",")
```

After knowing the position of the "next" comma, we use the `Mid()` function to parse out the characters between the "last" comma and the "next" comma. Again, if we are just starting to traverse the email, the position of the "last" comma is zero.

```
If pos <> 0 Then
    strSngEmail = Trim(Mid(strTemp, LastCommaPos + 1, _
                      NextCommaPos - LastCommaPos - 1))
```

NOTE

The `Trim(str)` function removes any whitespace characters that occur before or after a string.

After we have used the "next" comma position to get the length of the string to parse out, we reset the "last" comma to be the value of the "next" comma. We need to do this to make sure that when we run the loop again, the `Instr()` function moves its start position up to the comma it just found:

```
LastCommaPos = NextCommaPos
```

Figure 15.8 illustrates the dynamics of this code.

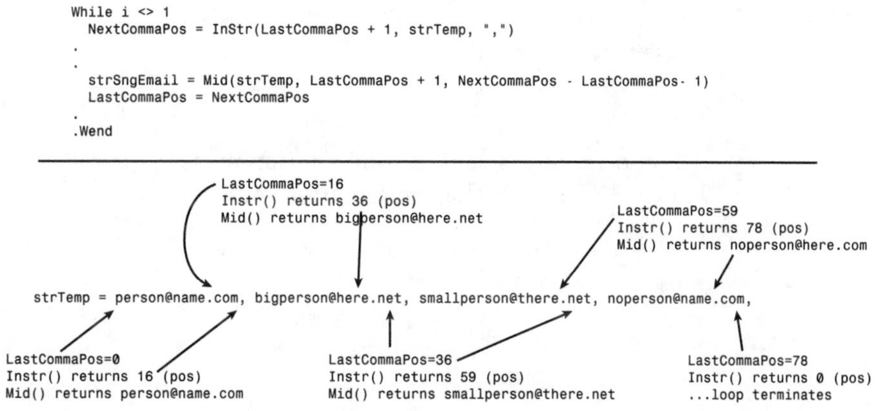

Figure 15.8: *You can use the* `Mid()` *function to return a substring from a larger string.*

We do some analysis on the single email address to make sure the supported domain characters are in the string. If the string contains characters indicating that the email address falls within the domain types we are supporting (.com, .net, .org, or .edu), we continue the loop. Otherwise, we set the function return value to False and exit the function. If all the email addresses comply with the supported domain types, the function returns True.

We keep the loop in force as long as we can parse out email addresses from a given email string or until an address reveals itself to be malformed. Figure 15.6, which you saw earlier in this chapter, shows the error message the application returns if a malformed email address is discovered.

As you read previously, if all the data that were submitted proves valid, we create an instance of the NewMail object. Then we assign the submitted values to the respective properties of the object and call the NewMail object's send method. An extract of the code from Listing 15.3 is shown below.

```
        .
        .
If IsDataOK = True then
    Set ml = CreateObject("CDONTS.NewMail")
    'Prep the NewMail object
    ml.From = Request.Form("From")
    ml.To = Request.Form("To")
    ml.Subject = Request.Form("Subject")
    ml.Body = Request.Form("Body")
    ml.Cc =  Request.Form("Copy")
    'Send the mail
    'ml.Send
    'Clean Up
    Set ml = Nothing
        .
        .
```

After the email is sent, a confirmation message is returned to the browser. Figure 15.9 shows the confirmation message.

OUTPUT

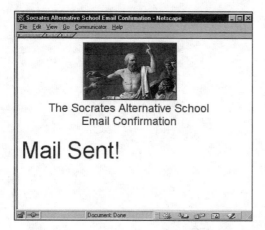

Figure 15.9: *A confirmation message is returned to the browser upon a successful send.*

What's Next

This chapter has shown you how to use the NewMail object of the CDONTS ActiveX Component. Also, you learned how to use the Instr() and Mid() functions to perform string parsing. You applied your string parsing skills to validate data that has been submitted to the NewMail object for mailing.

The next chapter is going to show you how to apply your knowledge about the NewMail object to the Attendance taking application you developed in Chapter 14. You'll use the NewMail object to notify a student's parents, via email, that their son or daughter was absent from or late to a class.

16

Adding a Mail Feature to the Attendance List

The promise of distributed computing means the ability to communicate with anyone, anywhere. A significant benefit that ASP brings to fulfilling the promise is the ability to use a variety of communication protocols transparently. Although it is true that the core protocol that ASP uses is HTTP, you can make it so your Active Server Pages work with other protocols. In an earlier chapter, you learned that it is possible to use the Collaborative Data Object for NT Server (CDONTS) as way to have your Active Server Pages send email using the Web Server. The work in this chapter is to incorporate SMTP into your Web site to provide the ability to send automatic email notification into the attendance-taking application that we built earlier for the Socrates Alternative School. In addition, we'll address another fundamental issue in distributed computing using ASP—how to maintain information that is organized according to groups of client-side HTML elements on the server side within the scope of one HTML form.

In this chapter you will learn how to

- Determine the values of specific types of HTML elements from the server side

- Create and mail form letters on the server side

- Use the JavaScript String object to parse strings on the client side

- Use an HTML element to share a common event procedure on the client side

Enhancing a Web Site

In Chapter 14, "Creating a Class Attendance Page," we made a Web site that allowed a teacher to log in to the site and select a class from a list of classes he or she teaches. After the teacher selected a class, a class roster was displayed from which a teacher could record the attendance for that class on that day. After attendance was taken, the teacher submitted the roster back to the Web site, at which time the attendance status for the class was recorded. After the attendance status was recorded, a summary report was created by the Web site and returned to the teacher.

All the logic and data-write functionality for this Web site was contained in a custom ActiveX Object Library.

Now we are going to add some features to enhance the site. First, we are going to make it so that each student in the class has a set of parents associated with him or her. A student might have one or many parents. We are going to make a secondary Web page that allows a teacher to view the set of parents for a given student in a class.

Next, we are going to enhance the attendance-taking page so a teacher can check off students in the roster. When a teacher checks off a student on the roster, an email letter is sent to the student's parent(s). This email letter contains a summary of the student's attendance record for the class. To implement the enhancements, we need to redesign the attendance-taking page (see Figure 16.1). In addition, the ActiveX Object Library that encapsulates the Web site's functionality will be expanded. New objects will be introduced. Listing 16.1 shows the code for the enhanced attendance page. The attendance page code has been enhanced to provide a common, client-side event procedure, written in JavaScript, that captures the click event for all the "Parent Info" buttons.

EXAMPLE

Listing 16.1: The Enhanced Attendance Page (SocClassAttendEx.asp/16asp01.asp)

```
<%'====================================
'Page: SocClassAttendEx.asp
'
'Presents an enhanced list of students in a selected class
'
'Programmer: Bob Reselman
'
'Created 2/05/2000
'====================================
Option Explicit 'Make it so we must declare variables
%>

<HTML>
<HEAD>
```

```
<TITLE>
<%=Request.Form("ClassID")%> Class Roster
</TITLE>
</HEAD>
<SCRIPT ID=clientEventHandlersJS LANGUAGE=javascript>
<!—
///////////////////////////////////////////////////////
//Funtion: btnProc(btn)
//
//Purpose: To display window that contains parent
//         info.
//
//Arguments: btn, The HTML Button element that made
//                the button click
//
//Return: None
//
//Remarks:
//
//Programmer: Bob Reselman
//
//Created: 2/5/2000
//
//History:
//
///////////////////////////////////////////////////////
function btnProc(btn) {
    var str = btn.name; //assing the nameo to a local var
    var len = 0; //length buffer
    var startPos = 0; //integer that indicates the start
                      //position of the substring
    var buttonPrefix = "btn";
    var stdID = "";

    len = str.length;
    startPos = buttonPrefix.length;
    //parse out the studentID out of the
    //button's name using the String object's
    //substring method
    stdID = str.substring(startPos, len);
    //open a new window to show the Active
    //Server Page that allows you to show parent
    //data. You pass the studentID to this page as
    //a query string value
```

continues

Listing 16.1: continued

```
        window.open(document.MyForm.SiteURL.value +
                    "/SocParentRec.asp?studentID=" + stdID,null,
                    //style the window
                    "height=200,width=500,status=yes,toolbar=no,
                    ➥menubar=no,location=no,resizable=yes");
    }

    //-->
    </SCRIPT>
    <BODY>
    <CENTER>
    <%'=======Beginning of Services Buttons========%>
    <TABLE>
    <TR>
    <TD>
    <A HREF="<%Response.Write Application("SiteURL") & _
                    "/ServiceProc.asp?Serv=1"%>">
    <Img src="./images/attendance.jpg" border=0></A></TD>

    <TD>
    <A HREF="<%Response.Write Application("SiteURL") & _
                    "/ServiceProc.asp?Serv=2"%>">
    <Img src="./images/students.jpg" border=0></A></TD>

    <TD>
    <A HREF="/<%Response.Write Application("SiteURL") & _
                    "/ServiceProc.asp?Serv=3"%>">
    <Img src="./images/reportcards.jpg" border=0></A></TD>
    </TR>
    <%'=======Beginning of Services Text========%>
    <TR>

    <TD Align=Center>
    <A HREF="<%Response.Write Application("SiteURL") & _
                    "/ServiceProc.asp?Serv=1"%>">
    <FONT FACE=Arial>Attendance</FONT></A></TD>

    <TD Align=Center>
    <A HREF="<%Response.Write Application("SiteURL") & _
                    "/ServiceProc.asp?Serv=2"%>">
    <FONT FACE=Arial>Students</FONT></A></TD>

    <TD Align=Center>
    <A HREF="<%Response.Write Application("SiteURL") & _
                    "/ServiceProc.asp?Serv=3"%>">
```

```
<FONT FACE=Arial>Report Cards</FONT></A></TD>
</TR>
</TABLE>
<%'=======End of Services menu========%>
<HR>
     <!—Let's use an HTML form to submit
     'class request data—>
<FORM Name=MyForm Method=Post
        Action="<%=Application("SiteURL") & "/SocClassAttendProcEx.asp"%>">
<FONT SIZE = 4 FACE=ARIAL COLOR=Purple>
<%
     Dim socApp 'a variant the stores the App object
     Dim socStudents 'a variant the stores the Students Collection object
     Dim socStudent 'a Student object
     Dim i 'counter var
     Dim clr 'color variable
     'Create an App object
     Set socApp = CreateObject("SocNewAlternate.clsSocApp")
     'Use the getStudents method to return a Collection
     'class full of student objects
     Set socStudents = socApp.getStudents(Request.Form("ClassID"))
%>

<BR>Socrates Alternative School <%=Cstr(Date())%><BR></FONT>
<TABLE WIDTH=80%>
<TR>
<TD bgcolor=#cd854f align=center>
<FONT Size=4 Face=Arial> </FONT></TD>
<TD bgcolor=#cd854f align=center>
<FONT Size=4 Face=Arial>ID</FONT></TD>
<TD bgcolor=#cd854f align=center>
<FONT Size=4 Face=Arial>Last Name</FONT></TD>
<TD bgcolor=#cd854f align=center>
<FONT Size=4 Face=Arial>First Name</FONT></TD>
<TD bgcolor=#cd854f align=center>
<FONT Size=4 Face=Arial>Status</FONT></TD>
<TD bgcolor=#cd854f align=center>
<FONT Size=2 Face=Arial>Notify<BR>Parent?</FONT></TD>
</TR>
<%

i = 0
'Traverse the Collection class of
'Students
```

continues

Listing 16.1: continued

```
For Each socStudent in socStudents
    'Alternate the background color of each
    'row in the HTML <TABLE>. Use the
    'MOD operator to distinguish even rows from
    'odd rows.
    If i Mod 2 = 0 then
        clr = "#ffd700"
    Else
        clr = "#ffff88"
    End if
%>
<TR>
<TD bgcolor=<%=clr%> align=middle>
<FONT Face=ARIAL Size=3>
<%'Add an HTML button element that, when clicked
'calls the common click event procedure that opens
'a new window and displays a page containing the parents
'of the given student. %>
<INPUT type="button"
        value="Parent Info"
        name=btn<%=Cstr(socStudent.StudentID)%>
        LANGUAGE=javascript
        <%'Use JavaScript's ability to direct
            'a click event call a common event handler.
            'In this case call the event procedure btnProc.
            'btnProc passes one argument, "this". "this" is
            'the JavaScript keyword which references the
            'object making the call, in this case the
            'specific button
        %>
        onclick="return btnProc(this)">
</FONT></TD>
<TD bgcolor=<%=clr%>>
<FONT Face=ARIAL Size=3>
<%'Get the Student ID%>
<%=Cstr(socStudent.StudentID)%></FONT></TD>
<TD bgcolor=<%=clr%>><FONT Face=ARIAL Size=3>
<%'Get the Student's Last Name%>
<%=socStudent.LastName%></FONT></TD>
<TD bgcolor=<%=clr%>><FONT Face=ARIAL Size=3>
<%'Get the Student's First Name%>
<%=socStudent.FirstName%></FONT></TD>
<TD bgcolor=<%=clr%> align=center><FONT Face=ARIAL Size=3>
```

```
<%'Construct a dedicated <SELECT> element for
'for each student. Make it so the teacher can
'select either Present, Absent or Late
'from the SELECT ComboBox%>
<SELECT Name="<%=Cstr(socStudent.StudentID)%>">
<Option value=Present>Present
<Option value=Absent>Absent
<Option value=Late>Late
</SELECT></TD>
<TD bgcolor=<%=clr%> align=center><FONT Face=ARIAL Size=2>
<%'Add a checkbox that indicates that the student's
'parents is to receive an email.%>
<INPUT type="checkbox"
       name=ck<%=Cstr(socStudent.StudentID)%>>
</FONT></TD>
</TR>
<%
        'Increment the counter integer
        'in order to keep track of the
        'number of students in the class as
        'well as the number of rows in the <TABLE>.
        i = i + 1
    Next%>
</TABLE>


<%'Persist the enrollment for the class%>
<INPUT Type=Hidden Name=Enrollment Value=<%=Cstr(i)%>>
<%'Persist the class date%>
<INPUT Type=Hidden Name=MyDate Value="<%=Cstr(Date())%>">
<%'Persist the ClassID%>
<INPUT Type=Hidden
       Name=ClassID
       Value="<%=Request.Form("ClassID")%>">
<INPUT Type=Hidden
       Name=SiteURL
       Value="<%=Application("SiteURL")%>">
<%'Resport the class entrollment%>
<FONT Face=Arial Size=3>Enrollment: <%=Cstr(i)%> </FONT>
<BR><INPUT Type=Submit
           Name=Submit
           Value="Submit Attendance">
</FONT>
</FORM>
</BODY>
</HTML>
```

CAUTION

Remember that JavaScript code is case sensitive. VBScript code is not.

OUTPUT

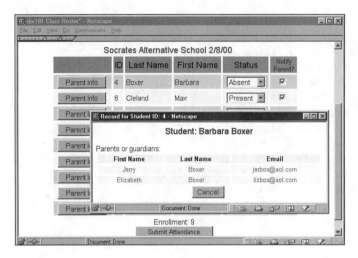

Figure 16.1: *The enhanced Attendance Page allows a teacher to view information about the parents of a student as well as send an attendance summary via email.*

Reconfiguring the Web Site

The entire set of ASP pages that you need to create this ASP application can be found in the code you download from the *by Example* Web site (http://www.quecorp.com/series/by_example/).

Some of the code you'll see in this chapter references Active Server Pages that are not shown in this chapter. For example, ServiceProc.asp is referenced in Listing 16.1, yet not displayed in this chapter. This page is not listed because none of the page's code has been changed in this enhanced version of the application. However, please be advised that these pages are part of the chapter download. Also, unchanged pages can be viewed in the previous version of this application in Chapter 14, "Creating a Class Attendance Page."

Be sure that when setting up the application, you create a Virtual Directory named SocAlternatEx. Also, please make sure that you install the MS Access database as an ODBC System DNS datasource named AriMiddleData. (Both the Socrates Alternative School and the Aristotle Middle School simulation used earlier in this book share the same datasource.)

You need to register the application's Visual Basic ActiveX DLL, SocAltObjLib.dll on the server. If you are using the prior version of this DLL from Chapter 14, you must unregister the older version and register the new version using Regsvr32.exe. (For details about using Regsvr32.exe, see the section, "Installing an ActiveX DLL on an IIS Computer using Regsvr32.EXE" in Chapter 14.)

Finally, make sure that you reconfigure the application variable, `Application("SiteURL")` in `global.ASA` to the IP address of the server from which you are running this application. The variable, `Application("SiteURL")` ships as

```
Application("SiteURL") = http://000.000.000.000/SocAlternateEx
```

You should change the IP address from `000.000.000.000` to the IP address of your server.

Working with the JavaScript Event Procedures

Notice that the Attendance Page in Figure 16.1 has a number of HTML button elements, one for each student, and that each of these buttons displays parents unique to each student. In addition, notice that the buttons on the page are created dynamically, that we never really know how many buttons will be generated until the code determines the number of students in the class. The dynamic nature of button generation for the page introduces an interesting problem. We need to have a button click event procedure that opens a new window containing unique parent information. However, if we don't know how many buttons we will have, how do we write an event procedure for each button? The answer is to create a common event procedure that is used by all buttons and to build smarts into this common event procedure that identifies the button that was clicked.

How JavaScript References an Event Procedure

Unlike VBScript, JavaScript has the ability to allow you to define any function as an event procedure for a given event for a given HTML element. For example, when you create an HTML button element in the body of your Web page, you can define a JavaScript event procedure that is called when the user clicks a button. HTML provides an `onclick` attribute that allows you to associate the event with the function. The following code is an extract from Listing 16.1 illustrating this concept:

```
<INPUT type="button"
       value="Parent Info"
       name=btn<%=Cstr(socStudent.StudentID)%>
.
.
       %>
       onclick="return btnProc(this)">
```

Please notice in the code above that the `<INPUT>` tag has an `onclick` attribute and that the value attached to the attribute is `"return btnProc(this)"`.

What the code actually does is make sure the button element executes the function btnProc(this) when the user clicks the button. Every button element created assigns the btnProc(this) function to the onclick attribute. Thus, all buttons share the event procedure.

The word this is a JavaScript keyword equivalent to the VBScript keyword Me. The keyword this means "this object,"—in this case, the button—to which the attribute onclick is attached. As you can see, the keyword is used as an argument to the bthProc function. When the user clicks the button, the bthProc function is called and the button being clicked is passed as an argument to the function. This is done so that the function knows which button invokes the event. The design of the program requires the event function to know which button invoked it and to determine the particular parent information to display. This is covered in detail in the next section.

Implementing a Common Event Procedure

The btnProc(this) function—which serves as the common event procedure for all onclick events of the button elements in the Attendance page—opens a window containing the data listing the parent information for the given student associated with the button. How does the event procedure know for which student to display data?

The event procedure knows which student's parents list to display because we built the student identification number into the name attribute of the HTML button. Please remember that the common btnProc(this) event procedure knows the button that invoked it. Therefore, the function can examine any of the properties of the button object. We'll take advantage of this fact to pass student identification information into the event procedure by embedding it into the value of the name attribute.

The Attendance Page builds the name attribute of the button object according to a special custom convention unique to this application. All HTML buttons are named with the btn prefix to which the student's identification number is concatenated. For example, a student with the identification number 4 has a number name of btn4, a student with the identification 34 has a button name of btn34, an so forth. The following code, extracted from Listing 16.1, shows how HTML buttons are created and named dynamically using server-side, inline VBScript:

```
name=btn<%=Cstr(socStudent.StudentID)%>
```

The event procedure function looks at the name value of the button passed to it and then separates the btn prefix from student identification number. After the separation takes place, the student ID number is attached as a query string variable value to the URL parameter of the window.open method. The window.open method calls a Web page containing the logic that retrieves and displays the parent list for a given student. This Web page uses the student ID value to determine the specific parent data to return.

(See the client-side `btnProc(this)` function in Listing 16.1.) We'll look at the Web page that retrieves parent data shortly. First, let's learn how JavaScript separates the `btn` prefix from the student identification number.

Working with the JavaScript `String` Object

JavaScript is an object-oriented scripting language and has been since its inception. As such, it has shipped with intrinsic objects from the beginning. One of these objects is the `String` object.

The `String` object contains properties and methods that allow you to manipulate and transform strings of characters. You create a string in JavaScript by creating a variable and then assigning a string to it. For example, to create a `String` object, `str`, in JavaScript, that contains the string, `"Hard Day's Night"`, you write the following:

```
var str = "Hard Day's Night";
```

NOTE

The keyword `var` indicates that you are declaring a variable.

After you have a `String` object created, you can use the various methods of the object to manipulate the characters within the string. For example, if you want to turn all the characters in the string to uppercase, you call the `toUpperCase()` method of the object, like so:

```
var str = "Hard Day's Night";
var newStr = str.toUpperCase();
```

The variable `newStr` evaluates to `"HARD DAY'S NIGHT"`.

The `String` object has more than 20 methods with which you can work. The `String` object contains methods that convert strings to upper- and lowercase. There are methods that extract substrings. In addition, the object contains methods that allow you to change the graphical display of a string. You can find a complete listing of the methods of the `String` object on the Microsoft Developers Network.

TIP

For a detailed description of the JavaScript String object, refer to the online documentation on the Microsoft Developers Network Web Site at
`http://msdn.microsoft.com/scripting/jscript/doc/jsobjstring.htm`.

Parsing Strings in JavaScript

As you read previously, the Attendance page builds the student identification number into the `name` attribute of its associated "Parent Info" button. We'll use two methods of the `String` object to extract the student ID from the button's `name` attribute.

The `btnProc()` function uses the `length` property and the `substring()` method of the `String` object to parse out the student ID number.

The `length` property reports the number of characters within a string. For example, in the code

```
var str = "Bob";
var i = str.length;
```

the variable i evaluates to 3.

The `substring(start, lastPosition)` method returns a substring within a given string. The `substring()` method takes two arguments. The first argument, `start`, indicates the starting position within the string from which to start the substring. (In a JavaScript string the initial position value is zero.) The `lastPosition` argument indicates the last position within the string to be included in the substring. For example,

```
var str = "Bob Reselman"
var newStr = str.substring(0,3) //returns "Bob"
var newStr = str.substring(2,3) //returns "b"
var newStr = str.substring(3,3) //returns ""
var newStr = str.substring(3,5) //returns " R"
var newStr = str.substring(3,9) //returns " Resel"
var newStr = str.substring(4,str.length) //returns "Reselman"
```

Thus, to extract the student ID from the name attribute we pass the `length` of our custom button prefix, `btn`, as the `start` argument for the substring method. In addition, we pass the `length` of the string of the given button's name as the `lastPosition` argument.

The following function is an abridged copy of the `btnProc(this)` function. Notice that the function defined the string variables `str` and `buttonPrefix`. The `str` variable stores the value of the passed button's name. The variable `buttonPrefix` stores the `btn` prefix value. The length of `buttonPrefix` is used as the value of the start argument for the `substring` method. The length of the variable, `str`, is assigned as the value of the `lastPosition` for the `substring` method. When the `substring` method executes, the student ID number is extracted from the button's name `attribute`.

```
function btnProc(btn) {
    var str = btn.name; //Pass the name to a local var
    var len = 0; //set a length buffer
    var startPos = 0; // an integer that indicates the start
                      //position of the substring
    var buttonPrefix = "btn";
    var stdID = "";

    len = str.length;
    startPos = buttonPrefix.length;
```

```
.
.        stdID = str.substring(startPos, len);
.
.
window.open(document.MyForm.SiteURL.value +
                "/SocParentRec.asp?studentID=" + stdID,null,
                //style the window
                "height=200,width=500,status=yes,toolbar=no,
                ➥menubar=no,location=no, resizable=yes");
}

//-->
</SCRIPT>
```

Figure 16.2 illustrates this concept.

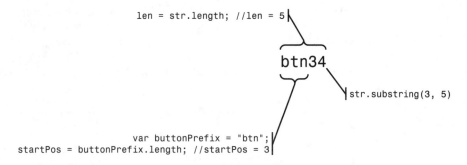

Figure 16.2: *You can use the* String *object's* length *method to identify a start position from which to return a substring from a string.*

After a function determines the student ID number, that number is passed to the URL parameter of the window.open method. The method calls an Active Server Page that retrieves and the displays the specific parent information for a given student. As you read previously, the student ID number is passed to the Active Server Page as a variable value on the submitted query string.

✔ For a review of the window.open method, please read "Working with a Built-In Object's Methods," in Chapter 5, "Fundamentals of Object-Oriented Programming" on page 117.

Retrieving a Student's Parent Data

The logic that retrieves the parent data and the parent data itself is stored in the ActiveX Object Library that was created especially for this application. As you learned in Chapter 14, the name of this object library is SocNewAlternate. We access objects in this Object Library using the CreateObject() method.

In addition to enhancing the Web pages within this application to accommodate the features we are adding, it's necessary to add new objects to the ActiveX Object Library. Also, we added a new method to an existing object, clsSocApp. Table 16.1 shows the enhancements to the SocNewAlternate Object Library. Notice that the objects clsSocParent and clsSocParents are new. Refer to Table 14.1 for a listing of the existing objects in the Object Library.

Table 16.1: **SocNewAlternate** *Object Library Enhancements*

Object	Property/Method	Description
clsSocParent	Email	A string indicating a parent's email address.
	FirstName	A string indicating the first name of a parent or guardian.
	LastName	A string indicating the last name of a parent or guardian.
	StudentID	The student ID of the student associated to the parent.
clsSocParents		A collection class containing clsSocParent objects.
clsSocApp	getParents(StudentID)	Returns a collection class of clsSocParent objects based on the integer passed in the StudentID argument.

NOTE

The ActiveX DLL and the Visual Basic source code for this new version of the SocAlternate object library can be found in the code you download from the companion Web site for this book.

Listing 16.2 shows the code for the Active Server Page SocParentRec.asp. This page retrieves and displays a list of parents for a given student. The page is displayed in Figure 16.1.

Listing 16.2: Displaying Parent Information (SocParentRec.asp/16asp02.asp)

```
<%Option Explicit%>
<HTML>
<HEAD>
<TITLE>Record for Student ID:
<%=Request.QueryString("studentID")%>
</TITLE>
</HEAD>
<SCRIPT LANGUAGE=javascript>
<!—
function btnCancelProc(){
////////////////////////////////////
//This function closes the window
```

```
//when the user clicks the cancel
//button.
//Created 2/5/2000
//
//Programmer: Bob Reselman
//////////////////////////////////////
        window.close();
    }
//-->
</SCRIPT>
<BODY>
<%
Dim socApp 'Application var
Dim pnts 'parents var
Dim pnt 'parent var
Dim std 'Student var
Dim i 'counter var
'Init the counter
i = 1
Set socApp = CreateObject("SocNewAlternate.clsSocApp")
'Get the parents for a given student
Set pnts = socApp.getParents(Request.QueryString("studentID"))
'Also, get the student object too.
Set std = socApp.getStudent(Request.QueryString("studentID"))
'Keep a HTML form in play. Netscape needs the form in
'in order to display elements within the form%>
<FORM action=""      method=POST      name=MyForm>
<CENTER>
<FONT FACE=ARIAL Size=4 Face=Purple>
Student: <%=std.FirstName%> <%=std.LastName%><BR>
</FONT>
</CENTER>
<P>
<FONT FACE=ARIAL Size=3 Face=Blue>
Parents or guardians:
<CENTER>
<TABLE width=100%>
<TR>
<TD Align=Center bgColor=yellow>
<FONT Color=Black Face=Arial Size=2>
<B>First Name</B>
</FONT>
</TD>

<TD Align=Center bgColor=yellow>
```

continues

Listing 16.2: continued

```
<FONT Color=Black Face=Arial Size=2>
<B>Last Name</B>
</FONT>
</TD>

<TD Align=Center bgColor=yellow>
<FONT Color=Black Face=Arial Size=2>
<B>Email</B>
</FONT>
</TD></TR>
<%
For Each pnt In pnts
'Traverse the parents collection, creating a
'new row in the table.
%>
<TR>
<TD Align=Center bgColor=#ffff88>
<FONT Color=Brown Face=Arial Size=2>
<%'Enter the parent's first name in a cell%>
<%=pnt.FirstName%>
</FONT>
</TD>

<TD Align=Center bgColor=#ffff88>
<FONT Color=Brown Face=Arial Size=2>
<%'Enter the parent's last name in a cell%>
<%=pnt.LastName%>
</FONT>
</TD>

<TD Align=Center bgColor=#ffff88>
<FONT Color=Brown Face=Arial Size=2>
<%'Enter the parent's email address in a cell%>
<%=pnt.Email%>
</FONT>
</TD></TR>
<%
i = i + 1
Next
'Clean up after yourself
set pnt = Nothing
set pnts = Nothing
%>
</TABLE>
```

```
<INPUT type="button"
       value="Cancel"
       name=btnCancel
       LANGUAGE=javascript
       onclick="return btnCancelProc()">
</CENTER>
</FORM>

</BODY>
</HTML>
```

All the detailed data retrieval work that the page requires is encapsulated in the clsSocApp object of the Object Library. The getParents(StudentID) method retrieves a clsSocParents collection object based on the value of the StudentID parameter. This collection object contains clsSocParent objects. The code traverses the collection object using a For...Each loop, creating a display of a parent's first name, last name, and email address during each trip through the loop. The actual data for each parent was entered in the object's database at a previous time.

Now that you have learned how to view the parent data of a student, let's move on to the features of the program that sends email notifications to the parents of students selected in the Attendance page.

Adding Email Data to the Student Roster

The email feature of the Attendance page of the Socrates Alternative School application uses the CDONTS Object Library that you learned about in Chapter 15, "Creating an Email Page with the CDONTS Component." The new enhancement allows the teacher to send email to selected parents for a student or students. The teacher selects a parent to notify by checking the check box in the "Notify Parent?" column of the attendance roster table (see Figure 16.1). The selected parent data, along with the attendance statistics, is submitted to the server-side Active Server Page for processing. If a student is checked, an email is sent to the student's parent.

Determining which students have been checked presents an interesting problem. The check box elements are a client-side entity. Data is not passed to the server in terms of HTML elements. Data is passed as name=value pairs. All the server-side script knows about is a value attached to an item in the Request.Form collection. The server doesn't know what type of client-side HTML element created the value. The server-side script doesn't know whether the element that created the value was a Text element or a Check box element. The question we need to answer is how do we let the server-side script know that a check box element for a specific student was checked?

Identifying Students Selected on the Client Side

As you've read, when the "Notify Parent?" check box for a student is checked, that student's parent is sent an email. The way that the server-side script knows that the data it is processing is indeed from a check box, and that the check box relates to a specific student, is through a custom naming convention. This "identification by naming convention" technique is similar to the earlier one we used to determine the student identification number from within the value of the button's name attribute.

In this case, the naming convention we use for an HTML check box element is to write the prefix ck before the student ID number. Thus, a check box for a student with an identification number of 34 is ck34, a student with an ID of 4 is, ck4, and so forth. The following code extract shows how check boxes are added to the student roster table in Listing 16.1:

```
<INPUT type="checkbox"
       name=ck<%=Cstr(socStudent.StudentID)%>>
```

One of the features of HTML is that only check boxes that are checked are submitted to a server. Unchecked check boxes are not sent on. The server-side Active Server Page looks at all the items in the Request.Form collection to identify those with a ck prefix. The ASP script knows that items in the Form collection with such a prefix are check boxes that relating to a specific student. Thus, the logic in the script notes that the student's parents are to be sent an email. A user defined function SendEmail() sends the email.

Listing 16.3 shows the extract of code that identifies the check boxes.

EXAMPLE

Listing 16.3: Determining the Sending of an Email (16asp03.txt)

```
Dim IDBuffer 'Buffer for studentID from checkbox
  For Each k in Request.Form
    'Check to see if the name of the form
    'variable begins with a "ck". This means that
    'it is a check box.
    If UCase(Left(k,2)) = "CK" then
      'Get the StudentID out of the checkbox name
      IDBuffer = Trim(Mid(k,3))
      'If the checkbox ID and the student ID matchup
      'then send an email!!!
      If CInt(IDBuffer) = CInt(socAttSum.StudentID) then
          IsMailed = SendEmail(socAttSum, _
                    socApp.getParents(socAttSum.StudentID))
      End if
    End e if
  Next
```

Emailing Attendance Status

As you can see, the real meat of the emailing enhancement is encapsulated into a user-defined function, SendEmail. Listing 16.4 shows the code for the function.

EXAMPLE

Listing 16.4: Encapsulating the Use of the CDONTS NewMail Object (16asp04.txt)

```
Function SendEMail(SocSumObj, prntsObj)
'===================================
'Sends a student's class attendance record
'to the parents on record.
'
'Created 2/6/2000
'Programmer: Bob Reselman
'===================================
    Dim ml 'CDONTS mail var
    Dim prnt 'Parent object var
    Dim m 'Mail message buffer
    Dim std 'Student buffer

    On Error Resume Next
    For Each prnt In prntsObj
      'Create a form letter to send to the parent
      m = "Dear Mr/Ms " & prnt.LastName & ":" & vbCrlf & vbCrLf
      m = m & "The following is a summary of the attendance "
      m = m & "statistics for your son/daughter, "
      m = m & SocSumObj.Firstname & " in class code: "
      m = m & SocSumObj.ClassID & "." & vbCrlf & vbCrlf
      m = m & "Days Present: " & SocSumObj.SumPresent & vbCrlf
      m = m & "Days Absent: " & SocSumObj.SumAbsent & vbCrlf
      m = m & "Days Late: " & SocSumObj.SumLate & vbCrlf
      m = m & vbCrlf & vbCrlf
      m = m & "Please feel free to contact us at: "
      m = m & Application("OrgEmail") & ", if you need more "
      m = m & "information." & vbCrlf & vbCrlf
      m = m & "Yours truly," & vbCrlf
      m = m & "The staff at the " & Application("OrgName")
      'Create the CDONTS Mail object
      Set ml = CreateObject("CDONTS.NewMail")
      'Prep the NewMail object
      ml.From = Application("OrgEmail")
      ml.to = prnt.Email
      std = SocSumObj.FirstName & " " & SocSumObj.LastName
      ml.Subject = "Attendance Status: " & std
      ml.body = m
      'Send the mail
      ml.Send
```

continues

Listing 16.4: continued

```
      If Err Then Exit Function
      'Clean Up
      Set ml = Nothing
    Next
    SendEmail = True
End Function
```

Figure 16.3 shows the mail that is sent by the code in the function
`SendEmail` from the previous example.

`SendEmail` takes two arguments, a `clsSocAttendSum` (`SocSumObj`) summary
object, which contains attendance summary information (days present,
absent, and late as well as first name, last name, and ID of the student)
and a parents collection object, `clsSocParents` (`prntsObj`). The `collection`
object stores a collection of `clsSocParent` objects. The parent object contains
the first name, last name, and email address of a student's parent.

OUTPUT

Figure 16.3: *You can use the CDONTS* NewMail *object within ASP to create
and send a form letter email.*

The function runs a For...Each loop against the `parents` collection object to
work with each `parent` object that the collection contains. The function creates
a form letter using information in the given parent object and `attendance`
summary object. This form letter is concatenated into a single variable, `m`. After

the form letter is created, a `CDONTS` `NewMail` object is created. Mail information is assigned to the various properties of the mail object. Some of the mail information such as `Application("OrgEmail")`, which is the organization's email address, is stored in application-level variables that the code references. After the email is addressed, the variable m, which contains the attendance summary form letter, is assigned to the `Body` property of the `NewMail` object. Then the letter is delivered using the `NewMail` object's `Send` method.

Listing 16.5 shows the complete code for the server-side ASP that processes the attendance information for each student, creates the attendance summary, and sends the email notification to selected students. This code is very similar to the attendance processing code in Chapter 14. However, the email notification enhancements have been added.

Listing 16.5: Using the CDONTS `NewMail` Object to Send Attendance Information (SocClassAttendProcEx.asp, 16asp05.asp)

EXAMPLE

```
<%'===================================
'Page: SocClassAttendProcEx.asp
'
'Passes the Attendance data to the App
'object to writing to the data datasource.
'Also, displays a report that summarizes
'the attendance activity for a given class
'at the Socrates Alternative School
'
'Programmer: Bob Reselman
'
'Created 1/15/99
'History: Mail features added 2/5/2000 BR
'===================================
Option Explicit 'Make it so we must declare variables

Function SendEMail(SocSumObj, prntsObj)
'===================================
'Sends a student's class attendance record
'to the parents on record.
'
'Created 2/6/2000
'Programmer: Bob Reselman
'===================================
   Dim ml 'CDONTS mail var
   Dim prnt 'Parent object var
   Dim m 'Mail message buffer
   Dim std 'Student buffer

   'On Error Resume Next
```

continues

Listing 16.5: continued

```
  For Each prnt In prntsObj
    'Create a form letter to send to the parent
    m = "Dear Mr/Ms " & prnt.LastName & ":" & vbCrlf & vbCrLf
    m = m & "The following is a summary of the attendance "
    m = m & "statistics for your son/daughter, "
    m = m & SocSumObj.Firstname & " in class code: "
    m = m & SocSumObj.ClassID & "." & vbCrlf & vbCrlf
    m = m & "Days Present: " & SocSumObj.SumPresent & vbCrlf
    m = m & "Days Absent: " & SocSumObj.SumAbsent & vbCrlf
    m = m & "Days Late: " & SocSumObj.SumLate & vbCrlf
    m = m & vbCrlf & vbCrlf
    m = m & "Please feel free to contact us at: "
    m = m & Application("OrgEmail") & ", if you need more "
    m = m & "information." & vbCrlf & vbCrlf
    m = m & "Yours truly," & vbCrlf
    m = m & "The staff at the " & Application("OrgName")
    'Create the CDONTS Mail object
    Set ml = CreateObject("CDONTS.NewMail")
    If Err Then Exit Function
    'Prep the NewMail object
    ml.From = Application("OrgEmail")
    ml.to = prnt.Email
    'ml.to = "reselbob@pionet.net"
    std = SocSumObj.FirstName & " " & SocSumObj.LastName
    ml.Subject = "Attendance Status: " & std
    ml.body = m
    'Send the mail
     ml.Send
    If Err Then Exit Function
    'Clean Up
    Set ml = Nothing
  Next
  SendEmail = True
End Function
%>


<HTML>
<HEAD>
<TITLE>
<%Response.Write Request.Form("lstClassID") + " Class Roster" %>
</TITLE>
</HEAD>

<BODY>
<CENTER>
```

```
<TABLE>
<%'=======Beginning of Services menu========%>
<TR>
<TD>
<A HREF="<%Response.Write Application("SiteURL") & _
                    "/ServiceProc.asp?Serv=1"%>">
<Img src="./images/attendance.jpg" border=0></A></TD>

<TD>
<A HREF="<%Response.Write Application("SiteURL") & _
                    "/ServiceProc.asp?Serv=2"%>">
<Img src="./images/students.jpg" border=0></A></TD>

<TD>
<A HREF="/<%Response.Write Application("SiteURL") & _
                    "/ServiceProc.asp?Serv=3"%>">
<Img src="./images/reportcards.jpg" border=0></A></TD>
</TR>

<TR>

<TD Align=Center>
<A HREF="<%Response.Write Application("SiteURL") & _
                    "/ServiceProc.asp?Serv=1"%>">
<FONT FACE=Arial>Attendance</FONT></A></TD>

<TD Align=Center>
<A HREF="<%Response.Write Application("SiteURL") & _
                    "/ServiceProc.asp?Serv=2"%>">
<FONT FACE=Arial>Students</FONT></A></TD>

<TD Align=Center>
<A HREF="<%Response.Write Application("SiteURL") & _
                    "/ServiceProc.asp?Serv=3"%>">
<FONT FACE=Arial>Report Cards</FONT></A></TD>
</TR>
</TABLE>
<%'=======End of Services menu========%>
<HR>
<FONT SIZE = 4 FACE=ARIAL COLOR=Purple>
<%
Dim socApp 'Custom App object var
Dim socStudents 'Students Collection class object var
Dim socAttends 'Attendance Status Collection class object var
Dim socAttSums 'Attendance Summary Collection class object var
Dim socAttSum 'Attendance Summary object var
```

continues

Listing 16.5: continued

```
Dim CId 'Holds the ID for a class at the Alternative School
Dim IsMailed 'Var to hold state me email notifications
Dim i 'integer buffer
Dim k 'key buffer

'Create an App object
Set socApp = CreateObject("SocNewAlternate.clsSocApp")
'Create a Collection class of attendance objects
Set socAttends = CreateObject("SocNewAlternate.clsSocAttends")

'Get the classID for this submission
CId = Request.Form("ClassID")

'Go through all the elements in the form
'collection and identify the ones that have
'numeric keys. The elements are student ID's.
'These are the guys we want to add to the
'clsSocAttends collection of clsSocAttend objects
For Each k in Request.Form
    'Go through all the elements in the Request
    'object's Form collection. If it is a number, you
    'know that you have a studentID. Remember,
    'we named the <SELECT> elements in the previous
    'page with the StudentID. The studentID is a numeric
    'value.
    If Isnumeric(k) then
        Select Case UCase(Request.Form(k))
            Case "PRESENT": i = 1
            Case "ABSENT": i = 0
            Case "LATE": i = 2
        End Select
    'Add the data to the socAttends collection
    'Make sure you do proper typecasting or you will
    'get a type mismatch from the collection object's
    'Add method!!!!
    socAttends.Add Cstr(CId), Cint(k), Date(), Cint(i)
    End if
Next

Dim clr 'color variable
i = 0
'Have the App object write the attendance
If socApp.setAttendance(socAttends) then %>
  <FONT Size=6 Color=Purple Face=Arial>
  Attendance Taken
  </FONT>
  <BR>
```

```
   <FONT Size=5 Color=Purple Face=Arial>
Here is a summary of your class's
attendance statistics to date:
   </FONT>
   <P>
   <CENTER>
<!—Create a TABLE —>
   <TABLE Width=80%>
<!—TABLE header——·>
   <TR>
   <TD><FONT Face=Arial Color=Blue Size=3>
<B>First Name</B></FONT></TD>
   <TD><FONT Face=Arial Color=Blue Size=3>
<B>Last Name</B></FONT></TD>
   <TD><FONT Face=Arial Color=Blue Size=3>
<B>Present</B></FONT></TD>
   <TD><FONT Face=Arial Color=Blue Size=3>
<B>Absent</B></FONT></TD>
   <TD><FONT Face=Arial Color=Blue Size=3>
<B>Late</B></FONT></TD>
   </TR>
<%
'Use the App object's getAttendSummary method
'to get a Collection class of Summary objects.
'Each Summary object contains the FirstName,
'LastName, Number of Days Present, Number of Day Absent
'and Number to Days Late.
Set socAttSums = socApp.getAttendSummary(CStr(Cid))
'Traverse the Collection class
For each socAttSum in socAttSums
    'Make rows of alternating colors
    If i Mod 2 = 0 then
        clr = "#ffd700"
    Else
        clr = "#ffff88"
    End if%>
<TR>
<%'Embed the LastName, FirstName, Number of Days Present
'Number of Days Absent and Number of Days Late within
'cells of an HTML <TABLE>%>
<TD bgcolor=<%=clr%>><FONT Face=Arial Color=Blue Size=3>
<%=socAttSum.LastName%></FONT></TD>
<TD bgcolor=<%=clr%>></FONT><FONT Face=Arial Color=Blue Size=3>
<%=socAttSum.FirstName%></FONT></TD>
<TD bgcolor=<%=clr%>></FONT><FONT Face=Arial Color=Blue Size=3>
<%=socAttSum.SumPresent%></FONT></TD>
<TD bgcolor=<%=clr%>></FONT><FONT Face=Arial Color=Blue Size=3>
<%=socAttSum.SumAbsent%></FONT></TD>
```

Listing 16.5: continued

```
<TD bgcolor=<%=clr%>></FONT><FONT Face=Arial Color=Blue Size=3>
<%=socAttSum.SumLate%></FONT></TD>
</TR>
<TR><TD>
<%
  'Now send the emails
  Dim IDBuffer 'Buffer for studentID from checkbox
  For Each k in Request.Form
   'Check to see if the name of the form
   'variable begins with a "ck". This means that
   'it is a check box.
   If UCase(Left(k,2)) = "CK" then
     'Get the StudentID out of the checkbox name
     IDBuffer = Trim(Mid(k,3))
     'If the checkbox ID and the student ID matchup
     'then send an email!!!
     If CInt(IDBuffer) = CInt(socAttSum.StudentID) then
        IsMailed = SendEmail(socAttSum, _
                   socApp.getParents(socAttSum.StudentID))
     End if
   End if
Next
'Increase the row counter
i = i + 1
Next
%>
</TD></TR>
</FONT>
<% End If%>
</TABLE>
<%
'Tell the user the status of the email notifications
If IsMailed Then
%>
<P>
<FONT Face=Arial Size=4 Color=Purple>
Email Notifications Sent
</FONT>
<%Else%>
<FONT Face=Arial Size=4 Color=Red>
There were problems with the Email notifications
</FONT>
</CENTER>
<%End If%>
</BODY>
</HTML>
```

Listing 16.6 shows the `global.ASA` file for the application.

Listing 16.6: The `global.ASA` File for the Enhanced Application (`16asp06.asp, global.ASA`)

```
<SCRIPT LANGUAGE=vbscript RUNAT=Server>
'*********************
'Filename: Global.ASA
'Application: Socrates Alternative School
'
'Programmer: Bob Reselman
'
'*********************
    Sub Application_OnStart()
        Application("SiteURL") = "http://147.100.100.100:9080/SocAlternateEx"
        Application("DBSource") = "AriMiddleData"
        Application("LogonErrFile") = "LogonErr.asp"
        Application("AccessErrFile") = "AccessErr.asp"
        Application("OrgName") = "Socrates Alternative School"
        Application("OrgEmail") = "Support@SocAltSchool.edu"
    End Sub

    Sub Session_OnStart()
        Session("LoginID") = ""
    End Sub

    Sub Application_OnEnd()
    End Sub

    Sub Session_OnEnd()
        Session.Abandon
    End Sub
</SCRIPT>
```

What's Next

This is the final chapter of *Active Server Pages 3.0 by Example*. The goal of this book was to help you learn the fundamentals of ASP programming clearly, using examples to demonstrate the concepts and techniques discussed with its chapters. A secondary goal of the book was to help you learn how to create programs that are designed to be run in a distributed environment, an environment in which any user could use any computer—any where—to interact with your application at any time.

This chapter brought together all the different facets of Active Server Page technology that we have been studying. You worked with server-side script in VBScript. You worked with client-side script in JavaScript. We used the

CDONTS ActiveX Component Library that ships with Windows NT to implement email functionality. We used a custom Object Library created with Visual Basic to encapsulate functionality that was special to our site. Finally, we combined email and Web browsing technology to make a distributed application that was useful and labor saving.

Today creating a presence in a distributed environment is a relatively inexpensive undertaking. Technology that was available previously only to enterprises with substantial financial resources can now be had for less than the price of a used car. The question before us isn't whether you can afford to be in the game. Rather, the question is what game do you want to play?

Inexpensive distributed computing means schools can provide every student with an up-to-date textbox that can never be lost or damaged. Inexpensive distributed computing means small, independent retailing can again become a viable business. In cyberspace all real estate is prime real estate. Inexpensive distributed computing means we'll all get smarter. Museums are now open to everyone 24 hours a day. Libraries never close.

Democratic society is by nature based on the free exchange of ideas in an open and distributed environment. The greatest threat to a democratic people is the monopolization of the creation and distribution of information by a select few. Modern distributed computing gives each of us a presence that can be seen and heard around the planet. Our present time really can be the Golden Age of humanity that mankind has dreamed about. I hope this book has in some small way contributed to realizing this dream.

Part V

Appendixes

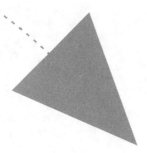

Appendix A

ASP Object Model

Application Object

The Application object refers to an ASP Application. An ASP Application is a group of Active Server Pages contained in an IIS virtual directory. The name of the virtual directory is the name of the ASP Application.

Methods

Lock

Locks up the Application-level variables so other scripts cannot change them.

EXAMPLE

```
Application.Lock
Application("Votes") = Application("Votes ") + 1
Application.Unlock
```

Unlock

Unlocks Application-level variables so others can use them. Unlock is called implicitly when a page is exited or a page times out.

Collections

STATICOBJECTS

```
Application.StaticObjects(key)
```

key is the name of an item in the StaticObject collection.

The StaticObject collection refers to all of the objects created with the <OBJECT> tags within the Application object. You use this collection if you want to find out about the objects within an ASP Application.

CONTENTS

```
Application.Contents(key)
```

key, the name of the item in the Contents collection.

The Contents collection refers to all the Application-level variables is in an ASP Application.

METHODS OF THE Contents COLLECTION

Remove(name|index) removes an item from the Contents collection.

`Application.Contents.Remove("SomeVar")`

EXAMPLE

RemoveAll removes all the objects from a collection.

`Application.StaticObjects.Contents.RemoveAll`

EXAMPLE

Events Procedures

`Application_OnStart`

This event procedure is called when an application starts. The event is captured in Global.ASA.

`Application_OnEnd`

This event procedure is called when an application ends. An application ends when IIS is stopped or when the Global.ASA file is replaced.

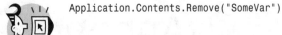

ASPError Object

An ASPError object contains the information about an error condition that has occurred in script in an Active Server Page. You access an ASPError object by calling Server.GetLastError. The properties of the ASPError object are read only.

Properties

ASPCode

Returns a string that is the error code for the ASPError object.

Number

Returns a long integer that is the error number of the given error.

Source

Returns a string indicating the source in which the ASPError occurs. For example, the text of the line of code that caused the error.

Category

Returns a string indicating where the error was generated: by Internet Information Server, a scripting language such as VBScript, or an ActiveX component.

File

Returns a string indicating the filename of the Active Server Page in which the ASPError was generated.

Line

Returns a long integer indicating the line number in the Active Server Page in which the ASPError was generated.

Column

Returns a long integer indicating the column number in the Active Server Page in which the ASPError was generated.

Description

Returns a string that describes the ASPError.

ASPDescription

Returns a string that provides a more detailed description of the ASPError should one be provided.

ObjectContext Object

The ObjectContext object represents the Context Object for an object registered within Microsoft Transaction Server. A Context Object is a shadow object of your Active Server Page should you indicate that it be used under Microsoft Transaction Server. You make your Active Server Page transactional by using the tag <@ transaction = Required> in the first line of your Active Server Page.

Methods

SetAbort

Indicates to MTS that the transaction has failed and that MTS should do failure cleanup. Also, invokes the event procedure, ObjectContext_OnTransactionAbort.

ObjectContext.SetAbort

SetComplete

Indicates to MTS that the transaction has succeeded and that MTS should commit the transaction. Also invokes the event procedure, ObjectContext_OnTransactionCommit.

ObjectContext.SetComplete

Events

OnTransactionAbort

The event procedure called when the ObjectContext object's SetAbort method is called.

```
Sub OnTransactionAbort()
    Response.Write "Transaction failed. All data is restored."
End Sub
```

OnTransactionCommit

The event procedure called when the ObjectContext object's SetComplete method is called.

```
Sub OnTransactionCommit()
    Response.Write "Transaction was successful"
End Sub
```

EXAMPLE

Request Object

The Request object represents the HTTP data sent from a browser to an Active Server Page via Internet Information Server.

Properties

TotalBytes

Total number of bytes sent in the request Server.

Methods

BinaryRead

Request.BinaryRead(*count*)

> where *count* is the number of bytes to read from client.

Binary Read returns an array of unsigned bytes. You use the method to get low-level byte data when the request is made using the Post method. If you use this method, the Request.Form collection is rendered inoperative. If you use the Request.Form collection, this method is made inoperative and an error will result.

EXAMPLE

```
Dim vPosted
lNum
lNum = Request.TotalBytes
vPosted = Request.BinaryRead(lNum)
```

Collections

ClientCertificate

Request.ClientCertificate(*key*[*subKey*])

where *key* is the name of the field to retrieve.

where *subKey* is the name of the subField to retrieve.

The ClientCertificate collection contains information about the digital security certificate on the client browser.

The following table shows you the fields that you can read.

Field	Description
Certificate	A string containing the entire contents of the certificate.
Flags	Additional information
	ceCertPresent—A client certificate is present.
	ceUnrecognizedIssuer—unknown issuer.
	Note: You need to include the certification include files in your Active Server Page in order to use these flags, ceCertPresent and ceUnrecognizedIssuer. Include cervbs.inc, for scripts in VBScript. Include cerjavas.inc for scripts in JScript. These include files are installed in the \Inetpub\ASPSamp\Samples directory.
Issuer	A string that containing user information. If the Issuer flag is specified without a *SubField*, the ClientCertificate collection returns a list of subfields separated by commas. For example, C=US, O=QUE, and so on.
SerialNumber	A string that indicates the certification serial number. This string is an ASCII representation of hexadecimal bytes separated by hyphens (-). For example, FF-55-F3-A2.
Subject	A string that contains a list of subfield values. The value of each sub-field contains information about the subject of the certificate. If the Subject flag is specified without a *SubField*, the ClientCertificate collection returns a comma-separated list of subfields. For example, C=US, O=QUE, and so on.
ValidFrom	A date that indicates when the certificate becomes valid. This date follows VBScript format and varies according to international settings. For example, within the U.S. you note the ValidFrom date as 10/31/97 10:20:00 PM.
ValidUntil	Expiration date of the certificate.

The following table shows subField values.

subField	Description
C	Indicates the name of the country/region of origin.
CN	Indicates the common name of the user. (Use this subField with the Subject key.)
GN	Indicates a given name.
I	Indicates a set of initials.
L	Indicates a locality.
O	Indicates the company or organization name.
OU	Indicates the name of the organization.
S	Indicates a state or province.
T	Indicates the title of the person or organization.

EXAMPLE

The following example shows you how to use the organization name from a client certificate collection.

```
<% If Request.ClientCertificate("SubjectO") = "QUE" Then
    Response.Write "You can buy books"
End If %>
```

Cookies

```
Request.Cookies(key)(subKey).attributes
```

where

> *key* is a string indicating the name of the cookie.
>
> *subKey* is a string indicating a subkey for a given cookie. You use subKeys to organize many cookie values under one name.
>
> *.attributes*. At the present time the attributes property allows you to read the value, .HasKeys. If cookie has subKeys, .HasKeys returns TRUE.

The Cookies represents a collection of cookies forwarded from a calling browser.

EXAMPLE

The following code shows you how to list the subKeys in the cookie "BooksBought" if the cookie should have subKeys:

```
If Request.Cookies("BooksBought").HasKeys Then
    For Each sKey In Request.Cookies("BooksBought").
        Response.Write "Here are the books you bought:"
        Response.Write Request.Cookies("BooksBought")( sKey) & "<BR>"
    Next End
End If
```

Form

```
Request.Form(element)[(index)|.Count]
```

> where *element* is a string indicating the Name of the element within the form
>
> where *index* is an optional index number that identifies items with an element.
>
> where *.Count* returns the number of items for an element. If the element does not have any items, .Count returns 1.

When you submit an HTML <FORM> on the client side, these elements appear to your Active Server Page as elements with the Form collection. You can use the Form collection to access the value within a particular HTML <FORM> element. For example, an element can be a Text element or a <SELECT> element, to name two.

EXAMPLE

The following example shows you how to find the value of an element, FirstName:

```
str = Request.Form("FirstName")
```

QueryString

```
Request.QueryString(variable)[(index)|.Count]
```

> where *variable* is a string indicating the name of the name=value pair within the QueryString.
>
> where *index* is an optional index number that identifies items with a name=value pair.
>
> where *.Count* returns the number of items for a name=value pair.

The QueryString collection indicates the variables that are submitted from a browser using the Get method or after a "?" character in the URL, when using an HTML anchor. For example

```
<A HREF="http://www.mysite.com/procname.htm?firstName=Bob>
Click me to submit a name</A>
```

EXAMPLE

The following example uses the QueryString collection to determine the value of the variable, firstName.

```
Str = Request.QueryString("firstName")
```

ServerVariables

```
Request.ServerVariables(varName)
```

> where *varName* is the name of the server variable.

The collection of environmental server variables that provide information about the browser making the request and the server upon which the Active Server Page is running. These variables are predefined and conform to the HTTP standard.

The following table shows a list of Server Variables.

Variable	Description
ALL_HTTP	All HTTP headers sent by the client.
ALL_RAW	Returns all headers in raw form.
	Note: ALL_HTTP places an HTTP_ prefix before the header name. In addition, the header name is always capitalized. If you use ALL_RAW, the header name and values appear as they are sent by the client.
APPL_MD_PATH	Returns the metabase path for the Application for the ISAPI DLL.
APPL_PHYSICAL_PATH	Returns the physical path corresponding to the metabase path. IIS converts the APPL_MD_PATH to the physical (directory) path to return this value.
AUTH_PASSWORD	Returns the value entered in the client's authentication dialog box. This variable appears if Basic authentication is used.
AUTH_TYPE	Indicates the authentication method that the server uses to validate users.
AUTH_USER	Indicates a raw authenticated user name.
CERT_COOKIE	Indicates a unique ID for a client certificate. This value is returned as a string.
CERT_FLAGS	Bit 0 is set to 1 if the client certificate is present. Bit 1 is set to 1 if the Certification authority of the client certificate is invalid. This means the CERT_FLAG value is not in the list of recognized CAs on the server.
CERT_ISSUER	Indicates issuer field of the client certificate.
CERT_KEYSIZE	Indicates the key size of Secure Sockets Layer connection in bits.
CERT_SECRETKEYSIZE	Indicates the number of bits in server certificate private key.
CERT_SERIALNUMBER	Indicates the serial number field of the client certificate.
CERT_SERVER_ISSUER	Indicates the issuer field of the server certificate.
CERT_SERVER_SUBJECT	Indicates the subject field of the server certificate.
CERT_SUBJECT	Indicates the subject field of the client certificate.
CONTENT_LENGTH	Indicates the length of the content as given by the client.
CONTENT_TYPE	Indicates the data type of the content. You use this server variables with queries that have attached information, such as the HTTP queries GET, POST, and PUT.

Variable	Description
GATEWAY_INTERFACE	Indicates the the revision of the CGI specification used by the server. The structure for this variable is CGI/*revision*.
HTTP_<HeaderName>	Indicates the value stored in the header *HeaderName*. If you want to use a header other than those listed in this table, you must prefix the header with the HTTP_ for the ServerVariables collection to retrieve its value.
	Note: The server interprets any underscore (_) characters in *HeaderName* as dashes in the actual header. For example, if you specify HTTP_A_HEADER, the server searches for a header sent as A-HEADER.
HTTP_ACCEPT	Indicates the value of the Accept header.
HTTP_ACCEPT_LANGUAGE	Indicates a string describing the language to use for displaying content.
HTTP_USER_AGENT	Indicates a string describing the browser that sent the request.
HTTP_COOKIE	Indicates the cookie string that was included with the request.
HTTP_REFERER	Indicates a string containing the URL of the original request when a redirect has occurred.
HTTPS	Set to ON if the request came in through secure channel (SSL). Returns OFF if the request is for a non-secure channel.
HTTPS_KEYSIZE	Indicates the number of bits in Secure Sockets Layer connection key size.
HTTPS_SECRETKEYSIZE	Indicates the number of bits in server certificate private key.
HTTPS_SERVER_ISSUER	Indicates the Issuer field of the server certificate.
HTTPS_SERVER_SUBJECT	Indicates the Subject field of the server certificate.
INSTANCE_ID	Indicates the ID for the IIS instance in textual format. This value appears as a string, if the instance ID is 1.
INSTANCE_META_PATH	Indicates the metabase path for the instance of IIS that responds to the request.
LOCAL_ADDR	Indicates the Server Address on which the request came in. Useful in multiserver environments.
LOGON_USER	Indicates the Windows account that the user is logged into.
PATH_INFO	Indicates extra path information as given by the client.
PATH_TRANSLATED	Performs any necessary virtual-to-physical mapping necessary in a translated version of PATH_INFO.
QUERY_STRING	Indicates the query information stored in the string following the question mark (?) in the HTTP request.

continues

continued

Variable	Description
REMOTE_ADDR	Indicates the IP address of the remote host (client browser) making the request.
REMOTE_HOST	Indicates the name of the host making the request. Returns the REMOTE_ADDR if no value is present in the REMOTE_HOST variable.
REMOTE_USER	Indicates the unmapped user-name string sent in by the user.
REQUEST_METHOD	Indicates the method used to make the request. For HTTP, this is GET, HEAD, POST, and so forth.
SCRIPT_NAME	Indicates the virtual path to the script being executed.
SERVER_NAME	Indicates the server's host name, DNS alias, or IP address of the server upon which your Active Server Page is running.
SERVER_PORT	Indicates the port number to which the request was sent.
SERVER_PORT_SECURE	Indicates a string that contains either 0 or 1. If the request is being handled on the secure port, then the variable value will be 1. Otherwise, it will be 0.
SERVER_PROTOCOL	Indicates the name and revision of the request information protocol. The structure for this variable is *protocol/revision*.
SERVER_SOFTWARE	Indicates the name and version of the server software that answers the request and runs the gateway. The structure for this variable is *name/version*.
URL	Indicates the base portion of the URL.

EXAMPLE

The following example shows you how to use the ServerVariables collection to report the IP address of a calling browser:

```
str = ServerVariables ("REMOTE_HOST")
```

Response Object

The Response object contains properties and methods that allow a server to send data back to a calling browser.

Properties

Buffer

You set the Buffer property to buffer page output. If you set the property to True, the server does not send any response data to the client browser until all of the server scripts on the current page have been processed. In addition, Buffering will continue until the Flush or End method has been called.

CacheControl

You set this property to Public if you want a proxy server to cache ASP data. Set the property to Private to deny proxy server's caching capability.

Charset

Sets the character set for the Active Server Page.

ContentType

Sets the content type(s) of the Response object. For example, to indicate that the Active Server Page response is supporting JPEG, you write

Response.ContentType = "image/JPEG"

Expires

Sets the time in minutes before a cached page will expire in the browser. If you want the page to expire immediately in the browser cache, set the value to −1.

ExpiresAbsolute

Sets the expiration time of a page in the browser's cache in exact data/time format.

The following example specifies that the page will expire 10 seconds after 4:30 PM on July 29, 2001:

```
<%Response.ExpiresAbsolute=#July 29,2001 16:30:10# %>
```

EXAMPLE

IsClientConnected

Read-only property that reports if the client is connected to the server.

PICS

Allows you to set the PICS value for your page. PICS is a parent advisory coding system that rates the content of your Active Server Page.

The following example adds a PICS rating to your Active Server Page:

```
Response.PICS(_
"(PICS-1.1 <http://www.rsac.org/ratingv01.html> labels on " _
& chr(34) & "1997.01.05T08:15-0500" & chr(34) & " until" & chr(34) _
& "1999.12.31T23:59-0000" & chr(34) & " ratings (v 1 s 1 l 1 n 1))")
```

EXAMPLE

You must use the chr(34) function to indicate a quotation mark.

Status

Sets and gets the Server status as determined by HTTP specification.

Methods

AddHeader

Response.AddHeader Name, Value

where Name is the name of the header.

where Value is the value of the header.

Adds a new HTML header to a page. It does not remove one. An HTML header is information that is sent to the browser as part of the page, but is not displayed within the browser. HTML headers are part of the HTTP specification.

The following example adds a Header to a `Response`:

```
Response.AddHeader "ACCESSERR", "Caution, unauthorized user"
```

AppendToLog

```
Response.AddToLog SomeString
```

where *SomeString* is log entry; adds an entry to the server's log.

BinaryWrite

```
Response.Binary SomeBinaryData
```

where *SomeBinaryData* is non-character converted data; outputs non-string data, such as graphics.

Clear

```
Response.Clear
```

Erases HTML body data from the buffer. If the `Response.Buffer` property is not set to `True`, an error occurs.

End

```
Response.End
```

Causes the server to stop processing the script and send the data.

Flush

```
Response.Flush
```

Causes the data being processed by ASP to be sent immediately from the server. If the `Response.Buffer` property is not set to `True`, an error occurs.

Redirect

```
Response.Redirect URL
```

where *URL* is the location of the Web site or file on the server to where the response should be redirected.

You use the method to pass a response onto another server on the Web or a page on the local server.

The following example passes the response to an external Web site:

```
Response.Redirect www.mcp.com
```

The following example passes the response to a page on the local server:

```
Response.Server ".\data\GoodStuff.htm"
```

```
Write
Response.Write SomeString
```

where `SomeString` is a string to pass to the calling browser; sends a string to be displayed in the browser.

The following example writes the current time to a calling browser:

```
Response.Write Time()
```

EXAMPLE

Collections

```
Cookies
Response.Cookies(cookie) [(key)|.attribute] = value
```

where `cookie` is the name of the cookie.

where `key` is a key that indicates sub fields within the cookie. Optional.

where `.attribute` is a cookie's attributes.

You use the `cookies` collection to set a cookie(s) to a client browser. You can create cookies that have multiple subfields under the same cookie name.

The following table shows you the attributes that the `Response.Cookies` collection supports:

Attribute	Description
Domain	Write-only. Specifies the requested domain that the cookie honors. You use this attribute to control responses to requests made on various domains throughout the server.
Expires	Write-only. The date on which the cookie expires. If you want the cookie to be stored on the browser's hard disk, this value must be set. If this attribute is not set to a date beyond the current date, the cookie vaporizes when the session ends.
HasKeys	Read-only. Specifies that the cookie contains keys.
Path	Write-only. If specified, indicates the requested path that the cookie respects, If this attribute is not set, the application path is used. You use this attribute to control responses to requests made on various files throughout the server's hard drives.
Secure	Write-only. Indicates whether the cookie is secure.

The following example sends a cookie, `BooksBought`, to the browser:

```
<% Response.Cookies("BooksBought")("Book1") = "Tom Sawyer"
Response.Cookies("BooksBought")("Book2") = "The Yearling"
%>
```

EXAMPLE

Server Object

The Server object represents the IIS server controlling the processing and traffic on your Web site.

Properties

ScriptTimeout

Sets the amount of time, in seconds, that a script can run before the server stops it. The default value is 90 seconds.

Methods

CreateObject

Server.CreateObject("*MyLibDll.MyObject*")

> where *MyLibDLL* is an ActiveX DLL or EXE.

> where *MyObject* is an object within the ActiveX Library.

You use this method to create server components. The following example shows you how to create a MyInfo component with page-level scope:

Set in = Server.CreateObject("MSWC.MyInfo")

Execute

Server.Execute *FilePath*

> where *FilePath* is the location of the ASP file to execute.

You use this method to work with scripts and data on other pages. The Execute method pass control to the page indicated by the FilePath parameter. Once execution is complete, control is passed back to the calling page.

The following example shows you how to call a page using the Execute method:

<%Server.Execute " Errors\BigError.asp"%>

GetLastError

Server.GetLastError

Returns an ASPError object. Make sure that you use the method before you send any data onto the calling browser.

The following example shows you how to return an ASPError object:

<%Set obj = Server.GetLastError%>

HTMLEncode

Server.HTMLEncode(*SomeString*)

> where *SomeString* is the string to encode.

The HTMLEncode method substitutes HTML tag and keyword characters with characters that are not subject to HTML interpretation by the browser. This method is useful if you want to display actual HTML in the browser.

The following example shows you how to use the HTMLEncode method to display the string "This is
" in the browser:

```
<%Response.Write Server.HTMLEncode("This is <BR>")
```

MapPath

```
Server.MapPath(ThePath)
```

where *ThePath* is a string indicating a relative or virtual path.

The method MapPath transforms a relative or virtual path into the actual physical path on the server.

The following example shows you how to use the method to return the physical path of the file, QueAps\chp14\default.asp:

```
<%=Server.MapPath("QueAsp\chap14\default.asp")%>
```

The output is, C:\Inetpub\wwwroot\QueAsp\chp14\default.asp

Transfer

```
Server.Tranfer ThePath
```

where *ThePath* is a string indicating a relative or virtual path.

Transfers all information created and processed on one Active Server Page to another Active Server Page. Unlike the Server.Execute method, control does return to the calling page when you use Server.Transfer.

The following example shows you how to use Server.Transfer to pass control of a page onto the Active Server Page, MyPage.asp:

```
Server.Transfer "MyPage.asp"
```

URLEncode

```
Server.URLEncode(URL)
```

where *URL* is a Web address to encode.

This method transforms the non-alphabetic HTML characters in a URL into encoded characters. Use this method to eliminate space characters and other extraneous characters from a URL. This method protects your URL calls from being malformed.

The following example encodes a URL:

```
<%Response.Write(Server.URLEncode("http://www.mcp.com")) %>
```

The output of this script is

```
http%3A%2F%2Fwww%2Emcp%2Ecom
```

Session Object

The Session object refers to page interaction that a user has with your ASP Application during one sitting. A session starts when the user enters and calls a page within your ASP Application's virtual directory. A session ends if the user has not called a page in your application or refreshed an existing one during a given amount of time. This time is determined by the time set in the Session.TimeOut property, or by the default value of 20 minutes as set on the server side in the Internet Information Server configuration. You can adjust this default setting. Finally, a session is terminated if the Session.Abandon method is called.

Properties

CodePage

The CodePage property sets or retrieves the number of the code page used for your Active Server Pages. The code page determines the Language glyphs, punctuation marks, and numerals that your Active Server Page uses.

LCIDSets the Locale Identifier. You use an LCID for localization, for example to use the " when indicating British currency.

SessionID

The SessionID property indicates the unique number the Internet Information assigns to each session upon startup.

TimeOut

Set the duration, in minutes, for a session. The default value is 20 minutes.

Methods

Abandon

Releases all session variables created during a given session, effectively ending the session.

Collections

StaticObject

Session.StaticObjects(key)

where key is the name of an item in the StaticObject collection.

The StaticObjects collection refers to all of the objects created with the <OBJECT> tags within the Session object. You use this collection if you want to find out about the objects within an ASP session.

Contents

```
Session.Contents(key)
```

where *key* is the name of the Session variable.

The Contents collection contains all the Session variables for a given session.

EXAMPLE

The following example shows you how to list the contents of the Contents collection:

```
<%
For Each k in Session.Contents
  Response.Write _
    "The key, " & k & " contains " & Session.Contents(k)
Next
%>
```

Methods

Remove(name|index) removes an item from the Contents collection.

```
Session.Contents.Remove("SomeVar")
```

RemoveAll removes all the objects from the Contents collection

```
Session.Contents.RemoveAll
```

Events

```
Session_OnStart
```

This event procedure is called when a new user enters your ASP application.

```
Session_OnEnd
```

This event procedure is called when a session expires.

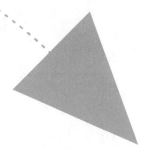

Appendix B

ADO Object Model

In this appendix you will learn the ActiveX Data Objects and the properties, methods, and collections of the

- Connection Object
- Recordset Object
- Command Object
- Parameters Object
- Error Object
- Field Object
- Property Object

Understanding ActiveX Data Objects

Microsoft ActiveX Data Objects (ADO) are a set of tools that make it easy to create client-server and Web-based applications that access and manipulate data. ADO is very powerful because it abstracts all data structures into a common set of objects. It serves as a "shell" for OLE DB, a set of standard interfaces exposed to a given datasource.

OLE DB interacts with data through a layer of software called the OLE DB Provider. The OLE DB Provider offers a mechanism of translating data structures using a common standard that has wide industry support. This means a common set of objects and methods work with many different data sources, including

Datasource	Provider string
ODBC Data Sources	Provider=MSDASQL
Microsoft Index Server	Provider=MSIDXS
Microsoft Active Directory Service	Provider=ADSDSOObject
Microsoft Jet databases	Provider=Microsoft.Jet.OLEDB.3.51

continues

continued

Datasource	Provider string
Microsoft SQL Server	`Provider=SQLOLEDB`
Oracle databases	`Provider=MSDAORA`

Together, ADO and OLE DB allow you to access data quickly and easily, because it makes no difference whether the datasource is a database or an email system: the same ADO objects are used to access either one. Data is data, regardless of datasource, and you generally won't have to worry about differences between datasources.

Seven ADO objects exist within a hierarchy known as the ADO Object Model:

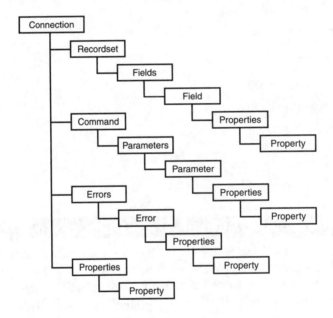

Figure C.1: *Here is a graphical representation of the ADO Object Model.*

The ADO Object Model represents the various components needed to perform data access within a given data environment. Each of the ADO objects has properties and methods that allow the manipulation of both the object as well as its contents. Some properties and methods are specific to one object, and others can be used by multiple objects.

ADO Object	Description
`Connection`	The main object in the ADO object model, a connection is a link to a datasource through the OLE DB Provider.
`Recordset`	Contains all records in a table within a datasource or a subset of the data (a set of records) returned from a command, such as a query or stored procedure call.

ADO Object	Description
Command	Maintains information about commands sent to a Connection object, such as a query or stored procedure. Allows you to perform a command, such as a data insertion, on a datasource.
Parameters	Individual parts of Command objects, such as a single condition of a query or a single argument of a stored procedure.
Error	Contains information about errors raised by the OLE DB Provider.
Field	Information describing a single field (column) within a Recordset.
Property	A characteristic of an ADO object, as defined by the data provider.

The most important thing to know about the ADO object model is that everything happens through the Connection object. The Connection object provides the link to the OLE DB Provider, and all of the other ADO objects have a Connection object as a parent somewhere within the object hierarchy. In other words, the other objects need a link to the data source before they can manipulate it, and the Connection object supplies the link. It defines the data source that has the data you want to access.

After a Connection is made, a Recordset object is used to retrieve and manipulate data from the data provider. You can use the Open method of the Recordset object to populate a Recordset with data. In addition, you can use a Command object in conjunction with a SQL database query or a stored procedure call to retrieve data for a Recordset. Command objects can be used to add or delete records from a table within the datasource, or to retrieve a set of records without returning a Recordset object.

Parameter objects are parameters or arguments passed to a Command object, such as a clause from a query or an argument of a stored procedure call. Not all Command objects have parameters.

Error objects contain information about data access errors (not ADO errors) that pertain to a single operation with a specific data provider.

Finally, Property objects represent characteristics of ADO objects, as defined by the data provider.

Refer to MSDN for more information about the ADO Object Model.

Connection Object

A Connection object is an open connection to a datasource. The Properties, Methods, and Collections of a Connection object allow you to manipulate the connection itself or the datasource.

Note that the Properties, Methods, and Collections described here might not be available with all datasources.

Properties

The Connection object has 11 properties:

Property	Description
Attributes	Used to read or set characteristics of a Connection object.
CommandTimeout	Used to read or set the length of time to wait for a response when a command is executed.
ConnectionString	Contains information required to initiate a connection to a datasource, such as the type of data provider, username, and password.
ConnectionTimeout	Used to read or set the length of time to wait for a connection to occur before generating an error.
CursorLocation	Used to read or set the position of the cursor.
DefaultDatabase	Used to read or set a string describing a database available from a data provider.
IsolationLevel	Used to read or set the level of isolation for transactions with the data provider.
Mode	Used to read or set permissions for modifying data.
Provider	Used to read or set the name of a data provider.
State	Used to determine whether a connection object is open or closed.
Version	Used to determine the version of ADO being used.

Methods

The Connection object has seven methods:

Method	Description
BeginTrans	Used to begin a new transaction with a Connection object.
Close	Used to close an open object.
CommitTrans	Used to save and end the current transaction, and to optionally start a new transaction.
Execute	Used to execute a query, stored procedure, or SQL statement.
Open	Used to open a datasource.
OpenSchema	Used to gather information about the datasource, such as a description of the tables and columns it contains.
RollbackTrans	Used to cancel and end the current transaction, and optionally start a new transaction.

Collections

The Connection object has two collections:

Collection	Description
Errors	Contains all of the Error objects pertaining to failures of the data provider.
Properties	Contains all of the Property objects for a single instance of a Collection object.

Recordset Object

A Recordset object is used to manipulate data from a provider. It represents the set of records returned from a base table because of a database query or a call to a stored procedure. All Recordset objects are constructed using records (rows) and fields (columns), and at any time, the Recordset object refers to a single record within the set as the current record.

Note that the Properties, Methods, and Collections described here might not be available with all datasources.

Properties

The Recordset object has 20 properties:

Property	Description
AbsolutePage	Used to read or set the page within the Recordset on which the current record exists.
AbsolutePosition	Used to read or set the position of the current record within a Recordset.
ActiveConnection	Used to read or set the connection to which the current Recordset belongs.
BOF	Used to see whether the current record is the first record in a Recordset.
Bookmark	Used to set the position of the current record and to return to it at any time.
CacheSize	Used to read or set the number of records cached in memory.
CursorLocation	Used to read or set the location of the cursor.
CursorType	Used to read or set the type of cursor.
EditMode	Used to determine whether the current record has been modified or whether a new record has been created.
EOF	Used to see whether the current record is the last record in a Recordset.

continues

continued

Property	Description
Filter	Used to read or set a filter, to show only those records that meet specified criteria.
LockType	Used to read or set the type of record locking within a datasource.
MarshalOptions	Used to read or set which records (modified or all) are to be sent back to the server.
MaxRecords	Used to read or set the maximum number of records that will be returned from a query or stored procedure.
PageCount	Used to determine the number of pages of records within a Recordset.
PageSize	Used to read or set the number of records to a page.
RecordCount	Used to determine the number of records within a Recordset.
Source	Used to read or set the datasource for a Recordset.
State	Used to determine whether a Recordset is open or closed.
Status	Used to determine the status of the current record.

Methods

The Recordset object has 19 methods:

Method	Description
AddNew	Used to create a new record.
CancelBatch	Used to cancel any pending batch updates.
CancelUpdate	Used to cancel any changes made to the current record.
Clone	Used to create a new record that is a duplicate of an existing record.
Close	Used to close a Recordset object.
Delete	Used to delete the current record or group of records.
GetRows	Used to retrieve a group of records and place them in an array.
Move	Used to move the position of the current record.
MoveFirst	Used to move the position of the current record to the first record.
MoveLast	Used to move the position of the current record to the last record.
MoveNext	Used to move the position of the current record to the next record.
MovePrevious	Used to move the position of the current record to the previous record.
NextRecordset	Used to close the current Recordset and open the next Recordset returned by a complex command.

Method	Description
Open	Used to set a cursor that reflects the records returned from a query or stored procedure.
Requery	Used to update a `Recordset` by rerunning the query that created the `Recordset`.
Resync	Used to refresh a `Recordset` from the database.
Supports	Used to determine the functionality a `Recordset` object supports.
Update	Used to save changes made to the current record.
UpdateBatch	Used to save all pending updates to the database.

Collections

The `Recordset` object has two collections:

Collection	Description
Fields	Contains all of the `Field` objects (columns) of a `Recordset`.
Properties	Contains all the `Property` objects for a single instance of a `Recordset` object.

Command Object

A `Command` object is a definition of a specific command you will execute against a datasource. It can be used to query a database and return records in a `Recordset` object, to execute a bulk operation, or to manipulate the structure of a database.

Note that the Properties, Methods, and Collections described here might not be available with all datasources.

Properties

The `Command` object has seven properties:

Property	Description
ActiveConnection	Used to read or set the connection to which the current command belongs.
CommandText	Used to read or set a string containing a command (such as an SQL statement or a stored procedure call) for a datasource.
CommandTimeout	Used to read or set the length of time to wait for a response when a command is executed.
CommandType	Used to read or set the type of command.
Name	Used to read or set the name of a command.

continues

continued

Property	Description
Prepared	Used to determine whether a compiled version of a command should be saved after it is executed.
State	Used to determine whether a Command object is open or closed.

Methods

The Command object has two methods:

Property	Description
CreateParameter	Used to create a new Parameter object.
Execute	Used to executes a query, SQL statement, or stored procedure.

Collections

The Command object has two collections:

Property	Description
Parameters	Contains all the Parameter objects for a single instance of a Command object.
Properties	Contains all of the Property objects for a single instance of a Command object.

Parameters Object

A Parameter object represents a parameter or argument that is passed to a Command object, such as a clause from a query or an argument of a stored procedure.

Note that the Properties, Methods, and Collections described here might not be available with all datasources.

Properties

The Parameters object has eight properties:

Property	Description
Attributes	Used to read or set characteristics of a Parameters object.
Direction	Used to read or set how a parameter is passed: as input, output, or a return value from a stored procedure.
Name	Used to read or set the name of a Parameters object.
NumericScale	Used to read or set the number of decimal places numeric data will utilize.
Precision	Used to read or set the total number of digits numeric data will utilize.

Property	Description
Size	Used to read or set the maximum size of a `Parameters` object.
Type	Used to read or set the data type of a `Parameters` object.
Value	Used to read or set the value of a `Parameters` object.

Methods

The `Parameters` object has one method, `AppendChunk`, which writes new data over existing data within a Parameter object.

Collections

The `Parameters` object has one collection, `Properties`, which contains all of the `Property` objects for a single instance of a `Parameters` object.

Error Object

An `Error` object contains information about data access errors (not ADO errors) that pertain to a single operation with a specific data provider.

Properties

The `Error` object has seven properties:

Property	Description
Description	Used to read a string containing a description of an error.
HelpContext	Used to read the help topic associated with an error.
HelpFile	Used to read the help file associated with an error.
NativeError	Used to read a number that reflects a data provider-specific error.
Number	Used to read a number that reflects an error.
Source	Used to read a string containing the name of the object that generated an error.
SQLState	Used to read the code returned by the provider when an error occurs from processing an SQL statement.

Field Object

All `Recordset` objects have a `Fields` collection made up of `Field` objects. Each `Field` object represents a column of data (with a single data type) within the `Recordset`.

Note that the Properties, Methods, and Collections described here might not be available with all datasources.

Properties

The Field object has 10 properties:

Property	Description
ActualSize	Used to read the length of a value within a field.
Attributes	Used to read or set characteristics of a Field object.
DefinedSize	Used to read or set the length of a Field object.
Name	Used to read or set the name of a Field object.
NumericScale	Used to read or set the number of decimal places numeric data will utilize.
OriginalValue	Used to read the value of a field before any change were made to it.
Precision	Used to read or set the total number of digits numeric data will utilize.
Type	Used to read or set the data type of a Parameter object.
UnderlyingValue	Used to read the current value of a Field object.
Value	Used to read or set the value of a Field object.

Methods

The Field object has two methods:

Property	Description
AppendChunk	Used to write new data over existing data within a Field object.
GetChunk	Used to read data from a Field object.

Collections

The Field object has one collection, Properties, which contains all of the Property objects for a single instance of a Field object.

Property

A Property object represents a dynamic characteristic of an ADO object that is defined by the data provider.

Note that the Properties described here might not be available with all datasources.

Properties

The Property object has four properties:

Property	Description
Attributes	Used to read or set characteristics of a Property object.
Name	Used to read or set the name of a Property object.
Type	Used to read or set the data type of a Property object.
Value	Used to read or set the value of a Property object.

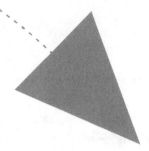

Appendix C

Common VBScript Functions

Array: Creates a Variant that contains an array of values.

Example:

```
'This statement creates an array with four elements: 5,10, 15, and 20
MyArray = Array(5,10,15,20)
```

Asc: Returns the ANSI character code of the first letter of a string.

Example:

```
MyString = "M"
'MyCharCode equals 77, the ANSI character code for M
MyCharCode = Asc(MyString)
```

Chr: Returns the character represented by a particular ANSI character code.

Example:

```
'MyChar equals "M", which is the character represented by ANSI code 77
MyChar = Chr(77)
```

Conversion Functions: Functions used to convert an expression to a Variant with a specific subtype:

Function	Converts expression to Subtype
CBool	Boolean
CByte	Byte
CCur	Currency
CDate	Date
CDbl	Double
CInt	Integer
CLng	Long
CSng	Single
CStr	String

Examples:

```
MyInteger = 15
MyString = CStr(MyInteger)      ' MyString equals the string "15"
MyDouble = 15.752
MyInteger = CInt(MyDouble)     'MyInteger equals the Integer 15
```

If the value returned by a conversion function is outside of the allowable range for the function's subtype, an error occurs.

CreateObject: Creates a reference to an Automation object.

Example:

```
'This code starts Microsoft Word,
'which creates a Document object called MyWordDocument
Set MyWordDocument = CreateObject("Word.Document")
```

Date: Returns the current date of the system.

Example:

```
'MyDate equals the date of the system at the time the command is executed
MyDate = Date
```

Day: Returns a number between 1 and 31 pertaining to the day of the month.

Example:

```
MyDate = #December 18, 1999#    ' Assign a date.
MyDay = Day(MyDate)    ' MyDay equals 18
```

Exp: Calculates the value of *e* (the base of natural logarithms, approximately 2.718282) raised to a power.

Example:

```
MyExpValue = Exp(5.5)     'MyExpValue equals (approximately) 1.704748
```

Formatting Functions: Functions used to format an expression in a specific way. Where applicable, formats are defined in the system's Control Panel.

Function	Formats expression as
FormatCurrency	A currency value (using the system's currency symbol)
FormatDateTime	A date or a time
FormatNumber	A number
FormatPercent	A percentage (multiplied by 100) with the suffix "%"

Example:

```
'MyCurrentDate equals the current system date and time,
'such as February 1, 2000 8:42:15 PM
MyCurrentDate = FormatDateTime(Date)
```

```
'MyPercent equals 65%
MyPercent = FormatPercent(.65)
```

Hex: Creates a string containing the hexadecimal value of an expression.

Example:

```
'MyHexValue equals 1AB
MyHexValue = Hex(427)
```

Hour: Returns the hour of a day as a number between 0 and 23.

Example:

```
MyTime = #3:57:27 PM#

'MyHour equals 15 (3:00 PM on a 24-hour clock)
MyHour = Hour(MyTime)
```

InStr: Determines the first location at which one string appears within another, from the beginning of the string.

Example:

```
'MyFirstPosition equals 4, the first position
'within "MyBigString" that "i" appears
MyFirstPosition = InStr(i,MyBigString)
```

InStrRev: Determines the first location at which one string appears within another from the end of the string.

Example:

```
'MyFirstPosition equals 3, the first position within
'"MyBigString" that "i" appears, as taken from the end of the string
MyFirstPosition = InStrRev(i,MyBigString)
```

Int: Determines the integer portion of a number.

Example:

```
MyInteger = Int(35.235)      'MyInteger equals 35
```

Is(Type) Functions: Functions that return a Boolean (true or false) value, to provide information about an expression.

Function	Returns true or false to indicate whether an expression
IsArray	Is an array
IsDate	Can be evaluated as a date or time
IsEmpty	Contains data (is initialized)
IsNull	Contains valid data
IsNumeric	Can be evaluated as a number
IsObject	Refers to an automation object

Examples:

```
'MyTest equals true, since MyDocument is an object
MyTest = IsObject(MyDocument)
```

```
'MyTest equals false, since 24 is not an object
MyTest = IsObject(24)
```

Join: Creates a string that is a concatenation of the elements in an array.

Example:

```
'Creates an array with three elements
MyArray = Array("ASP ","by ","Example")
```

```
'MyString equals "ASP by Example"
MyString = Join(MyArray)
```

LBound: Used with the UBound function, LBound can be used to determine the size of an array. LBound returns the lower bound of an array, which is always zero. *See also UBound.*

LCase: Converts a string to lowercase. *See also UCase.*

Example:

```
MyString = "This String Is Lowercase."
'MyLowerString equals "this string is lowercase."
MyLowerString = LCase(MyString)
```

Left: Returns a specified number of characters from the left side of a string. *See also Right.*

Example:

```
MyString = "Active Server Pages"
'MyLeftString evaluates to "Acti", the leftmost
'four characters of "Active Server Pages"
MyLeftString = Left(MyString,4)
```

Len: Returns the length (total number of characters) of a string.

Example:

```
MyString = "Active Server Pages"
MyStringLen = Len(MyString)      'MyStringLen equals 19
```

Log: Calculates the common logarithm (base 10) of a number.

Example:

```
MyLogValue = Log(5.5)     'MyLogValue equals (approximately)  .740362
```

LTrim: Removes leading spaces from a string. *See also RTrim.*

Example:

```
MyString = "   Active Server Pages      "
'MyStringTrim evaluates to "Active Server Pages      " (no leading spaces)
MyStringTrim = LTrim(MyString)
```

Mid: Returns the specified number of characters from within a string.

Example:

```
MyString = "Active Server Pages"
MyMidString evaluates to "tive Serve"
MyMidString = Mid(MyString, 3,10)
```

Minute: Returns the minute of an hour as a number between 0 and 59.

Example:

```
MyTime = #3:57:27 PM#
MyMinute = Minute(MyTime)     'MyMinute equals 57
```

Month: Returns the month of the year as a number between 1 and 12.

Example:

```
MyDate = #December 18, 1999#    ' Assign a date.
MyMonth = Month(MyDate)    ' MyMonth equals 12
```

MonthName: Returns the month of the year as a string.

Example:

```
MyDate = #December 18, 1999#    ' Assign a date.
MyMonthName = MonthName(MyDate)    ' MyMonthName equals "December
```

Now: Returns the time and date at the time the command is executed.

Example:

```
MyCurrentDate = Now     'MyCurrentDate equals the current system date and time
```

Replace: Replaces part of a string with a different substring.

Example:

```
'MyString equals "AAAAAAAAAA"
MyString = Replace("AABBAABBAA","A","B")
```

RGB: Returns an integer that represents an RGB (red, green, blue) color.

Example:

```
RedValue = 255
GreenValue = 255
BlueValue = 255
'MyRGB evaluates to the number representing white.
MyRGB = RGB(RedValue, GreenValue, BlueValue)
```

Right: Returns a specified number of characters from the right side of a string. *See also* Left.

Example:

```
MyString = "Active Server Pages"
'MyRightString equals "ages", the rightmost
'four characters of "Active Server Pages"
MyRightString = Right(MyString,4)
```

Rnd: Returns a random number, between 0 and 1, based on the system timer.

Example:

```
MyRandomNumber = Rnd
```

Round: Returns a number rounded to a specified number of digits.

Example:

```
MyNumber = 349.274
MyRoundNumber = Round(MyNumber, 2)      'MyRoundNumber equals 349.27
MyRoundNumber = Round(MyRoundNumber)     'MyRoundNumber equals 349
```

RTrim: Removes trailing spaces from a string. *See also LTrim.*

Example:

```
MyString = "    Active Server Pages    "
MyStringTrim = LTrim(MyString)    'MyStringTrim equals "    Active Server Pages"
(no trailing spaces)
```

Second: Returns the second of a minute as a number between 0 and 59.

Example:

```
MyTime = #3:57:27 PM#
MySecond = Second(MyTime)      'MySecond equals 27
```

Space: Returns a string containing a specified number of spaces.

Example:

```
MyString = Space(4)
'MyString equals "By    Example" (with four spaces
'between the two words)
MyString = "By" & Space(4) & "Example"
```

Split: Returns a one-dimensional array containing a number of substrings.

Example:

```
MyString = "Active Server Pages"
MySplitString = Split(MyString)
'MySplitString(0) equals "Active";
'MySplitString(1) equals "Server" ;
'MySplitString(2) equals "Pages"
```

Sqr: Calculates the square root of a number.

Example:

```
MyNumber = 625
MySqr = Sqr(MyNumber)      'MySqr equals 25
```

StrComp: Determines whether the value of one string is less than, greater than, or equal to another string.

Example:

```
MyString1 = "String 1"
MyString2 = "String 2"
'MyStrComp1 equals -1, since MyString1 is less than MyString2
MyStrComp1 = StrComp(MyString1, MyString2)
'MyStrComp2 equals 1, since MyString2 is greater than MyString1
MyStrComp2 = StrComp(MyString2, myString1)
'MyStrComp3 equals 0, since the strings are equal
MyStrComp3 = StrComp(myString1, myString1)
```

String: Returns a string of repeating characters in a specified length.

Example:

```
MyString = String(10, "A")     'MyString equals "AAAAAAAAAA"
```

StrReverse: Returns the reverse order of a specified string.

Example:

```
MyString = "Active Server Pages"
'MyStringReversed equals "segaP revreS evitcA"
MyStringReversed = StrReverse(MyString)
```

Time: Returns the current time of the system.

Example:

```
'MyTime equals the time of the system at the time the command is executed
MyTime = Time
```

Timer: Returns the number of seconds in the current day since midnight.

Example:

```
MyTime = Timer     'MyTime equals the number of seconds since midnight
```

TimeSerial: Returns a variant of subtype Date containing the time for an hour, minute, and second.

Example:

```
MyHour = 16          'MyHour equals 4:00 PM
MyMinute = -30          'MyMinute equals thirty minutes before MyHour
MySecond = 25- 20     'MySecond equals 25 minus 20, or 5, seconds
MyTime = TimeSerial(MyHour, MyMinute, MySecond)     'MyTime equals 3:30:05 PM.
```

TimeValue: Returns a variant of subtype Date containing the time.

Example:

```
'MyTimeString is a string with value "12:28:15 AM"
MyTimeString = "12:28:15 AM"
'MyTimeValue contains 12:28:15 AM
 MyTimeValue = TimeValue(MyTimeString)
```

Trim: Removes leading and trailing spaces from a string.

Example:

```
MyString = "    Active Server Pages    "
'MyStringTrim equals "Active Server Pages" (no leading or trailing spaces)
MyStringTrim = Trim(MyString)
```

TypeName: Returns a string containing the subtype of a variable.

Examples:

```
MyType = TypeName("Active Server Pages")    ' Returns "String".
MyType = TypeName(18)                ' Returns "Integer".
MyType = TypeName(NullVar)        ' Returns "Null".
```

UBound: Used with the LBound function, UBound can be used to determine the size of an array. UBound returns the upper bound of an array. *See also LBound*.

Example:

```
Dim MyArray(50)                'Create an Array with 50 elements
MyArrayLimit = UBound(MyArray)    'MyArrayLimit equals 50
```

UCase: Converts a string to uppercase. *See also LCase*.

Example:

```
MyString = "This String Is Uppercase."'MyUpperString equals "THIS STRING IS UPPERCASE."
MyUpperString = Ucase(MyString)
```

VarType: Determines the subtype of an expression, and returns a value according to the following table:

Constant	Value	Description
vbEmpty	0	Empty (uninitialized)
vbNull	1	Null (no valid data)
vbInteger	2	Integer
vbLong	3	Long integer
vbSingle	4	Single-precision floating-point number
vbDouble	5	Double-precision floating-point number
vbCurrency	6	Currency
vbDate	7	Date
vbString	8	String
vbObject	9	Automation Object
vbError	10	Error

Constant	Value	Description
vbBoolean	11	Boolean
vbVariant	12	Variant (used only with arrays of Variants)
vbDataObject	13	A data-access object
vbByte	17	Byte
vbArray	8192	Array

Example:

```
MySubType = VarType(MyString)      'MySubType equals 8
MySubType = VarType(MyCurrency)      'MySubType equals 6
```

Weekday: Determines the day of the week as a number between 1 and 7.

Example:

```
MyDate = #December 18, 1999#      ' Assign a date.
'MyWeekDay equals 7, because December 18, 1999 fell on a Saturday
MyWeekDay = Weekday(MyDate)
```

WeekdayName: Determines the day of the week as a string containing the name of the day.

Example:

```
MyDate = #December 18, 1999#      ' Assign a date.
'MyWeekDay equals "Saturday" because December 18, 1999 fell on a Saturday
MyWeekDay = WeekdayName(MyDate)
```

Year: Determines a number representing the year.

Example:

```
MyDate = #December 18, 1999#      ' Assign a date.
MyYear = Year(MyDate)      ' MyYear equals 1999
```

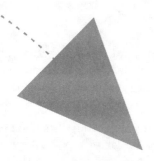

Glossary

Active Server Page (ASP)   A Web-based application containing a combination of HTML, ActiveX components, and VBScript code. Active Server Pages can be used to dynamically provide different content for different users when viewed through the user's Web browser from code generated on the server side.

ActiveX   A set of technologies based on Microsoft's Component Object Model (COM) for creating reusable binary objects.

ActiveX component   (Formerly OLE Automation Server) A physical file that contains classes from which objects can be defined. ActiveX components generally have file extensions `.exe`, `.dll`, or `.ocx`.

ActiveX control   An object that can be placed on a form so users can interact with applications. ActiveX controls have events, properties, and methods, and can be incorporated into other controls. ActiveX controls have an `.ocx` file extension.

ActiveX Data Objects (ADO)   An object model—including data connection, data manipulation, and recordset objects—used for data access.

ActiveX DLL   An ActiveX in-process component, an object that requires another application's process space. See also *ActiveX EXE*.

ActiveX document   A Visual Basic application that can be viewed within a container application such as Microsoft Internet Explorer (version 3.0 or later) or Microsoft Office Binder. ActiveX documents don't require HTML code to be viewed or manipulated.

ActiveX EXE   An ActiveX out-of-process component, an object that runs in its own address space. See also *ActiveX DLL*.

Add-in   A software component that extends Visual Basic's capability. Some add-ins, such as the Visual Basic Class Builder Utility add-in, are included with Visual Basic; many more are available from third-party sources. Within the IDE, you use the Add-In Manager to install and remove add-ins.

ANSI   Acronym for *American National Standards Institute*. ANSI provides a unique integer code for a character set that includes 256 characters. ANSI includes the 128-character ASCII character set and contains international letters, symbols, and fractions.

Application   One or more software components that do some action or provide some service; a compiled Visual Basic project. Other examples of applications include Microsoft Visual Basic and Microsoft Word. Also known as a *program*.

API   Acronym for *Application Programming Interface*. An API is a set of functions exposed by a software module that provide access to the services the module provides. In Windows, the API is a set of core functions that allow direct access to many operating system-provided services, such as window management and printer services. The Windows API consists of three main files: user32.dll, gdi32.dll, and kernel32.dll.

Argument   Data sent to a procedure. An argument can be a constant, a variable, or some other expression.

Array   An indexed group of related data. Elements within an array must be of the same data type (such as all integers or all strings), and each element has a unique, sequential index number.

ASCII   Acronym for *American Standard Code for Information Interchange*. ASCII provides a unique integer code for a character set that includes 128 numbers, letters, and symbols found on a standard U.S. keyboard. A subset of the ANSI character set. In Visual Basic, the ASC function returns the ASCII value of a character.

Authentication   The process by which the identity of a user is verified. In a distributed computing scenario, authentication can mean the user ID and password data that a user passes to the system matches the data on the server side.

Automation server   See *ActiveX component*.

Bind   To connect an object to a data source. See also *bound control*.

Bit   The smallest amount of data storage available on a computer. A bit is either 0 or 1.

Bookmark   A marker for a specific location. A bookmark can be a specific record in a database, a line of code within a project, or a specific Web page.

Boolean   A binary data type. Boolean values are 16-bit (2-byte) values that can hold the True or False constants or their equivalents (−1 and 0).

Bound control   A data-aware control attached to a database through a Data control. At runtime, when users manipulate the Data control by changing from one row of the database to the next, the bound control changes to display the data found in the columns of the new row. If users change the data stored in a row, the new data is saved to the database when the users switch to a new row.

Breakpoint A specific line within a block of code where program execution automatically stops (during runtime). Breakpoints are user-selectable. You can toggle them on and off during design time by pressing F9.

Browser An application used to browse content on the Web. Browsers, such as Microsoft Internet Explorer and Netscape Navigator, can show HTML pages, Active Server Pages, and various other types of content.

Buffer string A temporary holding location in memory for data that will be parsed or otherwise modified. For example, if an application is to take two string values from a user and then extract a specific section from their sum, each value would be placed in a buffer string. Then, these would be concatenated (and placed into another buffer string) before the desired value is parsed from the input data.

Byte An 8-bit data type that can hold numbers in the range 0–255. Bytes are the basis for all Visual Basic data types; for example, the `Single` data type is a 4-byte (32-bit) number.

CAB file Short for *cabinet file*. A CAB file is a group of files compressed into one larger file to conserve disk space. CAB files are often used to distribute applications. During installation, the Setup program extracts files from the CAB file and copies them to the appropriate location on the hard disk.

Call The keyword you use to transfer control of an application to a different `Sub`. Using the `Call` keyword is optional.

Child object An object contained within another object (its parent). See also *object*.

Class A template used to create user-defined objects. A class defines an object's properties and methods. All instances created from the class use the properties and methods defined by the class.

Class module A module that defines a class. See also *module*.

Client-side script Script embedded in a Web page that runs within a browser.

Code block A selection of code. A code block usually consists of all lines necessary to complete a specific task within the application.

COM Acronym for *Component Object Model*. A standard by which applications can expose objects to the system for use by other applications, and conversely a standard by which applications can use objects that have been exposed by other applications.

Compile   To prepare code for execution. In Visual Basic, code can be compiled into either P-code (which results in faster compilation) or native code (which results in faster execution). The type of compilation can be selected from the Compile page of the Project Properties dialog box.

Component object   An object that supports automation through exposed properties and methods. Examples of component objects include ActiveX controls, ActiveX documents, and ActiveX code components.

Compressed file   A file that has been modified to take up less space when stored on the hard drive. Generally, compressed files can't be opened or manipulated until they're decompressed.

Concatenate   To join two or more strings in an expression.

Conditional statement   A logical statement involving a comparison, which yields a Boolean (true or false) value.

Command Object   An ADO object that represents a command that you execute against a datasource. The command can be a SQL statement or a stored procedure. Also, the Command object can work with commands against custom datasources such as email systems.

Connection Object   An ADO object that represents a connection to an OLE DB datasource.

Constant   A variable or object whose value doesn't change.

Context-sensitive help   Information about a specific concept or object within an application that users can easily find. To access context-sensitive help, press Shift+F1 or click the What's This? help (question mark) button, and then select the confusing item.

Control   An object that can be manipulated at design time or runtime to present or change data. Controls are manipulated by changing properties during design time and by calling methods or responding to events during runtime.

Control array   An indexed group of similar controls that are of the same type and have the same name. Individual elements within the control array are identified by a unique index number.

Coolbar   A type of toolbar characterized by flat buttons that raise when the mouse is moved over them and depress when clicked. This is the type of toolbar found in the Visual Basic IDE. The Coolbar object is used to create user-modifiable coolbars.

Currency   A numeric data type particularly suited to store money data. Currency values are 64-bit (8-byte) integers, scaled by 10,000 to provide 4 digits to the right of the decimal point. Currency values use the prefix cur and the type declaration character @ (the "at" sign).

Data consumer An object that's bound to a data provider. A data consumer lets programmers connect to a datasource and manipulate information within it.

Data member Private variables of a class. Data members are seen only by the class that defines them.

Data provider A datasource that exposes information for data access, such as Microsoft Jet, Microsoft SQL, or Oracle.

Data type A set of rules describing a specific set of information, including the allowed range and operations and how information is stored. Data types in Visual Basic include Integer, String, Boolean, and Variant.

Date A numeric data type used to represent dates. Date values are 64-bit (8-byte) floating-point numbers which represent dates from January 1, 100 to December 31, 9999, and times from 0:00:00 to 23:59:59. The Date data type uses the prefix dat, and doesn't have a type-declaration character.

DCOM Acronym for *Distributed Component Object Model*. An extension of COM by which applications can expose objects to computers across a network; conversely, an extension by which computers can use objects that have been exposed from across a network.

Decimal A numeric data type, ranging from 0 to 28, used to specify the number of digits to the right of the decimal point. Decimal values are 96-bit (12-byte) unsigned integers, so with a scale of 28 the largest possible Decimal value is +/–7.9228162514264337593543950335; with a scale of 0, +/–79,228,162,514,264,337,593,543,950,335. The Decimal data type must be used with a Variant, uses the prefix dec, and doesn't have a type-declaration character.

Deployment The period during which an application is distributed for use by customers or by other applications.

Design time While creating an application, the time spent creating forms and writing functions. Forms and functions can be altered only during design time. See also *Runtime*.

Designer An object or application that's used as a basis for creating more advanced objects or applications.

Destination system The system on which an application will be installed and used.

Device independence The concept that software components don't directly control hardware devices. Device-independent software controls hardware by manipulating objects that abstract and expose the functionality of a class of hardware devices.

DLL   Acronym for *dynamic link library*. An executable file containing a set of functions that other applications can call during runtime. DLLs generally don't have a graphical user interface; instead, they're usually accessed by applications without user intervention.

Document Object Model (DOM)   The model that represents the relationships between the various objects that make up the Internet Explorer Browser and the HTML document within it.

Domain name   A unique name that identifies an Internet or network server, such as `www.mcp.com` or `www.microsoft.com`. Domain names are actually text representations of numeric IP addresses, and must be registered with international authorities such as InterNIC.

Domain Name Server (DNS)   A server on the Internet that keeps a list of IP addresses with a friendly domain name associated to each IP address. The DNS resolves a friendly domain name to an IP address.

Double   A numerical data type. `Double` values are 64-bit (8-byte) floating-point number. `Double` values use the prefix dbl, and the type declaration character # (the pound sign).

Datasource Name (DSN)   The name you assign to a datasource under ODBC. See also *ODBC*.

Dynamic   A changing object or expression.

Dynamic HTML (DHTML)   A series of extensions to the HTML language that allow an HTML page to be dynamically modified. A group of HTML pages that work together can be used to create a Web-based application. DHTML applications contain objects and events and are processed on the client within the Web browser.

Dynaset   A recordset that can include data from one or more tables from a database. A dynaset can be used to view or modify data contained in the underlying database.

Early binding   A technique an application uses to access an object. In early binding, objects are defined from a specific class. Early binding is often faster than late binding because the application doesn't have to interrogate the object at runtime to determine the object's properties and methods. In Visual Basic, early binding allows the AutoComplete features to work correctly.

Easter egg   A hidden signature within an application included by programmers to demonstrate that they wrote it. Easter eggs often require a complex set of user actions to activate.

Element   A single member of an array. Each element of an array is assigned a unique index value, which is used to locate and manipulate specific elements in an array. Within the context of HTML, an element is distinct entity in the Web page, such as an image or text input.

Encapsulation   The act of placing code or data in a location, such as a module or control, that is isolated from the rest of an application. Encapsulation hides both the implementation details and the internal complexity of an object, but still enables the application to use functions contained within it.

Enterprise computing   A computing model in which multiple users access applications and data stored on a server. In an enterprise computing environment, multiple servers and multiple networks may be linked together. This is an advanced form of "general" networking, in which users might share information directly, without the use of a dedicated server.

Entry point   The starting point in the code of an application. In Visual Basic 6, entry points include a `Sub Main` procedure or a `Form_Load` event.

Event   A signal fired by the operating system in response to a user action. For example, when a user clicks (and holds down) a mouse button, a `MouseDown` event is sent by the operating system. The active application intercepts this signal and executes the code attached to the `MouseDown` event.

Event-driven programming   A method of programming in which blocks of code are run as users do things or as events occur while a program is running. This differs from procedural programming, in which code blocks are contained within a module and called from other procedures.

Event procedure   The place in a project where code is written to respond to an event. Event procedures are named by joining the object name with the event name, such as `cmdButton_Click()`.

Extensibility   The capability to extend an object's or application's functionality through the use of a programming language or an add-in.

Field   A discrete element of a record in a database; a column in a database. For example, a database of music CDs might have many fields, including CD title, artist name, and CD label.

File   A unit of storage on an external storage device such as a hard disk retrievable block of data. Usually stored on a hard drive, files can contain executable programs, word processor documents, or bitmap picture files. In Visual Basic, each form, module, and project is saved as a file.

File handle   A structure that identifies and provides access to a file on disk.

FileSystemObject   An object that encapsulates the data and methods that allow you to work with files, folders and drives on a given computer. You create the `FileSystemObject` by using the `CreateObject` function to call the Script library like so: `CreateObject("Scripting.FileSystemObject")`

Flag   A `Boolean` (true or false) variable used to determine whether a condition has been met or an event has occurred. For example, the flag *blnPasswordSet* would be set to `True` when a password has been set, and to `False` when the password is cleared.

Flat-file database   A database file in which every record contains all the information required to describe it. Flat-file databases often contain redundant information; for example, every record in a flat-file database of music CDs would require multiple fields to describe the contact information for the artist's fan club. See also *Relational database*.

Form   The basis of an application's graphical user interface. Forms contain objects with which users manipulate data and otherwise control an application.

Focus   The state when an object can receive input from the mouse or keyboard. At any given time, only one object can have focus; this object is usually highlighted with a different color and contains the text cursor, where appropriate.

File Transfer Protocol (FTP)   A method used to transfer files between computers, across a network, or over the Internet by using the TCP/IP network protocol.

Function   A procedure, beginning with `Function` *functionname*`()` and ending with `End Function`, that returns a value to the calling procedure when it's complete.

Get   A Visual Basic keyword; the part of a `Property` procedure that gets the value of a property.

Global variable   A variable that can be accessed from anywhere within a program and which maintains its value while the program is being run. Global variables are defined within code modules with the `Public` keyword.

Gotcha   A detail that can cause problems when overlooked.

Graphical User Interface (GUI)   A set of forms and objects that allows users to view and manipulate data and otherwise control an application. A graphical user interface is the part of the application that sits between users and an application's underlying procedures.

Hard coding   The act of setting a value by directly coding it into the application, without allowing for a way to easily change it. For example, the hard coded statement `Set picPictureBox.Picture=LoadPicture("C:\windows\ bubbles.bmp")` will not work if the file `bubbles.bmp` is moved from the Windows folder, and it doesn't allow the user to change the image loaded into the `PictureBox`. To avoid this situation, it would be better to define a string variable that contains the image's path and filename, and then provide tools, such as an Open common dialog box, to allow the user to search for it.

Header   A commented section of code at the beginning of a procedure, usually placed before the `Sub` or `Function` statement. The header describes the purpose of the procedure, specifies all variables declared within it, and can contain information identifying the developer(s) who wrote it.

Help compiler   An application used to combine information into a help file.

Help context ID   A number that defines a position within a help file. The Windows help system uses context IDs to move to new locations within help files as users navigate through the help system.

High-level language   A computer language, such as Visual Basic, that can simplify coding by allowing programmers to write code with highly developed functions and keywords. See also *Low-level language*.

Hovering   The act of holding the mouse pointer over an object. For example, a ToolTip can appear when the pointer hovers over a command button.

HTML   Short for *Hypertext Markup Language*. HTML files are plain text files that include data and instructions for presenting it. When viewed with an Internet browser, an HTML file can contain text, multiple colors, and graphics. Using HTML files, which you can link via hyperlinks, is the primary way to display information on the Web.

HTML element   A portion of an HTML page, such as a graphic, a button, a text element, or a table.

HTTP   *Hypertext Transfer Protocol*. An Internet protocol used by Web browsers to exchange information and to receive and present data to the browser's user.

Hyperlinks   References between documents that, when selected by users, call and display other documents.

IDE   Acronym for *Integrated Development Environment*. The IDE includes all the tools necessary to create applications with Visual Basic 6.0 and Visual InterDev 6.0, such as the Form Layout window, Script Outline, and the Object Browser.

Index   A unique number that identifies a single element in an array or a control array.

Index (database)   A cross-reference of fields across the tables of a database that enables faster retrieval to specific records in the database.

Inheritance   The act of passing property values from a class to objects created by the class.

Initialization   The act of setting the value of a variable or expression to a specific starting value.

Input box   A dialog, created with the InputBox() statement, that waits for users to enter text or click a button. When users close an input box, a string containing the contents of the text box is returned to the calling procedure.

Instance   A single object created from a class. Also, a variable is an instance of a data type.

Instantiate   The act of creating an object. (An object is an instance of a class.)

Integer   A numerical data type. Integer values are 16-bit (2-byte) numbers within the range –32,768 to 32,767. Integer values use the prefix int, and the type declaration character % (the percent sign).

Integrated Development Environment (IDE)   See *IDE*.

Internet Information Server (IIS)   Microsoft's network file and application server. IIS is used primarily to support transmission of HTML pages using the HTTP protocol.

Internet Service Provider (ISP)   A company that provides access to the Internet via a dial-up or direct connection.

Interpreted language   A language, such as VBScript or Java, that doesn't enable compilation to native code. When an application created with an interpreted language is run, the application's code is passed through an interpreter, which modifies the code into a form the computer can understand and execute.

Intrinsic ActiveX control   An ActiveX control included with Visual Basic, such as the CommonDialog or Winsock control.

Intrinsic control   Also known as *standard controls*. A control included with Visual Basic, such as the Label or CommandButton controls. Intrinsic controls can't be removed from the ToolBox.

Intrinsic function   A predetermined function included with Visual Basic. Examples of intrinsic functions include the type conversion functions, such as CStr(), which usually converts a numeric expression to a string value.

IP Address   A number, structured in four groups with up to three digits in each group, separated by periods (`000.000.000.000`) that indicates a unique computer on the Internet.

JScript   The Microsoft implementation of the JavaScript scripting language.

Keycode   A constant value that represents a keystroke. Keycodes are sent to the application when a key on the keyboard is pressed, and are used to determine which keys the users pressed.

Key field   The field in a database table that uniquely describes each record. For example, the key field in a database table of employees might be the employee number. Also known as the primary key.

Keyword   A word (function, constant, or command) recognized by Visual Basic. You can't use keywords to name user-defined structures such as variables or constants. See *Name collision*.

Language independent   Any file, object, or other structure that can be used by any programming language. For example, the Windows API can be used by Visual Basic, C, or Visual C++.

Late binding   A method of using an object by an application. In late binding, objects are defined as `Object`. Late binding is slower than early binding because the application must interrogate the object to determine its properties and methods.

Let   A Visual Basic keyword; the part of a `Property` procedure that assigns a value to a property. Also used to assign a value to a variable, such as `Let x = 10`.

Literal statement   Any expression, consisting of ASCII characters and enclosed in quotation marks, that's used literally in a procedure. For example, if the code `MsgBox("This is a button")` was contained within the `Click` event of a command button, a dialog box containing the text `This is a button` would appear onscreen when the user clicked the button. Also known as a *literal* or *string literal*. Literals are also numbers used directly within code.

Local variable   A variable defined and used only within a specific procedure in an application. Other procedures can't see local variables.

Long   A numerical data type. `Long` (long integer) values are 32-bit (4-byte) numbers within the range –2,147,483,648 to 2,147,483,647. `Long` values use the prefix `lng` and the type declaration character & (the ampersand).

Loose typing   Defining and using variables without declaring or following a specific data type, such as when Variant values are used. This can lead to type-mismatch errors at compile time because expressions or values can encounter data types that they don't support. See also *Strict typing*.

Low-level language   A computer language such as machine language that requires a programmer to write code with lesser developed instructions that the computer can directly understand. C++ is an example of a low-level language.

Make   To compile code into a standard application (EXE), dynamic link library (DLL), or ActiveX control (OCX).

Member functions   See *Method*.

Menu   A list of user-selectable items within a program; also, a control used to add menus to an application.

Menu bar   The part of the Visual Basic IDE located directly below the title bar that lets you select functions and commands included with the application. Menu bars can be added to applications created with Visual Basic by using the Menu Editor.

Message box   A dialog created with the MsgBox() function that displays a message for users. Message boxes include one or more command buttons that enable users to either clear the dialog or respond with an answer to a query. A message box returns an integer value describing which button was selected.

Method   A procedure associated with a class that manipulates an object. For example, one method of a command button is SetFocus, which moves the focus to the command button that invoked the method.

MIME (Multipurpose Internet Mail Extension)   An extension to the email protocol that lets you embed data types other than text in an email message.

Name collision   An error that occurs when different structures are named identically. For example, if a variable is named string, a name collision will occur because the word String is a Visual Basic keyword. Name collisions also occur if identically named variables are defined within the same scope.

Naming convention   A specific style used to reference objects in code. See *Variable prefix* and *Variable suffix*.

Native code   Binary code that can be directly understood and executed by the computer's processor system. Visual Basic can be set to compile to native code by setting options on the Compile page of the Project Properties dialog.

Nesting   The act of including `Loop` or `Select Case` statements within similar statements. For example, a `Do...Loop` can be placed within one case of the `Select Case` statement. Then the repetitive action controlled by the `Do...Loop` executes only if the proper value is passed to the `Select Case` statement.

Network News Transfer Protocol (NNTP)   An Internet protocol used for reading, posting, and managing data posted to newsgroups.

N-tier architecture   The software design methodology that distributes the various parts of an application throughout the computing enterprise into an unlimited number of locations.

Object   A discrete combination of code and data, such as a `CommandButton` control or the Response object. Objects contain properties, methods, and events. Objects are defined by a class.

Object Browser   A part of the Visual Basic and Visual InterDev IDE, the Object Browser enables you to see all the objects (and all the properties, methods, and events of each object) available for use on the system. The Object Browser can be accessed by pressing F2, selecting Object Browser from the View menu, or by clicking the Object Browser button on the toolbar.

Object-oriented programming (OOP)   A programming style and a type of programming language that involves the use of software modules called *objects* to encapsulate data and processing.

ODBC (Open Database Connectivity)   A common standard that allows different databases to work together.

OLE Automation Server   See *ActiveX component*.

OLE DB   A Microsoft technology that allows access to data from multiple, different data sources.

Option Explicit   A Visual Basic keyword, the use of which forces each variable or expression in an application to be defined with a specific data type through the use of the `Dim`, `Private`, `Public`, `ReDim`, or `Static` keywords. Using `Option Explicit` can help reduce the likelihood of typographical errors when typing the names of existing variables. If `Option Explicit` isn't used, undefined variables automatically are defined as `Variants`.

P-code   Code that can't be directly understood and executed by the Windows operating system. In Visual Basic, code compiled to P-code is interpreted to native code at runtime. When creating an executable file, Visual Basic can be forced to compile to P-code by setting the appropriate options in the Compile tab of the Project Properties dialog box.

Parameter   A numeric or string value that can be changed to modify an expression.

Parse   To use string manipulation functions to change user-inputted string information. For example, the string `"Microsoft+Visual&Basic&6.0"` might be parsed into company (`"Microsoft"`) and application (`"Visual Basic 6.0"`) strings.

Pattern wildcards   Characters such as the asterisk (`*`) or question mark (`?`) that cause a query to broaden its result or that allow an expression to restrict inputted data. For example, a database query on all records containing `*ain` would return all records that end in `ain`, such as Spain, train, and so on. Note that SQL databases typically use the percent sign (`%`) instead of an asterisk.

Persistence   The concept of keeping an object's data stored in memory or on disk.

Pixel   The smallest and most commonly used screen-dependent measure of screen distance. Objects on a form, however, generally aren't sized and located using pixels because the number of pixels on a screen varies for different resolutions and for different types of display systems. See *Twips*.

Prefix   See *Variable prefix*.

Primary key   The field in a database table that uniquely describes each record. For example, the primary key in a database table of employees might be the employee number. Also known as the key `field`. **private**—a Visual Basic keyword. Variables or procedures defined with the `Private` keyword are available only in the module in which the variable or procedure is defined.

Procedural language   A programming language, such as Visual Basic, in which data is manipulated by calling procedures instead of proceeding line by line through all code contained in the application.

Procedure   A block of code that can be called from within an application. A procedure might be used to position objects on a form or to calculate information from a set of user data. Different types of procedures include `Functions` and `Subs`.

Program   See *Application*.

Project   A set of forms and modules that make up an application while it's being developed into an application.

Properties window   A part of the Visual Basic/Visual InterDev IDE. This window enables you to view and modify all the properties of a given object during design time. It's not available during runtime.

Property   An attribute of an object as defined by a class. For example, one property of a command button is `Caption`, which is the text that appears on the button's face.

Property bag An object that holds a set of property values and can restore those values to a new invocation of an object.

Property procedures Procedures used to view and modify the properties of an object, such as the Let and Get statements. The Get statement returns the value of a private variable of an object, while the Let statement modifies the value if the new value is of the correct type.

Protocol A formal set of rules that enables two computers to communicate (such as the HTTP or FTP protocols), or a set of rules used to define an action, such as argument passing or creation of an object from a class. See also *File Transfer Protocol (FTP)* and *HTTP*.

Prototype An application that simulates the behavior of another, more fully developed application. Visual Basic is often used as a prototyping tool—for example, to quickly develop a possible graphical user interface (GUI) for an application before the application is actually developed.

Public A Visual Basic keyword. Variables defined with the Public keyword can be seen by any procedure of any module contained in the application. If a public variable is defined within a class module, the object name must be specified to use the variable.

Query A subset of a database that fits specific criteria. For example, a query might be placed on a music CD database for all jazz CDs. The query would return a recordset that contains only jazz CDs and no classical or rock CDs.

Record All the data required to describe one retrievable item in a database; made up of one or more fields. A row in a database. For example, one record in a music CD database would contain all the data necessary to describe the CD, including artist, label, number of songs, and so on.

Recordset A set of records from a single database table that meets specific criteria.

Recordset object A specific ActiveX Data Object (ADO) object that represents a set of rows and column (recordsets) returned from a datasource.

Recursion The process of a procedure calling itself.

Relational database A database file in which records can include pointers to other tables that contain some of the information required to describe the record. Relational databases can be a more efficient means of storing information; for example, a relational database of music CDs would require only one field to describe the contact information for the artist's fan club. This field would hold a pointer to another table containing the fan club information for every artist in the database. Contrast with *Flat-file database*.

Request Object   An intrinsic, server-side Active Server Page object that represents the client browser calling the Internet Server for the given Active Server Page.

Response Object   An intrinsic, server-side Active Server Page object that represents the communication that a server makes back to a client browser requesting a given Active Server Page.

Robust   A term used to describe an application that can trap and react to errors that occur during execution. For example, a robust calculator application won't crash if users try to divide a number by zero. Instead, users might be see a dialog explaining that numbers can't be divided by zero.

Round   To change a value to a less precise value. When rounding a value, if the next most precise digit ends with 5 or higher, round up; otherwise, round down. For example, if rounding to the nearest tenth, the value 1.652 would be rounded to 1.7 (because the next most precise (one hundredth) digit is 5). If rounding to the nearest one hundredth, 1.652 would be rounded to 1.65. See *Truncate*.

Runtime   When creating an application, the time when the code is actually running. Forms and functions can't be altered during runtime. See also *Design time*.

Scope   An attribute of a variable or procedure that determines which sections of which module or script recognize it.

Server Object   An intrinsic, server-side Active Server Page object that represents the Internet Server.

Server-side   In a Web-based application, the part of the application run by the server instead of the client's Web browser.

Server-side components   In a Web-based application, the portions of the application located on and run by the server.

Server-side script   Script embedded in an Active Server Page that runs on the Internet server.

Set   A Visual Basic keyword; the part of a `Property` procedure that sets a reference to an object.

Single   A numerical data type. `Single` values are 32-bit (4-byte) floating-point numbers, within the range $-3.402823E38$ to $-1.4012989E-45$ for negative values, and $1.401298E-45$ to $3.402823E38$ for positive values. `Single` variables use the prefix sng, and the type declaration character ! (the exclamation point).

SMTP   *Simple Mail Transfer Protocol*. A protocol that allows you to send email over the Internet.

Secure Sockets Layer   A technology that allows you to transfer data between a browser and an Internet server in a safe manner using a public-private key encryption method.

Sniffing   The act of using software to monitor data moving on the Internet, usually with the hope of finding a particular piece of information.

SQL   Acronym for *Structured Query Language*. A set of rules that can control many different types of relational databases, including Microsoft Access and SQL Server databases.

Standard control   See *Intrinsic control*.

Standard EXE   A traditional executable application. A standard EXE is a self-contained application that doesn't expose objects to the system for use by other objects or applications.

Statement   A section of code that fully expresses a single declaration or action.

Static variable   A variable, defined with the Static keyword, that maintains its value between calls to different procedures.

Step   The act of moving through a section of code line by line. Stepping, used with a breakpoint, is useful in determining which line is causing a problem in code.

Stored procedure   A named set of programming statements that are stored and executed within a database server.

Strict typing   Always declaring and following a specific data type when defining and using variables. This can reduce the number of errors at compile time because expressions or values will only encounter data types that they support. Contrast with *Loose typing*.

String   An alphanumeric data type. String values are either variable-length (up to 2 billion characters) or fixed-length (approximately 64,000 characters); longer strings require more memory. Strings can include numbers, letters, and ASCII symbols. String values use the prefix str, and the type declaration character $ (the dollar sign).

Sub   A procedure, beginning with Sub *subname()* and ending with End Sub, that doesn't return a value to the calling procedure when it's complete.

Subscript   The index value of an element in an array.

Syntax   The specific method by which functions or lines of code are written. Important elements of syntax might include spelling, spacing, and punctuation.

System modal   A window or dialog that holds control of the entire system until the user responds to it.

Table   The basic mechanism of data storage in a database, made up of tables and rows. In a relational database, multiple tables might be used to store different categories of related information. For example, in a music CD database, one table might contain only artist information, whereas others might contain label information or fan club information.

Toolbar   A collection of buttons, contained either in a strip or in a dedicated window, that enables users to control an application.

Toolbox   A part of the Visual Basic 6 Integrated Development Environment. The Toolbox contains the objects and controls that are available for use in an application; objects are dragged from the Toolbox and added to forms during design time.

Traverse   To move through records in a database, elements in an array, or data contained within an object.

Truncate   To shorten or reduce a string value. For example, the value *This is My String* might be truncated to *My String*. Contrast with *Round*.

Twip   A screen-independent measure of screen distance equal approximately to 1/1440 of an inch. Objects on a form should be sized and located by using twips rather than pixels so they appear similarly on different types of display systems.

Type   The attribute of a variable that determines what kind of data it can contain. Different types of data include `Integer`, `Long`, `Variant`, and `String`.

Typecasting   Explicitly converting a variable or expression from one data type to another.

Type safety   The concept of keeping the data type of a variable or expression correct and consistent. In Visual Basic and ASP/VBScript, type safety can be forced through the use of the `Option Explicit` keyword.

User-defined data types   A data type not intrinsic to Visual Basic, defined by using the `Type` keyword, a list of declared elements, and the `End Type` keyword. User-defined data types can contain one or more elements of any data type. Not available under VBScript.

Validation   The act of ensuring that data is of an appropriate format before it's written to a database.

Variable   A named storage location that contains data and can be modified during runtime. Variables are generally defined to be a specific data type at design time.

Variable prefix   A combination of characters added to the beginning of a variable name, used to help describe the variable throughout your code. For example, a global variable used to accept user input might be called `gInput`; the prefix g is used to show that the variable is global. See also *Naming convention*.

Variant   A data type that can be either numeric or alphanumeric. A `Variant` is automatically created when a variable isn't defined to be a specific data type. `Variants` don't have a type declaration character. A `Variant` is the only explicit type available in VBScript.

VBA   Acronym for *Visual Basic for Applications*. Similar to but a subset of the Visual Basic language, VBA is the programming language included with such programs as Access and Excel. In these programs, VBA can be used to create macros.

VBScript   A scripting language, similar to but a subset of the Visual Basic language especially suited to be embedded into HTML files because it must be interpreted by a Web browser. VBScript enables objects to be added to Web pages to accomplish such tasks as password authentication or surveys for data collection.

Visual Basic runtime DLL   One of a set of files required to run an application developed in Visual Basic. Automatically installed with Visual Basic, the runtime DLLs must be copied to any machine on which an application is deployed.

Watch   A variable whose value is tracked during runtime. When a watch is set, it appears in the Watch window (part of the IDE). Watches are updated whenever a breakpoint is reached; thus, changes to values can be seen by placing breakpoints at specific events.

White space   When coding, the space within the code editor that doesn't contain text, such as blank lines or tab spaces. White space makes it easier to follow the flow of code—especially more complex structures such as nested loops—within a procedure.

Wintel   An abbreviation for Windows/Intel, the platform used by most computer users. Wintel refers to a computer running a version of Microsoft Windows on an Intel processor.

Wizard   An application, or a part of an application, that helps users complete a difficult task. For example, Visual Basic's Data Form Wizard consists of multiple steps, each of which asks for specific information required to create and bind a form to a database.

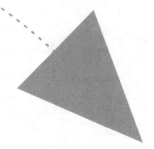

Index